# Information Security: Principles and New Concepts

# Volume III

# Information Security: Principles and New Concepts
# Volume III

Edited by **Fiona Hobbs**

CLANRYE
INTERNATIONAL

New Jersey

Published by Clanrye International,
55 Van Reypen Street,
Jersey City, NJ 07306, USA
www.clanryeinternational.com

**Information Security: Principles and New Concepts**
**Volume III**
Edited by Fiona Hobbs

International Standard Book Number: 978-1-63240-308-7 (Hardback)

Printed in the United States of America.

# Contents

# Preface

In contemporary times, there is no dearth of information. In fact, since the advent of technology and the World Wide Web, there has been an overload of information. All data needs to be recorded, saved and stored. However, some information is more crucial as compared to others. And this is where the concept of Information Security comes in. The origins of Information Security can be traced to the times of Julius Caesar in 50 B.C, when he invented the Caesar cipher. This mechanism was used to protect the confidentiality of correspondence and provided a means of detecting tampering, in case any. Regardless of the form that the data may take, electronic or physical, Information Security is a must in present times.

Information Security has grown and evolved significantly in recent years. Numerous occurrences of international terrorism, through disruption of data fuelled the need for better methods of Information Security. Today, it is an indispensable part of all the business operations across different domains. Protecting information has also become an ethical and legal requirement in many cases. Essentially, the practice of defending information from unauthorized access, use, disclosure and destruction is referred to as Information Security. The CIA triad of confidentiality, integrity and availability is one of the core principles of information security.

There are two important aspects to Information Security. These are Information Technology Security, which is concerned with technology security and Information Assurance, whose aim is to ensure that data is not lost during critical times.

I would like to thank all the contributors who have shared their knowledge in this book. I would also like to thank my family for their constant trust and support.

**Editor**

# Evaluation of Electrocardiogram for Biometric Authentication

**Yogendra Narain Singh**[1*], **S. K. Singh**[2]

[1]Department of Computer Science & Engineering, Institute of Engineering & Technology,
Gautam Buddh Technical University, Lucknow, India
[2]Department of Computer Engineering, Institute of Technology, Banaras Hindu University, Varanasi, India

## ABSTRACT

This paper presents an evaluation of a new biometric electrocardiogram (ECG) for individual authentication. We report the potential of ECG as a biometric and address the research concerns to use ECG-enabled biometric authentication system across a range of conditions. We present a method to delineate ECG waveforms and their end fiducials from each heartbeat. A new authentication strategy is proposed in this work, which uses the delineated features and taking decision for the identity of an individual with respect to the template database on the basis of match scores. Performance of the system is evaluated in a unimodal framework and in the multibiometric framework where ECG is combined with the face biometric and with the fingerprint biometric. The equal error rate (EER) result of the unimodal system is reported to 10.8%, while the EER results of the multibiometric systems are reported to 3.02% and 1.52%, respectively for the systems when ECG combined with the face biometric and ECG combined with the fingerprint biometric. The EER results of the combined systems prove that the ECG has an excellent source of supplementary information to a multibiometric system, despite it shows moderate performance in a unimodal framework. We critically evaluate the concerns involved to use ECG as a biometric for individual authentication such as, the lack of standardization of signal features and the presence of acquisition variations that make the data representation more difficult. In order to determine large scale performance, individuality of ECG remains to be examined.

**Keywords:** Electrocardiogram (ECG); Biometrics; Vitality Measures; Spoofing Attacks; Biometrics Fusion; Security

## 1. Introduction

The electrocardiogram (ECG) is a noninvasive tool used to measure irregularities present in the functioning of the heart. It is a recording of bioelectrical activity of the heart representing the cyclical contraction and relaxation of atrium and ventricle. The most important features of the ECG include the information lying in the P, Q, R, S, and T waves corresponding to atrial and ventricular depolarization or repolarization. Two heartbeats of a sample ECG signal and the labeled wave fiducials are shown in **Figure 1**. The ECG signals acquired from different individuals are heterogeneous, generally reflected in the change in morphology, amplitude and time interval of the heartbeats. The distinctiveness of ECG signals among individuals can be due to the difference in position, size and physical conditions of their hearts. The manner in which the heart's electrical phenomenon is led to individual's myocardium also plays an important role in producing unique features of heartbeat among individu-

als [1].

Different methods in support of using ECG as a candidate of biometric have been proposed in the literature [2-8]. Unlike conventional biometrics like face and fingerprint, ECG has inherent real-time vitality characteristic.

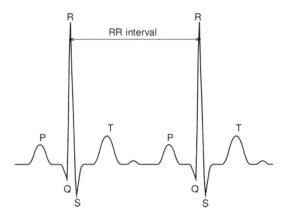

Figure 1. A sample of ECG signal that includes two heartbeats and the information lying in the *P, Q, R, S,* and *T* waves on each heartbeat.

*Corresponding author.

The presence of vitality signs in a biometric identity ensures that it is being collected from a live and legitimate individual at the time of enrollment. Besides the vitality feature, ECG as a biometric offers other advantages to an individual authentication system. The ECG information is intrinsic to an individual so it is highly secured and confidential; it is hard to steal and impossible to mimic. The ECG is universally present among all living individuals. However, the ECG is often used by physicians to diagnose cardiac and other related ailments. Through the deployment of ECG-enabled biometric system, the identity of an individual can be verified online during ECG monitoring or offline through the medical records. This identity verification is much more useful for the protection of person identification and protection of his/her privacy about the cardiovascular condition in particular to the cardiovascular patients [9]. Although the methods of using ECG as a biometric may not offer adequate accuracy, but it has potential to supplement the information for a multibiometric system. The inclusion of ECG to a multibiometric system not only improves the system accuracy but also it improves the robustness of the system against non-live samples to be enrolled.

In this paper, we evaluate the performance of an ECG-enabled biometric authentication system, both in a unimodal framework, and in a multibiometric framework where ECG is combined with the commonly used face biometric and the fingerprint biometric. Signal processing methods are used to delineate the ECG features and determine the dominant fiducials from each heartbeat. Performance of the unimodal system is evaluated on the proposed authentication strategy which uses the delineated features and taking decision about the identity of an individual with respect to the template database on the basis of match scores. We report that the system achieves the moderate performance in a unimodal framework. Further, we tested the feasibility of ECG in a multibiometric framework where it combines with the face biometric and with the fingerprint biometric as a supplement of information especially for assuring vitality detection from biometric sample. We report that the ECG can be effectively combined with the face biometric and with the fingerprint biometric for individual authentication. Transformation based score fusion technique is used to obtain the multibiometric systems and evaluated their performance using equal error rate (EER) and Receiver Operating Characteristic (ROC) curve. In order to test the operational viability of ECG-enabled biometric authentication system across a range of conditions, several concerns remain to be examined. We critically examine each of the concerns involved to use ECG as a biometric for example, lack of standardization of ECG features, variability of ECG features, individuality of ECG to a larger population and heritability of ECG features etc.

Briefly, the paper is outlined as follows. Section 2 presents a review of the existing methods that explore the feasibility of ECG as a biometric. The description of ECG-enabled biometric authentication system is presented in Section 3. The performance of the system is tested on the public database of ECG and the authentication results are given in Section 4. Section 5 describes the potential of ECG to supplement the information for a multibiometric system supported with the experimental results. The discussion on the concerns on the operational viability of ECG-enabled biometric authentication system is given in Section 6. Finally, the conclusions are noted in Section 7.

## 2. Related Works

Different studies in the recent past have shown the feasibility of ECG as a new candidate of biometric for individual authentication [2-8]. Israel et al. [2] demonstrated that ECG of an individual exhibits unique pattern. They performed ECG processing for quality check and a quantifiable metrics is proposed for classifying heartbeats among individuals. A total of 15 intrabeat features based upon cardiac physiology are extracted from each heartbeat and the classification is performed using linear discriminant analysis. The tests show that the extracted features are independent to electrode positions (e.g., around chest and neck), invariant to the individuals state of anxiety and unique to an individual.

One of the earliest studies that demonstrate the possible use of ECG for biometric application is reported by Biel et al. [4]. They conducted the biometric experiment on a group of 20 subjects where 30 features are extracted from each heartbeat. In order to reduce the amount of information the features with a relatively high correlation with other features are discarded and finally, 12 features are selected for classification. A multivariate analysis-based method is used for classification; however principle component analysis (PCA) score plot is utilized to interpret the similarities and differences of heartbeats among individuals. Shen et al. [5] conducted the biometric experiment for identity verification using appearance and time domain features of the heartbeat. However, most of the features are extracted from QRS complex that are stable with change in the heat rates. Template matching and decision-based neural network approaches are used to quantify the identity verification rates that are reported to 95% and 80%, respectively. After combining the classification approaches the result of identity verification is found to 100% for a group of 20 individuals.

Wang et al. [6] introduced two step fiducial detection framework that incorporates analytic and appearance based features from the heartbeat. The analytic features capture local information in a heartbeat which combines temporal and amplitude features while the appearance based features capture the holistic patterns in a heartbeat. To better utilize the complementary characteristics of analytic and appearance features, a hierarchical data integration scheme is presented. The method used for feature extraction is based on a combination of autocorrelation (AC) and discrete cosine transform (DCT) which is free from fiducial detection. The recognition performance of AC/DCT method is found between 94.47% and 97.8%.

Recently, Singh and Gupta [7,8] explored the feasibility of ECG to aid in human identification. Signal processing methods are used to delineate ECG wave fiducials from each heartbeat. The delineation results are found optimum and stable in comparison to other published methods. The proposed *P* and *T* wave delineators are used along with QRS complex to extract different features from dominant fiducials of the electrocardiogram on each heartbeat. The proposed system is tested on 50 subjects ECG and the matching decisions are taken on the basis of correlation between the stored credential and the test ECG signal. The system is achieved the classification accuracy ~98%.

## 3. ECG-Enabled Biometric Authentication System

The schematic description of ECG-enabled biometric authentication system is shown in **Figure 2**. ECG signal which is acquired from the individuals is preprocessed for quality check. It makes the necessary correction of the signal from noise and artifact. ECG delineation in-cludes detection of *P*, *Q*, *R*, *S*, and *T* waves with their dominant fiducials from each heartbeat. Feature extraction includes determination of time intervals, amplitudes and angle features from dominant fiducials of its waveforms. Finally, authentication and decision are taken by comparing the stored template and the query sample.

The heartbeats from the ECG trace are detected using QRS complex delineator which is implemented using the technique proposed in [10] with some improvements. It employs digital analysis of slope, amplitude and width information of ECG waveforms. Once the heartbeat is detected, temporal time windows are defined before and after QRS complex fiducials to seek for *P* and *T* wave delineations in each beat of the ECG.

### 3.1. *P* Wave Delineator

*P* wave represents the atrium function of the heart. The time derivative-based delineation technique is used to delineate the *P* wave fiducials from the heartbeats [11]. The time derivative of the ECG, $y_{nT}$ at time instant *T* is calculated using the following time difference equation,

$$y_{nT} = -2x_{(n-2)T} - x_{(n-1)T} + x_{(n+1)T} + 2x_{(n+2)T} \qquad (1)$$

where $x_{nT}$ represent the data sample of size *n* at discrete instance of time *T*. In order to determine *P* wave and its end fiducials, a time window is set heuristically which is extended from the beginning of QRS complex, $QRS_{onset}$ to the beginning of heartbeat, $Beat_{begin}$ as shown in **Figure 3(a)**. The $Beat_{begin}$ fiducial can be determined by searching of first isoelectric sample prior to the start

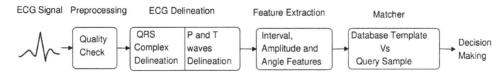

Figure 2. Schematic of ECG-enabled biometric authentication system.

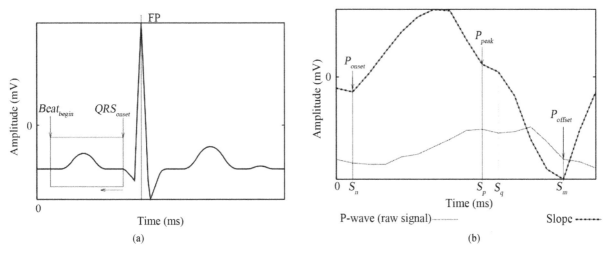

Figure 3. (a) Setting of a time window for *P* wave delineation and (b) detection of *P* wave fiducials in the time window.

of atrium deflection. For the detection of *P* waves, delineator computes the slope threshold, $\theta$. The slope threshold continuously adapts and set between the mean of most recently detected significant slopes, $\mu_{MS}$ and the mean of high frequency noise, $\mu_{HF\text{noise}}$ present in the detected beats.

$$\theta = 0.30\left(\mu_{MS} - \mu_{HF_{\text{noise}}}\right) \quad (2)$$

The level of high frequency noise present in the beat can be estimated, firstly, by passing the beat to highpass filter,

$$y'_{nT} = x_{nT} - 2x_{(n-1)T} + x_{(n-2)T} \quad (3)$$

which determines the presence of artifacts in the beat. The mean of filtered signal over a stream of samples is computed, next. Then noise metric, $HF_{\text{noise}}$ is estimated as the ratio to the maximum of averaged signal, $HF_{\text{noise}}^{MA}$ and the QRS amplitude, $h_{QRS}$ using the formula,

$$HF_{\text{noise}} = K \cdot \frac{HF_{\text{noise}}^{MA}}{h_{QRS}} \quad (4)$$

where $K$ is a constant which is set through the experiment.

The begin and the end fiducials of *P* wave, $P_{\text{offset}}$ and $P_{\text{onset}}$, respectively are determined by tracing the ECG signal in time-reverse order within the time window. The location of $P_{\text{offset}}$ is found at sample where the slope is most negative with some adjustment. The peak of *P* wave, $P_{\text{peak}}$ is found at the sample where the sign of slope is changed (zero crossing). After localization of peak, remaining signal is traced posteriorly for the detection of $P_{\text{onset}}$ fiducial. It is found at the sample where estimated value of $HF_{\text{noise}}$ exceeded to the slope. Found location $S_n$ shown in **Figure 3(b)** is the $P_{\text{onset}}$ fiducial.

## 3.2. *T* Wave Delineator

*T* wave represents ventricles repolarization. The problem with *T* wave delineation is its repolarization cycle which terminates faster while it has lower stimulation in comparison to the noise artifact present in the beat. This makes detection of *T* wave end fiducial, $T_{\text{offset}}$ more cumbersome. For the efficient detection of T wave end fiducials, the technique based on the analysis of waveform curvature is used [12]. It has corrected the signal from oscillatory patterns of reference potential using a recursive lowpass filter of following difference equation,

$$y_{nT} = 2y_{(n-1)T} - y_{(n-2)T} + x_n - 2x_{(n-4)T} + x_{(n-8)T} \quad (5)$$

where $x_n$ represents the data sample of size $n$ at discrete instant of time $T$. Prior to start of delineation process, a search window is set heuristically with respect to end position of QRS complex which is extended from

$QRS_{\text{offest}+80ms}$ to 1 as shown in **Figure 4**. The peak fiducial of *T* wave is determined using the technique of time derivative and adaptive threshold criterion, as similar to P wave with some adjustments.

The end fiducials of *T* wave are determined using the analysis of its waveform curvature that assumes the part of curvature near to its ends is convex. The signal is tracked downhill and finds the location of minimum radius of curvature as shown in **Figure 5**. After fixing the time difference between sample points *A*, *B* and *A*, *C*, the minimum radius of curvature is determined by maximizing *BL* using vector cross product between two directed line segments *i.e.*,

$$BL = \frac{|AC \times AB|}{|AC|}$$

## 3.3. ECG Feature Set

In order to validate ECG as a biometric for individual authentication, a feature set is prepared from the extracted fiducials of *P*, *Q*, *R*, *S*, and *T* waves from each heartbeat [8]. The feature set contains the attributes of different classes: interval features, amplitude features and angle features which are listed in **Table 1**. Thirteen interval features from different times instances of the dominant fiducials of *P*, *Q*, *R*, *S*, and *T* waves are computed which are shown in **Figure 6(a)**. Amplitude features are computed relative to the amplitude of *R* peak which is found invariant to change in the heart rate. We compute four amplitude features between the difference of amplitudes from P, *Q*, *S*, and *T* waves to *R* peak as

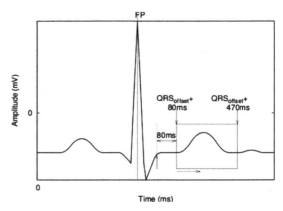

**Figure 4. Setting of a time window for *T* wave delineation.**

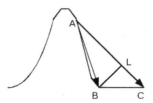

**Figure 5. Detection technique used to delineate *T* wave end fiducials.**

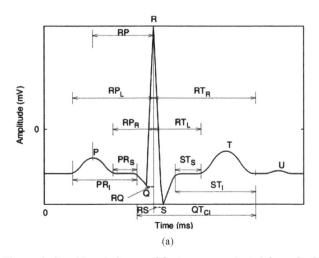
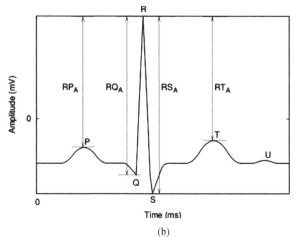

(a)             (b)

**Figure 6. Considered classes of features are selected from *P, Q, R, S* and *T* wave fiducials of heartbeat: (a) interval features and (b) amplitude features.**

**Table 1. Considered classes of features are selected from ECG wave fiducials. (Here *RR* interval is used to correct QT interval using Bazett's formula [13]).**

| Classes | Features | Representations |
|---|---|---|
| | *PR Interval* | $PR_1$ |
| | *PR Segment* | $PR_2$ |
| | *Corrected-QT Interval* | $QT_{CI}$ |
| | *ST Segment* | $ST_S$ |
| | *ST Interval* | $ST_1$ |
| | $R_{peak}$ *to* $P_{onset}$ *Segment* | $RP_L$ |
| Interval Features | $R_{peak}$ *to* $P_{peak}$ *Segment* | $RP$ |
| | $R_{peak}$ *to* $P_{offset}$ *Segment* | $RP_R$ |
| | $R_{peak}$ *to* $Q_{peak}$ *Segment* | $RQ$ |
| | $R_{peak}$ *to* $S_{peak}$ *Segment* | $RS$ |
| | $R_{peak}$ *to* $T_{onset}$ *Segment* | $RT_L$ |
| | $R_{peak}$ *to* $T_{offset}$ *Segment* | $RT_R$ |
| | *RR Interval* | $RR$ |
| | *RQ Amplitude* | $RQ_A$ |
| Amplitude Features | *RS Amplitude* | $RS_A$ |
| | *RP Amplitude* | $RP_A$ |
| | *RT Amplitude* | $RT_A$ |
| | *Angle Q* | $\angle Q$ |
| Angle Features | *Angle R* | $\angle R$ |
| | *Angle S* | $\angle S$ |

shown in **Figure 6(b)**. The angle class of features is related to angular displacement between different peak fiducials of *P, Q, R, S* and *T* waves. Here, the aim is to extract those features which are stable and consistent to

the change in heart rate. The angle features are shown in **Figure 7**.

### 3.4. Feature Normalization

Normalization is an important issue to obtain consistent features from change in the heart rate. The heart rate varies due to change in pressure inside the heart and ventricular volume. Change in heart rate consequently changes the duration of *P* wave, *PR* interval and *QT* interval. Thus the features of *P* and *T* waves are normalized by dividing them to the beat length, $PR_I + QT_{CI}$ while $RQ$ and $RS$ are used as raw features.

In order to investigate the effects of varying heart rate on peak fiducials of different waveforms, it is found that artial deflection do not change with the heart rate. Ventricular activation and the recovery of ventricles from stimulation are fairly invariant with change in heart rate. Therefore, raw amplitude and angle features are used in the experiment.

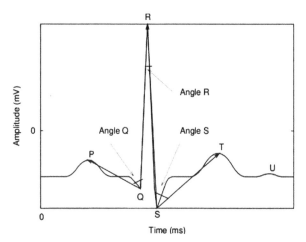

**Figure 7. Angle class of features are selected from *P, Q, R, S* and *T* wave fiducials of heartbeat.**

## 3.5. Generation of Scores from Feature Vectors

We have adopted statistical framework approach to generate match score from the feature vectors of the template and the query samples. Consider, $G_1$ and $G_2$ are two classes correspond to genuine and impostor. Let $f$ be a feature vector denoted as $f_1, f_2, \cdots, f_d$ of $d$-dimension. Using Bayesian decision theory [14] the risk of misclassification such as assigning of query sample $f$ to class $G_i$, $i = 1, 2$, for which the conditional risk defined as

$$R(G_i|f) = \sum_{j=1}^{2} L(G_i, G_j) \cdot P(G_i|f) \qquad (6)$$

is minimum where $L(G_i, G_j)$ is the loss incurred in deciding $G_i$ when the true class is $G_j$ and $(G_j|f)$ is the posterior probability. In the case of 0/1 loss function i.e., $L(G_i, G_j) = 1$, if $i \neq j$, otherwise it is 0, then conditional risks become the conditional probability of misclassification and the Bayesian decision rule can be simplified to maximum a posterior (MAP) rule stated as: Assign query sample $f$ to class $G_i$ if,

$$P(G_i|f) > P(G_j|f) \text{ for all } j \neq i \qquad (7)$$

Since the measures of query sample are independent conditionally to the class, therefore the required probability may be computed by combining different $P(G_i|f^{(k)})$ for each feature vector $k$. Then the system returns a score $s^{(k)}$ where

$$s^{(k)} = g\left(P(G_i|f^{(k)})\right) + h\left(f^{(k)}\right) \qquad (8)$$

where $g(\cdot)$ is a monotonic function and $h(\cdot)$ is the error of estimation caused by the matcher [15]. If we assume that $h$ is zero then $P(G_i|f^{(k)})$ is approximated to $P(G_i|s^{(k)})$. Therefore, the property of match score can be defined as: If $s^{(i)}$ and $s^{(j)}$ are two scores i.e., $s^{(i)} > s^{(j)}$ then the conditional probabilities for which the query samples and the templates are from the same user is given as $P(G_i|s^{(i)}) > P(G_i|s^{(j)})$; that means the claimed user belongs to class $G_i$.

## 3.6. Authentication Strategy

The computational procedure to generate the match scores from the comparison of query sample to the database template of ECG features is described as follows. Consider, an individual $i$ has an ECG data set of $t$ unit of time. The $m$ subdata sets of length $s$ unit of time ($s < t$) are arbitrarily selected from the complete trace of an ECG. A vector of $d$-features is extracted from each subdata set. Let $P^{(i)}$ be the pattern matrix consisting of $m$ vectors of individual $i$ of size $m \times d$ which can be defined as,

$$P^{(i)} = \begin{pmatrix} f_{1,1} & f_{1,2} & \cdot & \cdot & f_{1,d} \\ f_{2,1} & f_{2,2} & \cdot & \cdot & f_{2,d} \\ \cdot & \cdot & \cdot & \cdot & \cdot \\ \cdot & \cdot & \cdot & \cdot & \cdot \\ f_{m,1} & f_{m,2} & \cdot & \cdot & f_{m,d} \end{pmatrix} \qquad (9)$$

where element $f_{j,k}$ represents the $k$th feature of $j$th sub-data set. The purpose of arbitrarily selection of subdata set is to statistically analyze the variations present in different heartbeats of an individual ECG. Consider, the population size is $n$, so there are $n$ different ECG data sets. Thus, $n$ different pattern matrices $P^{(i)}$ are generated in the database where $i = 1, 2, \cdots, n$.

Let an individual have a query sample $Q$ that generates the feature vector $f' = \langle f_1', f_2', \cdots, f_d' \rangle$. Statistically, the distance between the attributes of a query sample and feature vectors of a pattern matrix of an individual $i$ is computed using Euclidean distance as follows,

$$d_j^{(i)} = \left( |f_{j,1} - f_1'| \quad |f_{j,2} - f_2'| \cdots |f_{j,d} - f_d'| \right) \qquad (10)$$

where $j = 1, 2, \dots m$. The sum of Euclidean distances between attributes of feature vectors gives the distance score measure for individual $i$, as

$$s_j^{(i)} = \sum_{k=1}^{d} |f_{j,k} - f_k'| \qquad (11)$$

for all subdata sets $j = 1, 2, \dots m$. In order to acknowledge the variations present in the ECG data set of an individual $i$, the mean of the distance scores, denoted as $s^{(i)}$ can be computed and determined as follows

$$s^{(i)} = \frac{1}{m} \sum_{j=1}^{m} s_j^{(i)} \qquad (12)$$

A smaller value of distance score indicates a good match while a higher value of distance score indicates a poor match. The distance scores is then, converted to the similarity scores by subtracting each from the maximum value of the score set.

## 4. Experimental Results

The performance of the ECG-enabled biometric authentication system is evaluated on the ECG database prepared from public database of PhysioBank archives [16]. ECG recordings of 73 subjects from the class European ST-T Database, MIT-BIH Normal Sinus Rhythm Database, MIT-BIH Arrhythmia Database and QT Database are selected and the template database is prepared. Since the database only offers one ECG signal for each subject, therefore the complete record is divided in two halves such that the first half is used for preparing the template set and the latter half is used for test set.

The match scores distributions of impostor and genuine cases are shown in **Figures 8(a)** and **(b)**, respectively while the equal error rate (EER) of the system is found to 10.8% as shown in **Figure 8(c)**. The performance of ECG-enabled biometric system is shown using Receiver Operating Characteristic (ROC) curve in **Figure 9**. It shows that the system has genuine acceptance rate (GAR) of 59% at zero false acceptance rates (FAR). The performance of the individual system gradually increases and reached to GAR of 82% at FAR of 7%. The EER result and the ROC curve show that the authentication performance of the ECG-based biometric system is low and hardly to compete the performance of the conventional biometrics (e.g., fingerprint and irises). However, ECG can be combined with other biometric and provide an excellent source of supplementary information in a multibiometric framework.

## 5. Fusion of ECG with Face and Fingerprint Biometrics

The ECG-based biometric system performs moderately in a unimodal framework. We show that ECG has the potential to supplement the information for a multibiometric system. In particular, we tested the performance of the multibiometric systems obtained from the fusion of ECG with face biometric and ECG with fingerprint biometric. The objective of the inclusion of ECG with face biometric and the ECG with fingerprint biometric is because; ECG is a physiological signal that has inherent real time vitality signs. In addition, the ECG information is intrinsic to an individual so it is hard to steal and impossible to mimic. Therefore, ECG as a biometric is robust enough against spoof attacks or falsification.

We hypothesis that ECG can be combined with face or fingerprint biometrics, effectively. Transformation based score fusion technique; in particular weighted sum rule is used to combine the match scores of different biometrics. Consider the performance of the fused biometric system is evaluated on the fusion technique that works on the assumption that weights of different identities are inversely proportional to their equal error rate (EER). Let $e_k$ be the EER of the biometric $k$, then weight ($w_k$) assigned to biometric $k$ can be computed as

$$w_k = \left( \sum_{k=1}^{t} \frac{1}{e^k} \right)^{-1} \cdot \frac{1}{e^k} \qquad (13)$$

where $0 \le w_k \le 1$, for all $k$ and $\sum_{k=1}^{t} w_k = 1$. Finally, the fused score, $f_i$ of an individual $i$ is computed as,

$$f_i = \sum_{k=1}^{t} w_k \cdot S_k^{(i)}; \quad (\forall i) \qquad (14)$$

Where $S_k^{(i)}$ is the similarity score of individual $i$ for biometric identity $k$ i.e., $1 \le k \le t$. Consequently, the total similarity measure of a multibiometric system for $n$

genuine ($G$) scores and $n'$ impostor ($I$) scores is given as $\left(f_1, f_2, \cdots, f_n\right)_G \cup \left(f_1, f_2, \cdots, f_{n'}\right)_I$ where

$$\left(f_1, f_2, \cdots, f_n\right)_G = \sum_{k=1}^{t} w_k \cdot \left(G_1, G_2, \cdots, G_n\right)_k \qquad (15)$$

$$\left(f_1, f_2, \cdots, f_{n'}\right)_I = \sum_{k=1}^{t} w_k \cdot \left(I_1, I_2, \cdots, I_{n'}\right)_k \qquad (16)$$

and $n' = n \times (n-1)$ for one-to-many comparison.

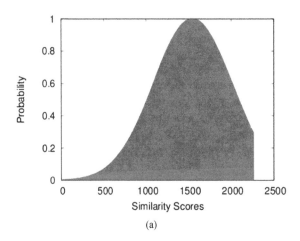

(a)

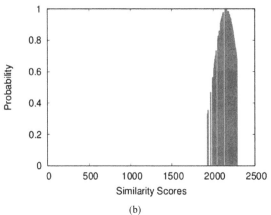

(b)

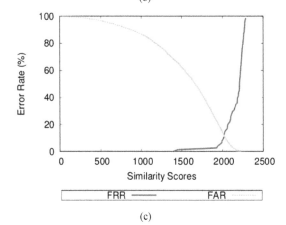

(c)

**Figure 8. ECG match scores distributions (a) impostor scores and (b) genuine scores; (c) Equal error rate (EER) curve.**

We acquired the face and the fingerprint biometrics information from the public database of NIST-BSSR1 [17]. In particular scores Set 1 is used in this experiment. From this set, the fingerprint scores are generated from the comparison of two right index fingerprints and the face scores are generated from the comparison of two frontal faces by the face recognition system labeled C. Since the databases of ECG, face and fingerprint biometrics are different, therefore we can assume that an individual in ECG database has a face and fingerprint information in other database and thus creating a virtual multibiometric system. From these sets, we prepare the face and fingerprint biometrics information of 73 subjects, where the individuals are selected arbitrarily from the given list of users. The equal error rate (EER) results of the unimodal systems of face and fingerprint biometrics is found 4.52% and 2.12%, respectively.

The performance of fused biometric systems of ECG with face and ECG with fingerprint are shown in **Figures 9** and **10**, respectively. The EER results of the aforementioned systems are reported 3.02% and 1.52%, respectively for the fused system of ECG with face and ECG with fingerprint biometric. The performance of the individual systems is face and fingerprint is reported to GAR of 87% and 95%, respectively for face and finger-print at zero FAR. The fused systems of ECG with face and ECG with fingerprint have achieved the performance to GAR of 94% and 96%, respectively at zero FAR. The performance of the fused systems improve further and reached to GAR of 99% and 100%, respectively for ECG with face and ECG with fingerprint at relatively higher values of FAR of 7%. These results confirm that the ECG can be fused with face and fingerprint biometrics, effectively for individual authentication.

## 6. Concerns of ECG-Enabled Biometric Authentication System

ECG-enabled biometric methods accomplish individual authentication task through statistical analysis of the ECG signal and perform quantitative comparison of the query signal to the enrolled signals. The performance of the cited methods depends heavily on the task of data representation that means how efficiently the ECG signal is delineated. The results presented by most methods have shown the uniqueness of ECG among humans and therefore can be used for biometric applications. But most experiments are done on modest data sets acquired under controlled conditions in laboratory demonstration. To be feasible, ECG-enabled biometric system must perform the authentication task across wide range of conditions, while following issues are to be addressed.

1) Lack of standardization of ECG features.
2) Variability of ECG features.

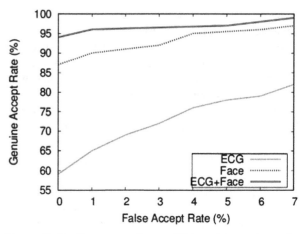

**Figure 9. Performance of a multibiometric system after fusing ECG with face biometric.**

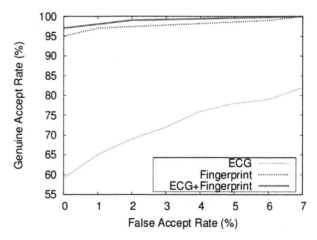

**Figure 10. Performance of a multibiometric system after fusing ECG with fingerprint biometric.**

3) Individuality of ECG.
4) Heritability of ECG waves.
5) Customization of ECG-enabled biometric system.

### 6.1. Lack of Standardization of ECG Features

Most methods that describe ECG as a biometric are based on the temporal or heuristic selection of wave boundaries on time and amplitude domain. Using the information of local maxima, local minima and zero crossings at different scales, the methods identify the significant fiducials of the ECG waves. The effectiveness of these methods rely on the accuracy of the detected fiducials which is a challenge due to the lack of any standardized definition of effective localization of ECG wave boundaries.

To use ECG as a biometric, the knowledge utilized by researchers is mainly based on medical findings of ECG information and they analyze the ECG on the approximate information of medical dominant fiducials. Although, the approximate localization of different waves fiducials may sufficient for clinical diagnosis but this information is certainly not sufficient for biometric decision making. Because the applications of using ECG as biometric expect the exact localization of ECG waves fiducials and a slight variation in localization of these fiducials may cause a misclassification *i.e.,* false acceptance or false rejection errors over a large data sets.

## 6.2. Variability of ECG Features

Another concern that limits the use of ECG for biometric applications is the variability of cardiac rhythm within the subjects or between the subjects. Heart rate varies with individual's physiological and mental conditions. Stress, excitement, exercise and other working activities may have impact on the heart rate and it can elevate. It is to be noted that other than changes in the rhythm of heartbeat, the morphology of an ECG remains unchanged. The changes in the heart rate consequently varying different patterns of the ECG, like RR interval, PR interval, and QT interval. These features are carefully transformed and make them free from the variations in the heart rate before using for biometrics applications [8]. An interesting discussion on the link between the individual's physiology and the heart rate has been given in [8]. Aging may impact heartbeat mainly up to the age of adolescence. Some features of heartbeat may vary due to the progressive change in individual's anatomy to the adolescence (~16 years of age).

Other factors like presence of artifacts and emergence of irregular beats may cause the changes in the morphology of the heartbeat. The dominant frequency of powerline interference 50 - 60 Hz can distort the ECG morphology while the presence of ectopic beats or premature beats can make the individual's classification harder. Most methods have employed the techniques that have been tested on a limited class of ECG patterns. Therefore, it is needed that the method can be extended to any number of morphologically distinct ECG waveforms for the operational viability of ECG-enabled biometric authentication system.

## 6.3. Individuality of ECG

Biometric individuality is a major concern to assess the performance of a biometric system. Individuality of a biometric refers the likelihood of interclass variability and intraclass similarity of testing patterns observed in a target population. For example, individuality of ECG refers that up to what extent the ECG patterns are scalable in a target population of sufficiently larger size. Statistically, the problem of individuality of ECG is yet to be studied.

Unlike to that, the feasibility of ECG for biometric use of individual authentication explored by most methods has been tested on a limited data size e.g., 20 subjects

[4,5]; 31 subjects [6]; 29 subjects [3]; and 50 subjects [8]. In order to assess large scale performance, the methods need to be tested on comparatively larger data size.

## 6.4. Heritability of ECG Waves

The heritability analysis of ECG has shown intraclass correlation between adult male twins (monozygotic and dizygotic). In particular, ventricular repolarization and heart rate are significant heritable components while composite $Q$, $R$, $S$ waves do not show a significant heritable component [18].

## 6.5. Customization of ECG-Enabled Biometric System

A customized ECG-enabled biometric system similar to an ECG analyzer which diagnoses cardiac ailments online is needed that can perform the authentication task across a range of conditions. The size of such a device is as small as a mobile phone so that it could be kept in the pocket and performs the authentication task during an individual's normal activity.

## 7. Conclusions

This paper has evaluated the feasibility of ECG as a biometric for individual authentication and proposed a method for ECG-enabled biometric authentication system. Unlike conventional biometrics that are neither secrets nor robust enough against falsification, ECG is inherited to an individual which is highly secure and impossible to be forged. Most importantly, ECG has an inherent real-time feature of vitality signs which ensures that an ECG cannot be acquired unless the person is not live or it can not be acquired unless the person to be authenticated is not present at the authentication desk. Therefore, it is robust enough against the falsified credentials to be enrolled in the system. We have shown that ECG has potential to provide an excellent source of supplementary information in a multibiometric system. The fusion of ECG with the face biometric and with the fingerprint biometric has shown a significant improvement in authentication performance of both of the fused systems. In addition, we have critically examined the research concerns of ECG-enabled biometric authentication system across wide range of conditions.

The laboratory demonstration of the biometric use of ECG has shown great promise, but the fruitful directions for further research include the following: 1) The ECG-enabled biometric system must perform the authentication task across wide range of conditions over a larger population including the data acquired at larger time intervals. 2) It is important to discover that up to what extent an ECG varies under different anxiety levels. An investigation of robustness to the subjects of different emotional states is still needed to validate the results of most methods. 3) The analysis methods of ECG signal is still in its infancy. The exploration of alternative classification techniques that are robust to handle variations in the features present that is to be claimed. 4) Specific efforts are needed to check the quality of the signals which is acquired abruptly. It may be because of noncooperation of the user or the presence of some artifacts in the signal. It would support the data representation methods which are working in non-standardized features framework.

# REFERENCES

[1]  B. P. Simon and C. Eswaran, "An ECG Classifier Designed Using Modified Decision Based Neural Networks," *Computer and Biomedical Research*, Vol. 30, No. 4, 1997, pp. 257-272.

[2]  S. A. Israel, J. M. Irvine, A. Cheng, M. D. Wiederhold and B. K. Wiederhold, "ECG to Identify Individuals," *Pattern Recognition*, Vol. 38, No. 1, 2005, pp. 133-142.

[3]  J. M. Irvin and S. A. Israel, "A Sequential Procedure for Individual Identity Verification Using ECG," *EURASIP Journal on Advances in Signal Processing*, Vol. 2009, 2009, Article ID: 243215, pp. 1-13.

[4]  L. Biel, O. Pettersson, L. Philipson and P. Wide, "ECG Analysis: A New Approach in Human Identification," *IEEE Transaction on Instrumentation and Measurement*, Vol. 50, No. 3, 2001, pp. 808-812.

[5]  T. W. Shen, W. J. Tompkins and Y. H. Hu, "One-Lead ECG for Identity Verification," *Proceedings of the Second Joint EMBS/BMES Conference*, Houston, 23-26 October 2002, pp. 62-63.

[6]  Y. Wang, F. Agrafioti, D. Hatzinakos and K. N. Plataniotis, "Analysis of Human Electrocardiogram for Biometric Recognition," *EURASIP Journal on Advances in Signal Processing*, Vol. 2008, 2008, Article ID: 148658, pp. 1-11.

[7]  Y. N. Singh and P. Gupta, "Biometric Method for Human Identification Using Electrocardiogram," *Proceedings of the 3rd IAPR/IEEE International Conference on Biometrics*, ICB 2009, LNCS, Springer-Verlag, Berlin, Vol.

5558, 2009, pp. 1270-1279.

[8]  Y. N. Singh and P. Gupta, "Correlation Based Classification of Heartbeats for Individual Identification," *Journal of Soft Computing*, Vol. 15, No. 3, 2011, pp. 449-460.

[9]  F. Sufi and I. Khalil, "An Automated Patient Authentication System for Remote Telecardiology," *Proceedings of the Fourth International Conference on Intelligent Sensors, Sensor Networks and Information Processing, ISSNIP* 2008, 15-18 December 2008, pp. 279-284.

[10] J. Pan and W. J. Tompkins, "A Real Time QRS Detection Algorithm," *IEEE Transactions on Biomedical Engineering*, Vol. 33, No. 3, 1985, pp. 230-236.

[11] Y. N. Singh and P. Gupta, "A Robust Delineation Approach of Electrocardiographic P Waves," *Proceedings of the 2009 IEEE Symposium on Industrial Electronics and Applications, ISIEA* 2009, Vol. 2, 2009, pp. 846-849.

[12] Y. N. Singh and P. Gupta, "A Robust and Efficient Technique of T Wave Delineation from Electrocardiogram," *Proceedings of the 2nd International Conference on Bio-Inspired Systems and Signal Processing, BIOSIGNALS*, 2009, pp. 146-154.

[13] H. C. Bazett, "An Analysis of the Time-Relations of Electrocardiograms," *Heart*, Vol. 7, 1920, pp. 353-370.

[14] R. O. Duda, P. E. Hart and D. G. Stork, "Pattern Classification," 2nd Edition, Wiley, New Delhi.

[15] P. Verlinde, P. Druyts, G. Cholet and M. Acheroy, "Applying Bayes Based Classifiers for Decision Fusion in a Multi-Modal Identity Verification System," *Proceedings of the International Symposium on Pattern Recognition in Memoriam Pierre Devijver*, Brussels, 12 February 1999.

[16] Physionet, "Physiobank Archives," Massachusetts Institute of Technology, Cambridge, 2011. http://www.physionet.org/physiobank/database/#ecg

[17] "Biometric Score Set," National Institute of Standard and Technology, 2011. http://www.itl.nist.gov/iad/894.03/biometricscores/

[18] M. W. Russell, I. Law, P. Sholinsky and R. R. Fabsitz, "Heritability of ECG Measurements in Adult Male Twins," *Journal of Electrocardiology*, Vol. 30, No. 1, 1998, pp. 64-68.

# 2

# Dynamic Identity Based Authentication Protocol for Two-Server Architecture

**Sandeep K. Sood**

Department of Computer Science & Engineering, Regional Campus Gurdaspur, Gurdaspur, India

## ABSTRACT

Most of the password based authentication protocols make use of the single authentication server for user's authentication. User's verifier information stored on the single server is a main point of susceptibility and remains an attractive target for the attacker. On the other hand, multi-server architecture based authentication protocols make it difficult for the attacker to find out any significant authentication information related to the legitimate users. In 2009, Liao and Wang proposed a dynamic identity based remote user authentication protocol for multi-server environment. However, we found that Liao and Wang's protocol is susceptible to malicious server attack and malicious user attack. This paper presents a novel dynamic identity based authentication protocol for multi-server architecture using smart cards that resolves the aforementioned flaws, while keeping the merits of Liao and Wang's protocol. It uses two-server paradigm by imposing different levels of trust upon the two servers and the user's verifier information is distributed between these two servers known as the service provider server and the control server. The proposed protocol is practical and computational efficient because only nonce, one-way hash function and XOR operations are used in its implementation. It provides a secure method to change the user's password without the server's help. In e-commerce, the number of servers providing the services to the user is usually more than one and hence secure authentication protocols for multi-server environment are required.

**Keywords:** Authentication Protocol; Smart Card; Dynamic Identity; Multi-Server Architecture; Password

## 1. Introduction

Most of the existing password authentication protocols are based on single-server model in which the server stores the user's password verifier information in its database. Password verifier information stored on the single server is mainly susceptible to stolen verifier attack. The concept of multi-server model removes this common point of susceptibility. The proposed protocol uses multi-server model consisting of two servers at the server side that work together to authenticate the users. Different levels of trust are assigned to the servers and the service provider server is more exposed to the clients than that of the control server. The back-end control server is not directly accessible to the clients and thus it is less likely to be attacked. Two-server model provides the flexibility to distribute user passwords and the authentication functionality into two servers to eliminate the main point of vulnerability of the single-server model. Therefore, two-server model appears to be a genuine choice for practical applications.

In a single server environment, the issue of remote login authentication with smart cards has already been solved by a variety of schemes. These conventional single-server password authentication protocols can not be directly applied to multi-server environment because each user needs to remember different sets of identities and passwords. Different protocols have been suggested to access the resources of multi-server environment. A secure and efficient remote user authentication protocol for multi-server environment should provide mutual authentication, key agreement, secure password update, low computation requirements and resistance to different feasible attacks.

A number of static identity based remote user authentication protocols have been proposed to improve security, efficiency and cost. The user may change his password but can not change his identity in password authentication protocols. During communication, the static identity leaks out partial information about the user's authentication messages to the attacker. Most of the password authentication protocols for multi-server environment are based on static identity and the attacker can use this information to trace and identify the different requests belonging to the same user. On the other hand, the dynamic identity based authentication protocols provide two-factor authentication based on the identity and password and hence more suitable to e-commerce applications. The aim of this paper is to provide a dynamic identity based secure and computational efficient authentication protocol with user's anonymity for multi-server environment using smart cards. It protects the user's identity in insecure communication channel and hence can be applied directly to e-economic applications.

This paper is organized as follows. In Section 2, we explore the literature on existing authentication protocols for multi-server environment. Section 3 reviews the dynamic identity based remote user authentication protocol for multi-server environment proposed by Liao and Wang. Section 4 describes the susceptibility of Liao and Wang's protocol to malicious server attack and malicious user attack. In Section 5, we present dynamic identity based authentication protocol for multi-server architecture using smart cards. Section 6 discusses the security analysis of the proposed protocol. The comparison of the cost and functionality of the proposed protocol with other related protocols is shown in Section 7. Section 8 concludes the paper.

## 2. Related Work

A number of smart card based remote user authentication protocols have been proposed due to the convenience and secure computation provided by the smart cards. However, most of these protocols do not protect the user's identities in authentication process. User's anonymity is an important issue in many e-commerce applications.

In 2000, Ford and Kaliski [1] proposed the first multi-server password based authentication protocol that splits a password among multiple servers. This protocol generates a strong secret using password based on the communications exchanges with two or more independent servers. The attacker can not compute the strong secret unless all the servers are compromised. This protocol is highly computation intensive due to the use of public keys by the servers. Moreover, the user requires a prior secure authentication channel with the server. Therefore in 2001, Jablon [2] improved this protocol and proposed multi-server password authentication protocol in which the servers do not use public keys and the user does not require prior secure communication channels with the servers.

In 2003, Lin et al. [3] proposed a multi-server authentication protocol based on the ElGamal digital signature scheme that uses simple geometric properties of the Euclidean and discrete logarithm problem concept. The server does not require keeping any verification table but the use of public keys makes this protocol computation intensive. In 2004, Juang [4] proposed a smart card based multi-server authentication protocol using symmetric encryption algorithm without maintaining any verification table on the server. In 2004, Chang and Lee [5] improved

Juang's protocol and proposed a smart card based multi-server authentication protocol using symmetric encryption algorithm without any verification table. Their protocol is more efficient than the multi-server authentication protocol of Juang [4]. In 2007, Hu et al. [6] proposed an efficient password authentication key agreement protocol for multi-server architecture in which user can access multiple servers using smart card and one weak password. The client and the server authenticate each other and agree on a common secret session key. The proposed protocol is more efficient and more user friendly than that of Chang and Lee [5] protocol.

In 2006, Yang et al. [7] proposed a password based user authentication and key exchange protocol using two-server architecture in which only a front-end server communicates directly with the users and a control server does not interact with the users directly. The concept of distributing the password verification information and authentication functionality into two servers requires additional efforts from an attacker to compromise two servers to launch successful offline dictionary attack. In 2008, Tsai [8] proposed a multi-server authentication protocol using smart cards based on the nonce and one-way hash function that does not require storing any verification table on the server and the registration center. The proposed authentication protocol is efficient as compared to other such related protocols because it does not use any symmetric and asymmetric encryption algorithm for its implementation. In 2009, Liao and Wang [9] proposed a dynamic identity based remote user authentication protocol using smart cards to achieve user's anonymity. This protocol uses only hash function to implement a strong authentication for the multi-server environment. It provides a secure method to update the user's password without the help of trusted third party. In their paper, they claimed that suggested protocol can resist various known attacks. However, we show in Section 4 that their protocol is insecure in the presence of an active attacker. In 2009, Hsiang and Shih [10] also found that Liao and Wang's protocol is susceptible to insider attack, masquerade attack, server spoofing attack, registration center spoofing attack and is not reparable. Furthermore, it fails to provide mutual authentication. To remedy these flaws, Hsiang and Shih proposed an improvement over Liao and Wang's protocol. In 2010, Sood et al. [11] found that Hsiang and Shih protocol is also found to be flawed for replay attack, impersonation attack and stolen smart card attack.

## 3. Review of Liao and Wang's Protocol

In this section, we describe the dynamic identity based remote user authentication protocol for multi-server environment proposed by Liao and Wang [9]. The notations used in this section are listed in **Table 1** and the protocol is shown in **Figure 1**.

## 3.1. Registration Phase

The user $U_i$ has to submit his identity $ID_i$ and password $P_i$ to registration center RC so that he can access the resources of the service provider server $S_J$. The RC computes

$$T_i = H(ID_i|x), V_i = T_i \oplus H(ID_i|P_i), B_i = H(P_i) \oplus H(x)$$

and $D_i = H(T_i)$. Then RC issues the smart card with secret parameters ($V_i$, $B_i$, $D_i$, H ( ), y) to the user $U_i$ through a secure communication channel.

## 3.2. Login Phase

The user $U_i$ submits his identity $ID_i^*$, password $P_i^*$ and the server identity $SID_J$ to smart card in order to login on to the service provider server $S_J$. The smart card computes $T_i^* = V_i \oplus H(ID_i^*|P_i^*)$, $D_i^* = H(T_i^*)$ and then verifies the equality of calculated value of $D_i^*$ with the stored value of $D_i$ in its memory. If both values of $D_i$ match, the legitimacy of the user is assured and smart card proceeds to the next step. Otherwise the login request from the user $U_i$ is rejected. Then smart card generates nonce value $N_i$ and computes

$$CID_i = H(P_i) \oplus H(T_i|y|N_i), P_{iJ} = T_i \oplus H(y|N_i|SID_J)$$

and $Q_i = H(B_i|y|N_i)$. Afterwards, smart card sends the login request message ($CID_i$, $P_{iJ}$, $Q_i$, $N_i$) to the server $S_J$.

## 3.3. Mutual Verification and Session Key Agreement Phase

The server $S_J$ computes

$$T_i = P_{iJ} \oplus H(y|N_i|SID_J), H(P_i) = CID_i \oplus H(T_i|y|N_i),$$
$$B_i = H(P_i) \oplus H(x)$$

and $Q_i^* = H(B_i|y|N_i)$, and then compares the computed

**Table 1. Notations.**

| | |
|---|---|
| $U_i$ | $i^{th}$ User |
| $S_J$ | $J^{th}$ Server |
| RC | Registration Center |
| $ID_i$ | Unique Identification of User $U_i$ |
| $P_i$ | Password of User $U_i$ |
| $SID_J$ | Unique Identification of Server $S_J$ |
| $CID_i$ | Dynamic Identity of User $U_i$ |
| H ( ) | One-Way Hash Function |
| x | Master Secret of Registration Center |
| y | Shared Secret Key of Registration Center & All Servers |
| $\oplus$ | XOR Operation |
| $|$ | Concatenation |

| User $U_i$ Knows | Smart Card Stores | Service Provider Server $S_J$ Knows H (x) and y | RC Knows |
|---|---|---|---|
| $ID_i$ and $P_i$ | $V_i = T_i \oplus H(ID_i|P_i)$ | | x and y |
| (Registration Phase) | $B_i = H(P_i) \oplus H(x)$ | | Computes $T_i = H(ID_i|x)$ |
| Submits | $D_i = H(T_i)$ , y | | $V_i = T_i \oplus H(ID_i|P_i)$ |
| $ID_i$ and $P_i$ | Where $T_i = H(ID_i|x)$ | | $B_i = H(P_i) \oplus H(x)$ |
| | | | $D_i = H(T_i)$ |
| (Login Phase) | Computes $T_i^* = V_i \oplus H(ID_i^*|P_i^*)$ | | |
| Enter $ID_i^*$, $P_i^*$ | Computes $D_i^* = H(T_i^*)$ | | |
| and $SID_J$ | Verifies $D_i^* \overset{?}{=} D_i$ | (Mutual Verification | |
| | Generate Nonce Value $N_i$ | & Session Key | |
| | Computes | Agreement Phase) | |
| | $CID_i = H(P_i) \oplus H(T_i|y|N_i)$, | Computes | |
| | $P_{iJ} = T_i \oplus H(y|N_i|SID_J)$, | $T_i = P_{iJ} \oplus H(y|N_i|SID_J)$, | |
| | $Q_i = H(B_i|y|N_i)$  $\xrightarrow{CID_i, P_{iJ}, Q_i, N_i}$ | $H(P_i) = CID_i \oplus H(T_i|y|N_i)$, | |
| | | $B_i = H(P_i) \oplus H(x)$, | |
| | | Computes $Q_i^* = H(B_i|y|N_i)$ | |
| | | Verifies $Q_i^* \overset{?}{=} Q_i$ | |
| | | Generate Nonce Value $N_J$ | |
| | $\xleftarrow{M_{iJ}1, N_J}$ | Computes $M_{iJ}1 = H(B_i|N_i|y|SID_J)$, | |
| Computes $M_{iJ}1^* = H(B_i|N_i|y|SID_J)$ | | | |
| Verifies $M_{iJ}1^* \overset{?}{=} M_{iJ}1$ | | | |
| Computes $M_{iJ}2 = H(B_i|N_J|y|SID_J)$ | | Computes $M_{iJ}2^* = H(B_i|N_J|y|SID_J)$ | |
| | $\xrightarrow{M_{iJ}2}$ | Verifies $M_{iJ}2^* \overset{?}{=} M_{iJ}2$ | |
| Computes Session Key | | Computes Session Key | |
| SK= $H(B_i|N_i|N_J|y|SID_J)$ | | SK= $H(B_i|N_i|N_J|y|SID_J)$ | |

**Figure 1. Liao and Wang's dynamic identity based on multi-server authentication protocol.**

value of $Q_i^*$ with the received value of $Q_i$. If they are not equal, the server $S_J$ rejects the login request and terminates this session. Otherwise, the server $S_J$ generates nonce value $N_J$ and computes $M_{iJ}1 = H(B_i|N_i|y|SID_J)$ and sends the message $(M_{iJ}1, N_J)$ back to smart card of the user $U_i$. On receiving the message $(M_{iJ}1, N_J)$, the user $U_i$'s smart card computes $M_{iJ}1^* = H(B_i|N_i|y|SID_J)$ and compares the computed value of $M_{iJ}1^*$ with the received value of $M_{iJ}1$. This equivalency authenticates the legitimacy of the service provider server $S_J$ else the connection is interrupted. Then the user $U_i$'s smart card computes $M_{iJ}2 = H(B_i|N_J|y|SID_J)$ and sends $M_{iJ}2$ back to the service provider server $S_J$. On receiving the message $M_{iJ}2$, the service provider server $S_J$ computes

$M_{iJ}2^* = H(B_i|N_J|y|SID_J)$ and compares the computed value of $M_{iJ}2^*$ with the received value of $M_{iJ}2$. This equivalency assures the legitimacy of the user $U_i$. After finishing mutual authentication, the user $U_i$ and the service provider server $S_J$ computes $SK = H(B_i|N_i|N_J|y|SID_J)$ as the session key.

# 4. Cryptanalysis of Liao and Wang's Protocol

Liao and Wang [9] claimed that their protocol provides identity privacy and can resist various known attacks. However, we found that this protocol is flawed for malicious server attack and malicious user attack.

## 4.1. Malicious Server Attack

The malicious legitimate server $S_J$ can compute the value of $T_i$, $H(P_i)$ and $B_i$ corresponding to the user $U_i$ during mutual verification and session key agreement phase. This malicious server $S_J$ also knows $H(\ )$ function, $y$ and $H(x)$ because Liao and Wang mentioned that $y$ is the shared key among the users, the servers and the registration center and $H(x)$ is used by the legitimate server $S_J$ to compute $B_i = H(P_i) \oplus H(x)$. The malicious server $S_J$ can record $CID_i = H(P_i) \oplus H(T_i|y|N_i)$, $Q_i = H(B_i|y|N_i)$, $N_i$ during login request message from the user $U_i$ and computes $P_{ik} = T_i \oplus H(y|N_i|SID_k)$ corresponding to the user $U_i$. Afterwards, the malicious server $S_J$ sends the login request message $(CID_i, P_{ik}, Q_i, N_i)$ to the service provider server $S_k$ by masquerading as the user $U_i$. The service provider server $S_k$ authenticates the received messages by calculating $Q_i^*$ from the received messages and checks its equivalency with the received value of $Q_i$. After that, the server $S_k$ generates a nonce value $N_k$ and computes $M_{ik}1 = H(B_i|N_i|y|SID_k)$ and sends the message $(M_{ik}1, N_k)$ back to the malicious server $S_J$ who is masquerading as the user $U_i$. On receiving the message $(M_{ik}1, N_k)$, the malicious server $S_J$ computes $M_{ik}2 = H(B_i|N_k|y|SID_k)$ and sends $M_{ik}2$ back to the service provider server $S_k$. On receiving the message

$M_{ik}2$, the service provider server $S_k$ computes $M_{ik}2^* = H(B_i|N_k|y|SID_k)$ and compares it with the received value of $M_{ik}2$. This equivalency assures the legitimacy of the user $U_i$. After the completion of mutual authentication phase, the malicious server masquerading as the user $U_i$ and the service provider $S_k$ computes $SK = H(B_i|N_i|N_k|y|SID_k)$ as the session key.

## 4.2. Malicious User Attack

The malicious privileged user $U_m$ can extract information like $y$ and $B_m = H(P_m) \oplus H(x)$ from his own smart card. He can also intercept the login request message $(CID_i, P_{iJ}, Q_i, N_i)$ of the user $U_i$ to the service provider $S_J$. This malicious user $U_m$ can compute

$$H(x) = B_m \oplus H(P_m), \ T_i = P_{iJ} \oplus H(y|N_i|SID_J),$$
$$H(P_i) = CID_i \oplus H(T_i|y|N_i)$$

and $B_i = H(P_m) \oplus H(x)$. Now this malicious user $U_m$ can choose random nonce value $N_m$ and computes

$$CID_i = H(P_i) \oplus H(T_i|y|N_m), \ P_{iJ} = T_i \oplus H(y|N_m|SID_J)$$

and $Q_i = H(B_i|y|N_m)$ and masquerade as the legitimate user $U_i$ by sending the login request message $(CID_i, P_{iJ}, Q_i, N_m)$ to the service provider server $S_J$. The service provider server $S_J$ computes

$$T_i = P_{iJ} \oplus H(y|N_m|SID_J), \ H(P_i) = CID_i \oplus H(T_i|y|N_m),$$
$$B_i = H(P_i) \oplus H(x), \ Q_i^* = H(B_i|y|N_m)$$

and compares the equality of calculated value of $Q_i^*$ with the received value of $Q_i$ to verify the legitimacy of the user $U_i$. Afterwards, the server $S_J$ generates nonce value $N_J$, computes $M_{iJ}1 = H(B_i|N_m|y|SID_J)$ and sends the message $(M_{iJ}1, N_J)$ back to the malicious user $U_m$ who is masquerading as the user $U_i$. On receiving the message $(M_{iJ}1, N_J)$, the malicious user $U_m$ computes $M_{iJ}2 = H(B_i|N_J|y|SID_J)$ and sends $M_{iJ}2$ back to the service provider server $S_J$. On receiving the message $M_{iJ}2$, the service provider server $S_J$ computes $M_{iJ}2^* = H(B_i|N_J|y|SID_J)$ and compares the computed value of $M_{iJ}2^*$ with the received value of $M_{iJ}2$ to verify the legitimacy of the user $U_i$. After finishing mutual authentication phase, the malicious user $U_m$ masquerading as the user $U_i$ and the service provider server $S_J$ computes $SK = H(B_i|N_m|N_J|y|SID_J)$ as the session key.

## 5. Proposed Protocol

In this section, we propose a dynamic identity based authentication protocol for multi-server architecture using smart cards that is free from all the attacks considered above. The notations used in this section are listed in **Table 2** and the protocol is summarized in **Figure 2**.

**Table 2. Notations.**

| | |
|---|---|
| $U_i$ | $i^{th}$ User |
| $S_k$ | $K^{th}$ Service Provider Server |
| RC | Control Server |
| $ID_i$ | Unique Identity of User $U_i$ |
| $P_i$ | Password of User $U_i$ |
| H ( ) | One-Way Hash Function |
| $SID_K$ | Unique Identity of $k^{th}$ Service Provider Server |
| $y_i$ | Random Value chosen by CS for User $U_i$ |
| x | Master Secret Parameter of Server CS |
| $N_1$ | Random Nonce Value Generated by User's Smart Card |
| $N_2$ | Random Nonce Value Generated by Server $S_k$ |
| $N_3$ | Random Nonce Value Generated by Server CS |
| $\oplus$ | XOR Operation |
| \| | Concatenation |

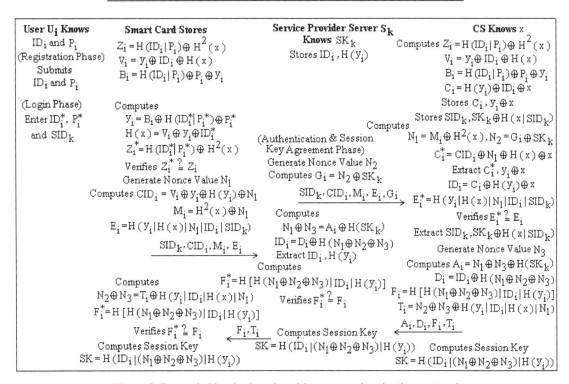

**Figure 2. Dynamic identity based multi-server authentication protocol.**

## 5.1. Registration Phase

The user $U_i$ has to submit his identity $ID_i$ and password $P_i$ to the control server CS for its registration over a secure communication channel.

Step 1: $U_i \rightarrow$ CS: $ID_i$, $P_i$

The control server CS computes the security parameters

$$Z_i = H\left(ID_i \big| P_i\right) \oplus H^2(x), \quad V_i = y_i \oplus ID_i \oplus H(x),$$

$$B_i = H\left(ID_i P_i\right) \oplus P_i \oplus y_i$$

and $C_i = H(y_i) \oplus ID_i \oplus x$, where x is the secret key of the CS and $y_i$ is the random value chosen by the CS for the user $U_i$. The server CS chooses the value of $y_i$ corresponding to the user $U_i$ in such a way so that the value of $C_i$ must be unique for each user. The server CS stores $y_i \oplus x$ corresponding to $C_i$ in its client's database. Then the server CS issues smart card containing security parameters ($Z_i$, $V_i$, $B_i$, H ( )) to the user $U_i$ through a secure communication channel.

Step 2: CS $\rightarrow$ $U_i$: Smart card

All service provider servers register themselves with

CS and CS agrees on a unique secret key $SK_k$ with each service provider server $S_k$. The server $S_k$ remembers the secret key $SK_k$ and CS stores the secret key $SK_k$ as $SK_k \oplus H(x|SID_k)$ corresponding to service provider server identity $SID_k$ in its service provider server's database.

Step 3: CS → $S_k$: $ID_i$, H ($y_i$)

The CS sends $ID_i$ and H ($y_i$) corresponding to newly registered user $U_i$ to all service provider servers. Each service provider server stores $ID_i$ and H ($y_i$) in its database.

## 5.2. Login Phase

The user $U_i$ inserts his smart card into a card reader and submits his identity $ID_i^*$, password $P_i^*$ and the server identity $SID_k$ to smart card in order to login on to the service provider server $S_k$. Then smart card computes

$$y_i = B_i \oplus H\left(ID_i^*|P_i^*\right) \oplus P_i^*, H(x) = V_i \oplus y_i \oplus ID_i^*,$$

$$Z_i^* = H\left(ID_i^*|P_i^*\right) \oplus H^2(x)$$

and compares the computed value of $Z_i^*$ with the stored value of $Z_i$ in its memory to verifies the legitimacy of the user $U_i$.

Step 1: Smart card checks $Z_i^*$ ?= $Z_i$

After verification, smart card generates random nonce value $N_1$ and computes

$$CID_i = V \oplus y_i \oplus H(y_i) \oplus N_1, M_i = H^2(x) \oplus N_1$$

and $E_i = H\left(y_i|H(x)|N_1|ID_i|SID_k\right)$. Then smart card sends the login request message ($SID_k$, $CID_i$, $M_i$, $E_i$) to the service provider server $S_k$.

Step 2: Smart card → $S_k$: $SID_k$, $CID_i$, $M_i$, $E_i$

## 5.3. Authentication and Session Key Agreement Phase

After receiving the login request from the user $U_i$, the server $S_k$ generates random nonce value $N_2$, computes $G_i$ = $N_2$ $SK_k$ and sends the login request message ($SID_k$, $CID_i$, $M_i$, $E_i$, $G_i$) to the control server CS.

Step 1: $S_k$ → CS: $SID_k$, $CID_i$, $M_i$, $E_i$, $G_i$

The control server CS computes

$$N_1 = M_i \oplus H^2(x), N_2 = G_i \oplus SK_k,$$

$$C_i^* = CID_i \oplus N_1 \oplus H(x) \oplus x$$

and finds the matching value of $C_i$ corresponding to $C_i^*$ from its client database.

Step 2: Server CS checks $C_i^*$ ?= $C_i$

If the value of $C_i^*$ does not match with any value of $C_i$ in its client database, the CS rejects the login request and terminates this session. Otherwise, the CS extracts $y_i$ from $y_i$ x corresponding to $C_i^*$ from its client database.

Then the CS computes

$$ID_i = C_i \oplus H(y_i) \oplus x, E_i^*$$
$$= H\left(y_i|H(x)|N_1|ID_i|SID_k\right)$$

and compares $E_i^*$ with the received value of $E_i$ to verifies the legitimacy of the user $U_i$ and the service provider server $S_k$.

Step 3: Server CS checks $E_i^*$ ?= $E_i$

If they are not equal, the CS rejects the login request and terminates this session. Otherwise, the CS extracts $SK_k$ from $SK_k \oplus H(x|SID_k)$ corresponding to $SID_k$ in its service provider server's database. Then the CS generates random nonce value $N_3$, computes

$$A_i = N_1 \oplus N_3 \oplus H(SK_k), D_i = ID_i \oplus H(N_1 \oplus N_2 \oplus N_3),$$

$$F_i = H\left[H(N_1 \oplus N_2 \oplus N_3)ID_i|H(y_i)\right],$$

$$T_i = N_2 \oplus N_3 \oplus H\left(y_i|ID_i|H(x)|N_1\right)$$

and sends the message ($A_i$, $D_i$, $F_i$, $T_i$) back to the service provider server $S_k$. The server $S_k$ computes

$$N_1 \oplus N_3 = A_i \oplus H(SK_k) \text{ from } A_i$$

and $ID_i = D_i \oplus H(N_1 \oplus N_2 \oplus N_3)$ from $D_i$.

Then the server $S_k$ extracts $H(y_i)$ corresponding to $ID_i$ from its database. Afterwards, the server $S_k$ computes

$$F_i^* = H\left[H(N_1 \oplus N_2 \oplus N_3)|ID_i|H(y_i)\right]$$

and compares $F_i^*$ with the received value of $F_i$ to verifies the legitimacy of the control server CS.

Step 4: Server $S_k$ checks $F_i^*$ ?= $F_i$

Then the server $S_k$ sends ($F_i$, $T_i$) to smart card of the user $U_i$. Then smart card computes

$$N_2 \oplus N_3 = T_i \oplus H\left(y_i|ID_i|H(x)|N_1\right),$$

$$F_i^* = H\left[H(N_1 \oplus N_2 \oplus N_3)|ID_i|H(y_i)\right]$$

and compares the computed value of $F_i^*$ with the received value of $F_i$.

Step 5: Smart card checks $F_i^*$ ?= $F_i$

This equivalency authenticates the legitimacy of the control server CS, the server $S_k$ and the login request is accepted else the connection is interrupted. Finally, the user $U_i$'s smart card, the server $S_k$ and the control server CS agree on the common session key as
$$SK = H\left(ID_i|(N_1 \oplus N_2 \oplus N_3)|H(y_i)\right).$$

## 5.4. Password Change Phase

The user $U_i$ can change his password without the help of control server CS. The user $U_i$ inserts his smart card into a card reader and enters his identity $ID_i^*$ and password $P_i^*$ corresponding to his smart card. Smart card computes

$$y_i = B_i \oplus H\left(ID_i^* \big| P_i^*\right) \oplus P_i^*, \ H(x) = V_i \oplus y_i \oplus ID_i^*,$$

$$Z_i^* = H\left(ID_i^* \big| P_i^*\right) \oplus H^2(x)$$

and compares the computed value of $Z_i^*$ with the stored value of $Z_i$ in its memory to verifies the legitimacy of the user $U_i$. Once the authenticity of card holder is verified, the smart card asks the card holder to resubmit a new password $P_i^{new}$. Finally, the value of

$$Z_i = H\left(ID_i \big| P_i\right) \oplus H^2(x) \text{ and } B_i = H\left(ID_i \big| P_i\right) \oplus P_i \oplus y_i$$

stored in the smart card is updated with

$$Z_i^{new} = Z_i \oplus H\left(ID_i \big| P_i\right) \oplus H\left(ID_i \big| P_i^{new}\right)$$

and $B_i^{new} = B_i \oplus H\left(ID_i \big| P_i\right) \oplus P_i \oplus H\left(ID_i \big| P_i^{new}\right) \oplus P_i^{new}$.

## 6. Security Analysis

Smart card is a memory card that uses an embedded micro-processor from smart card reader machine to perform required operations specified in the protocol. Kocher *et al.* [12] and Messerges *et al.* [13] pointed out that all existing smart cards can not prevent the information stored in them from being extracted like by monitoring their power consumption. Some other reverse engineering techniques are also available for extracting information from smart cards. That means once a smart card is stolen by the attacker, he can extract the information stored in it. A good password authentication scheme should provide protection from different possible attacks relevant to that protocol.

1) **Malicious server attack:** A malicious privileged server $S_k$ can monitor the authentication process of the user $U_i$ and can gather information related to the user $U_i$. The malicious server $S_k$ can gather information

$$CID_i = V_i \oplus y_i \oplus H\left(y_i\right) \oplus N_1, \ M_i = H^2(x) \oplus N_1$$

and $E_i = H\left(y_i \big| H(x) \big\| N_1 \big| ID_i \big| SID_k\right)$ during login phase corresponding to the legitimate user $U_i$. This malicious server $S_k$ can not compute $ID_i$, $y_i$ and $x$ from this information. This malicious server $S_k$ can compute the identity $ID_i$ from $D_i$ and can extract $H(y_i)$ corresponding to $ID_i$ from its database corresponding to the user $U_i$ during authentication and session key agreement phase. To masquerade as the legitimate user $U_i$, this malicious server $S_k$ who knows the identity $ID_i$ has to guess $y_i$ and $H(x)$ correctly at the same time. It is not possible to guess out two parameters correctly at the same time in real polynomial time. In another option, this malicious server $S_k$ has to get smart card of the user $U_i$ and has to guess the correct password $P_i$ in order to login on to the server $S_m$. It is not possible to guess the password $P_i$ correctly in real polynomial time even after getting the smart card of

legitimate user $U_i$ and after knowing the identity $ID_i$ of the user $U_i$. Therefore, the proposed protocol is secure against malicious server attack.

2) **Malicious user attack:** A malicious privileged user $U_i$ having his own smart card can gather information like

$$Z_i = H\left(ID_i \big| P_i\right) \oplus H^2(x), \ V_i = y_i \oplus ID_i \oplus H(x)$$

and $B_i = H\left(ID_i \big| P_i\right) \oplus P_i \oplus y_i$ from the memory of smart card. The malicious user $U_i$ can compute the value of $H(x)$ from this information. The value of $CID_m$, $M_m$ and $E_m$ is smart card specific and the malicious user $U_i$ requires to know the values of $H(x)$, $y_m$ and $ID_m$ to masquerade as the legitimate user $U_m$. Therefore, this malicious user $U_i$ has to guess $y_m$ and $ID_m$ correctly at the same time. It is not possible to guess out two parameters correctly at the same time in real polynomial time. Therefore, the proposed protocol is secure against malicious user attack.

3) **Stolen smart card attack:** In case a user $U_i$'s smart card is stolen by an attacker, he can extract the information stored in the smart card. An attacker can extract

$$Z_i = H\left(ID_i \big| P_i\right) \oplus H^2(x), \ V_i = y_i \oplus ID_i \oplus H(x)$$

and $B_i = H\left(ID_i \big| P_i\right) \oplus P_i \oplus y_i$ from the memory of smart card. Even after gathering this information, an attacker has to guess minimum two parameters out of $ID_i$, $H(x)$, $y_i$ and $P_i$ correctly at the same time. It is not possible to guess out two parameters correctly at the same time in real polynomial time. Therefore, the proposed protocol is secure against stolen smart card attack.

4) **Identity protection:** Our approach provides identity protection in the sense that instead of sending the real identity $ID_i$ of the user $U_i$ in authentication, the pseudo identification $CID_i = V_i \oplus y_i \oplus H\left(y_i\right) \oplus N_1$ is generated by smart card corresponding to the legitimate user $U_i$ for its authentication to the service provider server $S_k$ and the control server CS. There is no real identity information about the user during the login and authentication & session key agreement phase. This approach provides the privacy and unlinkability among different login requests belonging to the same user. The attacker can not link different sessions belonging to the same user.

5) **Offline dictionary attack:** In offline dictionary attack, the attacker can record messages and attempts to guess user's identity $ID_i$ and password $P_i$ from recorded messages. An attacker first tries to obtains identity and password verification information such as

$$Z_i = H\left(ID_i \big| P_i\right) \oplus H^2(x), \ B_i = H\left(ID_i \big| P_i\right) \oplus P_i \oplus y_i$$

and then try to guess the identity $ID_i$ and password $P_i$ by offline guessing. Here an attacker has to guess the identity $ID_i$ and password $P_i$ correctly at the same time. It is not possible to guess two parameters correctly at the same time in real polynomial time. Therefore, the proposed protocol is secure against offline dictionary attack.

**6) Replay attack:** In this type of attack, the attacker first listens to communication between the user and the server and then tries to imitate the user to login on to the server by resending the captured messages transmitted between the user and the server. Replaying a message of one session into another session is useless because the user's smart card, the server $S_k$ and the control server CS choose different nonce values ($N_1$, $N_2$, $N_3$) in each new session, which make all messages dynamic and valid for that session only. Therefore, replaying old dynamic identity and user's verifier information is useless. Moreover, the attacker can not compute the session key

$$SK = H\left(ID_i \big| \left(N_1 \oplus N_2 \oplus N_3\right) \big| H\left(y_i\right)\right)$$

because the user $U_i$'s smart card, the server $S_k$ and the control server CS contributes different nonce values ($N_1$, $N_2$, $N_3$) in each new session and the attacker does not know the value of $ID_i$, $N_1$, $N_2$, $N_3$ and $H(y_i)$. Therefore, the proposed protocol is secure against replay attack.

**7) Mutual authentication:** The goal of mutual authentication is to establish an agreed session key among the user $U_i$, the service provider server $S_k$ and the control server CS. All three parties contribute their random nonce values as $N_1$, $N_2$ and $N_3$ for the derivation of session key $SK = H\left(ID_i \big| \left(N_1 \oplus N_2 \oplus N_3\right) \big| H\left(y_i\right)\right)$. The control server CS authenticates the user $U_i$ using verifier information as $E_i^* = H\left(y_i \big| H(x) \big| N_1 \big| ID_i \big| SID_k\right)$, the service provider server $S_k$ authenticates the server CS using

$$F_i^* = H\left[H\left(N_1 \oplus N_2 \oplus N_3\right) \big| ID_i \big| H\left(y_i\right)\right]$$

and the user $U_i$ authenticates the server $S_k$ and the server CS using $F_i^* = H\left[H\left(N_1 \oplus N_2 \oplus N_3\right) \big| ID_i \big| H\left(y_i\right)\right]$. The proposed protocol satisfies strong mutual authentication.

## 7. Cost and Functionality Analysis

An efficient authentication protocol must take communication and computation cost into consideration during user's authentication. The cost comparison of the proposed protocol with the relevant smart card based authentication protocols is summarized in **Table 3**. Assume that the identity $ID_i$, password $P_i$, $x$, $y_i$, nonce values ($N_1$, $N_2$, $N_3$) are all 128 bit long and prime modular operation

is 1024 bits long as in most of practical implementations. Moreover, we assume that the output of secure one-way hash function and the block size of secure symmetric cryptosystem are 128 bits. Let $T_H$, $T_{SYM}$ and $T_{EXP}$ are defined as the time complexity for hash function, symmetric encryption/decryption and exponential operation respectively. Typically, time complexity associated with these operations can be roughly expressed as $T_{EXP} \gg T_{SYM} > T_H$. In the proposed protocol, the parameters stored in the smart card are $Z_i$, $V_i$, $B_i$ and the memory needed (E1) in the smart card is $384 \,(= 3*128)$ bits. The communication cost of authentication (E2) includes the number of communication parameters involved in the authentication protocol. The number of communication parameters is {$SID_k$, $CID_i$, $M_i$, $E_i$, $G_i$, $A_i$, $D_i$, $F_i$, $T_i$} and hence the communication cost of authentication (E2) is $1152 \,(= 9*128)$ bits. The computation cost of registration (E3) is the total time of all operations executed by the user $U_i$ in the registration phase. The computation cost of registration (E3) is $4T_H$. The computation cost of the user (E4) is the time spent by the user during the process of authentication. Therefore, the computation cost of the user (E4) is $8T_H$. The computation cost of the service provider server and the control server (E5) is the time spent by the service provider server and the control server during the process of authentication. Therefore, the computation cost of the service provider server and the control server (E5) is $12T_H$.

The proposed protocol uses the control server CS and the service provider server $S_k$ for the user's authentication that is why the computation cost of the servers (E5) is high as compared to Liao and Wang protocol [9]. On the other hand, the protocol proposed by Liao and Wang in 2009 totally relies on the service provider server $S_k$ for the user's authentication and hence susceptible to malicious server attack and malicious user attack. The proposed protocol maintains the user's anonymity by generating dynamic identity and free from different attacks. The proposed protocol requires very less computation as compared to other related protocols and also highly secure as compared to these related protocols. The functionality comparison of the proposed protocol with the relevant smart card based authentication protocols is summarized in **Table 4**.

**Table 3. Cost comparison among related smart card based authentication protocols.**

|     | Proposed Protocol | Liao & Wang [9] | Hsiang & Shih [10] | Chang & Lee [5] | Juang [4] | Lin *et al.* [3] |
|-----|-------------------|-----------------|--------------------|-----------------|-----------|------------------|
| E1  | 384 bits (0.375 \|n\|) | 512 bits (0.5 \|n\|) | 640 bits (0.625 \|n\|) | 256 bits (0.25 \|n\|) | 256 bits (0.25 \|n\|) | $(4t + 1)$ \|n\| bits |
| E2  | 9*128 bits (1.125 \|n\|) | 7*128 bits (0.875 \|n\|) | 14*128 bits (1.75 \|n\|) | 5*128 bits (0.625 \|n\|) | 9*128 bits (1.125 \|n\|) | 7*1024 bits (7 \|n\|) |
| E3  | $4T_H \ll T$ | $5T_H \ll T$ | $6T_H \ll T$ | $2T_H \ll\, < T$ | $T_H \ll\,< T$ | $5tT$ |
| E4  | $8T_H \ll T$ | $9T_H \ll T$ | $10T_H \ll T$ | $4T_H + 3T_{SYM} \ll T$ | $3T_H + 3T_{SYM} \ll T$ | $2T$ |
| E5  | $12T_H \ll T$ | $6T_H \ll T$ | $13T_H \ll T$ | $4T_H + 3T_{SYM} \ll T$ | $4T_H + 8T_{SYM} \ll T$ | $7T$ |

t: Number of servers; T: Time complexity of a modular exponential communication in $Z_n^*$ : \| n \| = 1024 bits.

**Table 4. Functionality comparison among related smart card based authentication protocols.**

|  | Proposed protocol | Liao & Wang [9] | Hsiang & Shih [10] | Chang & Lee [5] | Juang [4] | Lin et al. [3] |
|---|---|---|---|---|---|---|
| User's anonymity | Yes | Yes | Yes | No | No | No |
| Computation cost | Low | Low | Low | Low | Low | High |
| Single registration | Yes | Yes | Yes | Yes | Yes | No |
| Session key agreement | Yes | Yes | Yes | Yes | Yes | No |
| Correct password update | Yes | Yes | No | No | No | No |
| No time synchronization | Yes | Yes | Yes | Yes | Yes | No |
| Mutual authentication | Yes | Yes | Yes | Yes | Yes | No |
| Two factor security | Yes | Yes | Yes | No | No | No |
| Malicious server attack | No | Yes | No | Yes | Yes | No |
| Malicious user attack | No | Yes | Yes | Yes | Yes | No |

## 8. Conclusion

We presented a cryptanalysis of a recently proposed Liao and Wang's protocol and showed that their protocol is susceptible to malicious server attack and malicious user attack. An improved protocol is proposed that inherits the merits of Liao and Wang's protocol and resists different possible attacks. We have specified and analyzed a dynamic identity based authentication protocol for multi-server architecture using smart cards which is very effective to thwart different attacks. The proposed protocol helps the service provider servers and the control server to recognize the user's completely by computing their static identity and at the same time keeps the identity of the user dynamic in communication channel. The proposed protocol is practical and efficient because only one-way hash function and XOR operations are used in its implementation. Security analysis proved that the proposed protocol is more secure and practical.

## REFERENCES

[1]  W. Ford and B. S. Kaliski, "Server-Assisted Generation of a Strong Secret from a Password," *Proceedings of IEEE 9th International Workshop Enabling Technologies*, Washington DC, June 2000, pp. 176-180.

[2]  D. P. Jablon, "Password Authentication Using Multiple Servers," *Proceedings of RSA Security Conference*, London, April 2001, pp. 344-360.

[3]  I. C. Lin, M. S. Hwang and L. H. Li, "A New Remote User Authentication Scheme for Multi-Server Architecture," *Future Generation Computer System*, Vol. 19, No. 1, 2003, pp. 13-22.

[4]  W. S. Juang, "Efficient Multi-Server Password Authenticated Key Agreement Using Smart Cards," *IEEE Transactions on Consumer Electronics*, Vol. 50, No. 1, 2004, pp. 251-255.

[5]  C. C. Chang and J. S. Lee, "An Efficient and Secure Multi-Server Password Authentication Scheme Using

Smart Cards," *Proceedings of International Conference on Cyber Worlds*, Washington DC, November 2004, pp. 417-422.

[6]  L. Hu, X. Niu and Y. Yang, "An Efficient Multi-Server Password Authenticated Key Agreement Scheme Using Smart Cards," *Proceedings of International Conference on Multimedia and Ubiquitous Engineering (MUE'07)*, April 2007, pp. 903-907.

[7]  Y. Yang, R. H. Deng and F. Bao, "A Practical Password-Based Two-Server Authentication and Key Exchange System," *IEEE Transactions on Dependable and Secure Computing*, Vol. 3, No. 2, 2006, pp. 105-114.

[8]  J. L. Tsai, "Efficient Multi-Server Authentication Scheme Based on One-Way Hash Function without Verification Table," *Computers & Security*, Vol. 27, No. 3-4, 2008, pp. 115-121.

[9]  Y. P. Liao and S. S. Wang, "A Secure Dynamic ID-Based Remote User Authentication Scheme for Multi-Server Environment," *Computer Standards & Interface*, Vol. 31, No. 1, 2009, pp. 24-29.

[10] H. C. Hsiang and W. K. Shih, "Improvement of the Secure Dynamic ID Based Remote User Authentication Scheme for Multi-Server Environment," *Computer Standards & Interface*, Vol. 31, No. 6, 2009, pp. 1118-1123.

[11] S. K. Sood, A. K. Sarje and K. Singh, "A Secure Dynamic Identity Based Authentication Protocol for Multi-Server Architecture," *Journal of Network and Computer Applications*, Vol. 34, No. 2, 2011, pp. 609-618.

[12] P. Kocher, J. Jaffe and B. Jun, "Differential Power Analysis," *Proceedings of CRYPTO 99*, Springer-Verlag, August 1999, pp. 388-397.

[13] T. S. Messerges, E. A. Dabbish and R. H. Sloan, "Examining Smart-Card Security under the Threat of Power Analysis Attacks," *IEEE Transactions on Computers*, Vol. 51, No. 5, 2002, pp. 541-552.

# Secure Messaging Implementation in OpenSC

**Maurizio Talamo[1,2], Maulahikmah Galinium[3], Christian H. Schunck[2], Franco Arcieri[2]**

[1]Department of Engineering, University of Rome Tor Vergata, Rome, Italy
[2]Nestor Laboratory, University of Rome Tor Vergata, Rome, Italy
[3]Department of Information Science, University of Rome Tor Vergata, Rome, Italy

## ABSTRACT

Smartcards are used for a rapidly increasing number of applications including electronic identity, driving licenses, physical access, health care, digital signature, and electronic payments. The use of a specific smartcard in a "closed" environment generally provides a high level of security. In a closed environment no other smartcards are employed and the card use is restricted to the smartcard's own firmware, approved software applications, and approved card reader. However, the same level of security cannot be claimed for open environments where smartcards from different manufacturers might interact with various smartcard applications. The reason is that despite a number of existing standards and certification protocols like Common Criteria and CWA 14169, secure and convenient smartcard interoperability has remained a challenge. Ideally, just one middleware would handle the interactions between various software applications and different smartcards securely and seamlessly. In our ongoing research we investigate the underlying interoperability and security problems specifically for digital signature processes. An important part of such a middleware is a set of utilities and libraries that support cryptographic applications including authentication and digital signatures for a significant number of smartcards. The open-source project OpenSC provides such utilities and libraries. Here we identify some security lacks of OpenSC used as such a middleware. By implementing a secure messaging function in OpenSC 0.12.0 that protects the PIN and data exchange between the SC and the middleware, we address one important security weakness. This enables the integration of digital signature functionality into the OpenSC environment.

**Keywords:** Smart Card; Digital Signature; OpenSC; Secure Messaging

## 1. Introduction

The problem of secure Smartcard (SC) interoperability is one of the main issues that might limit the use of SCs in the future. The success of SC based online authentication and digital signature services critically depends on how this problem will be addressed: users expect SC based applications to work seamlessly in different environments (home, work, leisure) as well as in different countries (business travel, vacation). Existing ISO standards [1,2] and certification protocols like the Common Criteria (CC) [3] and CWA 14169 [4] do not yet facilitate such seamless use in a sufficiently secure setting.

A certified middleware that facilitates the usage of a wide range of SCs for diverse applications could provide a solution. Studying the security requirements for and creating such a middleware is at the focus of our ongoing research and led us to develop the Crypto Probing System (CPS) with an integrated Murphi model checker [5-7].

OpenSC [8] supports cryptographic operations which are used in SC security operations according to the PKCS#15 standard such as digital signature, the applica-

tion on which we concentrate here. The PKCS#15 standard is based on the Digital Certificates on SCs and Secured Electronic Information in Society (SEIS) specifications for digital signature applications using SCs [9]. As OpenSC is easy to use and supports a wide range of SCs. OpenSC could be an ideal component of a universal middleware enabling SC interoperability. However, there are several security aspects that need to be addressed in order to ensure the security of such a middleware.

In an environment where several SCs are connected to various applications via a middleware, an evident security problem is that commands that are supposed to be executed on a certain SC are in fact executed on a different one. **Figure 1** illustrates this situation: SC applications give input to and receive an output from several SCs sharing a common middleware. The middleware translates the input into command sequences, *i.e.* into Straight Line Programmes (SLP), which are supposed to be executed on a corresponding SC. Dashed arrows indicate the possibility that commands can interleave between the straight line programs. As a result a command will be executed on a SC different from the intended one.

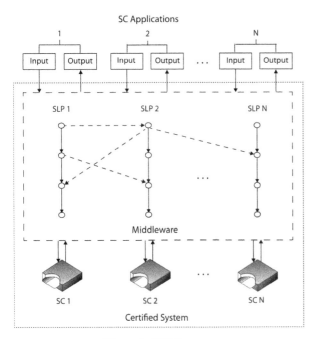

**Figure 1. Middleware.**

Such situations can arise inadvertently due to errors in the middleware but also be due to an attack. From a security perspective such events are particularly problematic if the SC executing a misdirected command does not immediately return an error message. This problem has been observed experimentally [10] and such a situation is called an "anomaly".

Any secure middleware must therefore be able to fully address the issue of misdirected or interleaving commands. There are several requirements that need to be fulfilled:

- The type of a SC must be securely identified.
- Sensitive information must be communicated using secure messaging (*i.e.* a protected channel between the SC application and the SC must be built and supported by the middleware).
- Anomalies must be efficiently detected and computational chains with two or more anomalies must be avoided [10].

The first problem of using OpenSC as part of a universal middleware is that the evaluation of a SC type is based on the Answer to Reset (ATR) and the file structure of the SC (**Figure 2**). As different SCs types may have the same ATR and file structure this method is not reliable. Apart from interoperability problems that may arise if a SC is actually of a different type than determined by OpenSC using the ATR, an attacker may engineer a SC so that it is recognized as being of a certain type (and serving a certain function) while it has been designed for malicious purposes. In the following we will not focus on this issue but we note that this problem needs to be addressed in future work.

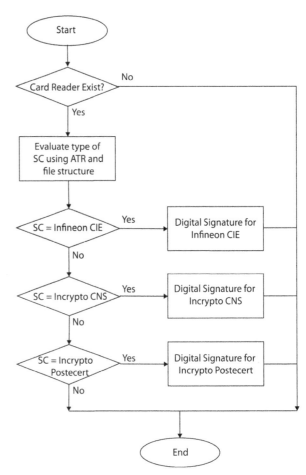

**Figure 2. Evaluation of smartcard type in OpenSC.**

The second problem of OpenSC is that the current OpenSC libraries do not support secure messaging operations which are required in most digital signature applications to protect the sensitive data exchange between software applications and the SC. In this work we extend the OpenSC libraries to include the secure messaging functionality (Sections 2 and 3). With this solution we facilitate the integration of commercially available digital signature SCs for example Postecert and Infocert into OpenSC 0.12.0 (Section 4). However, even after a "state of the art" integration of SM into OpenSC significant problems regarding the protection of the channel between SC applications and SCs persist as will be discussed in Section 5.

## 2. Digital Signature Process

The digital signature process as implemented in OpenSC 0.12.0 provides a basic functionality in the *iso*7816.*c* module for performing secure operation computing of a digital signature. However, this functionality does not support the secure messaging.

To meet the requirements of a complete digital signature process as implemented for example on the Incrypto chip based PosteCert and CNS (Carta Nazionale Servizi) the digital signature process [11] involves the following steps:

step 0 Reset the SC.

step 1 Change directory to the subdirectory containing the digital signature certificate which will be used (SELECT FILE command).

step 2 Activate the security environment for the digital signature (MSE RESTORE command).

step 3 At file system level, choose the private key to be used in the activated security environment (MSE SET command).

step 4 Ask the SC for a random number to be used as a challenge; the first step of activating SM (GET CHALLENGE command).

step 5 Transmit a random number to the SC as a challenge; the second step of activating SM (GIVE CHALLENGE command).

step 6 By using the two random numbers previously exchanged and ciphering 3DES with the shared 3DES key, transmit the PIN that is connected to the private key used for the digital signature operation (VERIFY PIN command). This closes the first SM operation.

step 7 Ask the SC for the random number to be used as (new) challenge; the first step of activating SM (GET CHALLENGE command).

step 8 Transmit a random number to the SC as a challenge; the second step of activating SM (GIVE CHALLENGE command).

step 9 By using the two random numbers previously exchanged and ciphering 3DES with the shared 3DES key, compute and send the input data buffer which is ciphered using the selected private key. Furthermore, receiving the result of the digital signature operation (PSO CDS—Perform Security Operation Compute Digital Signature command).

Extending the OpenSC capabilities to include the additional steps for SM in the digital signature process required modifications of the *pkcs15-tool.c* module of OpenSC 0.12.0 which will be detailed below. Integrating the digital signature functions of the digital signature SC into OpenSC also required to take the different file structures (e.g. different locations of PIN and PUK) into account.

## 3. Secure Messaging in OpenSC

Secure messaging (SM) is used to protect the exchange of sensitive data (e.g. the user's PIN) between the middleware and the SC. In digital signature processes SM is therefore used to protect the data exchanged in connection with the VERIFY PIN and PSO CDS commands

(steps 6 and 9 of the digital signature process detailed).

[12] presents a first but incomplete step towards integrating SM into OpenSC. While some of this work was useful as a starting point, achieving the SM functionality required substantial modifications and extensions. As seen in the steps of the digital signature process detailed in the previous section SM requires both the "Get Challenge" and "Give Challenge" functions. However, OpenSC provides only the Get Challenge function so the Give Challenge command was added to the *iso7816.c* module and registered in the *sc_card_operations* structure that consists of all the required SC operation commands. Any newly created SC command must be registered in this structure (**Figure 3**).

Furthermore the SM main module *sm.c* and a corresponding header file *sm.h* have been developed from scratch. The header file *sm.h* consists of interface functions used in the *sm.c* module. The *sm.c* module contains all essential functions related to SM operations.

As in [12], we created a SM hook in order to link the SM code into OpenSC. A *sc_sm_context* structure was set up in the header file *opensc.h*. **Figure 4** shows how the *sc_sm_context* structure is used in the *sc_card* structure in order to be recognized by the SC. The *sc_sm_context*

```
iso7816.c

static struct sc_card_operations ops2 = {
    ....
    iso7816_set_security_env,
    is07816_restore_security_env,
    iso7816_give_challenge,
    iso7816_get_challenge (),
    ....
};
```

**Figure 3. Structure of the SC operations.**

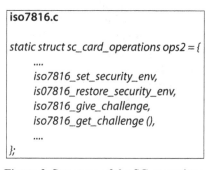

```
opensc.h

...

typedef struct sc_sm_context {
    int use_sm;
} sc_sm_context_t;

...

typedef struct sc_card {
    ...
    ...
    struct sc_card_operations *ops;
    struct sc_sm_context sm_ctx;
    ...
} sc_card_t;

...
```

**Figure 4. Secure messaging hook into OpenSC.**

structure contains the variable *use_sm* that will be used in the *apdu.c* module as a flag for SM. If the SC requires SM, this variable is flagged when the *pkcs15-tool.c* module calls the digital signature process.

For the SM operation, the original APDU serves as an input. The output of the SM operation is the encrypted APDU which is sent to the SC. This involves the following steps [13]:

step 1   Initialize the 24 bytes of SM key.

step 2   Set up and divide the SM key into three encryption and signature keys (8 bytes for each key) according to the 3DES algorithm.

step 3   Obtain two random numbers as challenges (get and give challenge functions—8 bytes for each random number).

step 4   Set up the header block for the APDU Command using the 8 byte random number generated by the get challenge function (**Figure 5(a)**). The header block also contains the mandatory header of the APDU command: the Class Byte (CLA), the Instruction Byte (INS) and two parameter bytes (P1,P2). Since the length of an object must be an integer multiple of 8 bytes, 4 byte padding is required.

step 5   Set up the Cipher Text Block (CTB) and the Cipher Text Object (CTO) by encrypting the data field of the original APDU using the 3DES algorithm. In the VERIFY PIN command, the data field contains the 8 byte PIN of the SC. In the PSO CDS command, the data field contains the input data (117 bytes) to be digitally signed. The CTO structure is a TLV (Tag-Length-Value) object containing a 1 byte Tag, a 1 byte Length variable and a Value variable (encrypted data and padding, either 16 or 120 bytes). **Figure 5(b)** shows the CTO structure using the VERIFY PIN (PSO CDS) commands as examples: the Value contains 16 (120) bytes of encrypted data from the 8 byte PIN (117 byte input data) and 8 (3) byte padding. Furthermore the CTB requires 5 byte padding to concatenate with the 19 (123) byte CTO (**Figure 5(c)**).

step 6   Set up the Net Le Object (if required—**Figure 5(d)**). The Net Le object is used in MAC (Message Authentication Code) Computation when the original APDU does not have a data field. In our experimentation, we do not use this object.

step 7   Set up MAC Computation (using 3DES algorithm), which requires a header block, the CTB and optionally the Net Le Object and set up the MAC object. **Figure 5(e)** shows the MAC Object structure: it is a TLV object containing a 1 byte Tag (0 × 8E), 1 byte Length (0 × 08) and an 8 byte Value (as a result of MAC Computation).

step 8   Create the SM APDU Command including CTO, MAC Object and the optional Net Le Object in the data field (**Figure 5(f)**).

step 9   Send the SM APDU Command and wait for SM APDU Response. SM APDU Response to the Verify PIN command is only a Status Word (SW) without a data field while the response to the PSO CDS command includes a data field as well as the SW (**Figure 5(g)**). This SW is a response code from the SC indicating whether or not the APDU command has generated an error.

These steps are coded in the *do_single_transmit* function of the *apdu.c* module. If SM is required, the *do_single_transmit* function calls the *applySM* function which is coded in the *sm.c* module. As shown in **Figure 6**, the *applySM* function supports the SM process from setting up the header block until composing the APDU

(a) Header Block Structure

| Random Number 8 bytes | CLA 1 byte | INS 1 byte | P1 1 byte | P2 1 byte | Padding 4 bytes |
|---|---|---|---|---|---|
| Header Block - 16 bytes | | | | | |

(b) CTO Stucture for VERIFY PIN (PSO CDS) Commands

| Tag (T) 0x87 | Length (L) 0x11 (0x79) | Value (V) | |
|---|---|---|---|
| | | Padding 0x01 | Encrypted Data 16 (120) bytes |
| CTO - 19 (123) bytes | | | |

(c) CTB Stucture for VERIFY PIN (PSO CDS) Commands

| CTO 19 (123) bytes | Padding 5 bytes |
|---|---|
| CTB - 24 (128) bytes | |

(d) Net Le Object Structure

| T 0x96 | L 0x01 | V |
|---|---|---|
| | | Le 0xFF |
| Net Le Object - 3 bytes | | |

(e) MAC Object Structure

| T 0x8E | L 0x08 | V |
|---|---|---|
| | | Result of MAC Computation 8 bytes |
| MAC Object - 10 bytes | | |

(f) SM APDU Command Structure for VERIFY PIN (PSO CDS) Commands

| CLA 0x0C | INS 1 byte | P1 1 byte | P2 1 byte | Lc 1 byte | Data Field | | | Le 1 byte |
|---|---|---|---|---|---|---|---|---|
| | | | | | CTO 19 (123) bytes | MAC Object 10 bytes | Net Le Object 0 or 3 bytes | |
| SM APDU Command sent to the SC - 35 (139) bytes (without Net Le Object) | | | | | | | | |

(g) SM APDU Response Structure for PSO CDS Commands

| Data Field | | SW 2 bytes |
|---|---|---|
| CTO 139 bytes | MAC Object 10 bytes | |
| SM APDU Response - 151 bytes | | |

**Figure 5. Structure of the objects in the SM operation.**

```
sm.c

...

void applySM(sc_apdu_t *apdu, sc_apdu_t *apduSM)
{
    ...

    Step I: Set up Header Block
    makeHeaderBlock (...);

    Step 2: Set up CTB and CTO
    makeCipherTextObjectBlock (...);

    Step 3: Set up Net Le Object
    makeNetLEObject(...);

    Step 4: Set up MAC Object
    makeMACObject (...);

    Step 5: Set up APDU SM
    apduSM->cla = apdu->cla | 0x0c;
    apduSM->ins = apdu->ins;
    apduSM->p1 = apdu->p1;
    apduSM->p2 = 0x80 | apdu->p2;
    #ifdef USE_NET_LE
        apduSM->lc = dwCipherTextObjLen + 0x03 + dwMacBlockLen;
    #else
        apduSM->lc = dwCipherTextObjLen + dwMacBlockLen;
    #endif

    apduSM->data = malloc((apduSM->lc) * sizeof(u8));
    apduSM->datalen = apduSM->lc;
    apduSM->resp = apdu->resp;
    apduSM->resplen = apdu->resplen;
    if(apduSM->ins == 0x2A)
        apduSM->le = apdu->le + 1;
    else
        apduSM->le = apdu->le;

    Step 6: Clear temporary variables

    ...
}
...
```

Figure 6. Secure messaging implementation in OpenSC.

which is sent to the SC (steps 4 - 8). In particular the *applySM* function implements padding, the 3DES encryption algorithm, MAC signing and the challenge functions.

## 4. Integrating Digital Signature Cards into OpenSC

OpenSC 0.12.0 recognizes three SCs with digital signature functionality which are approved in Italy [14]:

- The government issued official Italian electronic identity card (Carta Identita Elettronica—CIE).
- The digital signature card issued by the Italian Chambers of Commerce (InfoCert) but without supporting its digital signature functionality.
- The Carta Nazionale Servizi (CNS), which is available to citizens in some Italian regions.

In the previous section we have shown how the digital signature functionality of these cards can be supported

via the introduction of SM. Here we show how other digital signature SC can be integrated into OpenSC (including their digital signature functionality) using the example of the PosteCert card issued by the Italian Postal Service (Posteitaliane).

First, a file called *card-itaposte.c* was created which is used to initialize the Postecert card and to call the Postecert card driver (matching the ATR of the card). To recognize the driver, we add the Postecert card by defining *sc_card_type_itaposte_generic* variable and declaring a driver function *sc_get_itaposte_driver* in the file *cards.h*. Finally the driver *sc_get_itaposte_driver* is registered in file *ctx.c* which is used for context related functions.

In order to enable the digital signature functionality of the PosteCert card, the required PKCS#15 functions are provided in the *pkcs15-itaposte.c* module. All certificates, private keys and the PIN are created and their locations in the card's file structure are coded in function *sc_pkcs15emu_itaposte_init*. The *pkcs15-itaposte.c* module is a modified version of the *pkcs15-postecert.c* [15] and of the *pkcs15-itacns.c* [16] modules to match the current file structure of the Postecert card. We also register the function *sc_pkcs15emu_itaposte_init_ex* as built-in emulators in the *pkcs15-syn.c* module.

Furthermore an *itaposte.h* module is created in order to support the *card-itaposte.c* and *pkcs15-itaposte.c* modules. The *itaposte.h* module is derived from the *itacns.h* module of the CNS card. The *itaposte.h* module contains a structure called *itaposte_drv_data_t*, which consists of the IC manufacturer code, mask manufaturer code, operating system version, card type and SM key. The process of adding Postecert SC into OpenSC is shown in **Figures 7** and **8**.

Finally, the newly added and modified files are compiled together with the unchanged OpenSC files. To do that, the *itaposte.h*, *card-itaposte.c*, *pkcs15-itaposte.c*, *sm.h* and *sm.c* modules are registered in *Makefile.am*, and *card-itaposte.obj* and *pkcs15-itaposte.obj* are registered in *Makefile.mak*.

Other digital signature SCs [17] can be integrated into OpenSC analogously with minimal changes such as adjusting for different ATR and file structures.

## 5. Experimentation and Results

In this section we provide an overview of the digital signature process as we have implemented it in OpenSC. **Figure 9** shows the modules which are used in the digital signature process for a certain SC. OpenSC requires the following modules:

- *pkcs15-tool.c* module. This module is used to initialize the digital signature process. After calling this module, the digital signature process function is chosen according to the SC used. The digital signature

```
card-itaposte.c

...
static const struct sc_card_operations *default_ops = NULL;
static struct sc_card_operations itaposte_ops;
static struct sc_card_driver itaposte_drv = {
    "Italian Poste", "itaposte", &itaposte_ops, NULL, 0, NULL
};
/* List of ATR's for "hard" matching. */
static struct sc_atr_table itaposte_atrs[] = {
    { "3b:ff:18:00:ff:81:31:fe:55:00:6b:02:09:03:03:01:01:44:53:44:10:31:80:90",
        NULL, NULL, SC_CARD_TYPE_ITAPOSTE_GENERIC, 0, NULL},
    { NULL, NULL, NULL, 0, 0, NULL}
};
...
static int itaposte_match_card(sc_card_t *card)
{    ...
    itaposte_atr_match ();
    ...
}
static int itaposte_init(sc_card_t *card)
{    ...
    itaposte_match_card (card);
    ...
}
...
```

```
cards.h

...
enum {
    ...
        /* Italian CNS cards */
    SC_CARD_TYPE_ITACNS_BASE = 23000,
    SC_CARD_TYPE_ITACNS_GENERIC,
    ...
        /*Postecert Italian card */
    SC_CARD_TYPE_ITAPOSTE_GENERIC,
}
...
extern sc_card_driver_t *sc_get_itacns_driver(void);
extern sc_card_driver_t *sc_get_itaposte_driver(void);
...
```

```
ctx.c

...
static const struct _sc_driver_entry internal_card_drivers[] =
{
    ...
    { "itacns", (void *(*)(void)) sc_get_itacns_driver },
    { "itaposte", (void *(*)(void)) sc_get_itaposte_driver },
    ...
}
...
```

```
itaposte.h

typedef struct {
    u8 ic_manufacturer_code;
    u8 mask_manufacturer_code;
    u8 os_version_h;
    u8 os_version_l;
    u8 poste_version;
        u8 *sm_key;
} itaposte_drv_data_t;
```

**Figure 7. Adding postecert SC into OpenSC (1).**

```
pkcs15-itaposte.c

...
static int sc_pkcs15emu_itaposte_init(sc_pkcs15_card_t *p15card)
{
    ...
    const char *itaposte_auth_cert_path = "81108010";
    ...
        // add authentication PIN
    sc_format_path("3F008110", &path);
    ...
}
int sc_pkcs15emu_itaposte_init_ex(sc_pkcs15_card_t *p15card,
            sc_pkcs15emu_opt_t *opts)
{
    ...
    sc_pkcs15emu_itaposte_init(p15card);
}
...
```

```
pkcs15-syn.c

...
extern int sc_pkcs15emu_itaposte_init_ex(sc_pkcs15_card_t *,
            sc_pkcs15emu_opt_t *);

static struct {
    const char *        name;
    int        (*handler)(sc_pkcs15_card_t *, sc_pkcs15emu_opt_t *);
} builtin_emulators[] = {
    ...
    { "itacns", sc_pkcs15emu_itacns_init_ex},
    { "itaposte", sc_pkcs15emu_itaposte_init_ex },
}
...
```

**Figure 8. Adding postecert SC into OpenSC (2).**

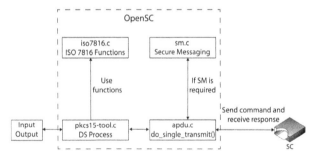

**Figure 9. Digital signature process in OpenSC.**

- *sm.c* module. This module is used to perform the SM operation.
- *apdu.c* module. This module is used to send the APDU Commands to and receive the APDU Responses from the SCs.

In our experimentation the data to be signed (string of 117 bytes) are provided to the middleware as a file (*input.c*).

While we have implemented "state of the art" secure messaging we note that the security provided by the SM functionality is limited. First, the SM key used to encrypt the input plaintext is generally the same for all SCs of a given type and therefore this key is essentially publicly known and therefore offers questionable protection. Second, the random numbers exchanged in connection with the Get and Give challenge commands are sent in clear between the middleware and SCs. An attacker who is

process function consists of all sequential required steps for the digital signature.
- *iso7816.c* module. This module contains ISO 7816 standard functions which are used in the digital signature process (Section 2).

able to sniff the exchanged random numbers and who has knowledge of the SC specific SM key can then easily decrypt the exchanged messages and/or inject his own commands into the "secured process".

In **Table 1** we summarize the complete digital signature process in terms of the exchanged APDU commands and responses for a digital signature SC using the Incrypto microprocessor. In the Verify (PSO CDS) command the PIN (Input data) are encoded in the byte se-

quences [09 0F...91 AE] ([5B 5E...3E F0]) and the last 8 bytes of the input data are the result of the MAC computation. Bytes [D6 E4...C1 DA] of the output data contain the digitally signed input data. For each APDU command, the microprocessor replies with an APDU response that consists of optional response data and a 2 byte of Status Word (SW). The SW [90 00] indicates that the APDU command has been processed by the microprocessor without error.

**Table 1. APDU command and APDU response for Incrypto CNS and postecert card (hexadecimal representation).**

| Command | APDU command | | | | | | | APDU response | |
| --- | --- | --- | --- | --- | --- | --- | --- | --- | --- |
| | CLA | INS | P1 | P2 | Lc | Data in CNS (postecert) | Le | Response data | SW |
| Select file | 00 | A4 | 08 | 00 | 04 (02) | 14 00 81 10 (81 10)<br>This indicates the certificate location of the SCs. | FF | 6F 34 81 02 00 00 83 02 81 10 86 0A<br>FF FF FF FF FF FF FF FF FF FF 8A 01<br>05 8B 18 FF FF FF FF FF FF FF FF FF<br>FF FF FF FF FF FF FF FF FF FF FF FF<br>FF FF FF FF 82 01 38<br>This indicates file control parameters that consist of a Tag [6F], a Length variable [34] and a Value variable [81 02... 01 38] | 90 00 |
| MSE restore | 00 | 22 | F3 | 03 | 00 | - | - | - | 90 00 |
| MSE set | 00 | 22 | F1 | B6 | 03 | 83 01 10 | - | - | 90 00 |
| Get challenge | 00 | 84 | 00 | 00 | 00 | - | 08 | 8 bytes random number | 90 00 |
| Give challenge | 80 | 86 | 00 | 00 | 08 | 8 bytes random number | - | - | 90 00 |
| Verify | 0C | 20 | 00 | 9A | 1D | 87 11 01 09 0F 0C EC CC 81 FB 91 F2 3A 45 96 7E 46 91 AE 8E 08 67 1E 69 C0 FA 33 BD 26<br>[87 11... 91 AE] is a TLV object of CTO structure which consists of a Tag [87], a Length variable [11] and a Value variable [01 09... 91 AE] that contains padding [01] and encoded PIN [09 0F... 91 AE]<br>[8E 08... BD 26] is a TLV object of MAC object structure which consists of a Tag [87], a Length variable [08]<br>and a Value variable [67 1E... BD 26] that indicates result of MAC Computation<br>(see **Figures 5(b), (e), (f)**) | 00 | - | 90 00 |
| Get challenge | 00 | 84 | 00 | 00 | 00 | - | 08 | 8 bytes random number | 90 00 |
| Give challenge | 80 | 86 | 00 | 00 | 08 | 8 bytes Random Number | - | - | 90 00 |
| PSO_CDS | 0C | 2A | 9E | 9A | 85 | 87 79 01 5B 5E 97 05 BD 43 96 B1 FA 8A 5B E5 C1 BC 2A 24 23 ED 5D 51 D4 DA D4 D5 AC F8 70 96 83 75 F7 38 41 00 0F 88 D1 A6 B3 7C F0 6C 1C 41 86 2A 05 1D 52 6B 2B 15 B9 FD AC ED 25 12 AC C0 2A C3 1C 7F 92 65 10 1D 89 52 5D A6 F1 F5 81 CE 6A 0C AE 3A F4 62 C4 ED BC 0E 89 27 1D 25 01 D7 18 5C E1 06 B1 E9 5A 7B 91 E6 D5 5F 47 72 B8 68 C0 B3 B1 50 17 58 BD A6 F5 A7 3E F0 8E 08 EC 51 AA 8D 9F AA 1A 3A<br>[87 79... 3E F0] is a TLV object of CTO structure which consists of a Tag [87], a Length variable [79] and a Value variable [01 5B... 3E F0] that contains padding [01] and encoded Input [5B 5E... 3E F0]<br>[8E 08... 1A 3A] is a TLV object of MAC object structure which consists of a Tag [8E], a Length variable [08] and a Value variable [EC 51... 1A 3A] that indicates result of MAC Computation<br>(see **Figures 5(b), (e), (f)**) | FF | 87 89 01 D6 E4 88 36 FE A7 AC F6 D7 46 4D E4 61 F2 E6 E2 4E 3D 04 F8 8B 00 DD B9 90 DD A0 0A D2 93 E5 91 46 C1 26 D1 32 BE 1E EC 03 FB FC 3C 12 FC 9F 16 6F 1A E6 E9 CD CA 42 72 CF 88 9A A5 7E 2D 4F F0 6D EC 11 AC 63 9B 2A 47 70 70 A6 81 59 8C 87 62 5B 45 8F 0A B8 35 23 BC 67 F4 AD 60 AC 73 19 7E C7 94 A2 29 78 45 E8 4A E7 D5 F2 68 68 32 52 BD BB 1C 14 EB 0F E5 9F E3 4C 63 0E E9 D9 7A EC 1D A1 C4 11 1F 13 34 C1 DA 8E 08 42 A9 5C 97 FE B9 07 FD<br>[87 89... C1 DA] is a TLV object of CTO structure which consists of a Tag [87], a Length variable [89] and a Value variable [01 D6... C1 DA] that contains padding [01] and encoded Output [D6 E4... C1 DA]<br>[8E 08... 07 FD] is a TLV object of MAC object structure which consists of a Tag [8E], a Length variable [08] and a Value variable [42 A9... 07 FD] that indicates result of MAC Computation<br>(see **Figure 5(g)**) | 90 00 |

## 6. Conclusion and Outlook

We have extended OpenSC 0.12.0 to include secure messaging so that the digital signature functionality of SCs can be supported in OpenSC. This will enable us to run extensive test on the interoperability of a wide class of digital signature SCs which are connected with their software applications via a single middleware [7]. We have identified several important security issues that must be addressed in future work. Part of this effort will include combining the OpenSC middleware with a model checker as a "watch-dog" to identify and prevent anomalies. The ultimate goal is to certify the secure interoperability of all SCs integrated into such an environment.

## 7. Acknowledgements

This project has been supported in part by MIUR under contract PRIN 2008ZE493H.

## REFERENCES

[1] International Organization for Standardization (ISO) "Identification Cards—Integrated Circuit Cards Part 4: Organization, Security and Commands for Interchange," International Organization for Standardization Std., Geneva, 2005.

[2] International Organization for Standardization (ISO) "Identification Cards—Integrated Circuit Cards Programming Interfaces—Part 3: Application Programming Interface," International Organization for Standardization Std., Geneva, 2008.

[3] The Common Criteria, "Common Criteria for Information Technology Security Evaluation," Common Criteria Std., 2009. http://www.commoncriteriaportal.org/cc/

[4] The European Committee for Standardization (CEN), "Secure Signature-Creation Devices 'EAL 4+'," European Committee for Standardization (CEN) Std., Brussels, 2004.

[5] M. Talamo, et al., "Robustness and Interoperability Problems in Security Devices," Proceedings of 4th International Conferences on Information Security and Cryptology, Beijing, 14-17 December 2008.

[6] M. Talamo, et al., "Verifying Extended Criteria for In-teroperability of Security Devices," Proceedings of 3rd International Symposium on Information Security, Monterrey, 10-11 November 2008, pp. 1131-1139.

[7] M. Talamo, M. Galinium, C. H. Schunck and F. Arcieri, "Interleaving Command Sequences: A Thread to Secure Smartcard Interoperability," Proceedings of the 10th International Conference on Information Security and Privacy, Jakarta, 1-3 December 2011, pp. 102-107.

[8] OpenSC, "OpenSC Tools and Libraries for Smartcard," 2001. http://www.opensc-project.org/opensc

[9] W. Rankl and W. Effing, "Smart Card Handbook," 4th Edition, Wiley, West Sussex, 2010.

[10] M. Talamo, M. Galinium, C. H. Schunck and F. Arcieri, "Interleaving Commands: A Threat to the Interoperability of Smartcard Based Security Applications," International Journal of Computer and Communication, Vol. 6, No. 1, 2012, pp. 76-83.

[11] M. Talamo, M. Galinium, C. H. Schunck and F. Arcieri, "Integrating Secure Messaging into OpenSC," Proceedings of the 2nd International Conference on Computer and Management, Wuhan, 9-11 March 2012, pp. 1222-1227.

[12] E. Pucciarelli, "Implementation of Secure Messaging," 2008. http://www.mail-archive.com/opensc-devel@lists.opensc-project.org/msg03034.html

[13] A. Villani, "Incrypto34v2 User and Administrator Guidance," ST. Incard, Marcianese, 2004.

[14] OpenSC. "Supported Hardware (Smart Cards and Usb tokens)," 2011. http://www.opensc-project.org/opensc/wiki/SupportedHardware

[15] O. Kirch and A. Iacono, "pkcs15-Postecert.c," 2004. http://www.opensc-project.org/opensc/browser/OpenSC/src/libopensc/pkcs15-postecert.c

[16] E. Pucciarelli, "pkcs15-Itacns.c," 2008. http://www.opensc-project.org/opensc/browser/OpenSC/src/libopensc/pkcs15-itacns.c

[17] Agencia per L'Italia Digitale, "Certificatori Firma Digitale. Ente Nazionale per la Digitalizzazione della Pubblica Amministrazione," 2011. http://www.digitpa.gov.it/certificatori_firma_digitale

# 4

# A Multi-Stage Network Anomaly Detection Method for Improving Efficiency and Accuracy

**Yuji Waizumi, Hiroshi Tsunoda, Masashi Tsuji, Yoshiaki Nemoto**
Graduate School of Information Sciences (GSIS), Tohoku University, Miyagi, Japan

## ABSTRACT

Because of an explosive growth of the intrusions, necessity of anomaly-based Intrusion Detection Systems (IDSs) which are capable of detecting novel attacks, is increasing. Among those systems, flow-based detection systems which use a series of packets exchanged between two terminals as a unit of observation, have an advantage of being able to detect anomaly which is included in only some specific sessions. However, in large-scale networks where a large number of communications takes place, analyzing every flow is not practical. On the other hand, a timeslot-based detection systems need not to prepare a number of buffers although it is difficult to specify anomaly communications. In this paper, we propose a multi-stage anomaly detection system which is combination of timeslot-based and flow-based detectors. The proposed system can reduce the number of flows which need to be subjected to flow-based analysis but yet exhibits high detection accuracy. Through experiments using data set, we present the effectiveness of the proposed method.

**Keywords:** Network Anomaly Detection; Timeslot-Based Analysis; Flow-Based Analysis; Multi-Stage Traffic Analysis; Flow Reduction

## 1. Introduction

In recent years, intrusions such as worms and denial of service attack have become a major threat to the Internet. In particular, novel intrusions such as novel worms and zero-day attacks are increasing and are responsible for a big damage to the Internet. For detecting intrusions, Network Intrusion Detection Systems (NIDSs) have gained attention. NIDSs are classified into misuse detection system and anomaly detection system.

In misuse detection systems such as Snort [1], intrusions are detected by matching signatures which are prepared manually in advance. They are highly popular in network security because they exhibit higher detection accuracy and generate fewer false positives for known intrusions than anomaly detection systems. However, developing signatures is cumbersome and time-consuming task because they have to be made by security experts manually. Therefore, novel intrusions can cause a significant damage to the Internet before signatures are developed.

On the other hand, anomaly detection systems such as NIDES [2] and ADAM [3] can detect unknown intrusions. This is because these methods detect intrusions based on the deviation from the normal behavior, and thus do not require a pre-hand knowledge of intrusions.

However, these methods tend to generate more false positives than signature base IDSs. Although a lot of researchers carried out to increase the detection accuracy, still higher detection accuracy is demanded. Therefore, we focus our research on anomaly detection systems.

In anomaly detection systems, network traffic is analyzed using observation units such as timeslot and flow. A timeslot-based detection has an advantage of being able to detect network anomaly states effectively. On the other hand, the flow-based analysis is capable of examining each communication in a more detail form. Our group has proposed a combination of timeslot-based and flow-based detections and shown its effectiveness [4]. However, in a flow-based analysis, a large number of buffers have to be prepared. Analyzing all flows of network traffic is not realistic, and the buffer size can be vulnerability to Denial of Service (DoS) attacks because all flow analysis can result in a buffer overflow.

In this paper, we propose a high accuracy multi-stage anomaly detection system which can reduce the number of flows necessary to be analyzed. The proposed system consists of two detection stages. The first stage is a timeslot-based detector which picks up flows need to be analyzed by flow-based detector in detail. It then inspects only these suspicious flows in the second stage, thus, computational load and buffer size to analyze flows can be reduced.

The remainder of this paper is organized as follows. Section 2 explains timeslot-based and flow-based analyses, and mentions issues in a combination of these analyses. In Section 3, we proposed a multi-stage anomaly detection system. Evaluation of the proposed system is presented in Section 4. Finally, Section 5 concludes this paper.

## 2. Combination of Timeslot-Based and Flow-Based Analyses

Anomaly detection systems generally analyze traffic in observation units such as timeslots and flows. In this section, we explain these units for the intrusion detection and introduce a conventional method which combines the two detectors. Furthermore, issues in the conventional method are also presented.

### 2.1. Timeslot-Based Analysis

Anomaly detection often uses timeslot-based analysis [4-6]. In this method, the overall traffic is separated into timeslots of fixed length and its features, which are numerical values representing the network state, are extracted from traffic in the timeslot. It has an advantage of low buffer storage since this analysis releases buffers after each timeslot. However, it is difficult for this method to specify anomalous communication flows.

### 2.2. Flow-Based Analysis

A flow is defined as a set of packets which have the same values for the following three header fields.
- Protocol (TCP/UDP)
- Source/Destination address pair
- Source/Destination port pair

A TCP flow ends with FIN or RST flags and UDP flows are terminated by time-out $(T_u)$.

A flow is often used in anomaly detection [4,7,8]. A flow-based analysis method can analyze each bidirectional communication in detail and can specify each anomalous communication. However, in this analysis, buffers must be prepared for every flow. The number of buffers to be prepared lineally increases with as increase in the number of flows. Thus, this method possesses a risk of buffer overflow. Therefore, storage of buffers is a bottleneck in the flow-based analysis and vulnerability to DoS attacks.

### 2.3. A Conventional Combination Method

Our research group has proposed a combined system using the timeslot-based and the flow-based analyses in parallel [4]. **Figure 1(a)** shows the overview of the conventional system, which we term as a parallel system.

Network traffic is inputted to both the timeslot-based and the flow-based detectors, and is analyzed by each detector. A combination of timeslot-based and flow-based detectors can detect intrusions effectively by taking advantage of the merits possessed by both of these methods. Therefore, the combination system is highly accurate in anomaly detection and [4] shows the effectiveness of the parallel system through some experiments using DARPA data set [9].

However, it is still necessary to address the problem of large buffer storage in the flow-based analysis. For reducing the amount of data to be analyzed by flow-based analysis, packet sampling [10-12] and setting short timeouts [13] have been proposed. However, by using the former, it is difficult to observe flows which consist of only few packets, and thus there is a high chance of missing important packets during detection. Since novel worms tend to be few packets in order to spread as fast as possible [14], such worms are difficult to be sampled. In the latter case, since long traffic flows will be split up if its interval of arrival time of packets exceeds the flow timeout, the short timeouts causes increasing the number of flows and declining efficiency and accuracy [11]. As a result, we consider that these approaches suffer from lack of information for detecting anomalous events and exhibit low detection accuracy.

Since packet sampling and setting short timeout diminish data of each flow without any regards for evaluating anomaly, it may result in lack of information needed to detect anomalous flows. For avoiding lack of information, not data of each flow but the number of flows should be reduced with appropriate criteria.

## 3. A Multi-Stage Anomaly Detection System

In this section, we propose a multi-stage network anomaly detection system. It uses fewer amount of buffer, but yet detects intrusions with high accuracy.

### 3.1. Outline

**Figure 1(b)** shows the overview of the proposed multistage

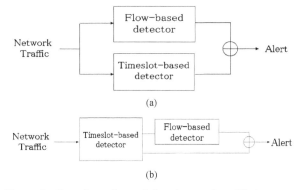

(a)

(b)

**Figure 1. Overview of parallel system and multi-stage system.**

system. The proposed system consists of timeslotbased detector in the first stage and flow-based detector in the second stage. The role of the first stage is to exclude flows that can be judged as obvious anomalous or obvious normal. For such flows, detailed analysis by the flow-based detector is not needed. By excluding such flows, the proposed method can achieve the both high efficiency and high accuracy in network anomaly detection.

Considering the role of the first stage, we utilize timeslot-based detector in it. In the timeslot-based detector, the anomaly level of a time slot basically depends on the number of anomalous flows. Therefore, if timeslots have extremely high or extremely low degree of anomaly, we can consider flows included in such timeslots as obvious anomalous or normal, respectively. Only flows included in the remaining timeslots need to be analyzed by the flow-based analysis. Therefore the proposed system can reduce the number of flows that need to be analyzed by the flow-based analysis.

The architecture of the proposed system is illustrated in **Figure 2**. Network traffic is input into both the timeslot-based detector and the dump module. The timeslot-based detector analyzes the network traffic for each timeslot. Based on the anomaly level of the timeslot, it classifies each slot into three levels which are anomalous, suspicious and normal. Normal slots are excluded from further analysis. For anomalous slots, this detector generates alerts to administrators to inform that anomalous traffic is detected. For suspicious slots, information needed to aggregate packets to assemble flows, which we term suspicious information, is sent to the dump module. This information includes start and end times of the suspicious slot, source/destination IP addresses and source/destina-

tion port numbers. The role of the dump module is to pick up packets based on the suspicious information, and to assemble them into suspicious flows. These flows are sent to the flow-based detector. The flow-based detector analyzes them and generates alarms if any anomaly is detected. As a result, it is not necessary to analyze flows in normal and anomalous slots. Therefore, the proposed system can reduce the number of flows that need to be stored in a buffer.

In Sections 3.2 and 3.3, we describe the timeslot-based detector and the flow-based detector respectively.

## 3.2. Timeslot-Based Detector

### 3.2.1. Outline

**Figure 3** shows the slot classification carried out by the timeslot-based detector. Firstly, each slot is classified into either anomalous slot candidate or normal slot by a threshold ($Th_{ac}$). Then the anomaly score of a slot exceeds the threshold ($Th_{ac}$), the slot is regarded as an anomalous slot candidate.

Next, the anomalous slot candidates are classified into anomalous slots or suspicious slots by another threshold ($Th_{as}$). When the anomaly score of an anomalous slot candidate exceeds the threshold ($Th_{as}$), this slot is judged as an anomalous slot.

For anomalous slots, the timeslot-based detector outputs alerts. For suspicious slots, this detector generates suspicious information. For normal slots, this detector outputs nothing. In the end, only the suspicious slots whose anomaly scores in the range from to are sent to second stage for a detail analysis. It is effective to detect anomaly based on packet header and payload individually [4]. Therefore, the timeslot-based detector has two modules, *header-based detection module* and *payload-based detection module*.

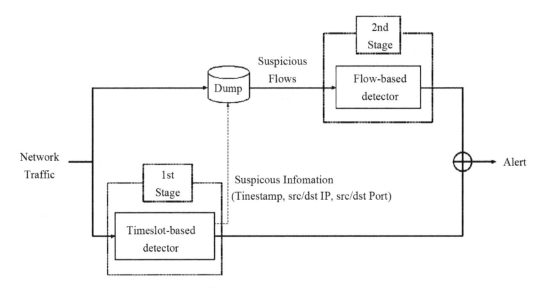

**Figure 2. Detailed architecture of the proposed system.**

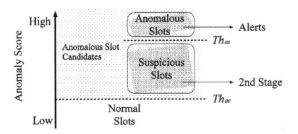

**Figure 3. Slot classification using two thresholds in timeslot-based detector.**

### 3.2.2. Header-Based Detection Module
The header-based detection module analyzes network traffic based on features mainly extracted from the header of each packet included in each timeslot. The features (37 types) extracted are as follows:

1) For all traffic.
a) Each number of packets of TCP/ UDP/ ICMP (3 types).
b) The number of TCP bytes.
c) The number of port varieties of TCP.
d) Each number of TCP flags (5 types).
e) The number of DNS packets.
f) The number of fragment packets.
g) The number of IP address varieties (each byte, 4 types).
2) For port #21, #22, #23, #25, #80 and #110.
a) Each number of TCP flags (3 types).
3) For port #80.
a) The maximum number of bytes between delimiter (space/line feed).
b) A ratio of the number of message headers per the number of request lines.
c) A ratio of the number of packets per the number of clients.

These features become elements of a feature vector. This detector calculates a projection distances from a feature vector to the first principal components using Principal Component Analysis (PCA) and defines the projection distance as the anomaly score of the flow from which the feature vector is extracted. Based on the anomaly score, slots are labeled as anomalous slots, suspicious slots, or normal slots.

### 3.2.3. Payload-Based Detection Module
The payload-based detection module analyzes network traffic by features extracted from payloads of a packet.

In the payload-based detection module, packet payloads are divided into 8-bit codes. Appearance and transition probabilities of each code are calculated using training data. Then, we assume that the code sequences in packet payloads of each port generate with Markov process. Hence, the appearance probability of a code sequence $(x_1, x_2, \cdots, x_n)$ in a packet payload is obtained from Equation (1)

$$P(x_1, x_2, \cdots, x_n) = P(x_1) P(x_2 | x_1) \cdots P(x_n | x_{n-1}) \quad (1)$$

where $n$ is the length of a packet.

Anomaly score $H$ for each packet is defined as the measure of information of code sequences and are obtained from Equation (2) because anomalous code sequences occur few many times. The anomaly of a slot is defined as the maximum value of in that slot.

$$H = -\log_2 P(x_1, x_2, \cdots, x_n) \quad (2)$$

Based on $H$, slots are labeled as anomalous slots, suspicious slots, or normal slots.

### 3.2.4. Output of Timeslot-Based Detector
**Table 1** summarizes the final outputs of the timeslot-based detector. When any one of the header-based and the payload-based detection modules label a slot as an anomalous slot, the timeslot-based detector outputs an alert. If header-based or payload-based detection modules label a slot as a suspicious slot, suspicious information is generated and sent to the dump module. When one detector labels a slot as an anomalous slot and the other labels a slot as a suspicious slot, the timeslot-based detector outputs both of alert and suspicious information. When both header-based and payload-based detection modules label a slot as a normal slot, the timeslot-based detector outputs nothing.

### 3.3. Flow-Based Detector

#### 3.3.1. Outline
The timeslot-based detector creates suspicious information when a slot is classified a suspicious slot. The flow-based detector analyzes suspicious flows which are assembled by the dump module using suspicious information. This detector classifies suspicious flows into anomalous flows or normal flows.

Similar to the timeslot-based detector, the flow-based detector consists of two analysis modules: header-based and payload-based detection modules. When any of the header-based and the payload-based detection modules classifies a flow as anomalous, the flow-based detector outputs an alert.

**Table 1. Output of the timeslot-based detector.**

| PDM \ HDM | Anomalous Slots | Suspicious Slots | Normal Slots |
|---|---|---|---|
| Anomalous Slots | Alert | Alert & SI | Alert |
| Suspicious Slots | Alert & SI | SI | SI |
| Normal Slots | Alert | SI | - |

HDM: Header-based Detection Module; PDM: Payload-based Detection Module; SI: Suspicious Information.

### 3.3.2. Header-Based Detection Module

The header-based detection module detects anomalous flows using features extracted from packet headers of a flow. It analyzes the following features (TCP: 19 types, UDP: 7 tyes):

1) For both of TCP and UDP flows.
a) The number of packets.
b) Inverse of the number of flows which have same port number.
c) The number of fragment packets.
2) For TCP flows (only sending packets from clients).
a) Each number of TCP flags (8 types).
b) Each number of packets with only a TCP flag (8 types).
3) For UDP flows.
a) Each number of sending/receiving packets for clients (2 types).
b) Each number of sending/receiving packets for clients (2 types).

The projection distance from a feature vector to the first principle component is calculated by PCA using these features. The projection distances are then used as anomaly scores of flows.

If some plural flows which have same source/destination IP addresses are observed in a short period of time, this module regards them as related flows and treats them as one set. Because some attacks, such as scan, consist of plural flows from single IP address, assembling the related flows can promotes the efficiency of detection.

When a flow $f$ is observed, flows which have the identical IP addresses with $f$ and meet the conditions below are regarded as the related flows of $f$

$$t_f - T_f < t_{f_i} < t_f \quad (3)$$

where $f_i$ denotes a related flow, $t_f$ and $t_{f_i}$ are the finish time of flow $f$ and $f_i$, respectively. A parameter $T_f$ is used to evaluate whether two flows $f$ and $f_i$ are observed in a short period of time.

Denoting the anomaly score of $f$ and $f_i$ as $a_f$ and $a_{f_i}$, respectively, the anomaly score of the set of the related flows $A_F$ can be expressed as:

$$A_F = a_f + \sum_{i=0}^{N-1} a_{f_i} \quad (4)$$

where $F$ denotes the set of the related flows and $N$ is the maximum size of buffer to store the related flows for evaluating $A_F$. Even if each flow of an intrusion has small anomaly score, we can detect such intrusion by evaluating $A_F$. Moreover, if an alert for $F$ is generated, this module does not generate more alerts for successive flows that have same source/destination IP addresses as $F$ during $t_f + T_f$. Thus, only one alert is generated for a single intrusion and we can avoid receiving redundant alerts.

### 3.3.3. Payload-Based Detection Module

For each TCP flow, a feature vector consists of 512 features which are the 256 codes from client to server and the 256 codes from server to client. For others, such as UDP flow, the feature vector consists of 256 features which are the 256 codes from client to server. Projection distances from the feature vector from the first principle component are calculated by PCA using these features. The flow-based detector defines the projection distances as anomaly scores of flows. This analysis is carried out for all TCP flows, port #20, #21, #23, #25 and #80 respectively.

## 4. Evaluation

### 4.1. Experimental Environment

We use the 1999 DARPA off-line IDS evaluation data set [9] to investigate the number of flows reduced by the timeslot-based detector and to evaluate of detection accuracy. The following information of intrusions is given in this data set.

- Intrusion instants.
- IP addresses and port numbers of intruders.
- IP addresses and port numbers of victims.
- Types of intrusions.

This data set consists of network traffic of 5 weeks. Week 1 and week 3 (10 days) traffic are attack-free while week 4 and week 5 (10 days) traffic include some intrusions. Data of week 1 and week 3 are used for training the detectors of the proposed system, and intrusions included in week 4 and week 5 are the detection targets. In week 4 and week 5, nearly 700,000 TCP and UDP flows are included.

**Table 2** shows the values of parameters $T_t, T_u, T_f$ and $N$, which are same as the parallel system [4]. A payload-based detection module in timeslot-based detector targets port #21, #25 and #80 on which the payload-based detection module is able to train effectively as the data set.

According to [15], and thresholds of flow-based detector are set such that the number of false positives does

**Table 2. Values of parameters set in evaluation.**

| Parameter | Description | Value |
|---|---|---|
| $T_t$ | Timeslot Length | 60 [sec] |
| $T_u$ | Timeout for Terminating UDP flows | 600 [sec] |
| $T_f$ | Available period of a base flow | 600 [sec] |
| $N$ | Maximum number of $f_i$ | 10 |

not exceed 10 for each day (100 in 10 days). Thresholds of detection module in the proposed system are set as shown in **Table 3**. The value of $Th_{ac}$ is set as explained in the next subsection.

## 4.2. Flow Reduction Performance

By using suspicious flow ratio per all flows in week 4 and week 5 ( $R_s$ ), and the ratio of detectable intrusions in anomalous slot candidates per all intrusions ( $R_{ac}$ ), we evaluate flow reduction effect of the proposed system. A low value of $R_s$ is preferred as it implies that the number of flows which will be analyzed in the flow-based detection modules are reduced. High $R_{ac}$ means that many intrusions included in the anomalous slots can be detected by the proposed method.

**Figure 4** shows changes in $R_s$ with respect to $R_{ac}$. This graph indicates that the bottom right portion of the line shows a high performance. **Figure 4** shows that $R_s$ is about 40 percent when $R_{ac}$ is about 90 percent. That is to say, it is possible to detect 90 percent intrusions by analyzing merely 40 percent of the total flows. This indicates the proposed system can effectively reduce flows to be analyzed.

Note that remained 10 percent intrusions become false negatives in the proposed method. However, after investigating these intrusions, we find that most of these intrusions cannot detect even by the flow-based detector. Since the behavior of these intrusions is almost same as normal communication, it is difficult to detect such intrusions by the already existed timeslot-based and flow-based detector. As a result, we conclude that there can be few additional false negatives caused by the proposed method. Therefore, $Th_{ac}$ is adjusted so that $R_{ac}$ becomes 90 percent in the next section.

## 4.3. Intrusion Detection Performance

In this section, the proposed system is evaluated in terms of detection accuracy. **Table 4** indicates the number of detected intrusions, the total number of intrusion and detection rate for existing IDSs and the proposed system. As shown in **Table 4**, the proposed system has higher detection rate than other IDSs except NETAD.

The proposed method achieves higher detection rate than the parallel system because the number of false positives are reduced by the proposed method. When flows are generated by mistaken operation of a user (e.g., access to closed service), these flows have a tendency to be detected by the flow-based detector and cause false positives. In case that some flows are included in normal slots in the proposed method, however, the flow-based detector does not need to analyze and detect such flows. This results in reduction of false positives.

**Table 3. A limitation number of false positives for each day set in evaluation for each detector.**

| Timeslot | | Flow | |
|---|---|---|---|
| Header | Payload | Header | Payload |
| 2 | 2 | 3 | 3 |

**Table 4. A comparison with other IDSs.**

| IDS | Detection rate (detected attacks/detectable attacks) |
|---|---|
| Expert-1 [16] | 50.3% (85/169) |
| Expert-2 [17] | 46.8% (81/173) |
| Dmine [18] | 40.2% (41/102) |
| Forensics [19] | 55.6% (15/27) |
| NETAD [20] | 71.4% (132/185) |
| Parallel system [4] | 60.8% (104/171) |
| Proposed system | 68.4% (117/171) |

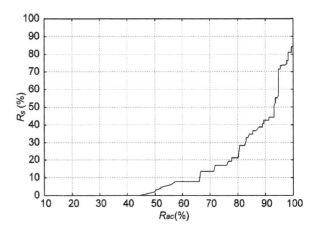

**Figure 4. Changes in $R_s$ with respect to $R_{ac}$.**

NETAD indicates higher detection ratio than the proposed system. However, NETAD has some drawbacks in practical situations. It detects intrusions using the appearance number of IP addresses. This causes many false positives in networks which provide services to any users. Moreover, intruders can easily evade the NETAD's detection because the IP addresses of intruders can be regarded as normal if they can access victims normally beforehand. In this regard, the proposed system can be applied to any networks because it does not use features such as IP addresses. Next, NETAD analyzes traffic using only the first few portion of payloads included in each packet. Therefore, NETAD is not able to detect intrusions which have anomalies the latter half of packet payloads. On the other hand, the proposed system analyzes all payloads, and can detect these intrusions. Consequently, the proposed system will work well in practical situations.

## 5. Conclusions and Future Works

In this paper, we proposed a multi-stage anomaly detection system which is combination of timeslot-based and flow-based detectors. To obtain high intrusion detection accuracy, a detection system should analyze each observed flow in detail. This flow-based analysis, however, needs high computational cost and large buffer to store flows. The computational cost and buffer size can be vulnerability for DoS attacks. To avoid this potential risk, the proposed system reduces the computational cost and buffer size by adopting timeslot-based detection modules, which can work with lower computational cost and smaller buffer size, at the stage of prior to flow-based detector. In the detection experiment, we demonstrated that the proposed system can reduce the number of flows which needs to be analyzed at the flow-based detection modules to 40 percent with high detection accuracy compared with existing intrusion detection systems. Thus, the proposed system can avoid the risk which arises from the computational cost and buffer size with high detection accuracy. But, some flows were classified as non attack flows at the first detection stage. This is a potential drawback of the proposed system and a future work.

## REFERENCES

[1]	M. Roesch, "Snort-Lightweight Intrusion Detection for Networks," *LISA'99 Proceedings of the 13th USENIX Conference on System Administration*, USENIX Association, Berkeley, 7-12 November 1999.

[2]	D. Anderson, T. F. Lunt, H. Javits, A. Tamaru and A. Baldes, "Detecting Unusual Program Behavior Using the Statistical Component of the Nextgeneration Intrusion Detection Expert System (NIDES)," Computer Science Laboratory SRI-CSL 95-06, May 1995.

[3]	R. Sekar, M. Bendre, D. Dhurjati and P. Bollineni, "A Fast Automaton-Based Method for Detecting Anomalous Program Behaviors," *Proceedings of the* 2001 *IEEE Symposium on Security and Privacy*, Oakland, 2001.

[4]	Y. Sato, Y. Waizumi and Y. Nemoto, "Improving Accuracy of Network-Based Anomaly Detection Using Multiple Detection Modules," *Proceedings of IEICE Technical Report*, NS2004-144, 2004, pp. 45-48.

[5]	P. Barford, J. Kline, D. Plonka and A. Ron, "A Signal Analysis of Network Traffic Anomalies," *Proceedings of ACM SIGCOMM Internet Measurement Workshop (IMW)* 2002, Marseille, November 2002, pp. 71-82.

[6]	T. Oikawa, Y. Waizumi, K. Ohta, N. Kato and Y. Nemoto, "Network Anomaly Detection Using Statistical Clustering

Method," *Proceedings of IEICE Technical Report*, NS-2002-143, IN2002-87, CS2002-98, Oct, 2002 pp. 83-88.

[7]	Y. Waizumi, D. Kudo, N.Kato and Y. Nemoto, "A New Network Anomaly Detection Technique Based on Per-Flow and Per-Service Statistics," *Proceedings of International Conference on Computational Intelligence and Security*, Xi'an, 15-19 December 2005, pp. 252-259.

[8]	A. Lakhina, M. Crovella and C. Diot, "Characterization of Network-Wide Anomalies in Traffic Flows," *Proceedings of the ACM/SIGCOMM Internet Measurement Conference*, Taormina, 25-27 October 2004, pp. 201-206.

[9]	"DARPA Intrusion Detection Evaluation," MIT Lincoln Labortory, Lincoln, 2011. http://www.ll.mit.edu/IST/ideval/index.html.

[10]	Inmon Corporation, "Flow Accuracy and Billing," 2011. http:// www.inmon.com/pdf/sFlowBillilng.pdf.

[11]	N. Duffield, C. Lund and M. Thorup, "Properties and Prediction of Flow Statistics from Sampled Packet Streams," *Proceedings of ACM SIGCOMM Internet Measurement Workshop (IMW)*, Marseille, 6-8 November 2002.

[12]	N. Duffield, C. Lund and M. Thorup, "Flow Sampling under Hard Resource Constraints," *Proceedings of ACM SIGMETRICS*, New York, 10-14 June 2004.

[13]	"NeFlow," 2011. http://www.cisco.com/warp/public/732/Tech/nmp/netflow/index.shtml.

[14]	P. Akritidis, K. Anagnostakis and E. P. Markatos, "Efficient Content-Based Detection of Zero-Day Worms," *Proceedings of the International Conference on Communications (ICC* 2005), Seoul, 16-20 May 2005.

[15]	R. Lippmann, J. W. Haines, D. J. Fried, J. Korba and K. Das, "The 1999 DARPA Off-Line Intrusion Detection Evaluation," *Computer Networks*, Vol. 34, No. 4, 2000, pp. 579-595.

[16]	P. Neumann and P. Porras, "Experience with EMERALD to DATE," *Proceedings of 1st USENIX Workshop on Intrusion Detection and Network Monitoring*, Santa Clara, 9-12 April 1999, pp. 73-80.

[17]	G. Vigna, S. T. Eckmann and R. A. Kemmerer, "The STAT Tool Suite," *Proceedings of the* 2000 *DARPA Information Survivability Conference and Exposition (DISCEX)*, Hilton Head, 25-27 January 2000.

[18]	S. Jajodia, D. Barbara, B. Speegle and N. Wu, "Audit Data Analysis and Mining (ADAM)," 2000 http://www.isse.gmu.edu/dbarbara/adam.html

[19]	M. Tyson, P. Berry, N. Willams, D. Moran and D. Blei, "DERBI: Diagnosis, Explanation and Recovery from computer Break-Ins," 2000.

[20]	M. Mahoney, "Network Traffic Anomaly Detection Based on Packet Bytes," *Proceedings of ACM-SAC*, Melbourne, 9-12 March 2003, pp. 346-350.

# 5

# Privacy Preserving Scheme for Location-Based Services

**Youssef Gahi[1], Mouhcine Guennoun[2], Zouhair Guennoun[1], Khalil El-Khatib[2]**

[1]Laboratoire d'Electronique et de Communications—LEC, Ecole Mohammadia d'Ingénieurs—EMI,
Université Mohammed V-Agdal—UM5A. BP, Rabat, Morocco
[2]University of Ontario Institute of Technology, Oshawa, Canada

## ABSTRACT

Homomorphic encryption schemes make it possible to perform arithmetic operations, like additions and multiplications, over encrypted values. This capability provides enhanced protection for data and offers new research directions, including blind data processing. Using homomorphic encryption schemes, a Location-Based Service (LBS) can process encrypted inputs to retrieve encrypted location-related information. The retrieved encrypted data can only be decrypted by the user who requested the data. The technology still faces two main challenges: the encountered processing time and the upper limit imposed on the allowed number of operations. However, the protection of users' privacy achieved through this technology makes it attractive for more research and enhancing. In this paper we use homomorphic encryption schemes to build a fully secure system that allows users to benefit from location-based services while preserving the confidentiality and integrity of their data. Our novel system consists of search circuits that allow an executor (*i.e.* LBS server) to receive encrypted inputs/requests and then perform a blind search to retrieve encrypted records that match the selection criterion. A querier can send the user's position and the service type he/she is looking for, in encrypted form, to a server and then the server would respond to the request without any knowledge of the contents of the request and the retrieved records. We further propose a prototype that improves the practicality of our system.

**Keywords:** Privacy; Location Based Services; Homomorphic Encryption

## 1. Introduction

The growth of smart phones and mobile devices in both software and hardware capabilities have resulted in the emergence of a set of new products and internet services that guarantee new promising business models. Location-Based Services (LBSs) have attracted the utmost importance in this regard. These services rely on the Global Positioning System (GPS) or Network-Based Positioning, which are mainly used to determine the current position of a user, in order to define his/her location relatively to a business or a service (banks, restaurants, universities etc). The user can enquire about that information by communicating wirelessly with an LBS server. The server uses the signal emitted by the user to locate him/her using Real-time Locating Systems (RTLS) [1]. Once the coordinates of the user are determined, the server responds with a list of all services surrounding the user's position.

LBSs have attracted the research and development community. However, LBSs suffer from a major security pitfall in terms of violating users' privacy. In other words, as the LBS server gains knowledge of the users' coordinates, this information can be manipulated by the server itself or by any malicious party to trace the movements of the users. Thereby, instead of using such a mechanism to facilitate lifestyle, it can easily turn over into an efficient tracking tool. This problematic urged the research community to find a secure way to use LBSs without disclosing users' private information.

Strong protection for users' information can be attained if the server is made capable of retrieving location-related information without being aware of the user's position or the point of interests he/she is requesting. It is challenging to achieve the latter target as the server needs to at least know this search criterion to retrieve the requested information. In this paper, we tackle this problem by using encryption schemes to retrieve data without violating the privacy of the users.

The remainder of this paper is organized as follows. In Section 2 we review the related work that aimed at securing location-based services. Section 3 provides a detailed description of the circuits that makes it possible to respond to requests in a blind fashion. Section 4 presents our prototype and the evaluation of its performance. Finally, Section 5 concludes our work and provides future research directions.

## 2. Related Work

There are a number of approaches in the literature to

solve the problem of privacy protection with location based services, including:

- Cloaking;
- Generation of dummies;
- Private information retrieval (PIR).

Gruteser and Grunwald [2] and Chow et al. [3] have based their approaches on K-anonymity [4-7]. The latter concept relies on hiding the user's location among K-1 neighbors. The main idea behind this concept is to send a box of locations instead of only the true one, whereby the probability to guess the user's location is always less than 1/K. Most of techniques relying on K-anonymity [2-7] use a middleware (the anonymizer). This anonymizer is a third party responsible for creating a Cloaking Region (CR), which contains the true user's location, as well as K-1 other neighbors. With such a technique, a typical scenario can be a user trying to localize the nearest bank. The user sends his/her requests (including his/her credentials) to the anonymizer through a wireless network. Thereafter, the anonymizer, which keeps the locations of all current users, authenticates the requester first and chooses a set of K-1 neighbors to create a CR that can be sent instead of the user's position. This way, the risk of violating the user's privacy is reduced by making it difficult to locate the position that has triggered the process (since the server is answering the whole CR). However, this approach suffers from several drawbacks. Firstly, the users' data is still revealed to a third party (the anonymizer) and thus the problem of preserving the user's privacy has not been solved. That is, we still have no guarantees that the anonymizer cannot be misused if a malicious hacker gains access to it. Secondly, the anonymizer needs to update the current location of all the subscribed users repeatedly, which will require a permanent communication and remote monitoring of the users, which is a clear violation of the users' privacy. Finally, the robustness of these approaches depends totally on having a relatively big number of neighbors at the time of receiving the requests. Therefore, depending on a middleware is far from being a perfect solution to secure location-dependent queries and hence any secure solution need to communicate directly with the Location Based Server without any intermediate parties.

Kido et al. [8] and You et al. [9] have proposed a new technique to hide users' location and trajectory by sending several queries instead of only one. The technique depends on creating several fake queries with fake identities in addition to the real query, thereby; the LBS server will not be able to identify. Apparently, the perfection of this mechanism depends on the number of fake requests generated; the more fake queries generated the more robust and secure the system becomes. The problem with this technique is that as the number of requests sent out by a user grows, the LBS may suspect that it is under an attack and thus the requests may be ignored. Moreover, receiving a big number of requests can slow down the server's response time significantly.

Ghinita et al. [10] have proposed a novel approach based on the Private Information Retrieval (PIR) scheme [11] as well as Grid Cells (GCs). The PIR scheme is used to retrieve data from a database without revealing the content of the queries or the identity of the user. GCs technique is used to request a reduced set of LBS which represents the area of interest to the user. The GCs firstly enquire from the server about the appropriate cells, and then retrieve anonymously suitable objects. Ghinita's technique succeeds in solving some of the issues associated with the abovementioned techniques. However, it relies on unguaranteed expectations like extensive data processing on the user's side. In most cases, the user is submitting the request through a mobile phone that has very limited processing capabilities.

Rebollo-Monedero and Forné [12] have proposed a mathematical model to minimize the risk of privacy violations in PIR's queries. They presented a promising system to enhance LBS exchange protocol and make communication more secure, despite using a TTP server as middleware between the users and the LBS server.

## 3. Secure Location-Based Services

To preserve the privacy of the user while interacting with the LBS server, we present in this section a novel approach based on homomorphic encryption scheme to preserve the privacy of the user while interacting with the LBS server.

Homomorphic encryption schemes allow performing arithmetic operations (additions and multiplications) over encrypted data, meaning that the result of an arithmetic operation would be the same whether applied over plain bits or encrypted bits. Our work uses a symmetric encryption scheme as a basis to request LBS services anonymously and guarantee retrieving only suitable data.

**Figure 1** depicts a high level architecture of the proposed Location Based Service. A user encrypts the request, which consists mainly of the user's geographical position and the category of the service (Bank, University, etc.) he/she is looking for, and then sends the encrypted request to the LBS server. This latter performs a search on the location database and produces an encrypted result that matches the search criterion. The encrypted records are returned to the user and upon decryption, the requesting party gets the location of the nearest services.

The encryption scheme is defined as: $c = m + 2r + s_k * Q$ where $c = \varepsilon_{sk}(m)$ is the cipher text of a bit m encrypted under the secret key $s_k$; r and Q are two random integers. 2r is called the noise of the cipher text. The decryption scheme uses the relationship $m = (c \bmod s_k) \bmod 2$. By carefully choosing the size of the secret key $s_k$ and the

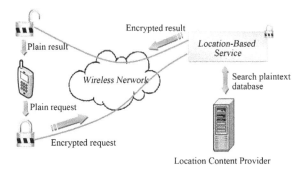

**Figure 1. Architecture of secure Location-Based Service.**

random values r and Q, this encryption scheme is proved to be semantically secure [13]. The size of each of these elements is based on a security parameter called $\lambda$, whereby $s_k$ is an odd $\lambda^5$-bit number, and r and Q are $\lambda$-bit and $\lambda^2$-bit numbers, respectively. As a consequence, each bit encrypted using this scheme would be represented in at most $(1 + \text{Log}_{10}(P))$ decimal digits, where P is $\lambda^7$-bit number. Furthermore, this scheme can support a finite number of arithmetic operations over the same ciphertexts, since it depends mainly on the ratio $s_k/r$. Thereby, we are able to decrypt successfully a bit c as long as the noise value is less than $s_k$. It is obvious to notice that this value doubles after each addition and squares after each multiplication. Therefore, our proposed process must be carefully executed such that it can terminate tasks before reaching the upper limit of the noise value. It is worth noting that the ability to support a high number of operations depends mainly on the parameter of security $\lambda$. If the latter is relatively large, then the ratio $s_k/r$ will be large enough to support a considerable number of computations. However, an encryption scheme that uses a big value of $\lambda$ produces big encrypted values, whereby the time needed to perform operations will be relatively long. In our system we use the Karatsuba algorithm [14] to manipulate big integer values. This algorithm allows performing more than $10^6$ integer operations in less than one second (tested on a personal computer with 2 GB memory with security parameter $\lambda = 5$). This is a practical situation, especially if we consider the size (order of $2^{78125}$) of the encrypted values generated by $\lambda$.

In our system, processing a user's request goes through the following four main steps:

1) Localizing category;
2) Localizing services;
3) Filtering services;
4) Generating results.

We demonstrate how these steps work by the following example. Assuming that the user needs to enquire about the nearby hospitals, he/she sends an encrypted request that represent both his/her current location (x,y) and the enquired category (hospital in this case). Once the server receives the request, it uses the user's position

to calculate distances and localize nearby services. Thereafter, it selects only the objects enquired about, and sends them back to the user in encrypted form. We note that encryption scheme, described, allows performing operations between plain and encrypted bits and the resulting record becomes encrypted.

In the next sub-sections, we provide complete details on each of these main processing steps.

### 3.1. Localizing Categories

The LBS database is structured as a tree, as shown in **Figure 2**. Thus, localizing suitable objects must be preceded by localizing the associated category. This process requires an exhaustive search, since the server doesn't have access to the content of the user's request since it's encrypted. The server needs to compare, bit by bit, the encrypted category, requested by the user, to all available categories in the database. The following formula is used for that comparison:

$$\forall C \in \text{LBS } I_C = \prod_{i=0}^{size-1} \left[\!\left[(1 \oplus c_i) \oplus v_i\right]\!\right] \qquad (1)$$

where *size* is the number of bits used to encode one category, $v_i$ is the $i^{th}$ bit in the enquired category, and $c_i$ is the $i^{th}$ bit in category $C$ that is available in the LBS's database.

This formula focuses on comparing the two categories c and v by verifying whether their sequences of bits are similar or not, knowing that c is encrypted. Towards that end, we compare separately each couple $(c_i, v_i)$ by calculating $1 \oplus c_i \oplus v_i$. The latter results in an encrypted value that either equals to $\varepsilon_{sk}(1)$, if $c_i$ is an encrypted form of $v_i$ or $\varepsilon_{sk}(0)$ otherwise. Then, it is possible to verify whether the compared categories are the same, by checking if all generated values are $\varepsilon_{sk}(1)$. Therefore, we calculate the product $I_C$ of these encrypted bits and if we get $\varepsilon_{sk}(1)$, then the categories are the same. Otherwise, we confirm that at least one pair $(c_i, v_i)$ exists such that $v_i \neq c_i$, meaning that the compared sequences are not the same. The values of $I_C$ are used by the server to filter out the objects that belong to the enquired category.

**Figure 2. LBS's structure.**

We should finally mention that each entry in $I_C$ will have a noise in the order of $\left[ size \times (\lambda + 1) \right]$-bit value, since it is the product of size encrypted bits, which are in the order of $(\lambda + 1)$-bit.

In **Figure 3** we show the noise values, produced from localizing categories, with respect to the bit sizes of these categories.

## 3.2. Localizing Services

In this sub-section we describe the mechanism that locates objects that surround the user's position.

The aim of our approach is to allow users to find the nearest targets while preventing LBS from identifying their positions. Therefore, we use the encrypted position $\left( \varepsilon_{sk}(X), \varepsilon_{sk}(Y) \right)$ and calculate, based on the Manhattan distance [15, 16], the distance separating them from the stored targets. This distance, depicted in **Figure 4**, is calculated between two points $A = (X_A, Y_A)$ and $B = (X_B, Y_B)$ as follows:

$$d(A, B) = |X_B + (1 \oplus X_A)| + |Y_B + (1 \oplus Y_A)| \qquad (2)$$

The relevant positions are presented as a set of bits, and therefore, binary addition is mandatory to calculate the distance. This arithmetic operation results in noise values ranging from $\lambda$-bit to $(sizeXY \times \lambda)$-bit values, which are produced when using the same encrypted bits for calculating both the current bit $S_i$ and the carry bit $S_{i+1}$. Here, $\lambda$, sizeXY, and $S_i$ are the original noise, the bit length of the coordinate $(X,Y)$, and the $i^{th}$ bit in the resulted addition S. In other words, this distance produces a noise value confined between $2\lambda$-bit and $(sizeXY^2 \times \lambda)$-bit, since it is the addition of two sequences with $(sizeXY \times \lambda)$-bit noise value.

In **Figure 5** we show the noise caused by this step in terms of the coordinate's bit length.

## 3.3. Filtering Targets

The distance that is separating the targets from the user

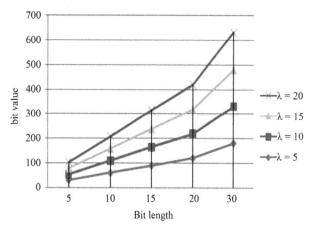

**Figure 3. Noise value produced while localizing categories.**

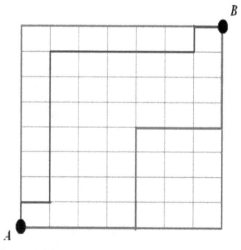

**Figure 4. Manhattan distance between two points.**

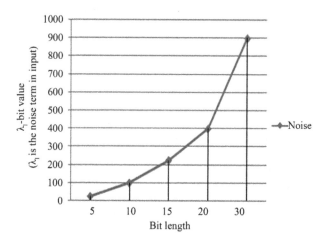

**Figure 5. Noise value when calculating distances.**

allows the server to decide which records to suggest for that user. Although the trivial solution is to send back all of the available targets and leave it for the user to filter these targets, this behavior may lead to an excessive processing time and transmission bandwidth. This is because the user must decrypt the results before filtering them which is a time-consuming procedure. Moreover, forcing a user to receive and process many objects irrelevant to his/her search may unnecessarily waste the resources of the user. Therefore, we propose here two novel approaches to mitigate this situation. in one approach, we use a blind sorting process that arranges the targets based on their encrypted distance, and then chooses the closest ones (number of records is known). In the second approach, we blindly localize the points that belong to a coverage area. In what follows we discuss these two approaches, the details about their functionality, and we highlight their benefits and drawbacks.

### 3.3.1. Blind Sorting

We exploit the PIR methodology and propose a novel

circuit that sorts encrypted values. That is, our circuit allows us to arrange the available locations based on their encrypted distance. Our novel circuit uses the principle of blind comparison. This principle compares two sequences of bits, of length n by performing binary subtraction between them. The $n^{th}$ bit resulting from this subtraction is used to check the nature of the comparison, since this latter is negative whether the bit value is $\varepsilon_{sk}(1)$ and positive otherwise. Blind comparison, however, suffers from a major drawback related to the value of noise that grows rapidly before finishing the process. Therefore, we enhance the model by proposing a novel technique that divides the set of bits into two parts, namely, low and high, and then compares these parts separately, as shown in **Figure 6**.

The partial comparisons conducted on the low and high parts of the targeted sequences are used to finalize the comparison between the two sequences using the following equation:

$$B_c = B_c'' + B_c' \times \overline{B_c''} \qquad (3)$$

where, $B_c$, $B_c'$ and $B_c''$ are the resulting encrypted bits of the comparison, the low part, and the high part, respectively. In **Table 1** we show the relation between these values, and **Figure 7** shows how our technique stabilizes the value of the noise, since in both low and high parts we reset the noise value.

Our comparison circuit is then used to arrange the selected objects in a certain order. We compare the two first elements to see if their associated bit $B_c$ is equal to $\varepsilon_{sk}(1)$. If so, we permute these elements, otherwise we keep them in their original order. This process is repeated for each adjacent pair of elements until all of the elements are compared. After that, the full comparison is repeated N times from the beginning, where N is the number of items available in R the set of targets belonging to a category.

We should mention here that having $B_c$ in an encrypted form may hinder the swap of bits described above. This problem is overcome by using a passkey formula that allows the executor to use the encrypted $B_c$ to apply the comparison. The passkey formula is defined as follows:

$\forall R1 \in R \ and \ R2 \in R \ :$

$$R1_{new} = B_c \times R1_{old} + \overline{B_c} \times R2_{old} \qquad (4)$$

$$R2_{new} = \overline{B_c} \times R1_{old} + B_c \times R2_{old} \qquad (5)$$

where $R1_{old}$, $R2_{old}$ and $R1_{new}$, $R2_{new}$ are the old and new values of the compared entries. **Figure 8** shows the performance of the latter technique in terms of the noise values it achieves. The technique generates high values of noise because of the fact that the same encrypted values are used $N^2$ times before arranging all of the items.

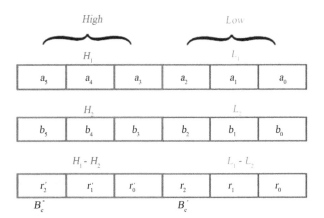

Figure 6. Translating the comparison of two set of bits to their low and high parts.

Table 1. Nature of comparaison from calculated bit value.

| $B_c'$ | $B_c''$ | $B_c$ | Order |
|---|---|---|---|
| $\varepsilon_{sk}(1)$ | $\varepsilon_{sk}(1)$ | $\varepsilon_{sk}(1)$ | $\geq$ |
| $\varepsilon_{sk}(1)$ | $\varepsilon_{sk}(0)$ | $\varepsilon_{sk}(1)$ | $\geq$ |
| $\varepsilon_{sk}(0)$ | $\varepsilon_{sk}(1)$ | $\varepsilon_{sk}(1)$ | $\geq$ |
| $\varepsilon_{sk}(0)$ | $\varepsilon_{sk}(0)$ | $\varepsilon_{sk}(0)$ | $<$ |

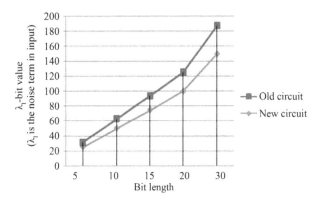

Figure 7. Noise value resulting from the new circuit compared to the old circuit.

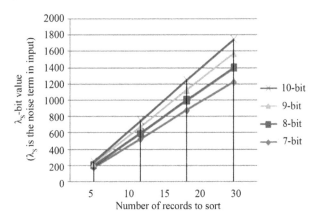

Figure 8. Noise value generated from arranging entries.

Therefore, unless the security parameter $\lambda$ is made big enough (*i.e.*, $\lambda > 15$), this circuit does not perform well due to the maximum noise that is reached before finishing the process. For that reason, we propose a lighter technique that focuses on finding the targets that belong to a specific area, instead of arranging all the objects and then choosing the nearest one, in such a way to filter out the suitable entries while keeping reduced noise values.

### 3.3.2. Coverage area

Objects can be chosen based on the specific area, surrounding the user's location within a radius P, as shown in **Figure 9**. For that purpose, we compare distances, calculated in the third step to P and then all associated $B_C$ will form a set of encrypted bits called $L_R$. Thus, the location belongs to the specified area only if $L_{R,i}$ is equal to $\varepsilon_{sk}(1)$. Furthermore, each category in the database T will have a corresponding $L_R$ that indicates anonymously whether a target is suitable or not.

The fact that the content of $L_R$ is encrypted forces us to find a special process to extract only $L_{R,i}$ that are equal to $\varepsilon_{sk}(1)$. Therefore, we need first to calculate the sum of $L_R$ using the equation:

$$\forall R \in T : S_R = \sum_{i \leq R} L_R \qquad (6)$$

This sum is calculated using elementary symmetric polynomials since this technique keeps the noise value at the order of n, whereby n is the size of $L_R$. It is then possible to localize the $i^{th}$ valid target by calculating the new sequence $L_R'$ as:

$$\forall R \in T L_R' = L_R \times \prod_{i=0}^{n} \left( 1 \oplus \eta_i \oplus S_{R,i} \right) \qquad (7)$$

where $\eta_i$ is the binary representation of the index of the element to select. Moreover, $L_R'$ contains only one bit value equal to $\varepsilon_{sk}(1)$ (the index to localize) while all others are equal to $\varepsilon_{sk}(0)$. This sequence leads to constructing a new database $T'$ of rows $R'$ that contains only the targets that belong to the coverage area. The new database $T'$ can be formed as follows:

$$\forall R \in T, \forall R' \in T' : R' = \sum_{i \leq R} (L_{R,i}' \times R_i) \qquad (8)$$

where $R_i$ is the $i^{th}$ target available in the enquired category.

Looking for objects in a specific area produces an acceptable noise value. This is achieved due to the fact that an important number of records can be supported and the circuit can be terminate before reaching the noise's limit. In **Figure 10** we show the noise produced in this stage.

### 3.4. Generating Results

The last step enables the server to select only the rows $R'$ that belong to the appropriate category. For that purpose

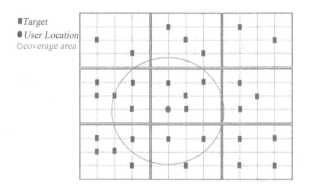

**Figure 9. Coverage area.**

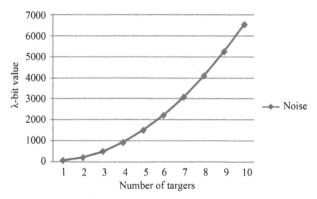

**Figure 10. Noise value generated while filtering objects in a specific category.**

we use the sequence of bits $I_C$ that is calculated during the first step, and then multiply it to the locations $R'$ that are available in the fixed perimeter. After that, we calculate the resulting location as follows:

$$\forall R' \in T' : R'' = I_C \times R' \qquad (9)$$

## 4. Implementation and Results

In this section we study the performance of our proposed system. In **Figure 11** we show the data flow of our proposed system. A user can auto-locate himself/herself (the region where he belongs as well as his position) using smart phone capabilities. Then, the user's software encrypts both his coordinate and the type of service he/she is targeting, and sends them to the server. The server retrieves the requested targets depending on the encrypted information. Thereafter, it sends these encrypted targets to the client to be decrypted and viewed by the user.

Our system has a limitation in terms of the number of records it can support. As the number of the stored targets grows, the system needs to conduct a significant number of arithmetic operations. We may even reach the upper limit of the noise value before extracting all the targets, and a successful decryption will not be guaranteed. We can overcome this problem by using large values of security parameter $\lambda$.

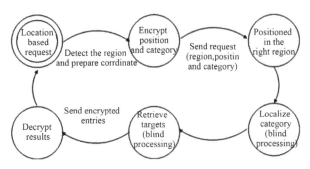

**Figure 11. Data flow.**

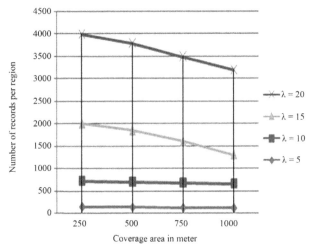

**Figure 12. Number of records supported for different values of $\lambda$.**

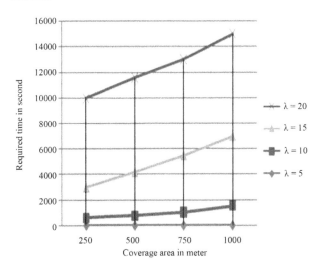

**Figure 13. Processing time.**

Our experimental results are shown in **Figures 12** and **13**. Our experiments are conducted on a personal computer with 2 GB memory and dual core CPU of 2 GHz. **Figure 12** depicts the performance in terms of the number of records per region we can support as a function of $\lambda$. **Figure 13** illustrates the performance in terms of the processing time consumed in each case. This figure shows

that whenever the coverage area gets bigger, the number of operations increases, while the number of records supported gets lesser.

## 5. Conclusions and Perspectives

The concept of answering location-related information for encrypted positions is promising to improve security needs. Indeed, such a mechanism can strongly attract the attention of researchers as it supports the preservation of the users' privacy.

In this paper we developed a novel fully secure location-based mechanism based on a homomorphic encryption scheme. We described the circuits that allow a LBS server to process encrypted inputs to retrieve targeted records that match the user's request. We also discussed the limitations and drawbacks of our proposed system and suggested some solutions to make it more practical. The performance of our system was tested through extensive experiments to extract useful results related to the noise generated and the processing time consumed.

As future work, we are planning to improve the performance of the encryption scheme to be able to support a large number of services. This step is mandatory to make it possible for a commercial deployment of our LBS system.

## REFERENCES

[1] Clarinox Technologies Pty Ltd., "Real Time Location Systems," 2009. http://www.clarinox.com/docs/whitepapers/RealTime_main.pdf

[2] M. Gruteser and D. Grunwald, "Anonymous Usage of Location-Based Services through Spatial and Temporal Cloaking," *Proceedings of the 1st International Conference on Mobile Systems, Applications and Services*, San Francisco, 5-8 May 2003, pp. 31-42.

[3] C. Y. Chow, M. F. Mokbel and X. Liu, "A Peer-to-Peer Spatial Cloaking Algorithm for Anonymous Location-Based Services," *Proceedings of the 14th Annual ACM International Symposium on Advances in Geographic Information Systems*, Arlington, 10-11 November 2006, pp. 171-178.

[4] B. Gedik and L. Liu, "Location Privacy in Mobile Systems a Personalized Anonymization Model," *Proceedings of the 25th International Conference on Distributed Computing System of the IEEE ICDCS*, Columbus, 10 June 2005, pp. 620-629.

[5] M. F. Mokbel, C. Y. Chow and W. G. Aref, "The New Casper: Query Processing for Location Services without Compromising Privacy," *Proceedings of the VLDB 2006*, Seoul, 12-15 September 2006, pp. 763-774.

[6] D. Reid, "An Algorithm for Tracking Multiple Targets," *IEEE Transactions on Automatic Control*, Vol. 24, No. 6, 1979, pp. 843-854.

[7]   B. Gedik and L. Liu, "A Customizable k-Anonymity Model for Protecting Location Privacy," *Technical Report*, Georgia Institute of Technology, Atlanta, 2004.

[8]   H. Kido, Y. Yanagisawa and T. Satoh, "An Anonymous Communication Technique Using Dummies for Location-Based Services," *Proceedings of the International Conference on Pervasive Services of the IEEE ICPS* 05, Santorini, 11-14 July 2005, pp. 88-97.

[9]   T. You, W. Peng and W. Lee, "Protect Moving Trajectories with Dummies," *Proceedings of the International Conference on Mobile Data Management*, Mannheim, 1 May 2007, pp. 278-282.

[10]  G. Ghinita, P. Kalnis, A. Khoshgozaran, C. Shahabi and K.-L. Tan, "Private Queries in Location-Based Services: Anonymizers Are Not Necessary," *Proceedings of the SIGMOD* 08, Vancouver, 9-12 June 2008, pp. 121-132.

[11]  C. Gentry and Z. Ramzan, "Single-Database Private Information Retrieval with Constant Communication Rate," *Proceedings of the 32nd International Colloquium on Automata, Languages and Programming*, Lisboa, 11-15 July 2005, pp. 803-815.

[12]  D. Rebollo-Monedero and J. Forne, "Optimized Query Forgery for Private Information Retrieval," *IEEE Transactions on Information Theory*, Vol. 56, No. 9, 2010, pp. 4631-4642.

[13]  C. Gentry, "A Fully Homomorphic Encryption Scheme," Ph.D. Thesis, Stanford University, Stanford, 2009.

[14]  http://en.wikipedia.org/wiki/Karatsuba_algorithm

[15]  http://en.wikipedia.org/wiki/Taxicab_geometry

[16]  Y. Gahi , M. Guennoun and K. El-khatib, "A Secure Database System Using Homomorphic Encryption Schemes," *Proceedings of the 3rd International Conference on Advances in Databases, Knowledge, and Data Applications*, St. Maarten, 23-28 January 2011, pp. 54-58.

# 6

# Simultaneous Hashing of Multiple Messages

**Shay Gueron[1,2], Vlad Krasnov[2]**
[1]Department of Mathematics, University of Haifa, Haifa, Israel
[2]Intel Corporation, Israel Development Center, Haifa, Israel

## ABSTRACT

We describe a method for efficiently hashing multiple messages of different lengths. Such computations occur in various scenarios, and one of them is when an operating system checks the integrity of its components during boot time. These tasks can gain performance by parallelizing the computations and using SIMD architectures. For such scenarios, we compare the performance of a new 4-buffers SHA-256 S-HASH implementation, to that of the standard serial hashing. Our results are measured on the 2nd Generation Intel® Core™ Processor, and demonstrate SHA-256 processing at effectively ~5.2 Cycles per Byte, when hashing from any of the three cache levels, or from the system memory. This represents speedup by a factor of 3.42x compared to OpenSSL (1.0.1), and by 2.25x compared to the recent and faster $n$-SMS method. For hashing from a disk, we show an effective rate of ~6.73 Cycles/Byte, which is almost 3 times faster than OpenSSL (1.0.1) under the same conditions. These results indicate that for some usage models, SHA-256 is significantly faster than commonly perceived.

Keywords: SHA-256; SHA-512; SHA3 Competition; SIMD Architecture; Advanced Vector Extensions Architectures; AVX; AVX2

## 1. Introduction

The performance of hash functions is important in various situations and platforms. One example is a server workload: authenticated encryption in SSL/TLS sessions, where hash functions are used for authentication, in HMAC mode. This is one reason why the performance of SHA-256 on modern x86_64 architectures was defined as a baseline for the SHA3 competition [1].

Traditionally, the performance of hash functions is measured by hashing a single message (of some length) on a target platform. For example, consider the 2nd Generation Intel® Core™ Processors. The OpenSSL (1.0.1) implementation hashes a single buffer (of length 8 KB) at 17.55 Cycles per Byte (C/B hereafter). Recently, [2] improved the performance of SHA-256 with an algorithm that parallelizes the message schedule, and the use of SIMD architectures, moving the performance baseline to 11.47 C/B (code version from April 2012 is available from [3], and will be updated soon) on the modern processors, when hashing from the cache.

In this paper, we investigate the possibility of accelerating SHA-256 for some scenarios, and are interested in optimizing the following computation: hashing a number ($k$) of independent messages, to produce $k$ different digests. We investigate the advantage of SIMD architectures for these parallelizable computations.

Such workloads appear, for example, during the boot process of an operating system, where it checks the integrity of its components (see [4] for example). This involves computing multiple hashes, and comparing them to expected values. Another situation that involves hashing of multiple independent messages is data de-duplication, where large amounts of data are scanned (typically in chunks of fixed sizes) in order to identify duplicates [5]. In these two scenarios, the data typically reside on the hard disk, but hashing multiple independent messages could also emerge in situations where the data is in the cache/memory.

A SIMD based implementation of hash algorithms was first proposed (in 2004) and described in detail by Aciiçmez [6]. He studied the computations of SHA-1, SHA-256 and SHA-512, and his investigation was carried out on Intel® Pentium™ 4, using SSE2 instructions. Two approaches for gaining performance were attempted: 1) Using SIMD instructions to parallelize some of the computations of the message schedule of these hash algorithms, when hashing a single message (see also later works (on SHA-1) along these lines, in [7,8]); 2) Using SIMD instructions to parallelize hash computations of several independent messages. Aciiçmez reports that he could not improve the performance of hashing a single buffer, using the SIMD instructions (while this could not be done on the Pentium 4, we speculate that it would be possible on more recent architectures). However, he reports speedup by a factor of 1.71x for simultaneous hashing of four buffers, with SHA-256 (speedup by a factor of 2.3x for SHA-512 is also reported, but it is less interesting in our context, because the comparison baseline was a (slow) 32-bit implementation).

In this paper we expand the study conducted by Aciiçmez, by demonstrating the performance of Simultaneous Hashing of multiple independent messages, on contemporary processors. We detail a method for a "Simultaneous Update" that facilitates hashing of independent messages of arbitrary sizes. To account for different usages, we investigate the performance of hashing multiple messages (of variable sizes) from different cache hierarchies, system memory, and from the hard drive.

## 2. Preliminaries and Notations

The detailed definition of SHA-256 can be found in FIPS180-2 publication [9]. Schematically, the computational flow of SHA-256 can be viewed as follows: "Init" (setting the initial values), a sequence of "Update" steps (compressing a 64 bytes block of the message, and updating the digest value), and a "Finalize" step (takes care of the message padding). The padding requires either one or two calls to the Update function, depending on the message's length (see more details in [2]). For SHA-256, the performance is almost linearly proportional to the number ($N$) of Update function calls, which. For a message of length bytes, the value of $N$ is:

$$N = \begin{cases} \left\lfloor \dfrac{length}{64} \right\rfloor + 2 & length \bmod 64 \geq 56 \\ \left\lfloor \dfrac{length}{64} \right\rfloor + 1 & else \end{cases} \quad (1)$$

For sufficiently long messages, we can approximate $N \sim$ floor (length/64). For example, this approximation for a 4 KB message gives floor (length/64) = 64, while actual hashing of a 4 KB message requires 65 Update function calls (i.e., a ~ 1.5% deviation).

## 3. Simultaneous Hashing (S-HASH) of Multiple Messages

SIMD architectures [10] are designed to execute, in parallel, the same operations on several independent chunks of data (called "elements"). Modern architectures have variants of SIMD instructions that operate on elements of sizes 1, 2, 4, or 8 bytes. By the nature of the algorithms, SHA-256 (and SHA-1) requires operations on 4 bytes elements, while SHA-512 requires operations on 8 bytes elements.

**Figure 1** describes the Simultaneous Hashing algorithm (S-HASH) that hashes $k$ messages and generates $k$

```
Algorithm 1: Simultaneous Hashing (S-HASH)
Input:
Buffers – a list with pointers to k buffers to be hashed.
Lengths – a list with the lengths (in bytes) of the k buffers.
Hashes – a list with pointers to store the k generated hash values.
Notations:
The number of t-bit "words" (elements) that fit in a register is m. (for SHA-256, t=32, and with AVX, m=128/32=4).
It is assumed that k > m.
The number of bytes, hashed by one "Update" operation is denoted by p.
Output: k hash values of the k buffers, stored the at memory locations pointed by Hashes.
Flow:
Init:
L[0] = Lengths[0]
L[1] = Lengths[1]
    …
L[m-1] = Lengths[m-1]
B[0] = Buffers[0]
B[1] = Buffers[1]
    …
B[m-1] = Buffers[m-1]
H[0] = Hashes[0]
H[1] = Hashes[1]
    …
H[m-1] = Hashes[m-1]
Last[0] = 0
Last[1] = 0
    …
Last[m-1] = 0
HashInit(Hashes[0])
HashInit(Hashes[1])
    …
HashInit(Hashes[m-1])
i = m;
Simultaneous Update:
Repeat
  n = min(L)/p
  S-UPDATE(H, B, n)
  L = L – [n×p|n×p|…|n×p]
  For j = 0 to m-1
    If L[j]<p AND Last[j]=0 then
      LastBlock[j] = PreparePaddingBlock(B[j])
      B[j] = LastBlock[j]
      Last[j] = 1
      L[j] = Length(LastBlock[j])
    Else If L[j]<p AND Last[j]=1 then
      If i=k then
        Break
      Else
        L[j] = Lengths[i]
        B[j] = Buffs[i]
        H[j] = Hashes[i]
        Last[j] = 0
        HashInit(Hashes[i])
        i++
      End If
    End If
  End For
End Repeat
If unfinished buffers still remain, finish hashing serially
```

**Figure 1. The simultaneous hashing (S-HASH) algorithm.**

digests, with some hash function. Suppose that the implemented hash function operates on $t$-bit "words" (elements), and that the architecture has $s$-bit SIMD registers. Then, the number of words that fit into a SIMD register is $m = s/t$, which we assume to be an integer. We also assume that $k > m$. Algorithm 1 starts with the Initialize step for the first $m$ buffers. Then, it invokes the "Simultaneous Update" function (for the specific hash function) every time there are $m$ blocks ready for processing. This is repeated until the shortest buffer (from the $m$ processed buffers) is fully consumed. At this point, a padding block is fed to the Simultaneous Update function, to "Finalize" (that buffer). If the hash is already finalized, a block from a new buffer is fed (after the proper "Init").

Here, we use the AVX architecture [10], with 128-bit registers (*i.e.*, $s = 128$). SHA-256 (and SHA-1) algorithms have $t = 32$, while SHA-512 has $t = 64$, implying $m = 4$ for SHA-1 and SHA-256, and $m = 2$ for SHA512. For our SHA-256 study, we can hash 4 buffers in parallel. We call this implementation 4-buffers SHA-256 S-HASH.

The near-future AVX2 architecture [11] has integer instructions that operate on 256-bit registers. This allows for doubling the number of independent messages that can be hashed in parallel and would lead to, for example, 8-buffers SHA-256 S-HASH or 4-buffers SHA-512 S-HASH.

# 4. Results

This section describes the 4-buffers SHA-256 S-HASH results.

## 4.1. The System's Characteristics

The system that was used for generating the reported measurements had the following characteristics:
- An Intel® Core™ i5-2500 processor (2nd Generation Intel® Core™ Processor; Sometimes referred to as Architecture Codename "Sandy Bridge").
- 8 GB RAM (DDR3 1600, 2 Channels).
- A RAID0 array of two Intel® SSD 320 drives, each one of 80 GB and combined throughput of 400 MB/sec (indicated by "hdparm-t" [12]).
- Fedora 16 OS.

All the runs were carried out on a system where the Intel® Turbo Boost Technology, the Intel® Hyper-Threading Technology, and the Enhanced Intel Speedstep® Technology, were disabled.

All of the performance numbers reported here, were obtained on the same system, ran on the same processor, and under the same conditions. In particular, we point out that all of the reported hash computations include the overhead of the proper padding, as required by the SHA-256 definition [9].

The tested codes were written in assembly language,

so their performance is compiler agnostic. The impact of the operating system is relevant only for hashing files from the hard disk, because some system calls (to access files/directories) are involved. However, we suggest that experiments with other operating systems would show the same performance traits that we report here.

## 4.2. Simultaneous Hashing of Multiple 4 KB Buffers, from Different Cache Levels and Main Memory

For profiling the performance of the 4-buffers SHA-256 S-HASH, we wrote a new implementation which processes four buffers in parallel. In order to estimate the advantage of the parallelization, we compare the resulting performance to serial implementations that hash the same amount of data.

To measure the performance of hashing data that resides in different cache levels, or in memory, we note that the processor has ([13]): 1) First Level Data Cache of 32 KB (per core); 2) Second Level Cache of 256 KB (per core); 3) Last Level Cache of 6 MB (shared among all the cores). Therefore,
- For data that resides in the First Level Cache, we hashed a total of 16 KB of data, split to 4 chunks of 4 KB each.
- For data that resides in the Second Level Cache, we hashed a total of 256 KB of data, split to 64 chunks of 4 KB each.
- For data that resides in the Last Level Cache, we hashed a total of 2 MB of data, split to 512 chunks of 4 KB each.
- For data that resides in the main memory, we hashed a total of 32 MB of data, split to 8192 chunks of 4 KB each.

Prior to the actual measurements, we ran the hash, in a loop, 500 times, in order to make sure that our data resides in the desired cache level (or memory).

For comparison, we used the OpenSSL (version 1.0.1) SHA-256 (serial) [14] implementation, and the faster implementation, based on the $n$-SMS method [2] (a version from April 2012, can be retrieved from [3]; An update will be posted soon).

The results, illustrated in **Figure 2**, show that hashing from all three cache levels can be performed at roughly the same performance, and there is only some small performance degradation when the data is hashed from the main memory. The 4-buffers SHA-256 S-HASH method is 3.42x faster than OpenSSL (1.0.1), and 2.24x times faster than the $n$-SMS method.

## 4.3. Simultaneous Hashing of Files from the Hard-Drive

The following results account for the performance of

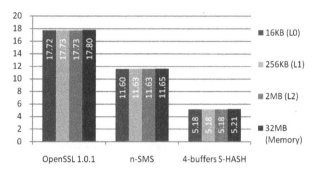

**Figure 2. SHA-256 hashing from different cache levels and memory, Intel® Core™ i5-2500 (Architecture Codename Sandy Bridge). The performance of the 4-buffers SHA-256 S-HASH is compared to the (standard) serial hashing with the OpenSSL 1.0.1 implementation, and to the *n*-SMS method (see explanation in the text).**

hashing from the disk. The numbers were obtained using the following methodology.

For the experiments, we prepared two directories with a different combination of files. The first directory (DIVERSE hereafter) contained 350 files occupying 79 MB (82,833,132 bytes) in total[1]. The files sizes range from 3 Bytes to 7.18 MB (7,533,568 bytes), with the average size of 0.22 MB (236,666 bytes). The detailed size distribution of the file is provided in **Table 1** in the Appendix. The second directory (UNIFORM hereafter) contained 8 (large) files of equal size, each one of 17.76 MB (18,623,835 bytes)[2]. For each directory, we prepared, in advance, the list of its files.

To measure the performance of hashing from the hard drive, we flushed the OS "pagecache" and "dentries" and "inodes" caches, before the measurements were taken (using the Linux directive
echo 3 > /proc/sys/vm/drop_caches) [15].

We measured the following operations: scanning the list (in the prescribed order), opening the files in the list, reading the size of each file, mapping the files to memory, calculating the SHA-256 values and storing them in appropriate location.

**Figure 3**, top panel, provides the performance for the "DIVERSE" directory in C/B (which is a frequency-agnostic metric). The performance is shown for several processor frequencies, to demonstrate how the hard-drive's throughput limits the overall observed performance. The figure shows that at the native processor speed (3.3 GHz), the S-HASH method outperforms the OpenSSL (1.0.1) implementation by a factor of 1.73x. When the processor is down-clocked to 1.6 GHz, all three implementations improve their C/B count, but the S-HASH

---
[1]These files were the drivers from a Windows 7 directory "Windows\System32\drivers\".
[2]The files were copies of the same file, namely "supercop-20120219.tar.gz", retrieved from http://hyperelliptic.org/ebats/supercop-20120219.tar.bz2

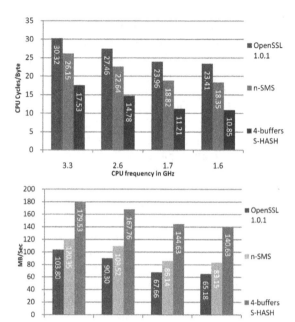

**Figure 3. Hashing the files in the directory DIVERSE (see explanation in the text). Measurements are taken on the Core i5-2500, operating at different CPU frequencies. Panel a shows the performance in Cycles per Byte. Panel b shows the performance in MB/sec.**

improves by a larger margin, becoming 2.16x faster than OpenSSL. The bottom panel of **Figure 3** shows the same performance, measured in MB/sec. It is interesting to observe that although the frequency of the processor is reduced by factor of two, from 3.3 GHz to 1.6 GHz, the S-HASH throughput reduces only by a factor of 1.28x.

**Figure 4** illustrates the performance for the UNIFORM directory. In this scenario, the performance of OpenSSL and of the *n*-SMS method are not limited by hard drive, because we see that reducing frequency does not improve the speed in C/B. On the other hand, the faster 4-buffers SHA-256 S-HASH implementation is affected by the hard drives. It improves (in C/B) when the frequency is reduced, although not as much as it does in the DIVERSE test. The figure shows that the 4-buffers S-HASH is 2.86x faster than OpenSSL, when the processor is clocked at 1.6 GHz, and 2.26x faster at the native processor's frequency.

In general, all implementations improve when the hashed files are large. The reasons are that the overheads for opening files are reduced, and the reads from hard drive are sequential. In addition, the S-HASH is faster when the processed files have equal lengths (UNIFORM directory). This happens because the computations for all the four buffers terminate concurrently, allowing four new buffers to be scheduled together. By contrast, in the DIVERSE directory, when a certain buffer is consumed, operations on the remaining buffers are stopped until a

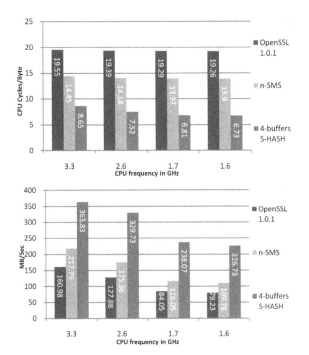

**Figure 4. Hashing the files in the directory UNIFORM (see explanation in the text). Measurements are taken on the Core i5-2500 operating at different CPU frequencies. Panel a shows the performance in Cycles per Byte. Panel b shows the performance in MB/sec.**

new buffer is scheduled.

## 5. Conclusions

We illustrated the general S-HASH approach, and demonstrated the advantage of a 4-buffers SHA-256 S-HASH, running on the AVX architecture. The speedups we observe depend on the location of the data, but are significant in all cases. When hashing equal length messages from any of the three levels of the processor's cache, or from main memory, the 4-buffers SHA-256 S-HASH performs at ~5.2 C/B. This is ~2.24x times faster than the best known serial hashing implementation. When hashing data from the hard-disk, the CPU performance is not the (only) limiting factor, because the disk's read performance becomes a bottleneck. Here, the 4-buffers S-HASH method executes at effectively 8.65 C/B at the native processor speed, 3.3 GHz. This performance is 2.26x faster than OpenSSL (1.0.1) and 1.67x faster than the $n$-SMS method [2] under the same conditions (19.55 C/B and 14.45 C/B, respectively).

We mentioned above two scenarios that require hashing of multiple messages, and can enjoy an S-HASH implementation: An OS check of the integrity of its components (during boot time), and data de-duplication. In addition, SSL/TLS servers that need to support multiple connections could also take advantage of an S-HASH implementation, if their software is set to process data from multiple connections in parallel. We suggest that the potential performance gain might be worth the hassle of tweaking the software to accommodate such parallelization.

Since the 4-buffers S-HASH operates on 4 buffers in parallel, one might wonder why it does not achieve the theoretical four-fold speedup factor, compared to the alternative implementation. We mention here two of the reasons: 1) The 2nd Generation Core™ Processors have an efficient ALU unit that can process data at a faster rate than the SIMD unit. This closes some of the theoretical four-fold gap that AVX can offer; 2) SHA-256 algorithm has a significant amount of rotations. Compared to a single ALU instruction (ROR), the S-HASH method needs to implement rotation by a flow of two (SIMD) shifts, followed by a (SIMD) xor.

Hashing from a hard-drive introduces a different consideration. The RAID array (of two Solid State Drives) that we used in our experiments had throughput of 400 MB/sec. At 3.3 GHz, this throughput is equivalent to processing at the rate of 7.15 C/B. This explains the results that we obtained: while the processor can hash data at 5.18 C/B with the 4-buffers S-HASH method if the data read from the cache (or memory), this performance cannot be reached when the data is fetched from the disk. This is why we get only 8.65 C/B (for the UNIFORM case), but as already noted, this is still significantly faster than the serial alternative. When the processor is clocked to 1.6 GHz, the same disk throughput becomes equivalent to processing at the rate of 3.81 C/B. Thus, on the under-clocked systems, we were able to hash at 6.73 C/B, which is closer (only 1.31x slower) to the processor's hashing capability (5.18 C/B). The remaining gap between the system-wise performance and the maximal processing capability can be attributed to OS overheads, and to the fact that the accessing data stored in the disk is non-sequential (but rather distributed between four areas).

The soon to be released Haswell architecture [11] will support AVX2 with integer instructions that operate on 256-bit registers. With this architecture, we could upgrade our method to implement 8-buffers S-HASH efficiently—in theory, doubling the performance of the 4-buffers S-HASH. However, for hashing data from the disk, we note that the SSD drives are not expected to double their throughput (at least in this time frame), so we should expect less than a twofold speedup.

Note that we intentionally did not study an S-HASH implementation of SHA-512. The reason is that SHA-512 operates on 64-bit "words", and therefore, the current AVX architecture can support only a 2-buffers SHA-512 S-HASH. This makes the S-HASH method less attractive because 1) The SHA-512 ALU implementations are already fast with the $n$-SMS method (8.72 C/B); 2) While each SHA-512 Update compresses 128 bytes of the message and a SHA-256 Update compresses only 64 bytes, SHA-512 involves 1.25x more rounds in the processing than SHA-256 (80 rounds versus 64). We therefore speculate that SHA-512 S-HASH implementations would become useful only on the AVX2 architectures (doing a 4-buffers S-HASH), but will be slower than 8-buffers SHA-256 S-HASH on that architecture.

We conclude this study by stating that our results show that for some usages, SHA-256 is significantly faster than commonly perceived.

Finally, we add a few related remarks on the five SHA3 finalists [1]. Skein and Keccak use 64-bit words, and the remark we made on SHA-512 holds similarly. J. H. Blake and Grostl already use SIMD instructions in their better performing implementations. Therefore, applying the S-HASH method to these algorithms would create a delicate tradeoff with the S-HASH and the benefits of their current use of the SIMD instructions. Such optimization would be an interesting study to carry out.

# REFERENCES

[1]   NIST, "Cryptographic Hash Algorithm Competition," 2012.
      http://csrc.nist.gov/groups/ST/hash/sha-3/index.html

[2]   S. Gueron and V. Krasnov, "Parallelizing Message Schedules to Accelerate the Computations of Hash Functions," 2012. http://eprint.iacr.org/2012/067.pdf

[3]   S. Gueron and V. Krasnov, "Efficient Implementations of SHA256 and SHA512, Using the Simultaneous Message Scheduling Method," 2012.
      http://rt.openssl.org/Ticket/Display.html?id=2784&user=guest&pass=guest

[4]   The Chromium Project, "Verified Boot," 2012.

[5]   C. Y. Liu, Y. P. Lu, C. H. Shi, G. L. Lu, D. H. C. Du and D.-S. Wang, "ADMAD: Application-Driven Metadata Aware De-Duplication Archival Storage System," *Fifth IEEE International Workshop on Storage Network Architecture and Parallel I/Os*, 22 September 2008, pp. 29-35.

[6]   O. Aciicmez, "Fast Hashing on Pentium SIMD Architecture," M.S. Thesis, School of Electrical Engineering and Computer Science, Oregon State University, 2004.

[7]   D. Gaudet, "SHA1 Using SIMD Techniques," 2012.
      http://arctic.org/~dean/crypto/sha1.html

[8]   M. Locktyukhin, "Improving the Performance of the Secure Hash Algorithm (SHA-1)," 2010.
      http://software.intel.com/en-us/articles/improving-the-performance-of-the-secure-hash-algorithm-1/

[9]   "Federal Information Processing Standards Publication 180-2: Secure Hash Standard."
      http://csrc.nist.gov/publications/fips/fips180-2/fips180-2.pdf

[10]  Intel, "Intel Advanced Vector Extensions Programming Reference," 2012. http://software.intel.com/file/36945

[11]  Intel (M. Buxton), "Haswell New Instruction Descriptions Now Available," 2011.
      http://software.intel.com/en-us/blogs/2011/06/13/haswell-new-instruction-descriptions-now-available/

[12]  Linux Manual, "Hdparm," 2012.
      http://linux.die.net/man/8/hdparm

[13]  Intel, "2nd Generation Intel® Core™ Processor Family Desktop Datasheet," 2012.
      http://www.intel.com/content/www/us/en/processors/core/2nd-gen-core-desktop-vol-1-datasheet.html

[14]  OpenSSL, "The Open Source Toolkit for SSL/TLS," 2012.
      http://openssl.org/

[15]  LinuxMM, "Drop Caches," 2012.
      http://linux-mm.org/Drop_Caches

## Appendix: Files size distribution for the "DIVERSE" directory

Table 1. The lengths (in bytes) of the 350 files in the DIVERSE directory, when they are sorted by an alphabetic order of the file-names (from left column top to right column bottom).

| | | | | | | | | |
|---|---|---|---|---|---|---|---|---|
| 14,336 | 122,960 | 15,440 | 73,280 | 6,150,304 | 77,312 | 183,872 | 80,464 | 100,352 |
| 5120 | 651,264 | 15,440 | 116,224 | 44,112 | 140,800 | 12,352 | 93,184 | 7936 |
| 68,096 | 277,624 | 64,512 | 5632 | 16,960 | 157,696 | 48,720 | 20,992 | 51,712 |
| 227,840 | 169,080 | 60,928 | 55,128 | 62,464 | 287,744 | 220,752 | 15,472 | 343,040 |
| 497,152 | 50,808 | 106,576 | 16,896 | 82,944 | 126,464 | 50,768 | 35,456 | 25,600 |
| 61,008 | 256,120 | 194,128 | 98,816 | 116,224 | 30,272 | 230,400 | 3,531,136 | 324,608 |
| 80,384 | 7680 | 28,752 | 982,912 | 120,320 | 140,352 | 60,416 | 19,008 | 25,088 |
| 18,432 | 7680 | 61,440 | 265,088 | 17,920 | 26,112 | 40,512 | 426,496 | 31,744 |
| 8704 | 8192 | 87,632 | 301,784 | 20,544 | 8192 | 1,524,816 | 461,312 | 30,720 |
| 286,720 | 41,472 | 97,856 | 294,064 | 119,680 | 15,424 | 128,592 | 401,920 | 184,832 |
| 47,104 | 303,464 | 23,040 | 530,496 | 50,768 | 224,832 | 46,592 | 161,792 | 36,432 |
| 14,976 | 307,560 | 24,128 | 9728 | 33,280 | 11,136 | 14,848 | 24,656 | 29,184 |
| 14,720 | 311,640 | 155,728 | 3,286,016 | 243,712 | 7168 | 130,048 | 185,936 | 29,184 |
| 293,376 | 311,656 | 270,848 | 195,072 | 95,312 | 6784 | 92,672 | 34,896 | 217,680 |
| 740,864 | 30,760 | 28,240 | 204,800 | 153,160 | 367,168 | 111,616 | 68,864 | 17,488 |
| 1,481,216 | 393,264 | 6656 | 29,696 | 20,992 | 32,320 | 83,968 | 12,496 | 129,024 |
| 178,752 | 13,104 | 45,056 | 70,224 | 60,928 | 8064 | 309,248 | 23,552 | 200,272 |
| 17,664 | 64,080 | 90,624 | 34,304 | 114,752 | 60,496 | 24,064 | 30,088 | 6656 |
| 38,912 | 64,592 | 95,232 | 24,576 | 106,560 | 947,776 | 165,376 | 199,168 | 46,672 |
| 30,320 | 32,896 | 41,984 | 290,368 | 65,600 | 35,328 | 204,800 | 199,168 | 71,760 |
| 27,008 | 89,600 | 72,192 | 23,104 | 115,776 | 24,064 | 214,096 | 192,256 | 363,584 |
| 28,736 | 21,760 | 118,784 | 55,376 | 113,152 | 56,320 | 158,720 | 192,256 | 294,992 |
| 288,336 | 292,864 | 552,448 | 223,448 | 22,016 | 164,352 | 55,296 | 29,184 | 24,248 |
| 48,840 | 740,864 | 98,344 | 3,440,660 | 17,024 | 57,856 | 145,920 | 1,897,328 | 161,872 |
| 65,088 | 1,485,312 | 132,648 | 646 | 35,392 | 44,544 | 11,264 | 44,544 | 24,576 |
| 70,168 | 146,036 | 35,104 | 31,232 | 158,712 | 259,072 | 76,800 | 26,624 | 59,904 |
| 143,792 | 112,128 | 21,160 | 122,368 | 228,752 | 374,864 | 104,016 | 15,872 | 17,920 |
| 350,208 | 172,544 | 468,480 | 26,624 | 9,984 | 51,264 | 29,696 | 23,552 | 27,776 |
| 195,024 | 654,928 | 92,160 | 100,864 | 481,504 | 44,032 | 171,600 | 99,840 | 88,576 |
| 77,888 | 42,064 | 147,456 | 76,288 | 642,952 | 24,576 | 109,056 | 62,544 | 42,496 |
| 78,848 | 412,672 | 45,568 | 46,592 | 75,672 | 1,659,984 | 23,040 | 38,400 | 21,056 |
| 158,720 | 10,240 | 17,488 | 32,896 | 100,904 | 6144 | 23,552 | 38,400 | 12,800 |
| 271,872 | 334,416 | 460,504 | 30,208 | 283,744 | 149,056 | 94,208 | 125,440 | 22,096 |
| 54,824 | 12,288 | 21,584 | 751,616 | 40,448 | 167,488 | 26,624 | 41,536 | 52,304 |
| 15,360 | 491,088 | 39,504 | 14,416 | 30,208 | 318,976 | 14,336 | 327,680 | 40,448 |
| 284,736 | 339,536 | 24,144 | 105,472 | 49,216 | 72,832 | 13,824 | 48,640 | 14,336 |
| 3 | 182,864 | 514,048 | 537,112 | 31,232 | 131,584 | 14,336 | 9728 | 16,464 |
| 7,533,568 | 499,200 | 102,400 | 410,688 | 94,784 | 97,280 | 16,896 | 19,968 | 21,504 |
| 7,533,568 | 60,416 | 40,448 | 39,024 | 155,216 | 75,840 | 43,584 | 98,816 | |

# Text Independent Automatic Speaker Recognition System Using Mel-Frequency Cepstrum Coefficient and Gaussian Mixture Models

**Alfredo Maesa[1], Fabio Garzia[1,2], Michele Scarpiniti[1], Roberto Cusani[1]**
[1]Department of Information, Electronics and Telecommunications Engineering, University of Rome, Rome, Italy
[2]Wessex Institute of Technology, Southampton, UK

## ABSTRACT

The aim of this paper is to show the accuracy and time results of a text independent automatic speaker recognition (ASR) system, based on Mel-Frequency Cepstrum Coefficients (MFCC) and Gaussian Mixture Models (GMM), in order to develop a security control access gate. 450 speakers were randomly extracted from the *Voxforge.org* audio database, their utterances have been improved using spectral subtraction, then MFCC were extracted and these coefficients were statistically analyzed by GMM in order to build each profile. For each speaker two different speech files were used: the first one to build the profile database, the second one to test the system performance. The accuracy achieved by the proposed approach is greater than 96% and the time spent for a single test run, implemented in Matlab language, is about 2 seconds on a common PC.

**Keywords:** Automatic Speaker Recognition; Access Control; Voice Recognition; Biometrics

## 1. Introduction

In last decades, an increasing interest in security systems has arisen. These systems are very useful since they allow managing security in a very efficient way, reducing the need of human resources. Most of them implement an access control system [1-4]. In particular, a huge number of research efforts were directed to speaker recognition problem [5-15]. In fact, many strategic places are of vital importance to the assessment of involved people. A simple way to verify people identity can consist in analyzing its voice. In fact, voice based recognition systems represent biometric systems that allow the access control in a very fast and low intrusive way, requesting a reduced collaboration of the people.

The human voice is peculiar to each person and this is due to the anatomical apparatus of phonation. The vocal tract consists of three main cavities: the oral cavity, the nasal cavity and the pharyngeal cavity [16]. The nasal cavity is essentially bony, hence static in time; furthermore it can be isolated through the soft palate. The oral cavity is formed by the bony structure of the palate and soft palate; its conformation can be altered significantly by the movement of the jaw, lips and tongue. The pharyngeal cavity extends to the bottom of the throat and it can be compressed retracting the base of the tongue towards of the wall of the pharynx. In the lower part it ends with the

vocal cords: a couple of fleshy membranes traversed by the air coming from the lungs. During the production of a sound, the space between the membranes (glottis) can be completely opened or partially closed.

Due to the peculiarity of the voice formation apparatus, it can be possible to recognize a particular individual from its voice. In addition, this operation can be evaluated in an automatic approach [13-15]. In literature, this problem is addressed as Automatic Speaker Recognition (ASR) [17], and it is widely discussed by the research community [13-15].

Speaker recognition is classified as a hybrid biometric recognition approach, as it has two components: the physical one related to the anatomy of the vocal apparatus, and the behavioral component, pertinent to the mood of the speaker just in the recording moment [15].

There are several approach to ASR based on features, vector quantization, score normalization, pattern matching, etc., but the most of them are text dependent [6,7,9-11, 13,14].

In this paper, we propose text independent ASR system based on Mel-Frequency Cepstrum Coefficients (MFCC) [18,19] and Gaussian Mixture Models (GMM) [20-22]. Then the model parameters are estimated with the maximum similarity making use of the Expectation and Maximization (EM) algorithm [23,24]. The novel combination of these two techniques, allows the system to reach high recognition rates and high operative velocities, as shown in the following, allowing to use the proposed system in real security context. In addition, unlike other works on ASR presented in literature, because the recorded speaker signal could be corrupted by environmental additive noise, a spectral subtraction algorithm [25,26] is also used. Comparisons with the state of the art demonstrate the effectiveness of the proposed approach in terms of accuracy rate.

The data acquisition can be performed through simple microphones which are well spread and their cost is negligible. However cheap instrumentation may be more affected by disturbances such as background noise and the spectral subtraction algorithm could be no more sufficient for efficient noise suppression.

The paper is organized as follows: Section 2 describes the ASR problem. Section 3 introduces the MFCC technique, while Section 4 introduces the GMM models. Section 5 describes the proposed ASR system and Section 6 shows some interesting experimental results. Finally Section 7 concludes the work.

## 2. System Description

A biometric recognition system generally consists of:
- A sensor which makes acquisition of data and its subsequent sampling: in the specific case the sensor is a microphone, possibly with a high Signal to Ratio (SNR) value. Since the input signal is essentially speech, the sampling rate is usually set to 8 kHz;
- A step of preprocessing that in the voice context is constituted by the signal cleaning: simply denoising algorithm can be applied to recorded data after a normalization procedure. In order to clean recorded speech signal from environmental additive noise, a spectral subtraction algorithm is used [23,24] in this paper;
- The extraction of the peculiar characteristics (feature extraction): in this stage Mel frequency cepstral coefficients are evaluated using a Mel filter bank after a transformation of the frequency axis in a logarithmic one;
- The generation of a specific template for each speaker: in this work we have decided to use the Gaussian Mixture Models (GMM) where model parameters are estimated with the maximum similarity making use of the Expectation and Maximization (EM) algorithm;
- In case of the user is registering (enrollment) for the first time to the system, this template will be added to the database, using some database programming techniques;
- Otherwise, in case of test among users already present in the database, a comparison (matcher) determines which profile matches the generated template of the

test speech. The matcher utilizes a similarity test, obtaining by a ratio value that can be accepted if it is higher than a decision threshold.

The typical ASR system is shown in **Figure 1**.

The technologies used for the development of the biometric system are the MMFCC for the extraction of the characteristics and the GMM for the statistical analysis of the data obtained, for the templates generation and for the comparison.

## 3. Mel Frequency Cepstral Coefficient

The term "cepstrum" is a pun where the first letters of the term "spectrum" are reversed. It was described in 1963 by Bogert *et al.* [27]. Cepstrum is defined as the inverse Fourier transform of the logarithm of the spectrum of a signal [28,29]:

$$x_c(n) = DFT^{-1}\left\{ \log \left| DFT\left\{ x(n) \right\} \right| \right\} \qquad (1)$$

The cepstrum transform the signal from the frequency domain into the quefrency domain.

When cepstrum is applied to the voice, its strength is to be able to divide excitation and transfer function. In a signal $y(n)$ based on the source-filter model, in this specific context, respectively the vocal cords and the vocal tract, cepstrum allows separation in $y(n) = x(n) * h(n)$, where the source $x(n)$ passes through a filter described by the impulse response $h(n)$. The spectrum of $y(n)$ obtained by the Fourier transform is $Y(k) = X(k) H(k)$ where $k$ index of discrete frequencies, *i.e.* the product of two spectra, respectively the source and the filter one. Separating these two spectra is complicated. On the contrary, it is possible to separate the real envelope of the filter from the remaining spectrum by formulating all the phase at the beginning. The cepstrum is based on the properties of the logarithm that can transform the product of the argument in sums of logarithms.

Starting from the logarithm of the modulus of the spectrum:

$$\log |Y(k)|$$
$$= \log \left( \left| X(k) H(k) \right| \right) = \log \left( X(k) \right) + \log \left( H(k) \right) \qquad (2)$$

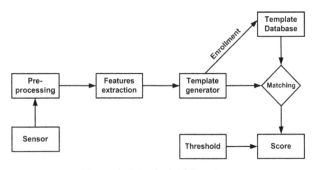

**Figure 1. A typical ASR system.**

it is possible to separate the fast oscillating component from the slow one, respectively by means of a high and low pass filter, obtaining:

$$c(n) = DFT^{-1}\left(\log|Y(k)|\right)$$
$$= DFT^{-1}\left(\log|X(k)|\right) + DFT^{-1}\left(\log|H(k)|\right) \quad (3)$$

that is the signal cepstrum in the quefrency domain. In the low quefrencies are described the transfer function information, in the high quefrencies there is data about excitation.

Hence the initial wave of percussion created by the vocal cords and shaped by the throat, nose and mouth can be analyzed as a sum of a source function (given by the excitation of the vocal cords) and a filter (throat, nose, mouth). The separation between high and low quefrency, can be obtained by a high pass lifter (filter) for the fast oscillation and a low pass lifter for the slow one.

Psychoacoustic studies [30-32] have shown that the mind perception of the frequency content of the sound follows a nearly logarithmic scale, the Mel scale, which is linear up to 1 kHz and logarithmic thereafter:

$$\text{mel}(f) = \begin{cases} f & \text{if } f \le 1\,\text{kHz} \\ 2595\log\left(1 + \dfrac{f}{7000}\right) & \text{if } f > 1\,\text{kHz} \end{cases}$$

The Mel scale is shown in **Figure 2**, where it is clear the compression of the Mel scale (reported in $y$-axis) with respect the Hertz scale (in $x$-axis) for frequencies greater than 1 kHz. In this scale pitches are judged by listeners to be equal in distance from one another.

Mel-cepstrum estimates the spectral envelope of the output of the filter bank. Let $Y_n$ represent the logarithm of the output energy from channel n, applying the discrete cosine transform (DCT) we obtain the cepstral coefficients MFCC through the equation:

$$c_k = \sum_{n=1}^{N} Y_n \cos\left[k\left(n - \frac{1}{2}\right)\frac{\pi}{N}\right] \forall k = 0, \cdots, K \quad (4)$$

The simplified spectral envelope is rebuilt with the

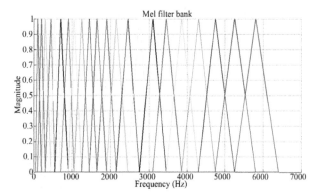

**Figure 2. Mel filter bank.**

first $K_m$ coefficients, with $K_m < K$:

$$C(\text{mel}) = \sum_{k=1}^{K_m} c_k \cos\left(2\pi k \frac{\text{mel}}{B_m}\right) \quad (5)$$

where $B_m$ is the bandwidth analyzed in Mel domain and $K_m = 20$ is a typical value assumed by $K_m$. $c_0$ is the mean value in d$B$ of the energy of the filter bank channels, hence it is in direct relation with the energy of the sound and it can be used for the estimation of the energy.

Schematically, the coefficients are derived in the following way: the spectrum of the original signal is computed with the Fourier transform; the obtained spectrum is mapped in Mel making use of appropriate overlapping windows; for each obtained function the logarithm is calculated; the discrete cosine transform is calculated (DCT); the coefficients are the amplitudes of the resulting spectrum. In order to emphasize the low quefrencies DCT is chosen.

## 4. Gaussian Mixture Model

Each arbitrary probability density function (pdf) can be approximated by a linear combination of unimodal Gaussian density [20]. Under this assumption, Gaussian mixture models have been applied to model the distribution of a sequence of vectors $X = x_1, x_2, \cdots, x_t, \cdots, X_T$ each one of dimension $D$, containing data on the characteristics extracted from the voice of a subject, according to:

$$p(x_t|\lambda) = \sum_{i=1}^{M} w_i p_i(x_t) \quad (6)$$

$$p(X_t|\lambda) = \prod_{t=1}^{T} p(s > t|\theta) \quad (7)$$

where $w_i$ are the weights of the corresponding mixtures to the unimodal Gaussian densities $p_i$ with $i = 1, \cdots, M$ and:

$$p_i(x_t) = \left(\frac{1}{\sqrt[D]{2\pi}\sqrt{\det(\Sigma_i)}}\right)^{-\frac{1}{2}\left((x_t - \mu_i)^T \Sigma^{-1}(x_t - \mu_i)\right)} \quad (8)$$

The weights of the mixtures satisfy the constraint:

$$\sum_{i=1}^{M} w_i = \quad (9)$$

Each speaker is identified by a $\lambda$ model obtained from GMM analysis. In particular lambda is defined as:

$$\lambda = \{w_i, \mu_i, \Sigma_i\} \quad (10)$$

where $\mu_i$ is the mean vector and $\Sigma_i$ is the covariance matrix.

Given a characteristic vector sequence of the speaker to be identified, the model parameters are estimated with the

Text Independent Automatic Speaker Recognition System Using Mel-Frequency Cepstrum Coefficient and Gaussian
Mixture Models

53

maximum similarity $\lambda$ making use of the Expectation and Maximization algorithm [23,24]. The $\lambda$ model is compared with a characteristic vector $X$ by calculating the log-likelihood similarity [23]:

$$\log P(X|\lambda) = \sum_T \log P(x_t|\lambda) \qquad (11)$$

In order to decide, it is utilized a similarity test obtained by the following ratio:

$$\frac{P(X|\text{ Speaker})}{P(X|\text{ Other Speaker})} > \sigma \qquad (12)$$

where $\sigma$ is the dec on the contrary, a collection of models of different speakers. The final score of a certain subject $S_c$ over an $X$ vector containing the voice features of the test is given by:

$$\log L(x) = \log p(X|S = S_c) - \log \sum_{S \in pop} p(X|S \neq S_c) \, (13)$$

where $L(X)$ represents the similarity value of $X$ vector with respect to $S_c$ compared with the characteristics of other individuals in the database (pop), excluding the one taken into account.

## 5. System Implementation

In the pre-processing phase, the signal has been improved using spectral subtraction [33,34] and segmented into frames partially overlying (50%) and relatively small. Frames not containing voice were skipped. The size of each frame is less than 20 ms in order to make the contained wave stationary. Each frame has been subjected to the Hamming window to minimize the discontinuities at the edges of the frame. For each frame 20 MFCC were calculated. The obtained data represents the characteristics of a speaker. This information, organized in a matrix containing a vector of Mel-Cepstral coefficients for each frame, is analyzed by the GMM using 32 mixtures. The result is a set of statistical data characterized by a mean vector, a covariance matrix and a weight vector which constitute the template itself. The template is employed when a speaker is added into the system or for the test step among the users already registered.

The public voice database *Voxforge.org* [35] was used in order to validate the system. *Voxforge* is an internet community including researchers and "donors" of human voice. The preset aims are to support who intends to realize and test an automatic speaker recognition system, a speech recognition engine, or any application related to analysis, to the recognition and more generally to the study of the human voice. Anyone can register on the website and send his own voice recordings to be made available to the whole community. For this study 450 speaker utterances were randomly extracted from Voxforge website. For each speaker two speeches were employed: the first one in order to perform the training

phase and the second one to test the system. Since the recognition system is text independent, each speech contains different words (typically reads paragraphs of popular books).

In the training step each template generated from the analysis of the speakers' utterances is stored into the system. This set of information represents the knowledge base of the system obtained in the training phase. The test stage was made utilizing the test templates of each speaker compared to the whole knowledge base of the system, *i.e.* all the templates stored in the training phase. This comparison was performed using the criterion of log-likelihood previously described. The output of the test phase is a matrix containing the similarity estimation of each test with respect to each profile stored in the system. This matrix is structured in this way: the rows represent the $i$th test and the column the $j$-training. Hence in position $(i,j)$ is contained the value representing the similarity likelihood of test speaker $i$ with respect to training speaker $j$. Since the comparison is made by log-likelihood, for each row (test) the system nominates the column (speaker in the system) containing the maximum value as the owner of the speech.

## 6. Experimental Results

As shown in **Table 1** there were 433 identifications on 450 subjects, this means that accuracy rate is 96.22%. Since the system creates a hierarchy of candidates owners of each test, if the top five were accepted as good results, it would be achieved a recognition rate of 97.78%.

With regard to temporal performances, it should be taken into account that the complete computation test involves the training data processing, the test data elaboration and the comparison from training and test data. Obviously it is also possible perform a single test and compare it to profiles in the system. These performance results in terms of time required, are specific to the database used, since the system developed can run with audio files containing variable size, speech length and sampling. The temporal performances are exposed in **Table 2**.

## 7. Comparison with the State of Art

This section discusses about the main speaker recognition systems found in scientific literature. In 1995 Reynolds [36] implemented an identification system based on spectral variability obtaining a 96.80% accuracy rate with 49 speakers. In 2009 Revathi, Ganapathy and Venkataramani [37] through an iterative clustering ap-

**Table 1. Accuracy performances.**

|          | Speakers | Hit | Accuracy |
|----------|----------|-----|----------|
| 1st      | 450      | 433 | 96.22%   |
| In top 5 | 450      | 440 | 97.78%   |

proach, PLP (Perceptual Linear Predictive cepstrum) and MF-PLP (Mel Frequency PLP) achieved 91% accuracy rate with 50 speakers randomly chosen from TIMIT database [38]. In 2009 Chakroborty and Saha [39] combining MFCC and IMFCC (Inverted MFCC) based on gaussian filter, reached 97.42% accuracy rate with 131 subjects of YOHO database [40]. In 2010 Saeidi, Mowlaee, Kinnunen and Zheng-Hua [41] through Kullback-Leibler divergence achieved 97% accuracy rate with 34 speakers. In 2011 Gomez [42] implemented an identification system based on novel parametric neural network, reaching 94% accuracy with 40 speakers. In 2011 Rao, Prasada and Nagesh [43] made a study comparing GMM, HMM (Hidden Markov Models) and MFCC. The accuracy rate obtained in best test condition was 99% on 200 subjects taken from TIMIT database.

**Table 3** summarizes the accuracy rates reached by the previous approaches.

## 8. Conclusions

In this paper we have introduced an ASR system based on MFCC and GMM. The accuracy of the proposed system is greater than 96% and with 450 speakers.

*I*th, as shown as a high recognition rate on a wide number of subjects, together with a high operative velocity, make it useful for real security access control applications.

**Table 2. Time performances.**

|  | Time (min:sec) |
| --- | --- |
| Whole computation | 17:03 |
| Training | 00:48 |
| Test & comparison | 16:15 |
| Single test | 00:02 |

**Table 3. Comparison with the state of the art.**

| Approach | Accuracy rate |
| --- | --- |
| Reynolds [36] | 96.80% |
| Revathi *et al.* [37] | 91% |
| Chakroborty and Saha [39] | 97.42% |
| Saeidi *et al.* [41] | 97% |
| Gomez [42] | 94% |
| Rao *et al.* [43] | 99% |
| Proposed | 97.98% |

## REFERENCES

[1]  F. Garzia, E. Sammarco and R. Cusani, "The Integrated Security System of the Vatican City State," *International Journal of Safety & Security Engineering*, Vol. 1, No. 1, 2011, pp. 1-17.

[2]  G. Contardi, F. Garzia and R. Cusani, "The Integrated Security System of the Senate of the Italian Republic," *International Journal of Safety & Security Engineering*, Vol. 1, No. 3, 2011, pp. 219-247.

[3]  F. Garzia and R. Cusani, "The Safety/Security/Communication System of the Gran Sasso Mountain in Italy," *International Journal of Safety & Security Engineering*, Vol. 2, No. 1, 2012, pp. 13-39.

[4]  F. Garzia, E. Sammarco and R. Cusani, "Vehicle/People Access Control System for Security Management in Ports," *International Journal of Safety & Security Engineering*.

[5]  H. Beigi, "Fundamentals of Speaker Recognition," VDM Verlag, Saarbrücken, 2011.

[6]  R. J. Mammone, X. Y. Zhang and R. P. Ramachandran, "Robust Speaker Recognition: A Feature-Based Approach," *IEEE Signal Processing Magazine*, Vol. 13, No. 5, 1996, pp. 1290-1312.

[7]  F. Soong, A. Rosenberg, L. Rabiner and B. Juang, "A Vector Quantization Approach to Speaker Recognition," *Acoustics, Speech and Signal Processing (ICASSP)*, 1985, pp. 387-390.

[8]  R. Auckenthaler, M. Carey and H. Lloyd-Thomas, "Score Normalization for Text-Independent Speaker Verification Systems," *Digital Signal Processing*, Vol. 10, No. 1-3, 2000, pp. 42-54.

[9]  S. Furui, "Recent Advances in Speaker Recognition," *Pattern Recognition Letters*, Vol. 18, No. 9, 1997, pp. 859-872.

[10] S. Pruzansky, "Pattern-Matching Procedure for Automatic Talker Recognition," *Journal of the Acoustical Society of America*, Vol. 26, No. 1, 1963, pp. 403-406.

[11] P. D. Bricker and S. Pruzansky, "Effects of Stimulus Content and Duration on Talker Identification," *Journal of the Acoustical Society of America*, Vol. 44, No. 3, 1968, pp. 1596-1607.

[12] D. Jurafsky and J. H. Martin, "Speech and Language Processing," Prentice Hall, Boston, 2008.

[13] M. Farrùs, "Prosody in Automatic Speaker Recognition: Applications in Biometrics and Voice Imitation," VDM Verlag, Saarbrücken, 2010.

[14] D. A. Reynolds, "An Overview of Automatic Speaker Recognition Technology," *Acoustics, Speech and Signal Processing (ICASSP)*, 2002, pp. 4072-4075.

[15] J. Mariani and F. Bimbot, "Language and Speech Processing," John Wiley & Sons, Chichester, 2010.

[16] I. R. Titze, "Principles of Voice Production," Prentice Hall, Boston, 1994.

[17] N. Morgan, H. Bourlard and H. Hermansky, "Speech Processing in the Auditory System, Chapter Automatic Speech Recognition: An Auditory Perspective," Springer,

Berlin, 2004.

[18] F. Zheng, G. Zhang and Z. Song, "Comparison of Different Implementations of MFCC," *Journal of Computer Science & Technology*, Vol. 16, No. 6, 2001, pp. 582-589.

[19] M. Sahidullah and G. Saha, "Design, Analysis and Experimental Evaluation of Block Based Transformation in MFCC Computation for Speaker Recognition," *Speech Communication*, Vol. 54, No. 4, 2012, pp. 543-565.

[20] C. Bishop, "Pattern Recognition and Machine Learning," Springer, Berlin, 2006.

[21] D. A. Reynolds, "Gaussian Mixture Models," Technical Report, MIT Lincoln Laboratory, Cincinnati, 2001.

[22] M. A. T. Figueiredo and A. K. Jain, "Unsupervised Learning of Finite Mixture Models," *IEEE Transactions on Pattern Analysis and Machine Intelligence*, Vol. 24, No. 3, 2002, pp. 381-396.

[23] D. A. Reynolds, T. F. Quatieri and R. B. Dunn, "Speaker Verification Using Adapted Gaussian Mixture Models," *Digital Signal Processing*, Vol. 10, No. 2, 2000, pp. 19-41.

[24] L. Xu and I. Jordan, "On Convergence Properties of the EM Algorithm for Gaussian Mixtures," *Neural Computation*, Vol. 8, No. 1, 1996, pp. 129-151.

[25] S. V. Vaseghi, "Advanced Digital Signal Processing and Noise Reduction," John Wiley & Sons, Chichester, 2006.

[26] S. Boll, "Suppression of Acoustic Noise in Speech Using Spectral Subtraction," *IEEE Transactions on Acoustics, Speech and Signal Processing*, Vol. 27, No. 2, 1979, pp. 113-120.

[27] B. P. Bogert, J. R. Healy and J. W. Tukey, "The Quefrency Analysis of Time Series for Echoes: Cepstrum, Pseudo-Autocovariance, Cross-Cepstrum, and Saphe Cracking," *Proceedings of the Symposium on Time Series Analysis*, 1963, pp. 209-243.

[28] C. Roads, "The Computer Music Tutorial," MIT Press, Cincinnati, 1996.

[29] J. G. Proakis and D. G. Manolakis, "Digital Signal Processing," Prentice Hall, Boston, 2007.

[30] D. O'Shaughnessy, "Speech Communication: Human and Machine," Addison-Wesley, Boston, 1987.

[31] S. Stevens, J. Stanley, J. Volkman and E. B. Newman, "A Scale for the Measurement of the Psychological Magnitude Pitch," *Journal of the Acoustical Society of America*, Vol. 8, No. 3, 1937, pp. 185-190.

[32] M. Gold, "Speech and Audio Signal Processing," John Wiley & Sons, Chichester, 2002.

[33] M. Berouti, R. Schwartz and J. Makhoul, "Enhancement of Speech Corrupted by Acoustic Noise, *Proceedings of IEEE International Conference on Acoustics, Speech, and signal Processing (ICASSP1979)*, 1979, pp. 208-211.

[34] R. Martin, "Noise Power Spectral Density Estimation Based on Optimal Smoothing and Minimum Statistics," *Speech and Audio Processing*, Vol. 9, No. 5, 2001, pp. 504-512.

[35] "Voxforge Database." www.voxforge.org

[36] R. Reynolds, "Robust Text-Independent Speaker Identification Using Gaussian Mixture Speaker Models," *IEEE Transactions on Speech and Audio Processing*, 1995, pp. 72-83.

[37] A. Revathi, R. Ganapathy and Y. Venkataramani, "Text Independent Speaker Recognition and Speaker Independent Speech Recognition Using Iterative Clustering Approach," *International Journal of Computer Science & Information Technology*, Vol. 1, No. 2, 2009, pp. 30-42.

[38] "TIMIT Speech Database." http://www.ldc.upenn.edu

[39] S. Chakroborty and G. Saha, "Improved Text-Independent Speaker Identification Using Fused MFCC and IMFCC feature Sets Based on Gaussian Filter," *International Journal of Signal Processing*, Vol. 5, No. 1, 2009, pp. 11-19.

[40] "Yoho Speech Database." http://www.ldc.upenn.edu

[41] R. Saeidi, P. Mowlaee, T. Kinnunen and Z. H. Tan, "Signal-to-Signal Ratio Independent Speaker Identification for Co-Channel Speech Signals," *Proceedings of International Conference on Pattern Recognition (ICPR2009)*, 2009, pp. 4565-4568.

[42] P. Gomez, "A Text Independent Speaker Recognition System Using a Novel Parametric Neural Network," *Proceedings of International Journal of Signal Processing, Image Processing and Pattern Recognition*, December 2011, pp. 1-16.

[43] R. R. Rao, V. K. Prasad and A. Nagesh, "Performance Evaluation of Statistical Approaches for Text-Independent Speaker Recognition Using Source Feature," *Inter-JRI Computer Science and Networking*, Vol. 2, No. 1, 2010, pp. 8-13.

# 8

# Determinants in Human Gait Recognition

**Tahir Amin**[*], **Dimitrios Hatzinakos**

Department of Electrical and Computer Engineering, University of Toronto, Toronto, Canada

## ABSTRACT

Human gait is a complex phenomenon involving the motion of various parts of the body simultaneously in a 3 dimensional space. Dynamics of different parts of the body translate its center of gravity from one point to another in the most efficient way. Body dynamics as well as static parameters of different body parts contribute to gait recognition. Studies have been performed to assess the discriminatory power of static and dynamic features. The current research literature, however, lacks the work on the comparative significance of dynamic features from different parts of the body. This paper sheds some light on the recognition performance of dynamic features extracted from different parts of human body in an appearance based set up.

**Keywords:** Biometrics; Feature Comparison; Feature Extraction; Gait Recognition

## 1. Introduction

The recognition of people by their physiological or behavioral characteristics is called biometrics. The use of biometrics in personal identification is not new and it has been used in criminology for a long time. Fingerprint databases are widely used by the law enforcement agencies from the early 19th century. Biometrics such as artistic drawings of facial features, color of eyes and footprints were routinely used in criminology even before the advent of modern technology. The invention of modern computers and digital technology have, however, transformed the way information is stored and processed. Digital technology has enabled us to store and process biometric data automatically without intervention or with our minimal input. The renewed focus on security in the past few years has brought the biometrics research into limelight. Recent developments in the biometric research have brought face, iris and fingerprint recognition from research labs to daily life. Biometric recognition systems are being installed as access control systems for granting access to offices, residential buildings and even laptop computers.

Gait is a behavioral biometric which can be perceived from a distance. It can be acquired without personal contact and cooperation. Iris and face biometrics have similar advantages but they need high resolution images and frontal view. However, it is possible to extract gait patterns from low resolution images. Human gait can vary over long durations due to many factors such as change in body weight, injuries and disease. However studies have indicated that it still possesses sufficient discriminatory power for personal recognition [1]. Gait is a complex function of skeletal structure, muscular activity, body weight, limb lengths, bone structures etc. This complexity of gait renders it difficult to imitate and hide if not impossible.

Human gait analysis can be used as a useful tool in a variety of applications. One such promising application is medical diagnostics of diseases that affect voluntary muscle activity such as walking. For example, Parkinson's disease that affects nerve cells in part of the brain controlling muscle movements. People with Parkinson's often experience trembling, muscle rigidity, difficulty in walking, and problems with balance and coordination. Early detection of walking disorders by motion analysis can be very helpful for the treatment of such diseases. Gait can also be used to generate early warning for law enforcement agencies by detecting suspicious motion activity in airports or subway stations.

The earliest work on human motion perception was performed by Johansson [1]. He used Moving Light Display (MLD) to study human motion perception. In his experiments, movements of bright spots on a display created impressions of walking, dancing and running persons to the viewers. Human gait analysis from digital video data can be broadly categorized into two classes; model based and appearance based. Model based approaches assume a priori geometric shape model of human body while no such assumption is taken in case of appearance based approaches. Initialization of human body model is performed at the start of tracking process in model

---

[*]Corresponding author.

based approaches. The majority of techniques use manual initialization of the model in the first frame with fixed lengths of body segments. There are no such initialization issues in appearance based methods. However, the appearance based method being holistic in nature can suffer from lack of correspondence between extracted gait signatures to the actual physical quantities. **Figure 1** shows the block diagram of a generic gait identification system.

The most critical step in gait recognition system is the extraction of gait features from video data. Human gait is cyclic in nature and this characteristic exhibits itself in cyclic appearance changes in the images when taken from a side view. Although gait is a dynamic process, studies have shown that static body parameters such as length and widths of limbs are also important in gait recognition. In appearance based methods, dynamics of lower half of the body are generally considered more important. Studies have been performed on the relative importance of static and dynamic features in gait recognition. But there is a lack of work in relative analysis of dynamic features from different parts of the body especially in an appearance based set up. Dynamics of different parts of the human body play a role in characterizing the human gait pattern. This paper analyzes the discriminatory power of features extracted from different parts of the body by applying area masks.

The rest of the paper is organized as follows. Section 2 gives a brief overview of the previous works in gait feature comparative analysis. In Section 3, we discuss preprocessing of silhouettes and provide details of dynamic feature extraction. Experimental results and discussion are given in Section 4. Section 5 draws conclusions with some directions to the future work. References are listed in Section 6.

## 2. Previous Works

We will briefly review the previous works on determination of characteristics that contribute to gait recognition and their relative importance. As mentioned earlier in the

preceding section, the current research literature lacks the comparative analysis of dynamic features extracted from different parts of the body. The comparison between static and dynamic features has, however, been studied in some of the works which will be summarized below.

Human locomotion has been widely studied by medical and physiological research community. Their main purpose is to determine the gait variations and distinguish between normal and pathological gait and rehabilitation of patients. Saunders *et al.* have defined human walking as the translation of the center of mass of the body from one point to another in a way that requires the least energy [2]. They also identified six gait determinants or variables that affect the energy expenditure. The six gait determinants are pelvic rotation, pelvic tilt, knee flexion at mid-stance, foot and ankle motion, knee motion and lateral pelvic displacement. The focus of this work as well as other similar ones was to study the movement of different muscles and limbs during the gait process. These types of studies are useful for detecting abnormalities in human walking and may also serve as a general guideline for recognition systems. The perception of human gait as well as its recognition involves much more than just the six determinants given in [2].

Wang *et al.* used both static and dynamic body biometrics for human recognition [3]. The static body features were derived from using the Procrustes shape analysis to obtain a compact appearance representation. The dynamic descriptors were estimated by recovering joint angle trajectories of the lower limbs using Condensation algorithm. The algorithm was evaluated by using a database consisting of 80 sequences from 20 subjects and four sequences per subject. They reported recognition of 83.75% at rank 1 by using only static features and a success rate of 87.5% when dynamic features were used. The combined features resulted in an increased recognition rate of 97.5% at rank 1. Wang *et al.* also performed comparative study between the dynamic and static features in their work reported in [3,4]. Their work showed that the dynamic information extracted from the video sequences is somewhat better for human identification than the static information. In [5], BenAbdelkader, Cutler and Davis, proposed a parametric technique for personal identification. Their gait signatures are based on the height and stride parameters extracted from low resolution video sequences. The experimental evaluations were performed on a database containing 45 subjects. A recognition rate of 49% was achieved by using both stride and height parameters and only 21% by using just the stride parameter. In [6], Bobick and Johnson used 4 static body parameters and averaged them to get mean walk vector for each gait sequence. The recognition results of this method are available in the form of CMC plots at the Georgia Tech human identification website [7]. Although

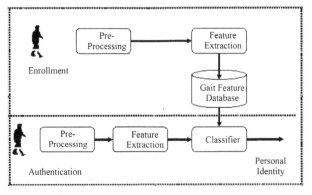

**Figure 1. Block diagram of the gait recognition system.**

the method is able to achieve a very compact representation of human gait (4-dimensional), its performance is low for lower rank recognition.

Veeraraghavan *et al.* [8] conducted a detailed comparison between shape and kinematic features for human recognition. Their experiments indicated that shape of the body carries more information than the kinematics for recognition of humans from video sequences. However, using kinematics in conjunction with shape features considerably improved the performance of the system. Similarly, gait analysis work carried out by R. Green and L. Guan also showed that anthropometric (static) features extracted by them were more discriminatory for human identification than the dynamic features in the shape of joint angle trajectories [9]. On the other hand, the experiments conducted by Johansson establish the importance of dynamic features for identification [1]. Contradicting results have been reported about the importance of dynamic and static features while dynamic feature comparison has not been performed explicitly. This work is poised to shed some light on the dynamic feature performance extracted from different parts of the binary silhouettes.

## 3. Extraction of Body Dynamics

In appearance based gait recognition systems, the first step usually involves segmentation of human subject from the background. This segmentation process is usually performed by background subtraction. The resulted silhouettes are noisy because of segmentation errors. We observe that silhouettes in the database contain outliers which should be removed to make the gait feature extraction more robust. We use median filtering with a mask of $5 \times 5$ to filter the silhouettes to get rid of outliers. The output from the median filter is binarized by simple thresholding to obtain smoothed silhouettes.

Human walking process is cyclic in nature. Gait cycle is the time between two identical events during human walking. It is usually measured from heel strike to heel strike of one leg. A complete gait cycle is shown in **Figure 2**.

The movement of arms and legs is the most prominent motion during gait cycle. Assuming that image plane is perpendicular to the direction of motion, the gap between two legs in 2D silhouettes changes during gait cycle. Similarly the gap between two arms and the rest of the body also changes in a cyclic fashion. This dynamic information can be captured by applying area masks at different parts of the binary silhouettes similar to the approach adopted by Foster *et al.* [10]. The number of pixels of the binary silhouettes under these masks is calculated. The process is repeated for each binary silhouette in the gait sequence and we obtain six area signals of length $N$, the number of frames in the gait sequence. The width of each area mask is 15 pixels. **Figure 3** shows the location of six area masks for an example silhouette from the database.

The following equations summarize the extraction of six area signals from the masks shown in **Figure 3**.

$$b[i,j] = \begin{cases} 1 & \text{if pixel } [i,j] \text{ belongs to foreground} \\ 0 & \text{if pixel } [i,j] \text{ belongs to background} \end{cases} \quad (1)$$

$$m_p[i,j] = \begin{cases} 1 & \text{for } L_p \leq i < L_p \\ 0 & \text{otherwise} \end{cases} \quad (2)$$

$$a_p(n) = \sum_{i,j} b_n[i,j] m_p[i,j] \quad (3)$$

where $b[i, j]$ is the binary silhouette, $m_p[i, j]$ is the area mask and $a_p(n)$ is the area under mask $p$ for frame $n$ of the silhouette sequence. $L_p$ is the starting row for mask $m_p$ and $p = [1, \cdots, 6]$ is the mask index. These area signals are shown in **Figures 4** and **5** for two typical silhouette sequences from the database.

The area signals extracted by applying the area masks are noisy due to the imperfections in the silhouette extraction process. It is observed that a high frequency riding wave is present in all of the area signals. We apply a newly proposed Empirical Mode Decomposition (EMD) algorithm to remove these riding waves to get cleaner area signals. EMD algorithm is described in the following subsection.

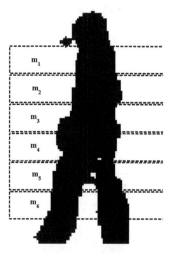

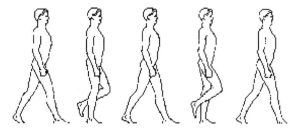

Figure 2. Human gait cycle.

Figure 3. Area masks.

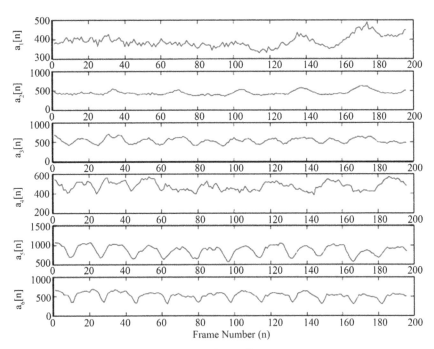

**Figure 4. Area signals for a silhouette sequence.**

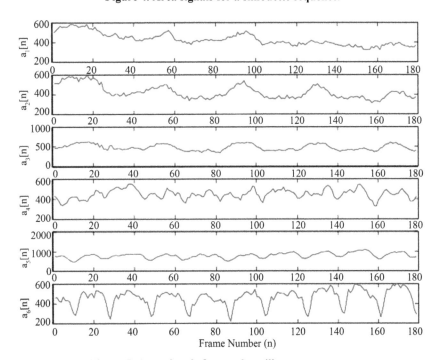

**Figure 5. Area signals for another silhouette sequence.**

### 3.1. Empirical Mode Decomposition (EMD)

The traditional data analysis methods such as Fourier transform have an inherent restriction to their application. They are suitable when the system is linear and the data is stationary. In most of the practical application scenarios these two conditions are rarely satisfied. But these traditional methods are still widely used because of their simplicity and well formed theoretical basis. In some cases, non linear and non stationary data can be transformed to linear and stationarity data before processing it with Fourier based methods. But in other cases new methods are needed which can analyze non linear and non stationary data. There has been some progress in the analysis of non stationary data in recent years. Wavelet analysis and Wagner-Ville distribution are the examples of data analysis tools for non stationary data. Huang *et al.*

proposed EMD to decompose non linear non stationary data into oscillatory modes called Intrinsic Mode Functions (IMF) [12]. The method separates IMFs from signals modulated in both amplitude and frequency. IMF is a function that satisfies two conditions:

- The number of extrema and the number of zero crossings are either equal or at most differ by one.
- The mean value of the envelope traced by the local maxima and the envelope defined by the local minima is zero.

IMFs are extracted by the sifting process which is applied iteratively until a predefined condition is satisfied or the residue becomes a monotonic function. The signal x(t) can be then represented in the following form:

$$a(t) = \sum_{i=1}^{k} e_i + r_k \qquad (4)$$

where $e_i$ denotes the $i$th extracted empirical mode and $r_k$ is the residue which is either a constant or mean trend. The sifting procedure to obtain the IMF is summarized in 6 steps as given in Algorithm 1.

---

**Algorithm 1: EMD Algorithm**

1) Extract all local extrema.
2) Determine the upper envelope by connecting all the local maxima by cubic spline interpolation.
3) Determine the lower envelope by connecting all the local minima by cubic spline interpolation.
4) Calculate the mean envelope $m_1$ from upper and lower envelopes.
5) Calculate the first component $h_1$ as follows:

$$h_1 = x(t) - m_1 \qquad (5)$$

6) Check if $h_1$ satisfies the IMF definition.
   a) If yes:

$$e_1 = h_1 \qquad (6)$$

Calculate residue as follows:

$$r_1 = x(t) - h_1 \qquad (7)$$

Go to step 1 and repeat the sifting process to extract more IMFs treating $r_1$ as the input data.
   b) if no: Calculate $h_{11}$

$$h_{11} = h_1 - m_{11} \qquad (8)$$

Where $m_{11}$ is the mean envelope of $h_1$. Repeat the sifting $k$ times until the stoppage criterion is met to get $h_1 k$.

$$h_{1k} = h_{1(k-1)} - m_{1k} \qquad (9)$$

$$e_1 = h_{1k} \qquad (10)$$

---

In order to illustrate the noise removal by EMD, we chose two area signals from **Figures 4** and **5** and decomposed them using the EMD algorithm. The input signals are plotted in **Figure 6** and their IMFs in **Figures 7** and **8**.

The high frequency noise appears as the first IMF, IMF₁ as shown in **Figures 7** and **8**. The area signals are

reconstructed by ignoring IMF₁ as given in the following equations.

$$a_1'(n) = \sum_{i=2}^{5} e_i[n] + r_k[n] \qquad (11)$$

$$a_2'(n) = \sum_{i=2}^{5} e_i[n] + r_k[n] \qquad (12)$$

The reconstructed signals are shown in **Figure 9**.

## 3.2. Correlation Analysis

After the noise removal from area signals by EMD algorithm, we compute autocorrelation of all six reconstructed area functions as follows:

$$R_{a_p'}[l] = \sum_n a_p'[n] a_p'[n+l] \qquad (13)$$

where $R_{a_p}$ represents the autocorrelation function of the reconstructed area signal $a_p'$ and $l$ is the time lag. $R_{a_p}$ is only calculated for positive lags *i.e.* $l = [1..N]$.

The dynamic gait features are then derived by taking the Discrete Cosine Transform (DCT) of the autocorrelation functions. The DCT of a discrete function $R_{a_p}$ is defined as:

$$T_p(k) = c(k) \sum_{l=0}^{N-1} R_{a_p'}(l) \cos\left(\frac{\pi(2l+1)k}{2N}\right) \qquad (14)$$

where $T_p(k)$ is the DCT transform of the original signal $R_{a_p}(l)$ of length N. The coefficient $c(k)$ is given by:

$$c(0) = \sqrt{\frac{1}{N}}, \quad c(k) = \sqrt{\frac{2}{N}} \qquad (15)$$

for $1 \le k \le M-1$.

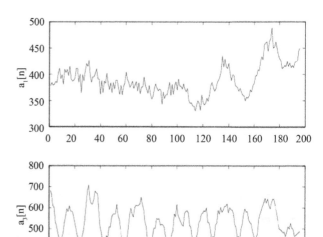

**Figure 6. Noisy area Signals.**

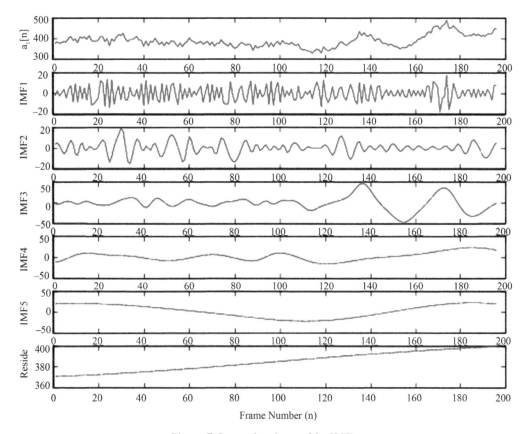

**Figure 7. Input signal $a_1$ and its IMFs.**

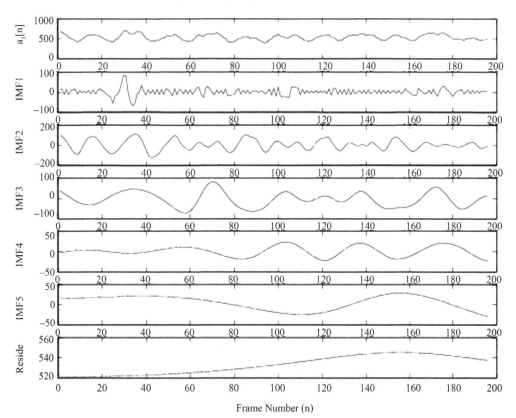

**Figure 8. Input signal $a_3$ and its IMFs.**

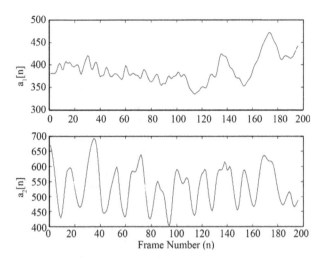

**Figure 9. Area signals after noise removal.**

# 4. Experimental Results

## 4.1. Database Description

We use the May 2001 version of Gait Challenge (GC) database from University of Southern Florida (USF) [12]. This database consists of 452 sequences from 71 subjects recorded under the following 5 covariates.

- shoe type, A or B
- surface type, Grass (G) or Concrete (C)
- carrying conditions, with Briefcase (BF) or without (NB)
- viewpoints, Left (L) or Right (R)
- time instants, $t_1$ or $t_2$

In order to assess the performance of gait recognition algorithms, the GC database also contains Human ID Challenge Experiments. There are total 11 experiments. We use experiment A (G, A, L, NB, $t_1$) to analyze the recognition potential of dynamic features extracted from different parts of the silhouettes. Experiment A is chosen due to the following reasons:

- Both Gallery (G, A, R, NB, $t_1$) and A set contain all the 71 subjects
- They are recorded under similar conditions except a different viewpoint. This eliminates the effect of other covariates which can skew the results.

## 4.2. Gait Features

Each silhouettes sequence is processed frame by frame for the extraction of dynamic gait features. The silhouette frames are processed by median filtering to reduce outliers. Next, we estimate the gait period from the autocorrelation function of the silhouette area signal. Speed normalization is achieved by ensuring the same number of frames in each gait cycle for all silhouette sequences. The six area signals are then extracted as explained in the preceding section and EMD algorithm is applied to reduce

the noise. DCT coefficients of autocorrelation functions of each of the six reconstructed area signals are computed. The first 35 DCT coefficients form our dynamic gait feature.

## 4.3. Feature Vector Normalization

We normalize the gait features by using Equation 16 to put equal emphasis on each component of the feature vector. Each of the components of 35-dimensional feature vector takes on different value for each silhouette sequence. These different values of each component form a sequence of numbers. We consider that these sequences are being generated by a Gaussian distribution. Mean $\mu_v$ and standard deviation $\sigma_v$ of each such sequence representing a component of the gait signature $v$ are calculated and then the sequence is normalized as follows:

$$v_i = \frac{v_i - \mu_v}{\sigma_v} \qquad (16)$$

This normalization process maps most of the values of the feature components $v$ in the range [−1, 1]. The advantage of this normalization is that a few abnormal values occurring in the sequence will not bias the importance of other values.

## 4.4. Feature Matching

Features are matched by nearest neighborhood using the simple City block distance. The City block distance between the two gait feature vectors is defined as:

$$d(\mathbf{p}, \mathbf{g}) = \sum_{i=1}^{P} |p_i - g_i| \qquad (17)$$

where $\mathbf{p}$ and $\mathbf{g}$ are the feature vectors of probe and gallery sequences respectively and p is the dimension of the signature vector.

## 4.5. Comparison of Dynamic Features

Cumulative Match Score (CMS) is used to evaluate the performance of different dynamic gait features. Each probe sequence feature is compared with the features of 71 sequences in the gallery. The gallery set consists of one sequence for each subject. The gallery sequence set is sorted according to the similarity to the probe sequences. The rank1 identification result is the total number of correct matches appearing on the top while Rank 5 value represents the correct identification obtained among the top 5 matches.

**Table 1** presents the performance evaluation of features extracted from the six area signals at Rank 1 and Rank 5. At Rank 1, the best performance of 97.18% is achieved from the features extracted from $a_6$. This area signal represents the dynamics of lower leg during the

**Table 1. Comparison of features at rank 1 and rank 5.**

| Area Signal | Rank 1 | Rank 5 |
|:---:|:---:|:---:|
| | (%) | (%) |
| $a_1$ | 53.52 | 94.37 |
| $a_2$ | 53.52 | 92.96 |
| $a_3$ | 78.87 | 100 |
| $a_4$ | 73.24 | 98.59 |
| $a_5$ | 73.24 | 98.59 |
| $a_6$ | 97.18 | 100 |

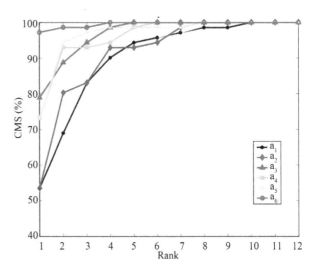

**Figure 10. CMC for six area features.**

gait motion. The second most significant results of 78.87% are achieved from $a_3$ which represents the lower arm dynamics. We achieve a recognition performance of 73.24% for both $a_4$ and $a_5$ features. Similarly, rank 1 recognition performance of $a_1$ and $a_2$ features is also the same at 53.52%. Rank 1 results indicate that thigh movement and knee movement is of equal importance in gait recognition. However, the performance of thigh and knee features is slightly lower than the features extracted from the lower arm dynamics.

Similar result pattern is obtained at rank 5. $a_6$ and $a_3$ features provide the best recognition performance of 100%. The recognition rate of $a_4$ and $a_5$ is slightly lower at 98.59%. The lowest performance of 92.96% is obtained from $a_2$ features. The recognition performance of $a_1$ features is slightly higher than $a_2$ feature set at 94.37%.

**Figure 10** shows the CMC plot for DCT features of six area signals. The recognition performance of the dynamic features extracted from $a_3$ and $a_6$ is superior to the other feature sets. These results partially support the traditional notion of significance of leg dynamics in gait recognition. It is also observed that the dynamics of the lower arm is very important in determining the gait pattern of the human subjects in an appearance based setup.

## 5. Conclusion

Human locomotion is a complex phenomenon involving the coordination of different limbs as the body translates from one point to another. The static configuration of the body such as the widths and lengths of different limbs have been shown of great importance in determining the gait pattern of the individuals. The contribution of dynamics of different parts of human body has not been studied explicitly in an appearance based recognition set up. In this paper, we have analyzed the recognition performance of dynamic features from different parts of the body. It is shown by experimental evaluation that dynamics of lower leg and lower arm are of utmost importance for building an efficient gait recognition system. The motion of lower half of the body has always been considered more important in the determination of gait pat-

tern. However, we have found that lower arm movement also plays an important role in gait recognition. The results from the present work can be used for building a better feature selection process for a more robust recognition system. Lower leg is usually very noisy in the extracted silhouettes because of shadows and walking surface issues. A set of better discriminatory features may be extracted from lower arm motion avoiding noisy data from lower leg.

## REFERENCES

[1]   G. Johansson, "Visual Perception of Biological Motion and a Model for Its Analysis," *Attention, Perception, & Psychophysics*, Vol. 14, No. 2, 1973, pp. 210-211.

[2]   J. B. dec. M. Saunders, V. T. Inman and H. D. Eberhart, "The Major Determinants in Normal and Pathological Gait," *The Journal of Bone and Joint Surgery*, Vol. 35-A, No. 3, 1953, pp. 543-558.

[3]   L. Wang, H. Z. Ning, T. N. Tan and W. M. Hu, "Fusion of Static and Dynamic Body Biometrics for Gait Recognition," *IEEE Transactions on Circuits and Systems for Video Technology*, Vol. 14, No. 2, 2004, pp. 149-158.

[4]   L. Wang, H. Z. Ning, T. N. Tan and W. M. Hu, "Fusion of Static and Dynamic Body Biometrics for Gait Recognition," *Proceedings of the 9th IEEE International Conference on Computer Vision (ICCV 03)*, Nice, 13-16 October 2003, pp. 1449-1454.

[5]   C. BenAbdelkader, R. Cutler and L. Davis, "Person Identification Using Automatic Height and Stride Estimation," *Proceedings of the IEEE 16th International Conference on Pattern Recognition*, Quebec, 11-15 August 2002, pp. 377-380.

[6]   A. F. Bobick and A. Y. Johnson, "Gait Recognition Using Static, Activity-Specific Parameters," *Proceedings of the*

2001 *IEEE Computer Society Conference on Computer Vision and Pattern Recognition*, Kauai, 8-14 December 2001, pp. 423-430.

[7]  "Georgia Tech GVU Center/College of Computing— Human Identification at a Distance," 2011. http://www.cc.gatech.edu/cpl/projects/hid

[8]  A. Veeraraghavan, A. K. Roy-Chowdhury and R. Chellappa, "Matching Shape Sequences in Video with Applications in Human Movement Analysis," *IEEE Transactions on Pattern Analysis and Machine Intelligence*, Vol. 27, No. 12, 2005, pp. 1896-1909.

[9]  R. D. Green and L. Guan, "Quantifying and Recognizing Human Movement Patterns from Monocular Video Images-Part II: Applications to Biometrics," *IEEE Transactions on Circuits Systems for Video Technology*, Vol. 14, No. 2, 2004, pp. 191-198.

[10]  J. P. Foster, M. S. Nixon and A. Prügel-Bennett , "Automatic Gait Recognition Using Area-Based Metric," *Pattern Recognition Letters*, Vol. 24, No. 14, 2003, pp. 2489-2497.

[11]  N. E. Huang, Z. Shen, S. R. Long, M. C. Wu, H. H. Shih, Q. Zheng, N. C. Yen, C. C. Tung and H. H. Liu, "The Empirical Mode Decomposition and the Hilbert Spectrumfor Nonlinear and Non-Stationary Time Series Analysis," *Proceedings of the Royal Society of London A*, Vol. 454, No. 1971, 1998, pp. 903-995.

[12]  S. Sarkar, P. J. Phillips, Z. Y. Liu, I. R. Vega, P. Grother and K. W. Bowyer, "The HumanID Gait Challenge Problem: Data Sets, Performance, and Analysis," *IEEE Transactions on Pattern Analysis and Machine Intelligence*, Vol. 27, No. 2, 2005, pp. 162-177.

# 9

# A Distributed Secure Mechanism for Resource Protection in a Digital Ecosystem Environment

**Ilung Pranata, Geoff Skinner, Rukshan Athauda**
Faculty of Science and IT, University of Newcastle, Callaghan, Australia

## ABSTRACT

The dynamic interaction and collaboration of the loosely coupled entities play a pivotal role for the successful implementation of a Digital Ecosystem environment. However, such interaction and collaboration can only be promoted when information and resources are effortlessly shared, accessed, and utilized by the interacting entities. A major requirement to promote an intensive sharing of resources is the ability to secure and uphold the confidentiality, integrity and non-repudiation of resources. This requirement is extremely important in particular when interactions with the unfamiliar entities occur frequently. In this paper, we present a distributed mechanism for improving resource protection in a Digital Ecosystem environment. This mechanism can be used not only for any secure and reliable transaction, but also for encouraging the collaborative efforts by the Digital Ecosystem community members to play a major role in securing the environment. Public Key Infrastructure is also employed to provide a strong protection for its access workflows.

Keywords: Digital Ecosystem; Authentication; Authorisation; Distributed Mechanism

## 1. Introduction

Information and resource protection is a de-facto requirement that must be advocated by every enterprise, organisation, and government entity. The importance of this requirement is further escalated when the entities are performing transactions in an online environment. Information security has been long considered as a crucial factor for e-commerce transactions. It is important to note that lack of sufficient security protection may limit the expansion of e-commerce technology [1]. However, although several e-commerce security mechanisms have been proposed and debated over a number of years, current internet technology still poses a number of incidents pertinent to the loss of information, unauthorized use of resources, and information hacking. These incidents generate an excruciating cost for the enterprises, ranging from the loss of revenue to the damage of their reputation. A recent survey [2] shows that the average cost resulted from the worst incident at about £280k - £690k per incident for a large organisation and £27.5k - £55k per incident for a small and medium organisation.

Similarly, Digital Ecosystem (DE) faces the identical issues due to its open environment where information and resources are exchanged over the network. With possibly thousands of Small and Medium Enterprises (SMEs) that form series of communities in a DE environment [3], protecting enterprise resources and acknowl-

edging which entities are trusted to access the resources become extensive tasks for each enterprise. While ensuring security protection is all about upholding the confidentiality, integrity, availability and non-repudiation of information, it is evident that the most consistent and effective way to ensure the preservation of these security properties is through the implementation of authentication, authorisation, encryption, and access control mechanisms [1,4]. Additionally, the provision of an efficient mechanism to measure the trustworthiness of entities will further strengthen the information and resource protecttion [5]. While authentication ensures only the right entities that are allowed to consume the resources, authorisation restricts the access over multiple hosted resources based on each entity's privileges. Nevertheless, current research in these areas for a DE environment is still very much limited or not attempted. This research gap further becomes our main motivation to focus our work in.

The remainder of this paper is structured as follows: Section 2 provides an introduction of Digital Ecosystem and its security challenges. Section 3 provides an overview of our proposed solution. Section 4 provides an implementation of our proposed solution. Section 5 presents an security analysis on the proposed solution. This is followed by Section 6 which shows the results of performance and scalability testing on our solution. To conclude the paper, Section 7 summarizes our present work and demonstrates several future works.

## 2. Digital Ecosystem & Its Security Challenges

Since its first inception, the newly emerging concept of Digital Ecosystem (DE) has received increasing attentions from researchers, businesses, IT professionals and communities around the world. A wide variety of researches and initiatives have been undertaken that aimed at the realization and implementation of a Digital Ecosystem concept. The enthusiasms were revealed inside numerous projects funded by European Commission under FP6 framework programme followed by FP7 framework programme as well as in numerous pilot regional workplans in Aragon, Tampere, Piedmont and West Midland [6,7]. The derived objective of DE primarily focuses on dynamic formation of a knowledge based economy [8]. Further, it was proposed that a knowledge based economy will lead to a creation of more jobs and a greater social inclusion in sustaining the world economic growth [6]. To realize this objective, it is critical to form an open framework infrastructure in promoting a wide use of Information and Communication Technology (ICT), as well as to solve the digital divide issues of internet and e-business adoption by small and medium enterprises [9].

The term "ecosystem" used inside DE notion is a fundamental biological science terminology to represent a dynamic interrelation between organisms and species that actively interact to conserve the environment [10]. Therefore, the similarity in concept and an analogy can be drawn between Digital Ecosystem and natural ecology community [9,11]. In a fundamental perspective, Digital Ecosystem is described as a digital environment and infrastructure where multiple digital components form a synergic correlation and collaboration with an evolutionary ability to adapt with its local circumstances [12]. Such digital components, or digital species used in other literatures, encompass various applications, services, frameworks, ontologies, knowledge, laws, taxonomies, reputation, training modules, trust relationships, and business models [9]. In a more technical term, Briscoe & Wilde [13] clearly define DE as the Multi-Agent Systems [14] that utilize distributed evolutionary computing [15,16] to combine the suitable agents in meeting user requests for applications. Further, the connectivity between the agents must be defined by the geography or spatial proximity unlike peer to peer [19] on which its peers' connectivity is based on bandwidth and information content.

In a DE environment where multiple interacting entities exist, the required efforts to enforce a strong authentication and authorisation mechanism are extensive. We identify three core issues that appear to be the challenging tasks to enforce such mechanisms. First, as the DE community expands its size to incorporate more entities,

the resource providers face a challenge to identify the legal entities that are able to access their resources. Second, the fact that each entity would have different set of access permissions to access multiple resources further complicates the implementation of an efficient mechanism. Third, it is probable that each resource provider would host multiple resources and services in a DE environment. This situation, in turn, creates a great issue to authorize the right entities to the right resources with the right permissions. The failure to assign the right permissions to the authorized entities would compromise the usage of resources which would bring negative impact to the resource provider. Therefore, it is apparent that enforcing strong and efficient authentication and authorisation mechanisms in a DE environment needs in-depth solutions on the core issues.

However, the current internet mechanisms are still far from adequate to provide a reliable authentication and authorisation processes for a DE environment. This view is reflected from our literature analysis over a number of internet mechanisms. Several prominent authentication mechanisms such as Identity Provider (IdP) or Credential Provider [20], Credential Server (CRES) [21], Grid Security Infrastructure (GSI) MyProxy [22] utilizes a centralised approach for creating user credential although their implementation differs between one another. These mechanisms could be implemented in DE, however the conspicuous issue of single server failure must be carefully considered. In an event where the credential provider server is down, there possibly a chaos in a DE community due to the unavailability of credential services for client authentication. Apparently, several authorisation mechanisms such as CAS [23], Akenti [24], and PMI [25] also take a similar centralised approach.

These mechanisms inherit several issues pertinent to the centralised management. First, the central management would face real issue with the bottleneck and failure on its servers. Security breach would occur if the central servers fail to perform their authorisation processes over the clients. This situation exposes the resources to the malicious attacks as there is no other authorisation mechanisms are in place. Although it is possible to replicate the central server, the replication process will bring abundance administrative issues and higher chances for compromising the resources, considering a huge amount of data that needs to be replicated. Second, challenges occur when the central server attempt to assign the access permissions to the DE member entities. As a large number of resource providers that host one or more resources, the central server needs to register each resource and its access permissions individually. Further, this situation becomes even more challenging as a single resource could be associated with multiple different access permissions, and each client may have different access permissions assigned to him. Therefore, the central management is not practical when there is huge number of entities in a DE environment. Third, serious administration issues would occur as a DE environment grows in size and diversity due to the great benefits that they can achieve. A central server will be experiencing huge burden to manage all client and resource providers' accounts and permissions even with the use of super computers or grid collections of computers.

Several DE literatures in [6,10,13] clearly reveal that DE is characterized as an open environment on which a centralized structure is minimized. DE must be engineered to provide a high resilience infrastructure while avoiding single point of control and failure. Therefore, a completely distributed control mechanism is required that immune to the super control failure. It is evident that the aforementioned internet mechanisms are inappropriate to be implemented in a DE environment due to its centralized management. We have dedicated a paper in [26] that derive the analogy of DE concept and further discuss its security challenges and requirements in detail. In this paper, we focus at the implementation and validation of our proposed DRPM solution [27,28] to solve the identified issues.

## 3. An Overview of DRPM

In this section, we provide a brief explanation of the important elements and workflows in in DRPM. Full discussion on these workflows could be found in [27,28].

### 3.1. Important Elements of DRPM

Two important elements of DRPM are client profile and capability token. A client profile is created in registration workflow when a client registers himself to access the resources. Its main function is to allow resource provider to capture all required, but voluntarily provided, client's information before any access to the resources is granted. The data that is contained in a client profile provides necessary information about who the client is and about their intentions for using the requested resources. Therefore, it ensures the resource provider that resources are not going to the wrong entities which would further impose the confidentiality and integrity of the resources. The use of client profiles also facilitates auditing process for the clients that are accessing a resource. For example, there may be a situation where a resource provider needs to make a trace back to determine which client was delegated access to the resource in case there was an incident involving a dispute or counterfeiting of the resource in question. Such implementation would reduce the risk of stolen data by the unauthorized entities.

At the end of registration process, an entity that is deemed eligible to access the resources would be issued a capability token. The purpose of this token is to simplify the management of access permissions that appear to be the challenge in collaborative environment, as have been pointed out by the number of literature from the previous section. A capability token functions as the authentication token for any subsequent access requests as well as for granting the access permissions. It contains the necessary right permissions for each client to perform a set of operations on a particular resource. This capability is produced by the resource provider on which a particular resource is hosted. On subsequent access request, this token is used by the resource provider to grant the client access to the resources and further provide the authorization process for the clients. Our basic design of capability token, as shown in **Figure 1**, contains the client profile identifier, resource provider identifier, resource identifier and list of access permissions, and it is expressed in XML [43] due to its simplicity, wide usability and self-descriptive characteristics. A time-stamp can be implemented in the capability token to determine the validity period of a user in accessing the resources. In the event where the trustworthiness of a new user is equivocal, a short-life capability token can be issued. Once the trustworthiness of the user gradually increases, resource provider can replace the short-life token with longer time-stamp validity. Additionally, the Uniform Resource Locator (URL) of resources is embedded in the token to provide an automatic and seamless connection to resource servers.

### 3.2. A Secure Registration Workflow

The DRPM registration portal is used to generate a client profile during the initial resource provisioning. The registration process comprises of three main stages: client registration, public key exchanges, and secure transfer of capability token. The resource provider endorsed certificate is utilized to identify the authentic resource provider

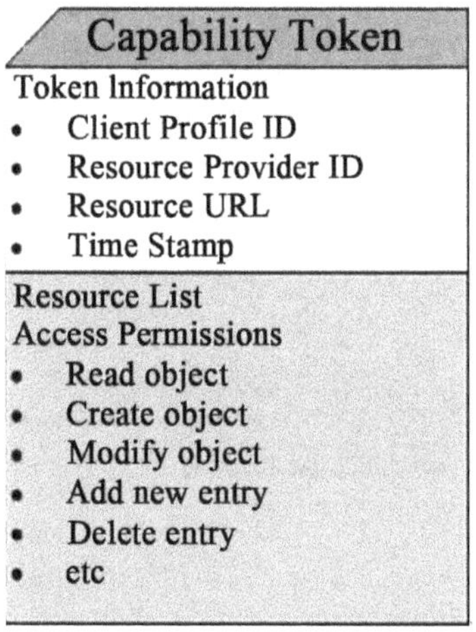

Figure 1. The structure of capability token.

based on its community endorsed public key certificate, which will be discussed in the next sub-section. The Public Key Infrastructure (PKI) is used to provide a secure communication between the client and resource provider. **Figure 2** shows the principal workflow for securing three stages of registration process.

The registration steps are detailed below:

1) A new client contacts the resource provider for requesting a resource. Resource provider sends its WoT endorsed public key to the client. Once the client determines and accepts the trustworthiness of the public key, he stores the resource provider trusted public keys and fills his information on the registration portal.

2) After the client information is filled, the registration portal creates a unique client and save this client profile.

3) Resource provider then requests for client certificate and stores the client public key on its repository. If required, WoT verification could be performed on client certificate to ensure the trustworthiness of the client.

4) The resource provider generates a client capability token based on client's allowed permissions.

5) Resource provider uses its own private key to sign the capability token. This process enhances the integrity of capability token over the untrusted network.

6) Resource provider then uses client's public key, received from step 3, to encrypt the signed message and send it to client end-point.

7) Client uses his own private key to decrypt the encrypted capability token.

8) Client then uses resource provider public key to gener-

ate the capability token from the signed message.

Note that at the final step of registration process, client will have his capability token and public key which was retrieved from the resource provider. The capability token and resource provider public key will be stored in client repository for subsequent requests. On another endpoint, the resource provider stores the client's public key in its own repository. We trust that the combination of both encryption and hashing mechanisms further uphold the confidentiality, integrity and non-repudiation of capability token during its transfer in the communication channel.

### 3.3. A Secure Resource Access Workflow

Once a client has been successfully registered with the resource provider, client will present his capability token to the resource provider on every access request. The capability token which contains client assertions and authorization permissions is primarily used as a base by the resource provider for authenticating the client and granting the resource access. Three foremost protection requirements for the resource access are the identification of resource provider, secured transfer of capability token, and authentication of a requesting client. A detailed workflow that ensures security protection on each resource access is provided in **Figure 3**.

The steps are as follow:

1) Client retrieves the resource provider capability token. The capability token contains the client access permissions and the resource URL. At this stage, the client

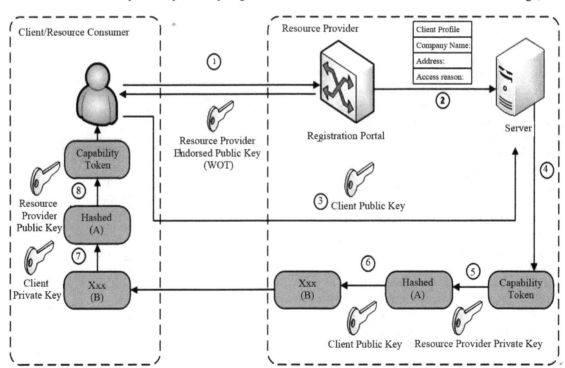

**Figure 2. DRPM secure registration workflow.**

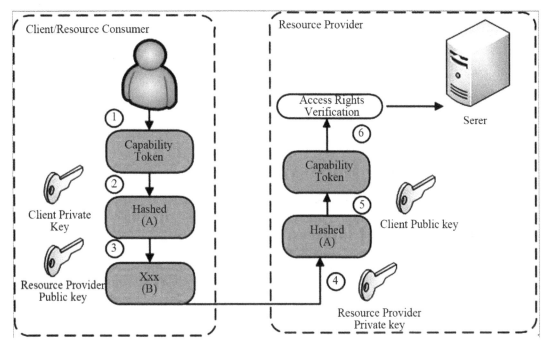

**Figure 3. DRPM resource access protection.**

also determines a symmetric pass key which will be shared with the resource provider and generate an Authentication Token which consists both symmetric pass key and capability token.

2) Client uses his private key to sign the capability token.

3) Client then encrypts the signed capability token using resource provider public key and he sends the encrypted message to the resource provider.

4) When resource provider received the encrypted message, it uses its own private key to de-crypt the message and retrieve the signed capability token.

5) Resource provider then verifies the signature of capability token using client public key. It then verifies the integrity of the capability token by generating the hash number from capability token.

6) Resource provider retrieves the access permissions listed in capability token.

Note that, on the step 1 of the workflow the client determines a symmetric pass key. This pass key will be utilized to generate a symmetric key for further communication after client is authenticated. In an event where the capability token is stolen due to man-in-middle attack, the unauthorized entity will still not be able to access the resource due as the symmetric key passphrase is shared between the legitimate client and resource provider only. This symmetric key would be used to secure communication after the authentication process. This is primarily due to the limitation of PKI which requires higher computation process. Further, a request for updating the resource provider public key could be made if the resource

provider generates a new pair of public-private keys due to an unforeseeable security breach.

## 3.4. Engaging Community Protection

As discussed in Section 2, DE must limit its centralized structure and promotes the involvement of Small and Medium Enterprises (SMEs) for its successful implementation. It is evident that centralized approach using either a Certificate Authority (CA) or Credential Provider (CP) must be minimized. For DRPM, we propose an idea to integrate the community trust services, such as Web of Trust (WoT) into DRPM workflow, particularly in client registration process. We present this idea as an alternative approach for protecting resources in a DE environment. Further, the implementation of WoT in DRPM encourages active participation of DE member entities to protect their environment.

Web of Trust (WoT) is a community endorsed certificate which provides a decentralized trust management in a digital community. In WoT, there is no central authority (such as CA) that every entity trust, instead each entity is able to sign others certificates or public keys to build an interconnected web of public keys. The identifycation of an entity is provided primarily by his public key which is digitally signed by any number of "introducers". Three degree of trustworthiness is introduced to reveal the reliability of the entity public key certificate: undefined, marginal and complete. Final decision for trusting the entity is rely on the user after examining the degree of trustworthiness. The prominent application of WoT is in Pretty Good Privacy (PGP) [30], which is used extensively to secure emails. The implementation of WoT in DRPM and the mechanism to ensure the trustworthiness of WoT entities is not within the scope of this paper. This issue becomes an inspiration for our future work.

## 4. DRPM Implementation

Our DRPM prototype is divided into two major applications: the resource provider application and the client application. The resource provider application consists of three main system components: listener component, registration component and resource component. The respective tasks of these components are to listen for any incoming connection from the client, to automatically create client profile and capability token, to securely exchange and host multiple resources. In contrast, client application is primarily utilized by resource consumer to securely register and access the hosted resources. Further explanation of each of the components that builds up our prototype architecture is provided.

### 4.1. Resource Provider Architecture

#### 4.1.1. Listener Server Component

The main functionality of listener server component is to accept any incoming HTTP requests from DE client members. Three main client requests on which this component handles are client registration, provider key signing and provider key retrieval. Upon receiving a client request, this listener component analyses the header of the incoming HTTP connection. This process has an objective to determine the nature of client request. Our client component, which would be discussed in detail in the following sub-section, was able to create unique HTTP headers to identify the objective of each request. **Figure 4** explains the activity workflow that reflects full functionalities of this listener server component.

In a case where an incoming HTTP request contains a registration header, the listener component constructs a certificate object that contains resource provider information and its public key. This certificate object is then sent to the client together with the registration page URL for redirection purposes. When client receives a token, he may verify the certificate to ensure the trustworthiness of resource provider and subsequently, he is redirected to the registration page. In a case where an incoming HTTP request contains a signed key header, the listener component sends provider public key to the client for signing process. We implemented a transaction lock on which other clients are not able to retrieve provider key during the signing process. Further, a configurable timeout of 5 minutes were adopted for each signing process. If the timeout is reached and client has not returned the signed key, the transaction lock will be released. In the last case where the client request is to retrieve provider key, this listener component would response back with provider public key.

When starting the listener server component, the system administrator would need to configure three URL addresses: URL address where the listener server is located, URL address of registration page component, and URL address of resource login component. These URLs are used by the clients to connect to the resource provider server and its resources, and for the listener server to redirect the client to the registration components. Another functionality of the listener server component is to generate both public and private keys. The KeyManager module of this component presents the existing resource provider public and private keys. It has a functionality to re-create both public and private keys. If the new keys are created, these keys will be stored securely in the key repository on the resource provider server.

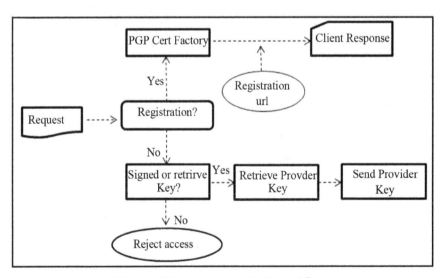

**Figure 4. Listener server activity workflow.**

#### 4.1.2. Registration Page Component

The registration page component contains a set of minimum information which needs to be filled in by the client. For our testing, we uploaded 4 resources on which the access permissions of each resource could be requested. In real implementation, types of resources and their access permissions are highly dependent on the configuretion that is set by each resource provider. During the registration process, client public key is obtained and stored by resource provider in its server repository. The obtained public key will be used in future access requests. That is to verify the signature of the presented capability token. When a client submits his information and indicates which resources that he intends to consume the registration page component then creates a client profile based on the supplied information. This client profile will be stored in resource provider's database. After the creation of client profile, this component constructs a capability token and generates a hash no of this token. The hash no is then stored in the database for subsequent resource access verification. The newly created capability token goes through encryption and signing process (by calling the *EncrypAndSignToken* method). **Figure 5** demonstrates the capability token that was taken before and after the encryption and signing process.

#### 4.1.3. Resource Page Component

This is the critical component where the resources and critical information are hosted. Therefore, a considerable amount of security must be implemented. When this component is requested by client, a series of validation checks are conducted to determine the availability of capability token, its originality and integrity. This component contains a login module that performs these checks. When resource component receives a HTTP request with access header, login module checks the availability of capability token in the request. It obtains client capability token from the incoming request. The module then calls the decryptFile and the verifySignature method to decrypt and verify the signature as showed in **Figure 3**. If any of these processes fails, access request will be rejected as a failed authentication process, otherwise the client will be redirected to the resource page component where he will be given access based on the permissions that is contained in his capability token.

Note that, when a client is able to access the resource page component, it means that he has been authenticated by the resource provider as a genuine client. However, at this stage the access permissions which are presented by the client in his capability token have not been authorised. A hash no verification of capability token is performed for this purpose (through createVerifyHash module). The hash no will be compared with the hash no that was obtained during the registration process. If hash no verification succeeds, the resource page component retrieves all access permissions from client's capability token, and it further granted the resource access based on these listed permissions. If the verification fails, a notification would be presented to the client and access to the resource would be disallowed.

### 4.2. Client Architecture

#### 4.2.1. Key Admin Component

Similar to the KeyManager module of resource provider listener component, this component allow clients to generate, manage and distribute his public and private keys. Any created keys would be stored in keys repository

c8261UUDDQ.xml


```
<?xml version="1.0"?>
<!--Resource capability token for accessing resources-->
<ResourceToken>
  <TokenInformation>
    <TokenID>c8261UUDDQ</TokenID>
    <IssuedBy>McArthur Logistic</IssuedBy>
    <ResourceUrl>http://localhost:50750/ServerResource/Resource.aspx</ResourceUrl>
    <ClientName>Initial Co</ClientName>
    <TimeStamp>4/4/2011 14:52:48</TimeStamp>
  </TokenInformation>
  <AccessPermission>
    <Resource id="1">
      <Permission>Access Data</Permission>
    </Resource>
    <Resource id="2">
      <Permission>Access Data</Permission>
      <Permission>Modify Data</Permission>
    </Resource>
  </AccessPermission>
</ResourceToken>
```


(a)

c8261UUDDQ.xml.asc


```
-----BEGIN PGP MESSAGE-----
Version: BCPG C# v1.6.1.0

hIsDnu5Qz3mHcKYBA/ihxZEEtX3kjj5Yrkn8RnYVbkVXZunD8K7VvvLAT8+Ue7D/
/4RoK9nEBc+0knWzavFw2fjAwyeflevY5vJtrcGQw9hRL8r99cfG6305CHix6OgN
q8AqSNJ7jQ/jZ3YXRZVv+gi0KaRYaFRR6GFK9xRSsZXQbALVLcfcDDO1x3qKycFb
w0JVGB/AD+Rx9kpxGfHOsoefVUI2jShGI1WAsxG1E6Mme2/TQzwdTudmjd8x4dCo
vZBgFbWI3/fVbpEiuDAOO9QJWbIfVTkaj72iPAkhHmp/fRk/+wB5SM3utcP0sPdW
TMKfgl5r+MKOzThYxjs6mua2F5+AGcIZoomplOODqW4LdevHksN+Q21Ny1TTGJ12
83Xw3x4QYfWHNTfHNub5j8AEEucstN8/2+5ADOOq0qkrZGOrcI6hMUCDILv31K4T
Cu4FKYIRCXBVyZX0VY62fBj0t6dpRfRYPDADJL41Bft3Fan721eAH9Zqbn6mRGyX
PM/xF3+dQpe5nd4z2914jPQZr3E8Dfp7DlpjQX55kDQ5K1VLBdJJ1ED02wsJ4U0s
HBWsMpHGNTMWrWvwKX8WZG49qRriQXps3YP8iaG6C/pTSa3extZjyLTJSY6X4/YI
NTebpA+J4OeCvD1E+YSo+31aUGYLcGrDWtEGxq6GdfDfHdOgg674mdvJxCxXSpMD
e/r+n7ACp6CItKqnenRTYjEsHihHW/6hwD5AEi1QgiRqafmDiAWDURn3ipXC2/Rq
pMSxNQtRcv9Cy/IH/uszYa8KThwY8qF9xqx+Z6khRPPGGV01b8N6VL8fDBATQDdJ
l1ELqBMF88jZhR9RUMCUM8xqzRVq00RNipgnNpdOvVLNRyVpDDuubTlIhTxZZ/Wt
R0dowC+kZmfD0bo=
=0JkU
-----END PGP MESSAGE-----
```


(b)

**Figure 5. The original (a) and the encrypted-signed (b) capability token.**

which is kept in client workstation. This component was proved to be very useful for client administrator to manage his own keys.

### 4.2.2. Client Registration Component

This component is a critical module for a client to Register for new resources. A client provides his intended resource provider listener server URL and its port for a secure communication. When a client registers for resource, a new HttpWebRequest will be created and sent to the resource provider listener server. This HttpWebRequest serves as a request message from client to listener component to process and return the provider's certificate and its registration page URL. Upon receiving the response, the component processes and de-serializes this response. in order to obtain the certificate object. The

requested client would then be able to view the WoT certificate, and simultaneously he is redirected to the resource provider registration page. **Figure 6** shows our implementation of client registration component.

We built this secure component in a windows application with a simple web browser interface. This component is equipped with a capability to generate a HTTP protocol request for its initial communication. We set a temporary listener which is started when the client clicks on "register" button. This objective of temporary listener is to receive the encrypted token and further decrypts the token with resource provider public key which is obtained from its certificate object. The signature verification process follows after the decryption process. **Figure 7** explains the entire activity workflow during resource registration from the client node point of view.

**Figure 6. Client registration component.**

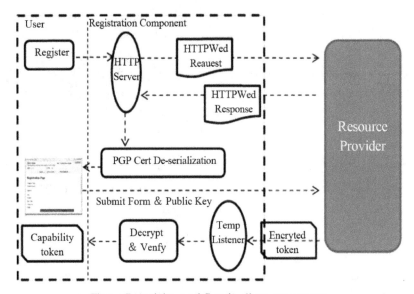

**Figure 7. Activity workflow in client component.**

### 4.2.3. Resource Access Component

DE client uses this component to access resources that are hosted in resource provider server. This component establishes communication and exchange processes of capability token and resources. A client is able to select which resource provider that he wants to access the resources based on his retrieved capability tokens. The component also lists all resources and their respective granted permissions. The lists of resource providers, resources, and permission types are retrieved from all capability tokens that are stored in client repository. When a client submits an access request, the capability token of its resource provider is retrieved and a symmetric key passphrase is generated. A temporary object will then be created to encapsulate this capability token and symmetric key passphrase. This object is further encrypted and signed as discussed previously in **Figure 3**.

## 5. Security Validation & Analysis

In order to validate our proposed solution, we developed several scenarios that showed various unauthorised attempts to access the resources. In each scenario, we focussed at how the existing prototype could mitigate any threats that were attempting to access the resources. The test outcomes of these scenarios would further attest the ability of our proposed solution to uphold the confidentiality, integrity and availability of resources and information while strengthening the authentication and authorisation mechanisms in a DE environment. These scenarios are detailed below:

- **Scenario 1:** If a capability token is stolen, would the unauthorised entity be able to read its content?

In our solution, a capability token is always encrypted and signed before it is being transferred in the network. The strongest encryption algorithm for e-commerce transactions (RSA algorithm) is utilized to prevent the unauthorised entity to read the content of capability token. Moreover, the Public Key Infrastructure (PKI) is fully utilized in our solution. With these measures in place, the confidentiality of capability token is always enforced. The unauthorised entity is only able to read the scramble data unless it has the corresponding private key to decrypt it. **Figure 7** above has showed the encrypted capability token before it is being sent in the network.

- **Scenario 2:** If an unauthorised entity attempts to use the stolen capability token to camouflage himself as a legitimate client, would he be able to access the resources?

In this situation, the unauthorised entity would not be allowed to access the resource for two reasons:

1) Resource provider always verifies the signature of capability token with the client public key on every access requests. Unless the unauthorised entity successfully obtained the client private key, the verification process of this capability token will be failed, and access will not be granted. **Figure 8** shows the failed verification processes of capability token signature.

2) In an event when an unauthorised entity performs the man-in-middle or relay attack during an active communication between client and resource provider, he would be able to obtain the capability token. However, the unauthorised entity will still not be able to access the resource due to the symmetric key passphrase that is shared between the legitimate client and resource provider only.

- **Scenario 3:** If an unauthorised entity or client modifies the capability token by adding or removing the resources or permission types, would he be able to consume the resources?

We implement a hashing mechanism for the resource provider to check the integrity of capability token. If there is any change, either minor or major change, in the capability token, the hash verification process will fail and the resource access will not be granted, as shown in **Figure 9**. This verification process further upholds the integrity of a capability token before any access to the resources is given.

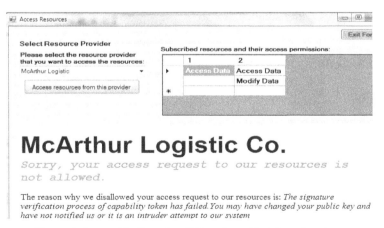

**Figure 8. Access disallowed as failure to verify token signature.**

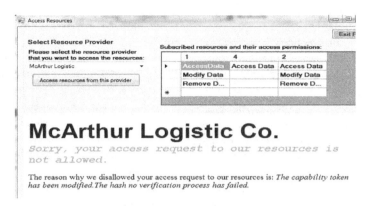

**Figure 9. Access disallowed as failure to verify the hash no.**

- **Scenario 4:** It is possible that a client is redirected to the unauthorized sites that claim to be the legitimate resource provider, how would DRPM prevent such situation?

This situation is known as phishing attack on which the client is redirected to the fraudulent link where he enters the personal details to the fraudster without any knowledge that he is the victim of the crime [31]. Our proposed capability token contains a ResourceURL field which functions to automatically redirect the client to the legitimate resource provider website. Further, the encryption method that is implemented before any token transfer is performed further upholds the confidentiality of a capability token during the transfer process. Therefore, our solution further reduces the possibility of phishing attack in a DE environment.

The verification and evaluation of DRPM proved to be successful, and it further resolved our main research issue of "authenticating the genuine client and managing multiple authorisation permissions over various resources". Our prototype implementation and testing has proved to solve several security concerns which were derived in section V as well as various threat scenarios that are likely to occur in a DE environment. Finally, the unique authentication and authorisation mechanisms offered by DRPM in conjunction with its secure architecture provide a complete and full fledge security solutions for a DE environment.

## 6. Performance and Scalability Analysis

### 6.1. Performance Testing

In this section, we briefly review our analysis on the computational cost of DRPM prototype. To measure the performance impact of DRPM, three different scenarios from the workflows are identified. They are: the overhead cost during initial registration process where provider's public key and its registration page are sent to the client, the overhead cost in processing client's registration that includes generating capability token and secure-

ing communication, and the overhead cost during resource access workflow. In addition, we compare the overhead cost of cryptography between two sets of machine.

All performance tests were conducted in two machines, and these machines respectively act as client and server. Our client machine run on a 1.86 GHz Intel Centrino with 1 Gb of RAM while our provider server machine run on a 2.26 GHz Intel Core2 Duo processor with 2 Gb of RAM and IIS 7 web server. Both machines were using NET framework 2.0 and MSSQL Server 2008 for the database. It is important to note that both client and provider server machines are below today's average of client and server computer standards. This configuration was taken to measure the performance of using DRPM prototype on the low end machines. As both client and provider server were connected via local high speed Ethernet LAN with 100 Mbps, we assume that the network latency during testing was insignificant. Therefore, it was not considered on the final performance results.

We conducted 52 repeated experiments for each scenario to obtain various performance results of DRPM. The result of the first two results was omitted due to the need for the application prototype to be compiled and the process workers to be started by the Just in Time (JIT) compiler in Net Framework 2.0. Therefore, only the results of subsequent 50 experiments were obtained. Due to the length limitation of the paper, we only present the mean and standard deviation of the experiment results. Further, the overhead costs derived from each scenario are calculated by applying the mean scores to the formula below:

$$\text{Overhead Cost}: \frac{\text{Processing Time}}{\text{Total Time Taken}} \times 100\%$$

The result of our performance testing on DRPM prototype is shown in **Table 1**.

The average total time take for initial registration reest was 226.18 milliseconds. This timing accounted for loading registration page and processing provider cerficate. Furthermore, the average total time for client regtration in our test was 593.24 milliseconds. This timing accounted for 134.56 milliseconds of server process and 458.68 milliseconds of client process. Our findings showed that token creation process accounted was accounted for the lowest time needed compare to other server processes such as encryption and signing process. The highest overhead cost (61.88%) was needed by other server process such as running complex stored procedures in database, forming response to client, and etc. In client process, the highest overhead cost was token decryption process. It was followed by signature verification process which was almost 88% faster than the former process. The rest client process accounted for 31.05 milliseconds (6.77%) was for processing response, storing token to repository, and etc.

As shown in **Table 2**, the overall time needed for accessing resource in our test was 701.28 milliseconds. This timing was account for 55.92 milliseconds for server login process and 645.36 milliseconds for client process and resource page loading. The result for server login process showed that the decryption process took the majority of server login time. This was followed by signature verification which was almost 88% faster than the decryption process aligned with the registration workflow decryption-signature process. Overall time take to retrieve the access permissions from token was 1.46 milliseconds for 1 Kb token size. As the capability token is intended for storing the access permissions in lightweight XML format, we expect that it only contains limited information; therefore its file size should not over than 5 Kb. Hash verification performance was a surprising result in our DRPM prototype testing. This was due to the process of hash verification method which involves generating hash no from the token (using SHA-1 algorithm) and comparing it with the original hash that is obtained from the database. The rest 5.34 milliseconds (9.54%) was needed for other server login processes such as reading private keys from key ring, forming HttpWebResponse message, writing logs, creating sessions and etc.

**Table 1. Registration workflow overhead cost (in milliseconds).**

| Scenario | Steps on Workflow | Processing Type | Mean | Standard Deviation | Overhead Cost |
|---|---|---|---|---|---|
| Registration: initial request | Server (Step 1) | Loading Page | 226.18 | 89.08 | N/A |
| | Server (Steps 2-6) | Creating Token | 6.84 | 6.89 | 5.08% |
| | | Encrypt and Sign | 44.46 | 6.84 | 33.04% |
| Registration: processing | | Total Server Time | 134.56 | 48.17 | N/A |
| | | Decrypt | 375.78 | 46.19 | 81.92% |
| | Client (Steps 7-8) | Verify Signature | 51.86 | 46.77 | 11.31% |
| | | Total Time | 458.68 | 55.32 | N/A |

**Table 2. Resource access workflow overhead cost (in milliseconds).**

| Scenario | Steps on Workflow | Processing Type | Mean | Standard Deviation | Overhead Cost |
|---|---|---|---|---|---|
| | | Decrypt | 43.48 | 4.04 | 77.75% |
| | | Verify Signature | 5.08 | 1.90 | 9.08% |
| | Server (Steps 4-6) | Verify Hash | 0.52 | 0.71 | 0.93% |
| Resource Access | | Retrieve Permissions From token | 1.5 | 0.50 | 2.68% |
| | | **Total Server Time** | 55.92 | 5.15 | N/A |
| | Client (Steps 1-3) | Encrypt & Sign | 435.84 | 55.75 | 67.53% |
| | | **Total Client Time** | 645.36 | 70.15 | N/A |

Token encryption and signature process accounts for the majority of total client process time. The rest 209.52 milliseconds (32.47%) was needed for other client processes including the activity to form HttpWebRequest, to retrieve token from repository, to process HttpWebResponse that was obtained from server, to redirect to resource page, to load resource page from server side and etc. Another finding from our testing was the overhead cost of cryptography processes which include decryption, encryption, sign and verification was reduced by almost 89% by doubling up the machine specification. This could be found by comparing any cryptography process between the client machine and server machine. **Figure 10** shows the overhead percentage of each process.

## 6.2. Scalability Testing

We tested the scalability of the listener server component to handle multiple HttpWebRequest requests as shown **Figure 11**. This test was conducted by utilizing the Apache JMeter [32] tool that specializes on the web scalability and performance testing. The purpose of this test was to review the scalability of the listener component to handle multiple client registration requests.

In our test bed, 1000 users were generated to access the listener component concurrently. Our test shows that the average elapsed time of this set of results was 162 milliseconds with the aggregate highest elapsed time of 327 milliseconds and the aggregate lowest elapsed time of 5 milliseconds. The scalability testing on other components such as registration, login, resource page, etc. were not able to be conducted by JMeter. This is primarily due to the need to utilize the prototype to create the request stream that holds the encrypted and signed capability token. We tested the scalability of other components only with a small number of machines (5 or less) and only a small number of clients (4 or less). Therefore, scalability of these components was not addressed in the experiment.

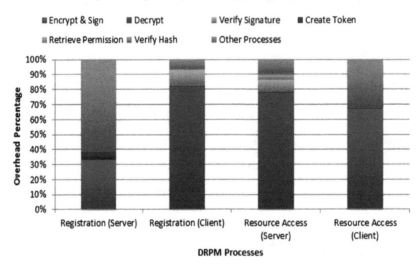

Figure 10. Overhead cost on DRPM prototype.

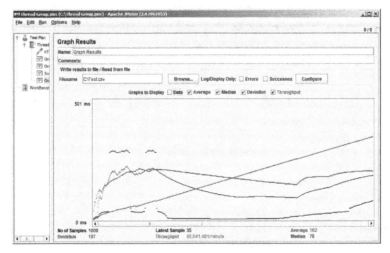

Figure 11. DRPM listener component scalability testing.

## 7. Conclusions

In this paper, we introduced the concept of Digital Ecosystem (DE), and we also outlined the challenges that are faced by DE, in particular the authentication and authorisation mechanism. We have also highlighted the requirement of DE to minimize the centralized structure and promoting the engagement of Small and Medium Enterprises (SMEs) for its successful adoption. We further propose a unique solution the Distributed Resource Protection Mechanism (DRPM) that attempt to solve the identified challenges. DRPM focuses on the creation of client profile and capability token to protect the critical resources. Moreover, we propose a secure DRPM architecture with adoption of Public Key Infrastructure (PKI). This further allows DRPM functions as a complete and full fledge security solution for Digital Ecosystem.

This paper also provides our implementation of secure DRPM which consists of two major system architectures: resource provider system and client system. Several scenarios of security threats are provided in this paper to analyse and evaluate the ability of our secure DRPM implementation to mitigate these threats. The analysis shows that the secure DRPM proposal is able to uphold the confidentiality, integrity, and non-repudiation of the resources. In addition, the performance and scalability analysis of DRPM are presented. Future works include the investigation of an effective trust mechanism in DRPM. As pointed in this paper, the utilisation of Web of Trust (WoT) would engage the interacting entities to actively protect their DE environment. At this point, however, DRPM does not include any trust mechanism that could allow the interacting entities to determine which resource providers are honest and which are not. The inclusivity of trust mechanism would significantly improve the overall security protection in DE environment. Therefore, investigation on the effective trust mechanism to improve the overall DRPM security is needed.

## REFERENCES

[1] D. Boughaci and H. Drias, "A Secure E-Transaction model for E-Commerce," *IEEE GCC Conference (GCC)*, Manama, 20-22 March 2006.

[2] C. Potter and A. Beard, "Information Security Breaches Survey 2010," *Technical Report*, PricewaterhouseCoopers, 2010.

[3] P. ltner and T. Grechenig, "A Joint Infrastructure of 'Digital Corporate Organisms' as Facilitator for a Virtual Digital Retail Ecosystem," *4th IEEE International Conference on Digital Ecosystems and Technologies (DEST)*, Dubai, 12-15 April 2010.

[4] Y.-L. Fang B. Han and Y.-B. Li, "Research and Implementation of Key Technology Based on Internet Encryption and Authentication," *International Conference on Networking and Digital Society (ICNDS'09)*, Guiyang, 30-31 May 2009.

[5] X. Tian and W. Dai, "Study on Information Management and Security of E-commerce System," *International Symposium on Intelligence Information Processing and Trusted Computing (IPTC)*, Huanggang, 18-20 November 2010.

[6] P. Dini, M. Darking, N. Rathbone, M. Vidal, P. Hernandez, P. Ferronato, G. Briscoe and S. Hendryx, "The Digital Ecosystems Research Vision: 2010 and Beyond," 2011. www.digital-ecosystems.org/events/2005.05/de_position_paper_vf.pdf

[7] EComm, "Technologies for Digital Ecosystems," 2005. www.digital-ecosystems.org/doc/flyer-de-sector.doc.

[8] F. Nachira, P. Dini and A. Nicolai, "A Network of Digital Business Ecosystems for Europe: Roots, Processes and Perspectives," 2011. http://www.digital-ecosystems.org/book/DBE-2007.pdf

[9] F. Nachira, E. Chiozza, H. Ihonen, M. Manzoni and F. Cunningham, "Towards a Network of Digital Business Ecosystems Fostering the Local Development," *Discussion Paper*, Bruxelles, 2002.

[10] H. Boley and E. Chang, "Digital Ecosystem: Principles and Semantics," *Inaugural IEEE International Conference on Digital Ecosystems and Technologies (IEEE DEST 2007)*, Cairns, 12-23 February 2007.

[11] M. Hadzic, E. Chang and T. Dillon, "Methodology Framework for the Design of Digital Ecosystem," *ISIC IEEE International Conference Systems, Man and Cybernetics*, Montreal, 7-10 October 2007.

[12] DigitalEcosystem.org, "Digital Ecosystems: The New Global Commons for SMEs and Local Growth," 2011. http://www.digital-ecosystems.org/de/refs/ref_books.html

[13] G. Briscoe and P. Wilde, "Digital Ecosystems: Evolving Service-Oriented Architectures," *1st International Conference on Bio Inspired Models of Network, Information and Computing Systems*, New York, June 2006.

[14] M. Wooldridge, "Introduction to MultiAgent Systems," Wiley, New York, 2002

[15] E. Cantu-Paz, "A Survey of Parallel Genetic Algorithms," *Reseaux et Systemes Repartis, Calculateurs Paralleles*, Vol. 10, 1998, pp. 141-171.

[16] J. Stender, "Parallel Genetic Algorithms: Theory and Applications," IOS Press, Amsterdam, 1993.

[17] A. Berson, "Client/Server Architecture," 2nd Edition, McGraw-Hill Companies, Upper Saddle River, 1996.

[18] W3C, "Web Services Architecture," 2011. http://www.w3.org/TR/ws-arch/

[19] R. Schollmeier, "A Definition of Peer-to-Peer Networking for the Classification of Peer-to-Peer Architectures and Applications," *Proceedings of 1st IEEE International Conference on Peer to Peer Computing*, Linkoping, 27-29 August 2001.

[20] H. Koshutanski, *et al.*, "Distributed Identity Management Model for Digital Ecosystems," *International Conference*

on *Emerging Security Information, Systems and Technologies* (*Securware*'07), Valencia, 14-20 October 2007.

[21] J. M. Seigneur, "Demonstration of Security through Collaborative in Digital Business Ecosystem," *Proceedings of the IEEE SECOVAL Workshop*, Athens, September 2005.

[22] J. Novotny, "An Online Credential Repository for the Grid: MyProxy," *Proceedings of the IEEE* 10*th International Symposium on High Performance Distributed Computing* (*HPDC*-10), San Fransisco, 7-9 September 2001.

[23] L. Pearlman, *et al.*, "A Community Authorization Service for Group Collaboration," *Proceedings of the 3rd International Workshop on Policies for Distributed Systems and Networks*, Monterey, 5-7 June 2002.

[24] M. Thompson, *et al.*, "Certificate-Based Access Control for Widely Distributed Resources," *Proceedings of the 8th Conference on USENIX Security Symposium*, Washington DC, 23-26 August 1999.

[25] J. Weise, "Public Key Infrastructure Overview," Sun Microsystem, Sun BluePrints Online 2001.

[26] I. Pranata, G. Skinner and R. Athauda, "A Survey on the Security Requirements for a Successful Adoption of Digital Ecosystem Environment," 2*nd International Conference on Information Technology Security* (*ITS* 2011), Singapore, 24-25 November 2011.

[27] I. Pranata, G. Skinner and R. Athauda, "Community Based Authentication and Authorisation Mechanism for Digital Ecosystem," 5*th IEEE International Conference on Digital Ecosystems and Technologies* (*DEST* 11), Seoul, 31 May-3 June 2011.

[28] I. Pranata, G. Skinner and R. Athauda, "Distributed Mechanism for Protecting Resources in a Newly Emerged Digital Ecosystem," 11*th International Conference on Algorithms and Architectures for Parallel Processing* (*ICA3PP* 2011), Melbourne, 24-26 October 2011.

[29] W3C, "Extensible Markup Language (XML)," 2011. http://www.w3.org/XML/

[30] P. R. Zimmermann, "The Official PGP User's Guide," MIT Press, Cambridge, 1995.

[31] FTSC, "FSTC Counter-Phising Initiative," Financial Services Technology Consortium, New York, 2004.

[32] Apache JMeter, 2011. http://jakarta.apache.org/ jmeter/

# 10

# Random but System-Wide Unique Unlinkable Parameters

**Peter Schartner**
System Security Group, Klagenfurt University, Klagenfurt, Austria

## ABSTRACT

When initializing cryptographic systems or running cryptographic protocols, the randomness of critical parameters, like keys or key components, is one of the most crucial aspects. But, randomly chosen parameters come with the intrinsic chance of duplicates, which finally may cause cryptographic systems including RSA, ElGamal and Zero-Knowledge proofs to become insecure. When concerning digital identifiers, we need uniqueness in order to correctly identify a specific action or object. Unfortunately we also need randomness here. Without randomness, actions become linkable to each other or to their initiator's digital identity. So ideally the employed (cryptographic) parameters should fulfill two potentially conflicting requirements simultaneously: randomness and uniqueness. This article proposes an efficient mechanism to provide both attributes at the same time without highly constraining the first one and never violating the second one. After defining five requirements on random number generators and discussing related work, we will describe the core concept of the generation mechanism. Subsequently we will prove the postulated properties (security, randomness, uniqueness, efficiency and privacy protection) and present some application scenarios including system-wide unique parameters, cryptographic keys and components, identifiers and digital pseudonyms.

**Keywords:** Randomness; System-Wide Uniqueness; Unique Cryptographic Parameters; Cryptographic Keys; Digital Identifiers; Digital Pseudonyms; UUID; Universally Unique Identifiers; GUID; Globally Unique Identifiers

## 1. Introduction

Concerning cryptographic parameters, cryptographic keys and digital identifiers, randomness is the foremost requirement. With respect to cryptographic applications, the lack of sufficient randomness causes security risks which may result in faster attacks or completely compromised systems. In the field of digital identifiers, the lack of randomness may cause privacy problems, when identifiers (and hence actions) become linkable to each other or to the identity of a specific instance or person.

Beside the positive effects of randomness mentioned above, random generation processes unavoidably come with the intrinsic risk of duplicates. Unfortunately, these duplicate cryptographic parameters, cryptographic keys and digital identifiers can put the security of safety- or security-critical systems at risk as well.

### 1.1. The Risks of Pure Randomness

**Digital Identifiers:** In our everyday electronic life, duplicate parameters used as digital identifiers may cause severe problems. Think of object and message identifiers or digital identities in e-business or e-government applications. In the first case, duplicate identifiers may cause inconsistencies in databases or the system's registry. In the second case, records of different instances or persons may become inseparably mixed up. Both situations may end up in disaster.

In the context of security systems like RSA encryption and signature schemes, ElGamal signature schemes and zero knowledge proofs, duplicates may cause the following problems (for details on the following attacks we refer the reader to [1,2]):

**RSA [3]:** Assume that two instances accidentally choose the same prime when generating the RSA key pair. Since this common prime is a factor of both moduli, an attacker can easily determine the second factor of the two affected moduli. Afterwards, he can determine the according private keys. If the key pairs have been used in an encryption scheme, the attacker can now decrypt messages he is not authorized for. In case of a signature scheme, he can sign on the victims' behalf and hence fake their identities.

**ElGamal [4]:** If a signing instance signs two different messages using the same randomizer, the attacker can retrieve the private signing key by solving two linear congruencies. Again, the signature scheme is broken.

**Zero Knowledge Proofs [5]:** Consider two rounds of a zero knowledge proof, where the same first message (based on the same random parameter) is sent to the verifier. If the verifier notices this fact, he will send two different second messages in order to extract the secret by use of the third messages. Again the attacker can now fake the identity of the victim.

## 1.2. The Problem of Randomness vs Uniqueness

In order to avoid the problems mentioned above, we need random *and* unique (cryptographic) parameters. Unfortunately, randomness and (system-wide) uniqueness are potentially conflicting requirements. Pure randomness includes the risk of duplicates and hence may violate uniqueness, whereas generation processes which guarantee system-wide uniqueness may reduce randomness or cause the generation to be either inefficient or prone to other attack scenarios.

## 1.3. Our Contribution

In this article we will propose a solution for the problem of randomness vs. uniqueness: a scheme to generate provably system-wide unique, but highly random and unlinkable numbers (called collision-free numbers—CFNs) which can be used as digital identifiers (or pseudonyms) and cryptographic parameters and keys.

As other approaches, our scheme is based on a unique identifier for the generating process and additional non-invertible (cryptographic) mechanisms to disguise it and hence protect the generator's privacy. Simply spoken, our approach is a counter-based pseudo-random number generator (PRNG) with a fresh (random) key for each call of the generator (see **Figure 6** for a PRNG (left) and our approach (right)). It is clear, that providing both properties at the same time, will not be achievable without extra costs. Based on a short discussion of related work, we will show that this overhead is quite low compared to the existing methods of generation (see **Table 1**), which in contrast to our approach do not provide randomness and uniqueness simultaneously.

The remainder of this article is structured as follows: In order to provide a base for our design and the subsequent analysis, we will first define five requirements on random number generators and provide the most essential cryptographic preliminaries. Based on the requirements we will briefly discuss existing approaches. The analysis will show that none of the existing generation methods simultaneously fulfills all requirements. Hence there is need for a new approach. After presenting the design principle of CFNGs we will prove the fulfillment of the stated requirements and close with a discussion of application scenarios for CFNGs.

## 2. Requirements on Random Number Generators

In order to avoid the risks of duplicates when generating and using cryptographic parameters or digital identifiers, we postulated two additional requirements on the em-

ployed secure and efficient generators for random numbers in [2]: Uniqueness and Privacy Protection. We called generators providing the following properties *collision-free number generators* (CFNG) and the outputs of such generators *collision-free numbers* (CFNs):

1) Security.
2) Randomness.
3) Efficiency.
4) Uniqueness.
5) Privacy Protection.

We are aware of the fact, that depending on the application scenario, not all of the above requirements may be necessary or there may be additional requirements. Nevertheless, in the scope of generating cryptographic parameters (like keys) and digital identifiers, these requirements are necessary to obtain a secure generating process and hence the existing methods of generation and our proposed approach will be analyzed with respect to the five requirements stated above.

### 2.1. Security

If one CFNG is compromised, all outputs previously generated by this specific generator should remain secure. Additionally, all other CFNGs in the system must not be affected. This means that there should not be a centralized CFNG (since compromising this CFNG immediately compromises the whole system) and distributed CFNGs must not use any common secrets like the secret key $k$ used by the compromised generator $G_1$ in **Figure 1**.

### 2.2. Randomness

Ideally, the outputs of CFNGs (see value 2 in **Figure 2**) are indistinguishable to the outputs of true random number generators (RNG—see value 1 in **Figure 2**).

In fact, the proposed generators will be based on true random numbers, but will be post-processed to fulfill the newly introduced requirement of uniqueness. Nevertheless, the only way to verify the randomness is to perform statistical tests (like the DIEHARD test suite [6]) on the generated sequences and compare the outputs to the properties of true random sequences.

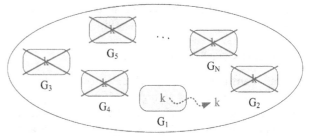

Set of all generators in the system

**Figure 1. Compromising generator $G_1$ compromises all generators.**

## 2.3. Efficiency

Concerning efficiency, minimal communications is the foremost requirement. Ideally, as depicted in **Figure 3**, there is no communication during the generation process and only one-time communication during the initialization. Nevertheless, to enable the usage of smart cards and other security token with limited resources, memory and computational demands should also be kept as low as possible.

## 2.4. Uniqueness

All outputs of all CFNGs within a system have to be unique, *i.e.*, there must not be any duplicates during the life-time of the system. As depicted in **Figure 4**, randomly generated values may be system-wide unique (e.g. outputs 1, 2 and 3), locally, but not system-wide unique (e.g. outputs 4 and 5) or not unique at all (e.g. outputs 6 and 7).

Local duplicates may be detected by storing all outputs and comparing the currently generated value against the stored ones. Obviously, this method will need a considerable amount of memory over the life-time of the generator. But even worse, global duplicates cannot be detected without communication with all the other generators or a centralized instance for checking. Besides a tremendous communication overhead, this again calls for local or centralized storage of all outputs for later comparison, which is obviously a bad idea with respect to the requirements "security" and "privacy protection".

## 2.5. Privacy Protection

Depending on the application scenario, outputs of CFNGs should not be linkable. As **Figure 5** shows, with respect to the protection of the generator's identity, especially two questions are of interest:

- Which CFNG has generated this (a specific) number?
- Have these numbers been generated by the same CFNG?

## 3. Cryptographic Preliminaries

Within this article the reader needs only a basic understanding of cryptography. So we will provide the most important facts and refer the reader to [7,8] for a detailed discussion of the basic concepts and more sophisticated cryptographic algorithms and protocols.

**Symmetric encryption** provides confidentiality. Encryption E and decryption D use the same key $k$: $c = E_k(m)$, $m = D_k(c)$ with plaintext $m$ and ciphertext $c$. Without the knowledge of $k$, $m$ cannot be efficiently retrieved from $c$. Most commonly, symmetric encryption algorithms are block-oriented, *i.e.*, they work on input blocks of fixed length. Candidates for symmetric encrypt

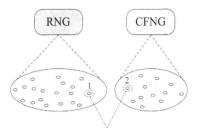

Generated by use of CFNG or random number?

**Figure 2. Outputs of a RNG and a CFNG.**

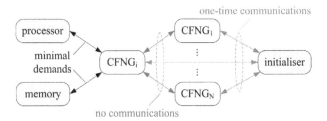

**Figure 3. Efficiency considerations.**

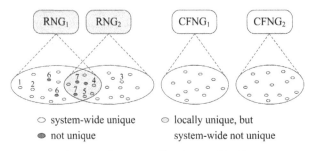

**Figure 4. Outputs of RNGs and CFNGs.**

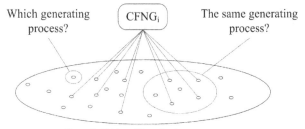

Set of all identifiers in the system

**Figure 5. Privacy protection.**

tion include DES [9] (Data Encryption Standard, 64 bit blocks and 56 bit keys), 3DES [10,11] (64 bit blocks and 112 bit keys), Skipjack [12] (64 bit blocks and 80 bit keys) and AES [13] (Advanced Encryption Standard, 128 bit blocks and 128,192 and 256 bit keys).

**Asymmetric encryption** also provides confidentiality, but uses different keys for encryption and decryption: $c = E_e(m)$, with public key $e$ and $m = D_d(c)$, with private key $d$. Without knowing $d$, $m$ cannot be efficiently retrieved from $c$, and $d$ cannot be efficiently derived from $e$ without additional (secret) knowledge. Candidates for asymmetric encryption include RSA [3] and ElGamal [4] (minimum key length 1024 bit) and ECC [8] (Elliptic Curve Cryptography, minimum key length 160 bit).

**Cryptographic Hash-functions** H are compressing one-way-functions, which convert a large, arbitrary sized input $m$ into a small, fixed size hash value $h$ (most commonly 128 or 160 bit): $h = H(m)$. Candidates for Hash-functions include SHA-1 [14] and RIPEMD160 [15], both with 160 bit outputs and the SHA-2 family [16] (224 to 512 bit outputs). Note that both, symmetric and asymmetric encryption and decryption functions are bijective for an arbitrary, but fixed key, whereas hashfunctions are by definition not injective!

## 4. Related Work

There exist at least three straight forward solutions for generating random *and* system-wide unique parameters:

The naive attempt of **centralized generation and check** obviously avoids duplicates but is quite inefficient concerning storage (all previously generated parameters have to be stored for later comparison) and communication (each instance which needs a parameter has to wait for the centralized generator to send it). Additionally, the centralized generator has full control over the generating process and knows all parameters. So, compromising this generator compromises the complete system.

With **local generation and check**, only the generation itself is done locally, but the comparison against all previously generated parameters has to involve all other generators or a centralized service. Again, efficiency and security are quite questionable.

**Local generation based on pseudo-random number generators** (PRNG, see [7]) can avoid centralized storage and comparison and is efficient in terms of memory and communications. But in order to avoid duplicates, all PRNGs have to use a common key or common secret parameters. So, if one of them is compromised, all of them become insecure. Additionally, the generated parameters are no longer random, but pseudo-random and

this approach is not suitable for software implementation, because by use of software, the system-wide key (or secret parameter) cannot be protected sufficiently.

A more sophisticated approach is the so called **location- and time-based generation** which simply uses location and time provided by a GPS receiver to derive a unique seed for the generation process. The idea behind this concept: two generation processes cannot take place at the same place *and* the same time. Besides the fact that the GPS signal will not be available at all locations, the according paper does not specify, how (pseudo-) randomness and uniqueness are maintained (see [17] for details).

A widely adopted approach for system-wide unique system parameters are **universally unique identifiers** (UUIDs, see [18]) and **globally unique identifiers** (GUIDs, see [19]), Microsoft's implementation of GUIDs. There exist several variants of GUIDs, but these variants either use the MAC address to guarantee uniqueness or they employ hash-functions or purely pseudo-random values. Except the first one, which violates the privacy requirement, none of them can guarantee uniqueness.

Besides the attempts mentioned above, there exist some **national methods** for the generation of identifiers used in e-business and e-government processes. Again, these methods employ hash-functions to protect the identity of the generating process and come with the unavoidable risk of duplicates (e.g. see [20]).

**Table 1** shows a summary of the discussed related work according the requirements stated in Section 2. Here "-" denotes, that the described generation method lacks a certain property, "??" denotes that it is unclear whether a generator provides a specific property (according to the publicly available specification) and "ok" denotes that the generator provides the property.

Note that none of the existing approaches shows "ok" for all five requirements. The analysis of our approach (see Section 6) will show that CFNGs (collision-free number generators) fulfill all requirements.

**Table 1. Related work—a short analysis and comparison.**

| Method | Security | Randomness | Efficiency | Uniqueness | Privacy |
|---|---|---|---|---|---|
| Centralized generation and check | - | ok | - | ok | ok |
| Local generation and check | ok | ok | - | ok | ok |
| Local PRNG-based generation | - | ok | ok | ok | ok |
| Location- and time-based generation (GPS-based) | ?? | ?? | ok | ok | ?? |
| UUIDs (MAC-based) | ok | ok | ok | ok | - |
| UUIDs (PRNG-based) | ok | ok | ok | - | ok |
| National method (Austria) | - | ok | ok | - | ok |
| Design goals of CFNGs (see Section 6 for proofs) | ok | ok | ok | ok | ok |

# 5. The Concept of Collision-Free Numbers

The core concept of collision-free number generators (CFNG) is closely related to pseudo-random number generators based on the CTR-mode of block-ciphers which uses a random but fixed key $k$ throughout its lifetime (see **Figure 6(a)**). The crucial difference of CFNGs compared to a PRNG in CTR-mode is that the key used by the CFNG is freshly chosen at random for each call of the generator (see **Figure 6(b)**).

Informally, our approach is based on three facts:

- Use counters that generate system-wide unique outputs $u$. This can easily be achieved by using counters of the following form: $u = ID\|cnt$, where $ID$ is a hierarchically structured identifier (e.g. the $ICCSN$ of a smartcard), unique for each generator, and $cnt$ is a locally stored value, which is incremented before each call of the generator.

- Employ some injective mixing function $f(u,r)$ which hides the value of $u$ by use of a so called randomizer $r$. This randomizer is freshly chosen at random for each call of the generator and deleted immediately after usage.

- In order to fix the uniqueness, embed the randomizer $r$ in the output $o$ of the generator by use of an injective bit permutation (or expansion). For the ease of discussion, we will use the concatenation ($\|$) throughout the remainder of this article.

More formally defined, the output $o$ of a basic—type 1—CFNG (denoted as CFNG1 in the remainder of this article) is of the form

$$o = f(u,r)\|r = f_r(u)\|r = \text{CFNG1}(\ ),$$

with $f$ being an injective mixing transformation for an arbitrary but fixed randomizer $r$ and $u$, $r$ defined as above. We suggest to either use an injective one-way mixing-transformation for $f_r$, according to Shannon [21] (e.g. symmetric encryption), or an injective probabilistic one-way function, based on an intractable problem (e.g. the discrete logarithm problem [7]).

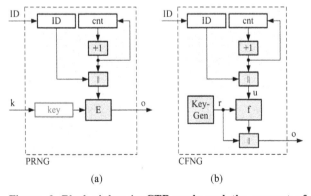

(a)                                   (b)

**Figure 6. Block-cipher in CTR-mode and the concept of CFNG (type 1).**

Note that originally, CFNGs have been called quasi-random number generators (QRNG). Since our generators provide numbers being neither pseudo-random nor random, QRNG—alphabetically and concerning the outputs being somewhat between PRNGs and true RNGs—would be the perfect name. Unfortunately the abbreviation QRNG collides with generators for quasi random sequences used for statistical testing. Hence to avoid this duplicate, we changed the name to CFNG.

# 6. Fulfillment of Requirements

## 6.1. Security

In our approach, all security critical parameters like randomizers or keys are nonces (numbers used once) generated on demand, *i.e.*, at each call of the generator. They are neither stored, nor transferred outside the generator. Hence, compromising one generator cannot affect any other generator in the system.

## 6.2. Uniqueness

In the following we will first give a proof for the uniqueness of outputs of Type 1 CFNGs. Based on this proof we will analyze Type 2 and Type 3 generators. Note that the lifetime of the system and especially of the generators employed within this system is defined by the time, none of the counters $cnt$ used inside of the CFNGs has an overflow.

**Theorem:** *Outputs of Type 1 CFNGs are unique during their lifetime.*

**Proof:** Consider two outputs of two arbitrary type 1 CFNGs: $o_1 = \text{CFNG1}_1(\ ) = f_{r1}(u_1)\|r_1$ and $o_2 = \text{CFNG1}_2(\ ) = f_{r2}(u_2)\|r_2$, with $r_1$, $r_2$ being random and $u_1 = ID_1\|cnt_1$ and $u_2 = ID_2\|cnt_2$. With respect to the randomizers $r_1$ and $r_2$, there are two cases:

1) $r_1 \neq r_2$: This directly means that $o_1 \neq o_2$.

2) $r_1 = r_2 = r$: Now, both calls of the generators employ the same randomizer and $f_r$ becomes injective. Hence $f_r(u_1)$ and $f_r(u_2)$ will be different if and only if $u_1 = ID_1\|cnt_1$ and $u_2 = ID_2\|cnt_2$ differ in at least one bit. This is always true, because

- Different generators use different identifiers $(ID_1 \neq ID_2)$, and

- If we call the same generator twice (*i.e.*, $ID_1 = ID_2$), the values $cnt_1$ and $cnt_2$ will differ, because the counter is incremented at each call of the generator.

Hence the outputs $o_1$ and $o_2$ will be different again. □

**Corollary:** *Outputs of type 2 and type 3 CFNGs are unique during their lifetime.*

**Proof:** Function $g$, applied to the unique inputs in type 2 and type 3 CFNGs is an injective one-way-function. Hence $g$ cannot destroy the uniqueness of the outputs. □

## 6.3. Privacy Protection

When analyzing CFNGs which employ a block cipher E for $f\left(o=E_r\left(ID\|cnt\right)\|r=c\|r\right)$, it is obvious that the identity of the generator is not protected sufficiently. Everybody who gets hold of an output $o$ can retrieve the identifier $ID$ of the according generator by simply decrypting $c$ by use of $r$: $ID\|cnt=D_r\left(c\right)$. We will later see that this may not be a problem in certain application scenarios, but in order to guarantee the protection of the generator's $ID$ we have either to change our requirements on $f$, or we have to slightly change the design of CFNGs.

- To provide privacy, $f$ has to be a cryptographic one-way function. Candidates include injective probabilistic one-way functions based on an intractable problem like the (ECC) discrete logarithm problem [7].
- In the case that $f$ is a (bijective) symmetric encryption function, we can employ an additional (injective) one-way-function $g$ to the output or to the randomizer of the original CFNG, which results in the variants depicted in **Figure 7**.

Both variants shown in **Figure 7** eliminate the attack described above. Now the attacker is faced with the problem of inverting function $g$, which is practically impossible. Hence, the output of function $f$ in case of type 2 CFNGs, and the randomizer $r$ in case of type 3 CFNGs, stays secure and the identity of the generator is safe again.

## 6.4. Randomness

Remember that in case of type 1 CFNGs, the second half of the output is the randomizer, which is—as the name implies—generated at random. Function $f$ is (with respect to the random input $r$) an injective mixing transformation, like a symmetric or asymmetric encryption function. Hence its output is pseudo-random.

Function $g$, applied in type 2 and type 3 CFNGs is a (injective) one-way-function. The randomness of its output depends on the randomness of its input, which is either the pseudo-random output of $f$ (type 2 CFNG), or the randomizer $r$ (type 3 CFNG).

Concerning the randomness of the outputs, we will briefly analyze the three types of CFNGs separately:

**Type 1 CFNGs**: The output is a concatenation of pseudo-random and random bits, and hence should "look random".

**Type 2 CFNGs**: The input of function $g$ is, as noted above, partially pseudo-random and random. So, the randomness of type 2 CFNGs should not be worse than the randomness of type 1 CFNGs.

**Type 3 CFNGs**: The output is a concatenation of pseudo-random and random bits, transformed by use of function $g$. So again, the output should "look random".

For all three types of generators, the statement "should

look random" has been verified by conducting statistical tests with the DIEHARD test suite [6]. See **Table 3** for exemplary DIEHARD results on 500.000 outputs $o$ of a type 1 CFNG (*i.e.*, 128.000.000 bit) of the form $o=AES_k\left(ID\|cnt\right)\|k$, where $ID$ is a 96 bit identifier (all zeros), $cnt$ is a 32 bit counter (which runs from 0 to 499.999) and $k$ is a 128 bit key randomly chosen for each encryption. Hence the length of one output $o$ is 256 bit. According to [22] we defined three areas: safe, doubtful, and failure, (see **Table 2**) where more results in the safe area indicate that the output is closer to randomness and more results in the failure area indicate that the tested sequence deviates from true randomness.

Analyzing **Table 3** with respect to the areas failure, doubt and safe we get 8, 13 and 26 entries, which is (as expected) quite close to the output of AES encrypted data (see [22]). Note that other test outputs and generators might have different outcomes, but this analysis of outputs of type 1 CFNGs strongly supports our brief theoretical analysis given above: the outputs "look random".

## 6.5. Efficiency

Our system is very effective with respect to communications. The only time we need to interact with a generator is during initialization, where the unique identifier $ID$ is loaded into the generator's memory. After that, especially during the generation of CFNs, there is no need for any communication at all.

Concerning the computation of CFNs, the approach is

**Table 2. Interpretation of DIEHARD $p$-values: safe—doubt—failure.**

| Area | $p$-value $p$ |
|---|---|
| Failure area (f) | $0<p\le0.10$ or $0.90\le p\le1$ |
| Doubt area (d) | $0.10<p\le0.25$ or $0.75\le p<0.90$ |
| Safe area (s) | $0.25<p<0.75$ |

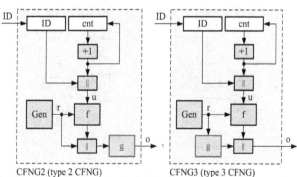

CFNG2 (type 2 CFNG)                    CFNG3 (type 3 CFNG)

**Figure 7.Variants of CFNGs ensuring privacy protection.**

**Table 3. DIEHARD test on type 1 CFNGs.**

| Test Name | p-value | Area | Test-Name | p-value | Area | Test-Name | p-value | Area |
|---|---|---|---|---|---|---|---|---|
| | 0.883838 | d | | 0.31904 | s | | 0.92747 | f |
| | 0.985774 | f | | 0.63408 | s | | 0.60832 | s |
| | 0.707886 | s | | 0.14583 | d | | 0.05893 | f |
| | 0.283701 | s | | 0.74402 | s | | 0.59841 | s |
| Birthday Spacing | 0.727969 | s | Monkey Test | 0.95016 | f | Monkey Test | 0.10172 | d |
| | 0.300982 | s | | 0.45042 | s | | 0.77173 | d |
| | 0.619710 | s | | 0.99874 | f | | 0.25175 | s |
| | 0.261471 | s | | 0.39829 | s | | 0.32827 | s |
| | 0.233554 | s | | 0.69937 | s | | 0.74176 | s |
| | 0.988664 | f | | 0.73568 | s | | 0.32743 | s |
| Overlapping Permutations | 0.256193 | s | Minimum Distance | 0.576871 | s | Overlapping Sums | 0.219271 | d |
| | 0.414570 | s | 3D-Spheres | 0.111133 | d | | 0.200393 | d |
| Binary Rank | 0.338007 | s | Squeeze | 0.215885 | d | Craps | 0.197837 | d |
| | 0.758256 | d | | 0.211515 | d | | 0.001859 | f |
| | 0.552591 | s | Runs | 0.829193 | d | Runs | 0.007574 | f |
| Count the 1s | 0.842024 | d | Parking Lot | 0.728020 | s | | | |

quite efficient, as well. See **Table 4** for a summary of different variants of type 1 CFNGs and **Table 5** for detailed timings of the CFNGs implemented in software on a SmartCafe Expert 2.0 JavaCard (see [23] and [24] for more details on the implementation of CFNGs). In case of Type 2 CFNGs, we used two different approaches to implement function $g$: elliptic curve scalar multiplication (SM) and modular exponentiation (ME).

As far as memory is concerned, each generator needs to locally store its $ID$ and the current value of the counter $cnt$. One may argue that compared to true random numbers or pseudo-random numbers, CFNs are quite long. The following comparison—which clarifies that CFNGs are worth consideration—is based on generating $2^n$ numbers of bit-length $N$ by use of RNGs, CFNGs, and PRNGs:

**RNG:** Remembering the birthday paradox, you will have a fair chance (~50%) to get a duplicate after generating approximately $2^{N/2}$ values (of bit-length $N$). Of course, keeping slightly below $2^{N/2}$ values will significantly reduce the probability of duplicates, but no matter how many outputs you generate, you cannot completely eliminate the risk of duplicates. In the worst case scenario, the second value generated is the first duplicate!

**CFNG:** Now think of CFNGs which generate the same number of CFNs. When employing a block cipher E for $f$, $|\mathrm{E}(ID\|cnt)| = |ID\|cnt| = |ID| + |cnt|$. If $|ID| = |cnt| = N/4$, the length of $r$ results in $|r| = N/2$. With this setup, the

**Table 4. Comparison of software- and hardware-based CFNGs.**

| | SW Implementation | HW implementation |
|---|---|---|
| Symmetric encryption | Quite low | Very low |
| Asymmetric encryption | Acceptable | Very low |

**Table 5. Time for generating a CFN.**

| CFNG | $f$ | $g$ | $|r|$ | $|output|$ | time |
|---|---|---|---|---|---|
| Type 1 | $DES_r(u)$ | - | 56 bit | 160 bit | 1.5 s |
| Type 1 | $Skipjack_r(u)$ | - | 80 bit | 160 bit | 2.0 s |
| Type 2 | $Skipjack_r(u)$ | ME | 80 bit | 160 bit | 3.4 s |
| Type 2 | $DES_r(u)$ | SM | 56 bit | 160 bit | 9.3 s |

$2^{N/4}$ generators in our system can generate $2^{N/4}$ outputs each, without any collisions. Note that if you need more generators and less outputs per generator, simply shift some bits from $cnt$ to $ID$ (i.e., increase the length of $ID$ and decrease the length of $cnt$) and vice versa. As long as $|ID\|cnt| = |ID| + |cnt| = N/2$ you will not get any duplicates when generating $2^{N/2}$ values.

**PRNG**: Obviously, PRNGs which use a common secret key and hierarchically structured counters can generate $2^N$ unique outputs of size $N$ without any duplicates. Nevertheless, since compromising one means compromising all, PRNGs are no option here.

Note that employing cryptographic mechanisms like hash-functions or encryption always slows down the generation process. But, when we want to protect the privacy of the generator's identity, the use of cryptographic primitives is mandatory. Modern smartcard microprocessors (like SmartCafe Expert 5.0 JavaCard from Giesecke and Devrient [25]) and modern CPUs (like Intels Westmere-based and Sandy Bridge processors [26]) provide encryption functions (like AES) implemented in hardware, but most commonly only provide software-based hash-functions.

Practical test on a SmartCafe Expert 5.0 JavaCards from Giesecke and Devrient [25] showed that hardware-based encryption is two to four times faster than hardware based hashing of the same data, and 10 to 15 times faster than hashing by use of software [27]. Hence, compared to the existing solutions like UUIDs or GUIDs which use hash-functions, our approach which uses encryption is quite competitive.

## 7. Fields of Application

Originally, CFNGs have been designed to eliminate the attack scenarios, briefly described in the introduction of this article. Besides that, we discovered that the concept of CFNGs could be quite useful in the field of unique identifiers as well. Additionally, by changing from symmetric to asymmetric algorithms, CFNGs can be used to generate unique pseudonyms, which can directly be used as keys in cryptographic protocols.

### 7.1. Unique Cryptographic Parameters and Keys

Reconsidering the attacks in Section 1.1 we will first describe how CFNGs will fix the problems with randomness in cryptographic protocols. Simply spoken, we will replace *random* parameters by *system-wide unique but random* parameters, generated by the use of application-specific CFNGs.

**Primes**: The security of an RSA scheme (used for encryption or digital signature) is based on the factorization problem, or more precisely, on the problem of factoring the modulus $n$ which is the product of two *random* primes: $n = pq$. If the randomness in the prime generation process is based on CFNGs, there will be no duplicates and no attacks based on common primes. Note that the attacker knows only $n$, so we have implicit privacy protection here. As a consequence we can use a type 1 CFNG with $f$ being a symmetric encryption algorithm. So the primes will be of the following form:

$$p = \text{CFNG1}(\ ) \| pad = \text{E}_k \big( ID \| cnt \big) \| k \| pad,$$

where *pad* is a sequence of random padding bits which ensures the required length (512 bit upwards). Padding the unique header simplifies the prime generation process. In a first step, we set the least significant bit of $p$ to 1, so that $p$ is an odd number. If $p$ is not prime, we can now simply add 2 and check again. This will be repeated until $p$ is prime. As long as this repeated adding 2 does not interfere with the unique header, our resulting prime will be unique.

**ElGamal Randomizers**: When using the ElGamal signature scheme, we need some *random* parameter $r$, called randomizer, to digitally sign a message. As above, this randomizer is protected by an intractable problem, the discrete logarithm problem. So, we can again use a type 1 CFNG to generate our randomizers:

$$r = \text{CFNG1}(\ ) \| pad = \text{E}_k \big( ID \| cnt \big) \| k \| pad,$$

where the padding bit sequence *pad* can be omitted, if $\text{E}_k \big( ID \| cnt \big) \| k$ is of sufficient length.

**Nonces**: *Random* numbers used once (nonces) are essential for the security of zero knowledge protocols (ZKP). So again, we employ a CFNG to generate the nonces $s$. Unfortunately, many ZKPs include messages that contain the nonce in unprotected form, or messages of a protocol round can be used to extract the nonce. Hence, to provide explicit privacy protection, we have to use a type 2 or type 3 CFNG:

$$s = \text{CFNG2}(\ ) = g\big(\text{CFNG1}(\ )\big) = g\big(f(u,r)\|r\big)$$
$$\text{or } s = \text{CFNG3}(\ ) = f(u,r)\|g(r).$$

### 7.2. Unique Identifiers and Pseudonyms

In specific scenarios, we do not care about the privacy protection of the generators identity. In this case, simply employ a type 1 CFNG based on symmetric encryption and where necessary, (randomly) pad the output to the appropriate length.

However, in the majority of cases, digital identifiers and digital pseudonyms (of the same generator) should be unlinkable to each other. This means that we have to provide privacy protection for the identifier, embedded in the CFNGs. So we can either use a type 1 CFNG with a one-way function $f$ or a type 2 or type 3 CFNG.

To explain the operating principle, we will first discuss an RSA-based type 1 generator of the form:

$$o = \text{CFNG1}(\ ) = \text{RSA}_{(e,n)}\big(ID\|cnt\big)\|e\|n$$

where $e$ is the public exponent of the RSA system and $n$ is the modulus. Although being quite long ($|n| \geq 1024$ bit), these identifiers contain a public key $(e,n)$ which can be used to

1) Authenticate the holder of the identifier by verifying his digital signature or to

2) Send encrypted messages to the holder of the identifier, provided that the holder has stored the according private key.

**Figure 8** shows the usage of digital pseudonyms in the context of an authentication scheme based on digital signatures. The prover employs an RSA-based type 1 CFNG to generate his unique digital pseudonym $o = \mathrm{RSA}_{(e,n)}\big(ID\|cnt\big)\|e\|n$. After the generation, $P$ sends $o$ to the verifier. The verifier extracts the public key $(e, n)$ and sends a challenge $r$ to the prover. The prover signs the challenge and sends the signature $s$ to the verifier, who finally verifies the signature with the public key of the prover.

In order to keep the identifiers as short as possible, but also protect the identity of the generator, we suggest to use CFNGs of type 2 or type 3 based on elliptic curve cryptography (ECC), elliptic curve scalar multiplication (SM) and point compression (PC). Generators with the shortest outputs, but still secure and privacy protecting are of the form:

$$o = \mathrm{CFNG2}(\ ) = \mathrm{PC}\Big(\mathrm{SM}\big(\big(\mathrm{DES}(u,r)\|r\big), P\big)\Big)$$

where $P$ is a so-called generator point of the elliptic curve (see [8] for details on ECC). By using this type of generator we can achieve outputs with a length form 128 bit upwards. Scenarios which only need short-term security may use 128 bit outputs, but the long-term security requires 160 bit or more. Since the output of the elliptic curve scalar multiplication (SM) is an ECC public key,

the key $(e,d)$ with public key $e = \mathrm{SM}\big(\mathrm{DES}(u,r)\|r\big), P\big)$ and private ECC key $d = \mathrm{DES}(u,r)\|r$, can be used as sketched above. For a detailed discussion of ECC-based pseudonyms we refer the reader to [28].

Finally, when replacing DES by Skipjack (SJ) with CBC mode and ciphertext stealing, these ECC-based type 2 CFNGs (see **Figure 9** and [29]) are a secure and efficient replacement for UUIDs which fulfills all requirements on UUIDs (*universally unique* identifiers). In particular, the generated identifiers, which are based on 48 bit user identifiers (UI), are system-wide (or in UUID's language universally) unique, whereas UUIDs are not!

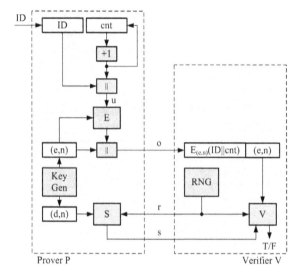

**Figure 8. Usage of digital pseudonyms.**

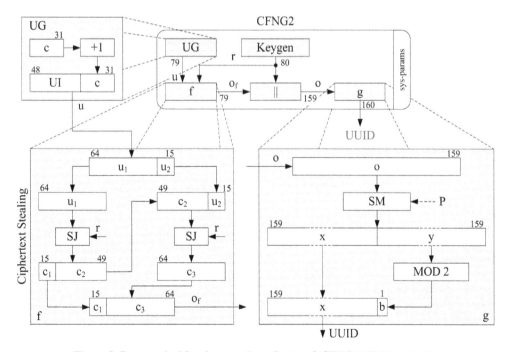

**Figure 9. Prototypical Implementation of a type 2 CFNG (160 bit output).**

## 8. Conclusion

Security critical parameters and identifiers, chosen purely random, come with the intrinsic risk of duplicates. These duplicates may cause severe problems in cryptographic schemes, cryptographic protocols and applications. In this article, we proposed an efficient mechanism which could replace true random number generators in the mentioned fields of application. In contrast to true random number generators, the so called collision-free number generators (CFNGs) provably do not generate any duplicates during their life-time. Nevertheless, the proposed generators are secure (compromising one or more generators does not compromise the whole system), efficient (in terms of computation, communications and memory) and they additionally protect the generator's identity (*i.e.*, outputs are unlinkable to each other and the generator's identity).

## REFERENCES

[1]   P. Schartner, "Security Tokens—Basics, Applications, Management, and Infrastructures," IT-Verlag, Sauerlach, 2001.

[2]   M. Schaffer, P. Schartner and S. Rass, "Universally Unique Identifiers: How to Ensure Uniqueness While Protecting the Issuer's Privacy," *Proceedings of Security and Management* 2007, CSREA Press, Las Vegas, 2007, pp. 198-204.

[3]   R. L. Rivest, A. Shamir and L. Adleman, "A Method for Obtaining Digital Signatures and Public-Key Cryptosystems," *Communications of the ACM*, Vol. 21, No. 2, 1978, pp. 120-126.

[4]   T. ElGamal, "A Public Key Cryptosystem and a Signature Scheme Based on Discrete Logarithms," *IEEE Transactions of Information Theory*, Vol. IT-31, No. 4, 1985, pp. 469-472.

[5]   S. Goldwasser, S. Micali and C. Rackoff, "The Knowledge Complexity of Interactive Proof Systems," *SIAM Journal on Computing*, Vol. 18, No. 1, 1989, pp. 186-208.

[6]   G. Marsaglia, "The DIEHARD Test Suite 2003," 2003.

[7]   A. J. Menezes, S. A. Vanstone and P. C. Van Oorschot, "Handbook of Applied Cryptography," CRC Press, London, 1996.

[8]   D. Hankerson, A. J. Menezes and S. A. Vanstone, "Guide to Elliptic Curve Cryptography," Springer-Verlag, Berlin, 2004.

[9]   National Institute of Standards and Technology—NIST, "FIPS Publication 46-3: Data Encryption Standard (DES)," NIST, Gaithersburg, 1999.

[10]  NIST, "FIPS Special Publication 800-38A: Recommendation for Block Cipher Modes of Operation—Methods and Techniques," NIST, Gaithersburg, 2001.

[11]  ISO/IEC, "ISO/IEC 10116: Modes of Operation of an n-bit Block Cipher," 1991. http://www.iso.org

12]  NIST, "SKIPJACK and KEA Algorithm Specifications," NIST, Gaithersburg, ver. 2.29, 1998.

[13]  NIST, "FIPS Publication 197: Advanced Encryption Standard (AES)," NIST, Gaithersburg, 2001.

[14]  NIST, "FIPS Publication 180-1: Secure Hash Standard (SHA)," NIST, Gaithersburg, 1995.

[15]  H. Dobbertin, A. Bosselaers and B. Preneel, "RIPEMD-160: A Strengthened Version of RIPEMD," *Proceedings of Fast Software Encryption* (*FSE*), *LNCS*, Springer, Berlin, Vol. 1039, 1996, pp. 71-82.

[16]  NIST, "FIPS Publication 180-2: Secure Hash Standard," NIST, Gaithersburg, 2002.

[17]  IPCOM, "Method of Generating Unique Quasi-Random Numbers as a Function of Time and Space," PriorArtDatbase, IPCOM#000007118D, 2002.

[18]  P. Leach, M. Mealling and R. Salz, "RFC 4122: A Universally Unique IDentifier (UUID) URN Name-Space," 2005. http://www.ietf.org/rfc/rfc4122.txt

[19]  Microsoft Developer Network, "Globally Unique Identifiers (GUIDs)," 2008. http://msdn.microsoft.com/en-us/librarycc246025.aspx

[20]  Republik Österreich, "Bundesgesetz über Regelungen zur Erleichterung des Elektronischen Verkehrs mit Öffentlichen Stellen (E-Government-Gesetz—E-GovG)," BGBl. I 10/2004, 2010. http://www.ris.bka.gv.at

[21]  C. E. Shannon, "Communication Theory of Secrecy Systems," *Bell System Technical Journal*, Vol. 28, No. 4, 1949, pp. 656-715.

[22]  M. Alani, "Testing Randomness in Ciphertext of Block-Ciphers using DIEHARD," *International Journal of Computer Science and Network Security—IJCSNS*, Vol. 10, No. 4, 2010, pp. 53-57.

[23]  M. Schaffer, P. Schartner and S. Rass, "Efficient Generation of Unique Numbers for Secure Applications," *Technical Report TR-Syssec-07-01*, Klagenfurt University, System Security Group, Klagenfurt, 2007.

[24]  P. Schartner and M. Schaffer, "Implementing Collision-Free Number Generators on JavaCards," *Technical Report TR-Syssec-07-03*, Klagenfurt University, System Security Group Klagenfurt, 2007.

[25]  Giesecke and Devrient, "Sm@rtCafe JavaCards," 2011. http://www.gi-de.com.

[26]  Intel, "Intel Processors Supporting AES-NI," 2011. http://www.intel.com.

[27]  P. Schartner, "A Low-Cost Alternative for OAEP," *Proceedings of International Workshop on Security and Dependability for Resource Constrained Embedded Systems SD4RCES*, *ICPS Series*, ACM Digital Library, in Print, 2011.

[28]  P. Schartner and M. Schaffer, "Efficient Privacy-Enhancing Techniques for Medical Databases, *BIOSTEC*, *Communications in Computer and Information Science*, Springer, Berlin, Vol. 25, 2008, pp. 467-478.

[29]  P. Schartner, "Unique Domain-Specific Citizen Identification for E-Government Applications," *Proceedings of the 6th International Conference on Digital Society—ICDS 2012*, Valencia, 30 January-4 February 2011.

# 11

# Towards a Comprehensive Security Framework of Cloud Data Storage Based on Multi-Agent System Architecture

**Amir Mohamed Talib, Rodziah Atan, Rusli Abdullah, Masrah Azrifah Azmi Murad**

Faculty of Computer Science & IT, University Putra Malaysia UPM, Serdang, Malaysia

## ABSTRACT

The tremendous growth of the cloud computing environments requires new architecture for security services. Cloud computing is the utilization of many servers/data centers or Cloud Data Storages (CDSs) housed in many different locations and interconnected by high speed networks. CDS, like any other emerging technology, is experiencing growing pains. It is immature, it is fragmented and it lacks standardization. Although security issues are delaying its fast adoption, cloud computing is an unstoppable force and we need to provide security mechanisms to ensure its secure adoption. In this paper a comprehensive security framework based on Multi-Agent System (MAS) architecture for CDS to facilitate confidentiality, correctness assurance, availability and integrity of users' data in the cloud is proposed. Our security framework consists of two main layers as agent layer and CDS layer. Our propose MAS architecture includes main five types of agents: Cloud Service Provider Agent (CSPA), Cloud Data Confidentiality Agent (CDConA), Cloud Data Correctness Agent (CDCorA), Cloud Data Availability Agent (CDAA) and Cloud Data Integrity Agent (CDIA). In order to verify our proposed security framework based on MAS architecture, pilot study is conducted using a questionnaire survey. Rasch Methodology is used to analyze the pilot data. Item reliability is found to be poor and a few respondents and items are identified as misfits with distorted measurements. As a result, some problematic questions are revised and some predictably easy questions are excluded from the questionnaire. A prototype of the system is implemented using Java. To simulate the agents, oracle database packages and triggers are used to implement agent functions and oracle jobs are utilized to create agents.

**Keywords:** Cloud Computing; Multi-Agent System; Cloud Data Storage; Security Framework; Cloud Service Provider

## 1. Introduction

Computer in its evolution form has been changed multiple times, as learned from its past events. However, the trend turned from bigger and more expensive, to smaller and more affordable commodity PCs and servers which are tired together to construct something called "cloud computing system". Moreover, cloud has advantages in offering more scalable, fault-tolerant services with even higher performance [1]. Cloud computing can provide infinite computing resources on demand due to its high scalability in nature, which eliminates the needs for cloud service providers to plan far ahead on hardware provisioning [2].

Cloud computing integrates and provides different types of services such as Data-as-a-Service (DaaS), which allows cloud users to store their data at remote disks and access them anytime from any place.

However, Determining data security is harder today, so data security functions have become more critical than they have been in the past [3]. However, there still exist many problems in cloud computing today, a recent re-search shows that cloud data storage security have become the primary concern for people to shift to cloud computing because the data is stored as well as processing somewhere on to centralized location called "data centers" or CDS. So, the clients have to trust the provider on the availability as well as data security. Even more concerning, though, is the corporations that are jumping to cloud computing while being oblivious to the implications of putting critical applications and data in the cloud. Moving critical applications and sensitive data to a public and shared cloud environment is a major concern for corporations that are moving beyond their data center's network perimeter defense. The problem of verifying correctness, confidentiality, integrity and availability for CDS security becomes even more challenging [4]. CDS systems are expected to meet several rigorous requirements for maintaining users' data and information, including high availability, reliability, performance, replication and data consistency; but because of the conflicting nature of these requirements, no one system implements all of them together. For example, availability, scalability and data consistency can be regarded as three conflicting goals. Security framework is proposed to facilitate the correctness, confidentiality, availability, and integrity of user' data cloud security. Data security on the cloud side is not only focused on the process of data transmission, but also the system security and data protection for those data stored on the storages of the cloud side. From the perspective of data security, which has always been an important aspect of quality of service, cloud computing inevitably poses new challenging security threats for a number of reasons:

> Firstly, cloud computing is not just a third party data warehouse. The data stored in the cloud may be frequently updated by the users, including insertion, deletion, modification, appending, reordering, etc. To facilitate storage correctness under dynamic data update is hence of paramount importance. However, this dynamic feature also makes traditional integrity insurance techniques futile and entails new solutions [4,5].

> Secondly, the deployment of cloud computing is powered by data centers running in a simultaneous, cooperated and distributed manner. Individual user's data is redundantly stored in multiple physical locations to further reduce the data integrity threats [4]. Therefore, distributed protocols for storage correctness assurance will be of most importance in achieving a robust and secure cloud data storage system in the real world [5].

> Thirdly, CDS systems offer services to assure integrity of data transmission (typically through checksum backup). However, they do not provide a solution to the CDS integrity problem. Thus, the cloud client would have to develop its own solution, such as a backup of the cloud data items, in order to verify that cloud data returned by the CDS server has not been tampered with.

> Finally, there is lack of fine-grained cloud data access control mechanism to security-sensitive cloud resources [6].

To alleviate these concerns, a cloud solution provider must ensure that cloud users can continue to have the same security over their applications and services by providing evidence to these cloud users that their organization and cloud users are secure.

In order to achieve these problems we proposed a comprehensive security framework based on MAS architecture, our security framework has been built using two layers: agent layer and cloud data storage layer. The MAS architecture has five agents: Cloud Service Provider Agent (CSPA), Cloud Data Correctness Agent (CDCorA), Cloud Data Confidentiality Agent (CDConA), Cloud Data Availability Agent (CDAA) and Cloud Data Integrity Agent (CDIA).

The term "agent" is very broad and has different mean-

ings to different researchers [7-9]. Genesereth et al. [7], has gone so far as to say that software agents are application programs that communicate with each other in an expressive agent communication language.

A multi-agent system (MAS) consists of a number of agents interacting with each other, usually through exchanging messages across a network. The agents in such a system must be able to interact in order to achieve their design objectives, through cooperating, negotiating and coordinating with other agents. The agents may exhibit selfish or benevolent behavior. Selfish agents ask for help from other agents if they are overloaded and never offer help. For example, agents serving VIP (Very Important Person) cloud users for CSP service never help other agents for the same service. Benevolent agents always provide help to other agents because they consider system benefit is the priority. For example, agents serving normal cloud users for CSP service are always ready to help other agents to complete their tasks [6].

## 1.1. Security Goals in Cloud Computing

Traditionally, cloud computing has six goals namely confidentiality, correctness assurance, availability, data integrity, control and audit. These six goals need to be fulfilling in order to achieve an adequate security. This paper focuses in the first four security goals:

### 1.1.1. Confidentiality

In cloud computing, confidentiality plays a major part especially in maintaining control over organizations' data situated across multiple distributed cloud servers. Confidentiality must be well achieved when employing a public cloud due to public clouds accessibility nature. Asserting confidentiality of users' profiles and protecting their data that is virtually accessible, allows for cloud data security protocols to be enforced at various different layers of cloud applications [10].

Data access control issue is mainly related to security policies provided to the users while accessing the data. In a typical scenario, a small business organization can use a cloud provided by some other provider for carrying out its business processes. This organization will have its own security policies based on which each user can have access to a particular set of data. The security policies may entitle some considerations wherein some of the employees are not given access to certain amount of data. These security policies must be adhered by the cloud to avoid intrusion of data by unauthorized users [11].

### 1.1.2. Correctness Assurance

Goal of correctness assurance in cloud computing is to ensure cloud users that their cloud data are indeed stored appropriately and kept intact all the time in the cloud to improve and maintain the same level of storage correctness assurance even if cloud users modify, delete or append their cloud data files in the cloud [4].

### 1.1.3. Availability

Availability is one of the most critical information security requirements in cloud computing because it is a key decision factor when deciding among private, public or hybrid cloud vendors as well as in the delivery models [10]. The SLA is the most important document which highlights the trepidation of availability in cloud services and resources between the CSP and client. Therefore, by exploring the information security requirements at each of the various cloud deployment and delivery models, vendors and organizations will have confidence in promoting a secured cloud framework.

### 1.1.4. Data Integrity

Integrity of the cloud data has to deal with how secure and reliable the cloud computing data. This could mean that even if cloud providers have provided secure backups, addressed security concerns, and increased the likelihood that data will be there when you need it. In a cloud environment, a certification authority is required to certify entities involved in interactions; these include certifying physical infrastructure server, virtual server, environment, user and the network devices [12].

## 2. Literature Review

Some argue that cloud user data is more secure when managed internally, while others argue that cloud providers have a strong incentive to maintain trust and as such employ a higher level of security. However, in the cloud, your data will be distributed over these individual computers regardless of where your base repository of data is ultimately stored. Industrious hackers can invade virtually any server. There are the statistics that show that one-third of breaches result from stolen or lost laptops and other devices. Besides, there also some cases which from employees' accidentally exposing data on the Internet, with nearly 16 percent due to insider theft [13].

Wang et al. [4], stated that data security is a problem in cloud data storage, which is essentially a distributed storage system. And explained their proposed scheme to ensure the correctness of user's data in cloud data storage, an effective and flexible distributed scheme with explicit dynamic data support, including block update, delete, and append relying on erasure correcting code in the file distribution preparation to provide redundancy parity vectors and guarantee the data dependability. Their scheme could achieve the integration of storage correctness insurance and data error localization, i.e., whenever data corruption has been detected during the storage correctness verification across the distributed servers, Could almost guarantee the simultaneous identification of the misbehaving server(s) through detailed security and performance analysis.

Takabi et al. [14], proposed a comprehensive security framework for cloud computing environments. They presented the security framework and discuss existing solutions, some approaches to deal with security challenges. The framework consists of different modules to handle security, and trust issues of key components of cloud computing environments. These modules deal with issues such as identity management, access control, policy integration among multiple clouds, trust management between different clouds and between a cloud and its users, secure service composition and integration, and semantic heterogeneity among policies from different clouds.

Yu et al. [15], formulated architecture of cloud that consists of two separated spaces that are the User Space and Kernal Space. These spaces connected through the network interface and provide different levels of interaction with in the cloud. The cloud's Kernal Space is used to regulate a physical allocation and access control. The cloud's User Space contains processes that are directly used by the cloud users.

Du et al. [16], presented the design and implementation of RunTest, a new service integrity attestation system for verifying the integrity of dataflow processing in multitenant cloud infrastructures. RunTest employs application-level randomized data attestation for pinpointing malicious dataflow processing service providers in large-scale cloud infrastructures. They proposed a new integrity attestation graph model to capture aggregated data processing integrity attestation results. By analyzing the integrity attestation graph.

Venkatesan and Vaish [17], proposed an efficient multi-agent based static and dynamic data integrity protection by periodically verifying the hash value of the files stored in the enormous date storage. Their proposed data integrity model is based on the multi-agent system (MAS). The reason for embedding the agent concept is known, that is the agent is having capability of autonomous, persistence, social ability and etc. The proposed MAS architecture has multiple agents to monitor and maintain the data integrity also the architecture includes three entities (respectively customer, service provider and the data owner).

Looking at the wider technological perspective of MAS and security in CDS environment has been studied by Talib et al. [5] proposed a security framework based on MAS architecture to facilitate security of CDS. Although the illustrative MAS architecture is not given, the above should describe the security framework for CDS. However, this model does not consider the technological perspective of CDS. Therefore, the main motivation for this study is to formulate a more detailed security framework based on MAS architecture for collaborative CDS environment. The long-term goal of this study is to formulate a tool to support MAS tasks within collaborative CDS environment. As such, the security framework shall place more emphasize on the technological perspective.

## 3. Methodology

Currently, there is a lack of formal a security framework for collaborative CDS environment [4,5], and there are no hard and fast rules on how to formulate a security framework. The investigation of the problems and then analyzed the formulation of the proposed framework is taking into account the problems identified from the survey result. This is very important to make sure the proposed framework is met the objective and the limitation. So in which there three steps are taken in the methodology, first conducted a survey and analyzed it, second analyzed the security framework and lastly the process of the formulation of the security framework.

A survey was conducted in selected 15 respondents (2 respondents from Information Security Department from MIMOS Berhad, 7 respondents from Information Security Group (ISG) from Faculty of Computer Science and Information Technology (FSKTM), UPM, 3 security experts and 3 programmers from different companies) participated in this research (pilot study). Thirty three questionnaires were distributed to the respondents, and fifteen questionnaires were returned. The questionnaire data were verified and was analyzed using Rasch Model. The result of the survey contributed to the formulation of the proposed security framework.

However, use of Rasch to analyze and validate questionnaires for theoretical constructs in other technical fields is still lacking. Whilst the usage of Rasch often deals with competency evaluation on people or objects, the usage could also be extended to evaluate another critical element of research—the research instrument construct validity [18]. The pilot data were tabulated and analyzed using WinSteps, a Rasch tool.

The main components derived from the questionnaire are: information security concept and understanding, cloud computing concept and understanding, software agent concept and understanding, cloud computing security and CDS based on MAS.

A new security framework shall be synthesized as follows:

- Structured cloud data, which includes in CDS. There are many potential scenarios where data stored in the cloud is dynamic, like electronic documents, photos, or log files etc.
- The collaborative CDS environment elements are derived.
- Cloud users and CSPs are considered the main part of

this framework, in which they have to make a SLA between them in term of facilitating the services by the CSP and renting these services to the cloud users.
- Agents will act as a tool to facilitate the security policies.

The proposed security framework based on MAS architecture is formulated especially to facilitate the confidentiality, correctness assurance, availability and integrity of CDS and consists of four main components: layers, cloud users, CSPs and data flow. The layers consist of the collaboration tools of agents and CDS.

## 4. Security Framework

**Figure 1** shows a schematic representation of security framework. The framework has been built by using two layers.

The functionality of those layers can be summarized as follows [4,19]:
- ➤ **Agent layer:** This layer has one agent: the User Interface Agent. User Interface Agent acts as an effective bridge between the user and the rest of the agents.
- ➤ **Cloud data storage layer:** Cloud data storage has two different network entities can be identified as follows:
- ✓ **Cloud user:** Cloud users, who have data to be stored in the cloud and rely on the cloud for data computation, consist of both individual consumers and organizations.
- ✓ **Cloud service provider (CSP):** A CSP, who has significant resources and expertise in building and managing distributed cloud storage servers, owns and operates live cloud computing systems.

## 5. MAS Architecture

In MAS architecture, we proposed five types of agents: Cloud Service Provider Agent (CSPA), Cloud Data Confidentiality Agent (CDConA), Cloud Data Correctness Agent (CDCorA), Cloud Data Availability Agent (CDAA) and Cloud Data Integrity Agent (CDIA) as illustrated in **Figure 2**.

The rest of agents are described as follows:

### 5.1. Cloud Service Provider Agent (CSPA)

Is the users' intelligent interface to the system and allow the cloud users to interact with the security service environment. The CSPA provides graphical interfaces to the cloud user for interactions between the system and the cloud user. CSPA act in the system under the behavior of CSP. CSPA has the following actions [6,19]:
- Provide the security service task according to the authorized service level agreements (SLAs) and the original message content sent by the CDCorA, CDConA,

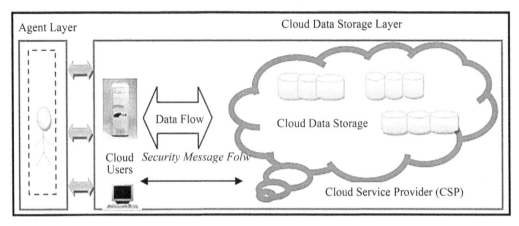

**Figure 1. Proposed security framework.**

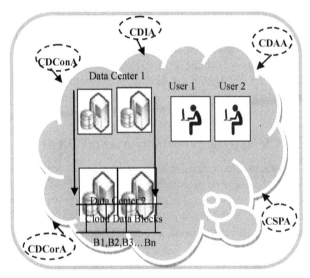

**Figure 2. Proposed MAS architecture.**

CDAA and CDIA.

- Display the security policies specified by CSP and the rest of the agents.
- Designing user interfaces that prevent the input of invalid cloud data.
- Receive the security reports and/or alarms from the rest of other agents to respect.
- Translate the attack in terms of goals.
- Monitor specific activities concerning a part of the CDS or a particular cloud user.
- Creating security reports/alarm systems.

## 5.2. Cloud Data Confidentiality Agent (CDConA)

This agent facilitates the security policy of confidentiality for CDS. Main responsibility of this agent is to provide a CDS by new access control rather than the existing access control lists of identification, authorization and authentication. This agent provides a CSP to define and enforce expressive and flexible access structure for each cloud user [6]. Specifically, the access structure of each cloud user is defined as a logic formula over cloud data file attributes, and is able to represent any desired cloud data file set. This new access control is called as:

- Formula-based cloud data access control (FCDAC).

This agent is also notifies CSPA in case of any fail caused of the techniques above by sending security reports and/or alarms.

Formula-Based Cloud Data Access Control (FCDAC) and also named as a SecureFormula it's an access policy determined by our MAS architecture, not by the CSPs. It's also define as access is granted not based on the rights of the subject associated with a cloud user after authentication, but based on attributes of the cloud user. In our system, CDConA provide access structure of each cloud user by defining it as a logic formula over cloud data file attribute. SecureFormula is an additional confidentiality layer used by our system to verify that the cloud users' login page is a genuine.

If you are a cloud user, you are required to register first to the system and write your valid email and enter your SecureFormula during your first login. Your SecureFormula will be sent to your email. Be ensured that, your SecureFormula is not your password. Do not set your SecureFormula to be the same as your password!

Sign in from your computer [6]:
1) Enter your Cloud User ID;
2) Verify that your SecureFormula image is correct;
3) Confirm by entering your password.

Our confidentiality layer guaranteed that, even if your password is correct and your SecureFormula is incorrect, then you will not be able to login.

The architecture of CDConA consists of five modules, as shown in **Figure 3**. Cloud Communication Module provides the agent with the capability to exchange information with other agents, including the CDConA, CDCorA, CDAA, CDIA and CSPA. Cloud Register Module facilitates the registration function for CDConA. Cloud Request Management Module allows the agent to

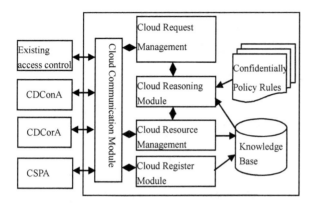

**Figure 3. CDConA architecture.**

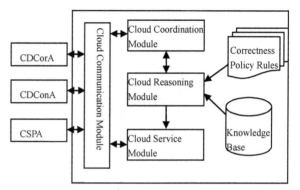

**Figure 4. CDCorA architecture.**

act as the request-dispatching center. Cloud Resource Management Module manages the usage of the cloud resources. Cloud Reasoning Module is the brain of the CDConA. When the request management module and resource management module receive requests, they pass those requests to reasoning module by utilizing the information obtained from the knowledge base and the confidentiality policy rule.

### 5.3. Cloud Data Correctness Agent (CDCorA)

This agent facilitates the security policy of correctness assurance for CDS. Main responsibility of this agent is to perform various block-level operations and generate a correctness assurance when the cloud user performs update operation, delete operation, append to modify operation or insert operation. This agent notifies CSPA in case of any fail caused of the techniques above by sending security reports and/or alarms.

The architecture of the CDCorA consists of four modules, as shown in **Figure 4**. Cloud Communication Module provides the agent with the capability to exchange information with CSPA. Cloud Coordination Module provides the agent with the following mechanisms. If the data is updated then the data encryption is performed. If the data is deleted then the data encryption is performed. If the data is Append then the data encryption is performed. If the data is inserted then the data encryption is performed. Cloud Reasoning Module calculates the necessary amount of cloud resources to complete the service based on the required service level agreements (SLA) by utilizing the information obtained from the knowledge base and the correctness assurance policy rule. Cloud Services Module performs the block-level operations of encryption and decryption when the cloud user update, delete, append and insert his/her data.

In CDS, there are many potential scenarios where data stored in the cloud is dynamic, like electronic documents, photos, or log files etc. Therefore, it is crucial to consider the dynamic case, where a cloud user may wish to perform various block-level operations of update, delete and

append to modify the data. Our proposed correctness assurance protocol is not going to be genuine if there is absent of SecureFormula. So in case of: Update operation: The cloud user needs to enter his/her SecureFormula plus 00, Delete operation: The cloud user needs to enter his/her SecureFormula plus 01, Append operation: The cloud user needs to enter his/her SecureFormula plus 10 and Modify operation: The cloud user needs to enter his/her SecureFormula plus 11.

### 5.4. Cloud Data Availability Agent (CDAA)

This agent facilitates the security policy of availability for CDS. Main responsibility of this agent is to receive and display the security issues that offer by its sub-agents of CDDPA and CDRA. CDAA facilitate two new techniques of file distribution preparation and file retrieval. This agent is also notifies CSPA in case of any fail caused of the techniques above by sending security reports and/or alarms.

Cloud data availability is to ensure that the cloud data processing resources are not made unavailable by malicious action. Our MAS architecture is able to tolerate multiple failures in cloud distributed storage systems.

To ensure the availability, we explain the notions of global and local cloud attack blueprints. To detect intrusions, the CDAA receives a set of goals representing the global cloud attack blueprints. To recognize this global cloud attack blueprint, it must be decomposed in local cloud sub-blueprints used locally by the different agents distributed in the CDS. In general agents can detect only local cloud attacks because they have a restricted view of the CDS. So, we make a distinction between a global cloud attack blueprint and local cloud sub-blueprints. A global cloud blueprint is an attack blueprint, derived from the security policies specified at a high level by the CSPs, that the MAS must detect and the detection of this blueprint will be notified only to CDAA. A local cloud blueprint is a blueprint derived from the global cloud blueprint but that must be detected by local agents. For a CDAA over-viewing the global cloud attack blueprint the probability of an attack is equal to 1, while for the local agent it is below 1.

The architecture of the CDAA consists of three modules, as shown in **Figure 5**. Cloud Communication Module provides the agent with the capability to exchange information with CDAA and CSPA. Cloud Servers Modules provides the agent with the following mechanisms: 1) Disperse the data file redundantly across a set of distributed servers; and 2) Enable the cloud user to reconstruct the original data by downloading the data vectors from the servers. Cloud Reasoning Module provides the CDAA with the specific misbehaving server(s) and server colluding attacks by utilizing the information obtained from the knowledge base and the availability policy rule.

## 5.5. Cloud Data Integrity Agent (CDIA)

This agent facilitates the security policy of integrity for CDS. It is used to enable the cloud user to reconstruct the original cloud data by downloading the cloud data vectors from the cloud servers. Main responsibility of this agent is backing up the cloud data regularly from "Cloud Zone" and sending security reports and/or alarms to CPSA when [20]:

✓ Human errors when cloud data is entered.
✓ Errors that occur when cloud data is transmitted from one computer to another.
✓ Software bugs or viruses.
✓ Hardware malfunctions, such as disk crashes.

Our proposed integrity layer named as "CloudZone". In CloudZone, we introduce the first provably-secure and practical backup cloud data regularly that provide reconstruct the original cloud data by downloading the cloud data vectors from the cloud servers.

### "CloudZone" Requirements

➤ "CloudZone" only backs up the MS SQL databases. It does not back up other MS SQL files such as program installation files, etc.
➤ "CloudZone" does not support component-based backup.
➤ "CloudZone" does not use Visual SourceSafe (VSS) for backup and restore.
➤ "CloudZone" supports backup and recovery of Windows Oracle 10 g.

### With "CloudZone" Cloud Backup, you can select any of the following as backup objects:

➤ Oracle Server 10 g running on Windows.
➤ Microsoft SQL Server 2000, 2005 and 2008.
➤ Microsoft Exchange Server 2003 and 2007.

The architecture of the CDIA consists of three modules, as shown in **Figure 6**. Cloud Communication Module provides the agent with the capability to exchange information with CDIA, CDConA, CDCorA, CDAA and CSPA. Cloud Resources Management Modules provides

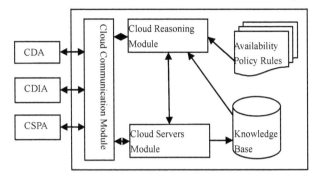

**Figure 5. CDAA architecture.**

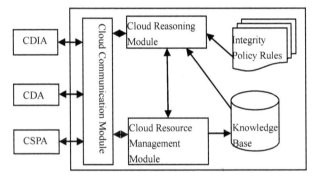

**Figure 6. CDIA architecture.**

the agent with the following mechanisms. If the CDIA registered as CDIA-VIP then back-up of the data is performed successfully. If the CDIA did not register as CDIA-VIP, it asks the cloud user to back-up the data manually. Cloud Reasoning Module shows the reasons of in case the result of the back-up the data is failed by utilizing the information obtained from the knowledge base and the integrity policy rule [20].

## 6. Implementation

Ganawa Security as a Service (GSecaaS) has been implemented (~30.000 lines of JAVA code) with Oracle 11 g. The implementation was based on structure-in-5 MAS architectures described above. We briefly describe the GSecaaS implementation to illustrate the role of the agents and their interaction. To simulate the agents, Oracle database packages and triggers are used to implement agent functions and Oracle jobs are utilized to create agents. Each agent is considered as an instance of the agent in the environment that can work independently, and can communicate with other agents in order to fulfill its needs or fulfill the others requests. To demonstrate the feasibility of the proposed system, a prototype is implemented using Java and PHP.

At the interface layer, the interaction of the system with the cloud user is based on a set of dialogues. These dialogues are implemented using Java and PHP. An example of an interface is shown in **Figure 7**.

# 7. Pilot Study

## 7.1. Result

The pilot data were tabulated and analyzed using Win-Steps, a Rasch tool. The results of Person and Item summary statistics and measures are tabulated in **Tables 1** and **2**.

The results of the survey are analyzed in three parts; data reliability, fitness of respondent and items data and determination of component groups cut-off points.

### 7.1.1. Data Reliability

Summary statistics for respondents (persons) and items (questions) are depicted in **Tables 1** and **2**, respectively. 15 respondents returned the survey questionnaire. Out of which, Rasch identified an extreme score which will later be excluded from further analysis.

From the summary of measured persons (**Table 1**), the

**Figure 7. An example of interaction window with a cloud user (confidentiality layer).**

spread of person responses is = 3.29 logit is fair. This is due to extreme responses by a participant. However, Reliability = 0.82 and Cronbach Alpha = 0.94 indicates high reliable data and hence the data could be used for further analyses.

On the questionnaire items, the summary of 15 measured questionnaire items (**Table 2**) reveals that the spread of data at 2.36 logit and reliability of 0.74 are good and fair, respectively.

Details on each measured items are listed in **Table 3**. The acceptable limits are 0.4 < Acceptable Point Measure Correlation < 0.8 and 0.5 < Outfit Mean Square < 1.5, and –2.0 < Outfit z-standardized value < 2.0). The previous pilot study is therefore proven helpful in making the questionnaire more reliable.

### 7.1.2. Fitness of Respondent Data and Questionnaire Items Data

A Person-Item Differential Map (PIDM) is used to reveal the "easiest" and "hardest" questions answered by respondents. Based on the summaries and PIDM, a few observations could be concluded. Person SU1 is at the leftmost of the person distribution. Rasch provides the Person Item Distribution Map (PIDM), which is similar to histogram (**Figure 8**). PIDM allows both person and items to be mapped side-by side on the same logit scale to give us a better perspective on the relationship of person responses to the items. PIDM indicates a higher Person Mean (0.64) compared to the constrained Item Mean. This indicates tendency to rate higher importance to the prescribed questionnaire items.

**Table 1. Summary of measured persons.**

|  | Raw score | Count | Measure | Model error | Infit | | Outfit | |
|---|---|---|---|---|---|---|---|---|
|  |  |  |  |  | MNSQ | ZSTD | MNSQ | ZSTD |
| MEAN | 133.8 | 42.8 | 0.49 | 0.27 | 1.02 | –0.2 | 1.01 | –0.2 |
| S.D. | 14.9 | 3.5 | 0.69 | 0.02 | 0.52 | 2.1 | 0.53 | 2 |
| MAX. | 167 | 45 | 2.64 | 0.34 | 3.14 | 6.4 | 3.37 | 6.7 |
| MIN. | 86 | 30 | –0.65 | 0.25 | 0.28 | –4.5 | 0.28 | –4.4 |

Real RMSE 0.30 Adj. S.D. 0.62 Separation 2.10 Person reliability 0.82 Model RMSE 0.27 Adj. S.D. 0.64 Separation 2.35 Person reliability 0.85 S.E. of person mean = 0.11 Maximum extreme score: 1 Person valid responses: 95.0%.

**Table 2. Summary of measured items.**

|  | Raw score | Count | Measure | Model error | Infit | | Outfit | |
|---|---|---|---|---|---|---|---|---|
|  |  |  |  |  | MNSQ | ZSTD | MNSQ | ZSTD |
| MEAN | 119.8 | 38.3 | 0.02 | 0.3 | 1 | 0 | 1 | 0.1 |
| S.D. | 16.7 | 3.2 | 0.64 | 0.08 | 0.12 | 0.6 | 0.15 | 0.7 |
| MAX. | 150 | 40 | 1.16 | 0.6 | 1.29 | 1.5 | 1.4 | 1.9 |
| MIN. | 88 | 29 | –1.2 | 0.2 | 0.83 | –1.3 | 0.74 | –1.3 |

Real RMSE 0.32 Adj. S.D. 0.54 Separation 1.69 Item reliability 0.74 Model RMSE 0.27 Adj. S.D. 0.64 reparation 2.35 Item reliability 0.75 S.E. of item mean = 0.09.

**Table 3. Items statistics—Measure order.**

| Item | | Raw | | | Model | Infit | | Outfit | | Pt Mea |
|---|---|---|---|---|---|---|---|---|---|---|
| No. | Item | Score | Count | Measure | S.E. | MNSQ | ZStd | MNSQ | ZStd | Corr. |
| A cloud data storage (CDS) | | | | | | | | | | |
| 1 | A1 roles | 139 | 15 | −1.18 | 0.3 | 0.98 | 0 | 1 | 0.1 | 0.31 |
| 2 | A2 resources | 127 | 15 | 0.12 | 0.22 | 0.88 | −0.7 | 0.84 | −0.8 | 0.44 |
| 3 | A3 infrastructure | 132 | 15 | −0.32 | 0.26 | 0.88 | −0.6 | 0.85 | −0.7 | 0.43 |
| 4 | A4 req analysis | 128 | 14 | −0.26 | 0.27 | 0.84 | −0.8 | 0.81 | −1 | 0.46 |
| 5 | A5 sys analysis | 129 | 15 | −0.4 | 0.23 | 0.97 | 0 | 1.13 | 0.6 | 0.37 |
| 6 | A8 implementation | 124 | 14 | −0.01 | 0.27 | 0.84 | −0.7 | 0.84 | −0.8 | 0.48 |
| 7 | A7 domain | 138 | 15 | −0.82 | 0.28 | 1.04 | 0.3 | 1 | 0.1 | 0.28 |
| B cloud user | | | | | | | | | | |
| 8 | B1 behavior | 106 | 11 | −0.56 | 0.39 | 1.06 | 0.3 | 1.1 | 0.4 | 0.24 |
| 9 | B2 awareness | 111 | 12 | −0.53 | 0.28 | 1.19 | 0.6 | 1.27 | 0.9 | 0.13 |
| 10 | B3 usage | 94 | 11 | 0.05 | 0.26 | 0.9 | −0.2 | 0.93 | −0.1 | 0.48 |
| C cloud service provider (CSP) | | | | | | | | | | |
| 11 | C1 facilitate | 150 | 15 | −0.72 | 0.38 | 0.89 | −0.6 | 0.8 | −0.7 | 0.31 |
| 12 | C2 encourage | 90 | 15 | 0.92 | 0.24 | 1.27 | 1.2 | 1.25 | 1.1 | 0.38 |
| 13 | C3 provide | 89 | 15 | 0.99 | 0.23 | 1.06 | 0.4 | 1.07 | 0.4 | 0.49 |
| 14 | C4 trust | 107 | 14 | 0.09 | 0.27 | 1.03 | 0.2 | 1 | 0.1 | 0.43 |
| D agent tools | | | | | | | | | | |
| 15 | D1 definition | 112 | 13 | 0.17 | 0.43 | 0.89 | −0.2 | 0.88 | −0.2 | 0.47 |
| 16 | D2 characteristic | 95 | 12 | 0.76 | 0.46 | 0.95 | 0 | 0.91 | −0.1 | 0.31 |
| 17 | D3 communication | 126 | 10 | 0.2 | 0.6 | 0.83 | −0.2 | 0.74 | −0.3 | 0.56 |
| 18 | D4 prosperity | 128 | 12 | 0.76 | 0.46 | 0.95 | 0 | 0.91 | −0.1 | 0.49 |
| 19 | D5 goal | 132 | 12 | 0.76 | 0.46 | 0.95 | −0.2 | 0.94 | −04 | 0.76 |
| E security goals in cloud computing | | | | | | | | | | |
| 20 | E1 confidentiality | 145 | 15 | −0.09 | 0.34 | 0.86 | −1.3 | 0.79 | −1.3 | 0.39 |
| 21 | E2 correctness assurance | 137 | 15 | 0.81 | 0.34 | 0.9 | −0.9 | 0.87 | −1 | 0.41 |
| 22 | E3 availability | 126 | 15 | −0.25 | 0.35 | 0.9 | −0.3 | 0.87 | −0.4 | 0.49 |
| 23 | E4 integrity | 116 | 15 | 0.75 | 0.26 | 0.95 | −0.2 | 0.96 | −0.2 | 0.45 |
| 24 | E5 data privacy | 131 | 39 | 1.13 | 0.35 | 1.1 | 0.8 | 1.14 | 0.9 | 0.26 |
| 25 | E6 multi-tenancy | 123 | 39 | −0.5 | 0.39 | 1 | 0.1 | 1.05 | 0.3 | 0.4 |
| 26 | E7 control | 134 | 15 | 1.16 | 0.35 | 1 | 0 | 1.01 | 0.1 | 0.35 |
| Mean | | 119.8 | 38.3 | 0.0 | 0.3 | 1.0 | 0.0 | 1.0 | 0.0 | 0.4 |
| S.D. | | 16.7 | 3.2 | 0.6 | 0.1 | 0.1 | 0.6 | 0.2 | 0.7 | 0.1 |

PIDM is used to reveal the "easiest" and "hardest" questions answered by respondents. Based on the summaries and PIDM, a few observations could be concluded. Person SU1 is at the leftmost of the person distribution. As the Customer Service Director, it's lonely up there and not many want to share with him information, hence the pattern of answers. Item F1—"Cloud user must pay in order to get the cloud services", and F5—"Agents have the ability to pass the parameters among them" are on the rightmost and leftmost of the Item distribution, respectively. The question for F1 is on "Cloud user must pay in order to get the cloud services" Strategy and F5 is on "Agents have the ability to pass the parameters among them" strategy. We believe that respondents might not understand the terms "Cloud user

must pay in order to get the cloud services" and "Agents have the ability to pass the parameters among them" in cloud computing concept and software agent concept. Layman-terms were used to better represent the questions. In this case, questions F1 and F5 were rephrased to F1—"both of these strategies the respondent must totally agreed". Determining the "Easy" questions is not as easy as portrayed in the Person-Item Variable map. It was envisaged that question F1 and F5 were revised.

### 7.1.3. Component Group Cut-Off Points
There are no hard and fast rules on how to determine which of the less important components should be excluded from the framework. The components are sorted into descending logit values. The list is then distributed

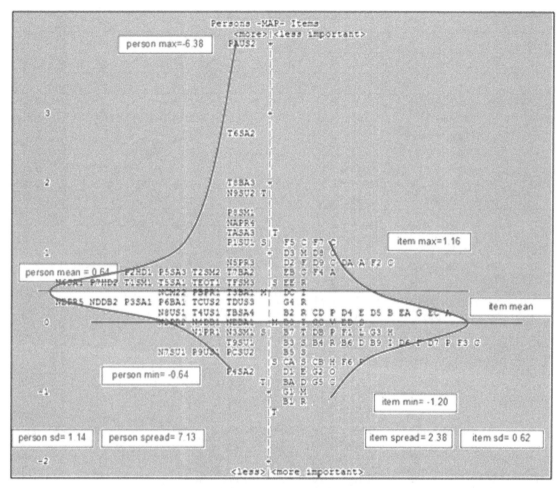

**Figure 8. Person-item distribution map.**

to four experts from software engineering fields, and three cloud computing security experts.

## 7.2. Discussion

Based on the overall experts' judgments, the following components are selected to be excluded from the model (**Table 3**):

- C2 Encourage/CSPs must encourage cloud users to use their trusted CDS.
- D1 CSPA—Provide the security service task according to the authorized service level agreements (SLAs)/ different area.
- E5 Data privacy/different area.
- E6 Multi-tenancy/different area.
- E7 Control/different area.

Based on the above reduced components, the revised framework is depicted in **Figure 1** and its MAS architecture in **Figure 2**. Based on the Pilot study results, the revised security framework based on MAS architecture is directly driven from the initial framework. This is because the most of the components are common and used to identify the respondent in the questionnaire.

The proposed security frameworks to facilitate security of CDS are based on Wang *et al.* [4], Talib *et al.* [5], Takabi *et al.* [14], Yu *et al.* [15], Du *et al.* [16] and Venkatesan and Vaish [17], they all runs in six main parts layers, functions, security goals, infrastructures, approaches, technologies and applications and overlaps on some specific components are architectures and collaborations. The major comparison on the major components of all above frameworks is depicted in **Table 4**.

## 8. Conclusion

In this paper, we investigated the problem of data security in cloud computing environment, to ensure the confidentiality, correctness assurance, availability and integrity of users' data in the cloud; we proposed a security framework and MAS architecture to facilitate security of CDS. This security framework consists of two main layers as agent layer and cloud data storage layer. The propose MAS architecture includes five types of agents: CSPA, CDConA, CDCorA, CDAA and CDIA. To formulate the security framework for collaborative CDS security, the components on MAS, cloud user and CSP

**Table 4. Comparisons between the frameworks.**

| Item/Framework | Wang *et al.* [4] | Talib *et al.* [5] | Takabi *et al.* [14] | Yu *et al.* [15] | Du *et al.* [16] | Venkatesan and Vaish [17] |
|---|---|---|---|---|---|---|
| Layer | Y | Y | Y | NA | Y | NA |
| Function | Y | Y | Y | NA | Y | Y |
| Security goal | Y | Y | Y | Y | Y | Y |
| Infrastructure | Y | Y | Y | Y | Y | Y |
| Approach | NA | Y | Y | Y | Y | Y |
| Technology | Y | Y | Y | Y | Y | Y |
| Application | Y | NA | Y | Y | Y | NA |
| Architecture | NA | Y | NA | NA | Y | Y |
| Collaboration | Y | Y | Y | Y | Y | Y |

are compiled from various literatures. An initial model of modified MAS components for collaborative CDS security is proposed. The relationships between these components are used to construct the questionnaire, which were tested in a pilot study. Rasch model was used in analyzing pilot questionnaire. Item reliability is found to be poor and a few respondents and items were identified as misfits with distorted measurements. Some problematic questions are revised and some predictably easy questions are excluded from the questionnaire. A prototype of the system (GSecaaS) is implemented using Java and PHP. The use of this system has shown how the system could be used to facilitate the security of the CDS.

# REFERENCES

[1] M. Zhou, R. Zhang, W. Xie, W. Qian and A. Zhou, "Security and Privacy in Cloud Computing: A Survey," *Proceedings of the Sixth International Conference on Semantics Knowledge and Grid* (*SKG*), Beijing, 2010, pp. 105-112.

[2] C. S. Aishwarya, "Insight into Cloud Security Issues," *UACEE International Journal of Computer Science and Its Applications*, 2011, pp. 30-33.

[3] J. W. Rittinghouse and J. F. Ransome, "Cloud Computing: Implementation, Management, and Security (Chapter 6)," 2009.

[4] C. Wang, Q. Wang, K. Ren and W. Lou, "Ensuring Data Storage Security in Cloud Computing," *IEEE*, Vol. 186, No. 978, 2009, pp. 1-9.

[5] A. M. Talib, R. Atan, R. Abdullah and M. A. A. Murad, "Formulating a Security Layer of Cloud Data Storage Framework Based on Multi-Agent System Architecture," *TGSTF International Journal on Computing*, Vol. 1, No. 1, 2010, pp. 120-124.

[6] A. M. Talib, R. Atan, R. Abdullah and M. A. A. Murad, "Towards New Access Data Control Technique Based on Multi Agent System Architecture for Cloud Computing in Software Engineering and Computer Systems Part II," In: V. Snasel, J. Platos and E. El-Qawasmeh, Eds., *Springer Series: Communications in Computer and Information Science* 189, Springer-Verlag, pp. 268-279.

[7] M. R. Genesereth and S. P. Ketchpel, "Software Agents," *Communication of the ACM*, Vol. 37, No. 7, 1994, pp. 48-53.

[8] E. H. Durfee, V. R. Lesser and D. D. Corkill, "Trends in Cooperative Distributed Problem Solving," *IEEE Transactions on Knowledge and Data Engineering*, 1989, pp. 63-83.

[9] H. Mouratidis, P. Giorgini and G. Manson, "Modelling Secure Multi-Agent Systems," ACM, 2003, pp. 859-866.

[10] S. Ramgovind, M. M. Eloff and E. Smith, "The Management of Security in Cloud Computing," Information Security for South Africa (ISSA), Sandton, Johannesburg, 2010, pp. 1-7.

[11] K. D. Bowers, A. Juels and A. Oprea, "HAIL: A High-Availability and Integrity Layer for Cloud Storage," 2009. http://eprint.iacr..org/2008/489.pdf

[12] D. Zissis and D. Lekkas, "Addressing Cloud Computing Security Issues," *Future Generation Computer Systems*, Vol. 28, No. 3, 2010, pp. 583-592.

[13] J. Yang and Z. Chen, "Cloud Computing Research and Security Issues," *International Conference on Computational Intelligence and Software Engineering* (*CiSE*), 2010, pp. 1-3.

[14] H. Takabi, J. B. D. Joshi and G. J. Ahn, "SecureCloud: Towards a Comprehensive Security Framework for Cloud Computing Environments," 34*th Annual IEEE Computer Software and Applications Conference Workshops*, 2010, pp. 393-398.

[15] H. Yu, N. Powell, D. Stembridge and X. Yuan. "Cloud Computing and Security Challenges," ACM, 2012, pp. 298-302.

[16] J. Du, W. Wei, X. Gu and T. Yu, "RunTest: Assuring Integrity of Dataflow Processing in Cloud Computing Infrastructures," *ASIACCS'*10, Beijing, 13-16 April 2010, pp. 293-304.

[17] S. Venkatesan and A. Vaish, "Multi-Agent Based Dynamic Data Integrity Protection in Cloud Computing," 2011, pp. 76-82.

[18] A. A. Aziz, A. Mohamed, A. Zaharim, S. Zakaria, H. A. Ghulman and M. S. Masodi, "Evaluation of Information Professionals Competency Face Validity Test Using Rasch," *Proceedings of the* 4*th Pacific Rim Objective*

*Measurement Symposiom* (*PROMS*), 2008, pp. 396-403.

[19] A. M. Talib, R. Atan, R. Abdullah and M. A. A. Murad, "Security Framework of Cloud Data Storage Based on Multi Agent System Architecture: Semantic Literature Review," *Computer and Information Science*, Vol. 3, No.

4, 2010, p. 175.

[20] A. M. Talib, R. Atan, R. Abdullah and M. A. A. Murad, "CloudZone: Towards an Integrity Layer of Cloud Data Storage Based on Multi-Agent System Architecture," *ICOS*, 2011, pp. 127-132.

# 12

# Security Policy Management Process within Six Sigma Framework

**Vijay Anand, Jafar Saniie, Erdal Oruklu**

Department of Electrical and Computer Engineering, Illinois Institute of Technology, Chicago, USA

## ABSTRACT

This paper presents a management process for creating adaptive, real-time security policies within the Six Sigma $6\sigma$ framework. A key challenge for the creation of a management process is the integration with models of known Industrial processes. One of the most used industrial process models is *Six Sigma* which is a business management model wherein customer centric needs are put in perspective with business data to create an efficient system. The security policy creation and management process proposed in this paper is based on the Six Sigma model and presents a method to adapt security goals and risk management of a computing service. By formalizing a security policy management process within an industrial process model, the adaptability of this model to existing industrial tools is seamless and offers a clear risk based policy decision framework. In particular, this paper presents the necessary tools and procedures to map Six Sigma *DMAIC (Define-Measure-Analyze-Improve-Control)* methodology to security policy management.

**Keywords:** Security Management; Security Process; Policy; Threat; Six Sigma

## 1. Introduction

A security policy [1] management process is necessary for refining existing policies or creating new policies as threats and computing services evolve. Security policy creation process gives an insight onto the quantification of risk. For high level management where it is necessary to make risk based decisions, this process provides a way to manage risk as threats change. There is always a need to maintain consumer trust for a successful computing service. A measure of an effective security policy creation process is the evaluation of risk. In this paper, we review existing policy creation models and propose our model based on Six Sigma $(6\sigma)$ [2] with quantification of the risk factors. We contend that threats have a direct implication on policies which are countermeasures to threats. Therefore, the efficacy of security policies needs to be measured against the modeled and analyzed threats in the security policy management system. As threats evolve so must the security policies since there is a direct correlation between threats and security policy.

There have been various processes proposed to create security policies for a secure system. The various aspects of the security policy creation models are 1) understanding threats for policy creation; 2) a monitoring process for existing internal or external threats; and 3) policy operations in the system.

In the current literature, the security policy manage-ment is generally referred to as a security policy process. A security policy process model given in [3] identifies various phases of a security policy creation and updates. Most of the policy creation models have a clear security goal perspective of creating or enhancing security policies. Some models [4] are created by taking into consideration what security professionals had to say about the various aspects of technology that needs to be addressed before a policy is created.

We propose to adapt the security policy creation process into a business management system wherein the efficacy of the policy management and risk based decisions can be easily quantified in the current models. For a policy management model to be effective in an industrial setting, it needs to be based on an industrial process. Institutionalizing any process has inherent cost [5] on usage of tools, learning curve to use the process effectively and integrating the process into the system. Hence, an effective integration of a security policy management process into an existing industrial process allows other processes to be integrated with security policy; thereby enhancing the effectiveness of the industrial system as a whole. In this paper, we use the Six Sigma model to base our security policy management process due to its widespread acceptance and effectiveness in an industrial setting. Our key contributions are:

- Creation of a security policy management process

with an explicit feedback mechanism so as to control the deployment of security policies with evolving threats,
- Using the Six Sigma process model for the security policy management process to ease integration with industrial processes,
- Quantification of risk in security policy management for making decisions.

## 2. Six Sigma in a Nutshell

The implementation of Six Sigma is generally done in two different approaches either for improving a product or creating a new product. For making changes to existing processes, the process used in Six Sigma is called *DMAIC (Define-Measure-Analyze-Improve-Control)*. The DMAIC project methodology has five phases: [6]
- Define: This step involves the quantification of high-level project goals and the process used.
- Measure: This step involves the quantification of important methods used in a current process from which relevant data is collected.
- Analyze: This step involves the identification of the causality effect between the process and factors influencing the process.
- Improve: This step involves the optimization of the current process.
- Control: This step involves the correction to any deviation associated with a particular process before it results into defects.

For new products, the *DMADV (Define-Measure-Analyze-Design-Verify)* system is generally used. The DMADV project methodology features five phases:
- Define design goals that are consistent with customer demands and the enterprise strategy.
- Measure and identify CTQs (characteristics that are Critical to Quality), product capabilities, production process capability, and risks.
- Analyze to develop and design alternatives, create a high-level design and evaluate design capability to select the best design.
- Design details, optimize the design, and plan for design verification.
- Verify the design, set up pilot runs, implement the production process and hand it over to the process owners.

In our approach, the security policy management within the Six Sigma framework 1) Defines security goals and quantifies digital assets, 2) Measures and assesses various threats to digital assets and quantifies risk, 3) Analyzes the overall security goals with the identification of the diversity of external and internal factors affecting the assets of a computing service, 4) Improves designs and optimizes the security policies with evolving threats, and

5) Controls threat mitigation with security policy implementation to guarantee the quality of service for gaining customer trust.

## 3. Security Policy Management Process

### 3.1. Existing Security Policy Creation Processes

Existing security policy creation processes identify the need to have a feedback mechanism in order to draft new policies. The two widely recognized processes are PFIRES (Policy Framework for Interpreting Risk in e-Business Security [3]) and the organizational process model [4] which initiate the following steps for security policy creation:
- Assess: Assessment phase is a trigger to evaluate security policies which is initiated by either: 1) Creation of new model or addition of a new feature such that the input/output characteristics of a computing service is altered leading to changes in the risk factors; or 2) Consequence of the review and management of existing policies affecting the risk parameters of the computing service. For either of the above cases, the reference for policy changes are existing policies and the assumptions made during the institutionalization of the policies. In the organizational process [4] model, this phase is blended in the task of Policy Awareness, Policy Review and Risk Assessment.
- Plan: Planning phase is where the requirements and strategy of rolling out a new security policy is created. This phase outlines the high level requirements of security policies for later implementation. In the organizational process [4] model this is primarily done in Policy Development.
- Deliver: Deliver phase is when the actual implementation of the policy is undertaken. The design of various control structures based on requirements is determined. The implementation part of the security policy updates is also integrated in this phase.
- Operate: Operate phase is persistent in which various external and internal businesses, regulatory and technology trends affecting the security policies are monitored and analyzed.

The above policy management mechanisms, although they are theoretically effective, do not integrate into known business processes such that effective decision making can be achieved from a management standpoint. They also lack correlation with known security tools such that effectiveness of a policy mechanism can be quantified for risk analysis. In the proposed security management framework we integrate security policy management within Six Sigma processes and correlate security tools with each phase of the management process.

## 3.2. Causality Framework for Security Policy Management

For a Six Sigma implementation, there is a need to establish a causal analysis [7] which is true for other process improvement methodologies. We make a case for causality with respect to security policy and threats. We propose that the objective of a security policy creation is to counter threats as shown in **Figure 1**.

For any security policy creation process, the objective is to counter all known (real world and modeled) threats. The set of all threats may be unknown but a security policy creation process strives to expand the knowledge base of known threats to all possible threats. The basis for this process model to work is to have a causality relationship between security policy and threats. Based on this premise, we contend:

***Theorem***: *A security policy "S" counters a threat "T" in a secure system. $S \rightarrow T$*

***Proof***: By contradiction.

Let's assume:

Threat T1 which exists in a system and there is no policy equivalent to counter it. The only way that can be done is if we counter this threat by institutionalizing a security policy represented as $T1 \rightarrow S1$. If in the presence of security policy S1, the threat still exists then it implies:

$S1 \nrightarrow T1$ exists then the creation of policy really did not alleviate the threat. Hence the only way to alleviate the threat is if $S1 \rightarrow \neg T1$. If we generalize this then $S \rightarrow \neg T$.

A security policy management process has to adapt security policies based on the feedback it receives on the threat information in order to mitigate threats in real-time. Hence, a key element stressed here is the ability of having feedback for countermeasures on threats [3]. The other aspect of security policy management is to operate the process within a known and respected industrial process. Hence, we stress the requirement of creating this process within a Six-Sigma framework.

## 3.3. Elements of the Proposed Security Policy Management Process

The elements of the proposed policy creation and execution process are:

- Security Policy: The security policy is the actual policy definitions [1,8] that are implemented. These definitions are invoked [9] before the computing logic is executed. This takes the feedback from a threat profile which was used to create the policies. The decision of countermeasures lies with this policy definition. In this Security Policy definition, the security policy is broken down into two parts: 1) a Directive part wherein the Security Policy implementation acts

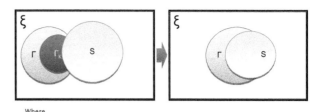

Where
$\xi$ = The set of all executions
$\Gamma$ = Set of threats, known and unknown
$\Gamma_K$ = Set of known Threats
S = Set of security policies created to counter threats
$S \cap \Gamma_K = \Gamma_K$ and $\Gamma \cup \Gamma_K = \Gamma_K$ for an ideal situation

**Figure 1. Threat—policy correlation.**

as a predictor for any existing threat by setting up the computing service; and 2) a Countermeasure part where the Security Policy implementation of countermeasures creates mitigation strategies based on known threat models after data has been processed.

- Threat Model: The threat model [10] is an important aspect of policy creation and also policy execution. In the previous section, the case was made for threat and policy as a cause and effect relation in a secure computing system.

- Risk Assessment using CVSS (Common Vulnerability Scoring System) [11] scores: Security policies protect digital assets that are essential to the commerce of digital assets. In an industrial setting of sale and usage of digital assets, the following are required:

1) Risk quantification on digital assets is well defined by security policies.

2) Simplicity of the decision system.

Common Vulnerability Scoring System (CVSS) provides a framework to convert threat data into applicable risk information. In this paper, we use CVSS as a basis to quantify various metrics within a Six Sigma framework. The metrics are grouped under base, temporal and environmental classes. The base metric deals with vulnerability characteristics that don't change over time, temporal metric with characteristics that change over time, and environmental metric deals with the operating user environment.

## 4. Security Policy Management Process with Six Sigma $(6\sigma)$ Integration

The various phases of Six Sigma are integrated with a security management process as shown in **Figure 2**. In this figure, each phase of Six Sigma is shown with various elements involved in the security process. A brief overview of the security policy management with Six Sigma is given below:

1) In the Define phase of Six Sigma, existing Security Policy is reviewed. This review of the policy is based on the cost of quality and effectiveness of existing policies with respect to various threats encountered and modeled.

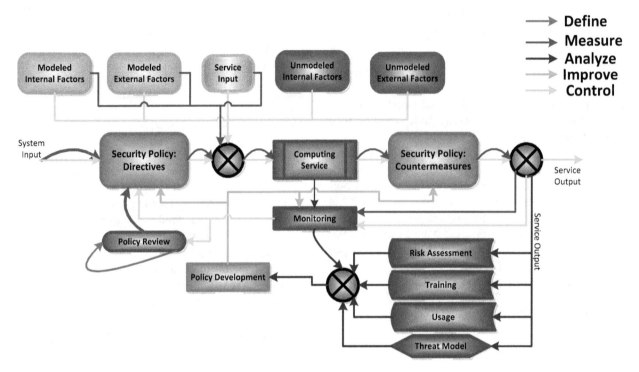

**Figure 2. Proposed security policy management process.**

2) In the Measure phase of Six Sigma, the various risks of a threat are measured for the existing security infrastructure. Based on the risk quantification, confidence level on existing infrastructure elements like the Security Policy Directives, Countermeasures and Threat Model is measured.

3) In the Analyze phase of Six Sigma, new security policies are proposed and their effectiveness is measured with respect to existing security policies to counter threats. This phase requires experimentation with various kinds of implementation and the cost effectiveness to mitigate risk.

4) In the Improve phase of Six Sigma, the actual implementation of the Security Policy Directives, Countermeasures and Monitoring mechanism based on a Threat Model is done such that the effectiveness of the newer model can be monitored.

5) In the Control phase of Six Sigma, the new policy effectiveness is tracked. Since the Security Policy is broken down into a directive part and a countermeasure part, the policy effectively tries to adapt to threats.

## 4.1. 6σ—DEFINE Phase for Security Policy

Define phase of Six Sigma is used to identify digital assets and quantify various design goals for the security policy management process. As shown in **Figure 2**, *Policy Review and Policy Development* reflects the define phase in security policy management process. This phase generally would involve the identification of security goals, assets, threats and factors involving security policy creation. Digital assets identified by the customer and service provider are important components of a computing service.

Asset identification is important to quantify the need to address a threat. If the severity of threat to an asset is high, then the product development needs to be done to address that deficiency. In this paper as an example we highlight the threats quantified in the CMLA (Content Management License Administrator) [12] service provider adopter agreement which needs to be addressed by security policies. The logical threats and the operational threats in this service agreement are of most importance on the software side. If PostgreSQL [13] database is used to create the service under the CMLA restrictions then:

- Threat identification to these digital assets needs to be assessed during this phase. The most important threats for the database that can be quantified from the CMLA agreement are:

  1) Improper or unauthorized creation, modification or deletion of user accounts.

  2) Improper or unauthorized creation, modification or deletion of database contents.

  3) Improper or unauthorized creation, modification or deletion of database access controls.

  4) Exploitation of input control (buffer overflows) to undermine availability and escalate privilege.

- With management approval, an appropriate threat alleviation systems needs to be identified as well as choice of the version of the database.

The tools used in the define phase are:

- Cost of Quality (CQ) where the cost of quality can be split into Cost of Good Quality (CGQ) [14] when a process conforms to certain guidelines, which in context of security, is to follow the best practices in managing security policies.
- Cost of Poor Quality (CPQ) [14] accrued due to non-conformance. A tool commonly used to focus on failures in CPQ is a Pareto Chart [15].

Pareto Chart [15] is used for identifying financial loss due to threats to digital assets denoting CPQ. A Pareto chart highlights the importance of a certain factor among various factors. In case of security, the Pareto chart highlights the importance of loss in revenue correlated to corresponding security vulnerability. A typical Pareto chart for CVSS severity of attacks for PostgreSQL database (Years 2001-2005) is shown in **Figure 3**. This chart represents the CVSS score of vulnerabilities when being prioritized for system integration. For security management processes, the severity of the rating of a threat is equated to financial dollars and a management data spread should clearly show where priorities lie.

Another way to highlight various aspects of process is by using a SIPOC (supplier, input, process, output, customer) [16] chart which identifies the workflow interaction of any service. For a security policy management process the SIPOC chart, identifies how security policy interacts with a computing service. The SIPOC chart for a security process is shown in **Figure 4**.

- Supplier of Input—System, Consumer, Malicious-

Content Provider, and Environment.
- Inputs—System Inputs, Consumer data input, Environmental input, and Malicious data input.
- Process—Computing Service for Content, Security Policy Directives and Countermeasures for Threats.
- Output—Processed Data and Monitoring Data.
- Customer—Consumer.

## 4.2. 6σ—MEASURE Phase for Security Policy

Measure phase involves measurement and quantification of risks to digital assets in the service.

- Threat Impact due to software is measured by a system similar to the CVSS score.
- Risk due to hardware which quantifies the level of trust the hardware can provide.
- Risk during operation of the computing service based on the threat model identified during the Define phase.

The CVSS base score consists of:

- Access Vector denoting how the vulnerability is exploited.
- Access Complexity denoting the complexity of the vulnerability once access is gained into the system.
- Authentication which highlights how many authentication steps an attacker has to attempt so as to exploit the vulnerability.
- Confidentiality Impact metric which highlights how the vulnerability effects unauthorized data.
- Integrity Impact which denotes the guarantees of trust on content.
- Availability Impact which denotes content accessibility in face of a successful attack.

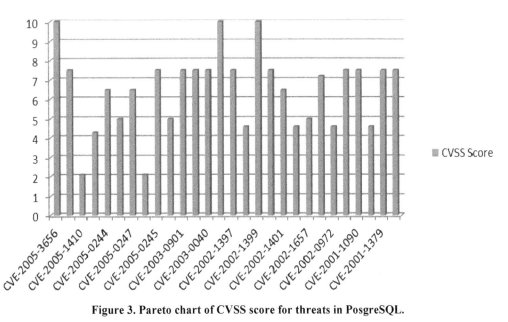

Figure 3. Pareto chart of CVSS score for threats in PosgreSQL.

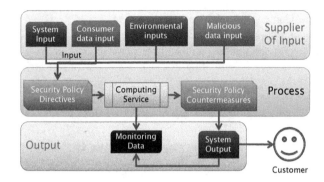

**Figure 4. Security SIPOC chart of a computing process.**

The tools used in the measure phase for Six Sigma are:

- Y = F(X) [6] tool as shown in **Figure 5**, which identifies malicious input (X) and related output (Y) for various threats identified to be included in the *Define Phase*. Typically this analysis shows the causality relation of threat vectors and corresponding vulnerability of a computing system. In **Figure 5**, the threat dataset (X) when processed by the computing system (F) identifies the vulnerability (Y). In this analysis, the Access Vector of CVSS is the threat dataset. Access Complexity and Authentication of the CVSS base score are measured.

- *FMEA* (Failure Mode and Effects Analysis) [17] tool identifies threat vectors, severity of threats, causes and current inspection methodology to evaluate the risks. Here, the Confidential Impact, Integrity Impact and Availability Impact of the CVSS base score are measured. The vulnerability data obtained from NVD (National Vulnerability Database) [18] of Post greSQL [13] identified in the *Define Phase* shows the number of threats each year as shown in **Figure 6**. Another important aspect of policy creation process is to train the people who would deal with the computing system and change the computing logic in any way. The score that affects the quality of the security of a product depends on how well they are trained.

- *Process Sigma* [19] tool quantifies whether current security policies are capable ($C_p$, $C_{pk}$) to meet identified threats by identifying the process sigma. $C_p$ indicates the capability of existing security policies to counter known and modeled threats. $C_{pk}$ indicates how effective a security policy in countering actual threats:

1) The important factors here are the consumer specification and operational specification. If the severity threats are quantified within these specifications, then the CVSS Risk score gives the value of risk.

2) This also has a bearing on the customer agreements. Difficult to stage attacks requiring the customer to be an active participant in the attack like hardware attacks will fall beyond the operational specification of a computing

service. Hence the customer agreement is drawn to limit liabilities for the computing service provide in such cases. The Cpk value of risk in case of hard to exploit attacks would be low which are then framed into consumer agreements.

- *GAGE* [6] tool is used to gage repeatability and reproducibility (Gage R & R) of threat identification, and to remove false positives from the approach data is collected.

The Six Sigma Measure phase chart shown in **Table 1** indicates the proposed mapping of various tools in Six Sigma to that of a security measures.

**Table 1. Measure phase mapping to security management.**

| Six Sigma | Security |
|---|---|
| $Y = F(X)$ | Input/Output |
| FMEA | Static Analyzers, Inspection Process and Education |
| Process Sigma | CVSS Scores |
| GAGE | Differential CVSS Scores |

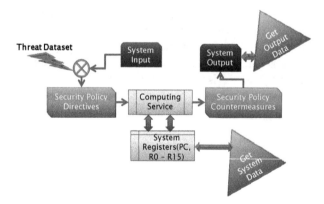

**Figure 5. Y = F(X) analysis for security.**

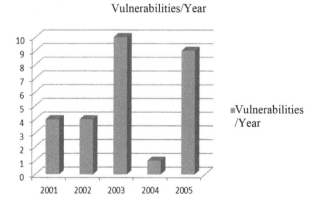

**Figure 6. Vulnerability rate each year of PostgreSQL [18].**

## 4.3. 6σ—ANALYZE Phase for Security Policy

Analyze phase determines the effectiveness of the security policies and threats models already in place. The goals of this phase are:

- Improvement to existing security policies.
- Identification of new threats and thereby changes to the threat model.

The CVSS temporal metrics provides measurements and analysis into:

- Exploitability which measures the techniques of exploits and the availability of code that can used to stage the exploit.
- Remediation Level which deals with the type of fix that is available for a given vulnerability.
- Report Confidence which deals with the existence of the vulnerability and quality of information about the technical details of the vulnerability.

The tools used in the analyze phase are:

- *Hypothesis testing* [20] on threat data to test efficacy of new security policies creating null hypothesis ($H0$) or alternate hypothesis ($Ha$). The alpha risk is still kept at an industrial risk standard of 5% for hypothesis testing. This is also used to test security flags in automated testing tools before deployment. This can be established by measuring the exploitability as defined in the CVSS temporal metric.
- *Correlation and Regression* to test known threat vectors to identify input output relationships. This part deals with lab based penetration and fuzz testing for software security and quality assurance [21]. The output is generally identified by Pearson coefficient. This can be highlighted by the remediation level and report confidence of the CVSS temporal score.
- *Analysis of Variance* (ANOVA) [22] is hypothesis testing with variations of input factors. It essentially states the effectiveness of security framework for variations in input and temperature, or input and clock etc.

Elements of the Analyze Phase are:

- *Risk Assessment*: Based on the available policy and threat models:

  1) Decisions can be made on the degree of risk that can be taken.

  2) Some policies maybe too expensive to implement and not worth implementing for the product at hand and this assessment of risk quantification helps make business and financial decisions.

  3) Usage of the policy and threat models combined with the computing logic determines how people utilize a security system and helps to focus on critical threats and policies. Eventually, it feeds into the risk assessment for any future decision.

- *Component Threat Model*: The threat model in the analysis phase gives an overview of any modeled threats and the modeling of any new threats.

  1) In a computing system built out of various components, a specific threat model for each component exists. For example some components in a computing service may experience network centric threats where as others might experience hardware centric threats.

  2) Monitoring is used to analyze effectiveness of the policies so as to discover various correlations between input output data and threats to digital assets.

- *Penetration Testing*: Simulating and staging an attack on a computing service requires understanding about how a computing service is used. It identifies various input output characteristics based on the component threat model.

Proposed Analyze Phase mapping to security principles is shown in **Table 2**.

## 4.4. 6σ—IMPROVE Phase for Security Policy

Improve phase within the context of security policies have to either create new security policies or improve existing security policies. The **tools** used in the improve phase are:

- Design of Experiments (DOE) [23] is essentially doing ANOVA [22] for the whole system. ANOVA measure in the analyze phase is used to get variations for components of a computing service. In DOE, all variations in a computing service are taken into account to understand the effectiveness of the security framework and recording risk value of a policy to a threat on any digital asset with variations. This needs to be done always after the GAGE measurement is conducted on the threats since it identifies the source of variations due to threats in various operating environments.

Elements of Improve Phase are:

- *Security Policy Directive*: The security policy directive is the actual policy definitions which are implemented. These definitions are invoked before the actual computing logic is executed. This takes the feedback from a threat profile which was used to create the policies.

**Table 2. Analyze phase mapping to security management.**

| Six Sigma | Security |
|---|---|
| Hypothesis Testing | Risk Assessment |
| ANOVA | Component Threat Model |
| Correlation and Regression | Penetration Testing |

- *Security Policy Countermeasures*: The countermeasure part of security policy acts on any modeled threat which has been encountered during operation. The effective decision of countermeasures lies with this policy definition.

The Improve Phase mapping to security management is shown in **Table 3**.

### 4.5. 6σ—CONTROL Phase for Security Policy

Control phase of security policy highlights the actual control of the computing service with security policies operating in a feedback mode. The **tools** used in the control phase are:

- Statistical Process Control (SPC) [24] measures the critical characteristics of the process in real-time and generates countermeasures if threats are identified to alleviate them.
- Mistake Proofing [25] also called Poka-Yoke wherein policy definitions are error-proofed so that they cannot be misinterpreted

Control Phase mapping to security principles is shown in **Table 4**.

## 5. Comparison of the Security Policy Models

A comparison of security policy management between the existing work presented in Section 3 (PFIRES model [3], and the organizational process model [4]) and the proposed Six-Sigma model is presented in **Table 5**. The various aspects of this comparison are:

- Refining of Security Policies—a security policy management process requires refinement of existing policies in a proactive and reactive manner. The primary objective of the existing models and the presented model is similar and all the models satisfy this requirement.
- Threat Profile—the threat profile on which the security policy is executed is done with an active threat profile in the Six-Sigma model. Due to the causality relationship between security policy and threat as a

part of the live computing service, an active threat profile is required to provide continuous monitoring and adaptation of security policy. The existing models in literature do indicate the need for threat modeling but do not propose it to be a part of the active system.

- External Factors—the external factors affecting a computing service is the unknown in any security architecture. Threats that are known and modeled can only be countered by design.
- Feedback—the feedback for the efficacy of a security policy due to changes in threats is addressed implicitly during policy evaluation and design in existing systems. In the Six-Sigma process, the feedback is explicit since we added an explicit threat monitoring system to adapt security policies.
- On the Fly Change—due to compartmentalization of security policies and threat profiles as an explicit part of the computing service, the proposed model can change on the fly as threats evolve. The threat monitoring system also allows us to adapt policies based on monitoring data. In the current models, due to the embedded part of policy in the computing service without explicit separation, on the fly change may be difficult to enact.

Table 3. Improve phase mapping to security management.

| Six Sigma | Security |
|---|---|
| DOE | System Threat Model |
| | Security Directives, Security Countermeasures and Threat Monitor |

Table 4. Control phase mapping to security management.

| Six Sigma | Security |
|---|---|
| SPC | Threat Data Monitor and Security Countermeasures |
| Poka-Yoke | Security Directives |

Table 5. Feature comparison of the security policy models.

| | PFIRES Model [3] | Organizational Process Model [4] | Proposed Six Sigma Model |
|---|---|---|---|
| Policy Output | Yes | Yes | Yes |
| Threat Profile | No | No | Yes |
| External Factors | Yes | Yes | Yes |
| Feedback | Implicit | Implicit | Explicit |
| On the Fly Change | No | No | Yes |
| Mathematical Model | No | No | Yes |
| Industrial Process Integration | No | No | Yes (Six Sigma) |

- Mathematical Model—the model presented here is based on the causality relationship between threat and security policy. Without having causality relationship, Six-Sigma tools cannot be used for analysis. Thereby, the framework we present in this model is different from others where the mathematical framework is not presented. The models compared against are based on well-known practices or experience whereas the proposed model is based on a mathematical approach.
- Industrial Process Integration—the model presented here integrates security policy management process within industrial processes which facilitates industry goals of risk quantification and assessment. The PFIRES model and Organizational Process model don't present integration with industrial processes.

## 6. Conclusions

In this paper, we presented a security policy management process within a Six Sigma framework. Furthermore, we contend that the design of secure computing systems is based on creating adaptive policies and their correlation to threats. We address various challenges in security policy management process including:

- Integration with a known management process thereby reusing tools already existing within an industrial setting.
- Integration of tools with security primitives to facilitate decision making.
- Quantification of risks to digital assets.

## REFERENCES

[1] F. B. Schneider, "Enforceable Security Policies," *ACM Transactions on Information and System Security*, Vol. 3, No. 1, 2000, pp. 30-50.

[2] Six Sigma Motorola University, 2011. http://web.archive.org/web/20051106012600/http://www.motorola.com/motorolauniversity.

[3] J. Rees, S. Bandyopadhyay and E. H. Spafford, "PFIRES: A Policy Framework for Information Security," *Communications of the ACM*, Vol. 46, No. 7, 2003, pp. 101-106.

[4] K. J. Knapp, R. F. Morris Jr., T. E. Marshall and T. A. Byrd, "Information Security Policy: An Organizational-Level Process Model", *Computers and Security*, Vol. 28, No. 7, 2009, pp. 493-508.

[5] W. Scacchi, "Process Models in Software Engineering," *Encyclopedia of Software Engineering*, 2nd Edition, John Wiley and Sons, Inc., New York, 2001.

[6] R. Shankar, "Process Improvement Using Six Sigma: A DMAIC Guide," ASQ Quality Press, Milwaukee, 2009.

[7] D. N. Card, "Myths and Strategies of Defect Causal Analysis", *Proceedings of Pacific Northwest Software Quality Conference*, Portland, 18-19 October 2006.

[8] G. Zanin and L. V. Mancini, "Towards a Formal Model for Security Policies Specification and Validation in the SELinux System," *Proceedings of the Ninth ACM Symposium on Access Control Models and Technologies (ACMAT'04)*, New York, 2-4 June 2004, pp. 136-145.

[9] S. Preda, F. Cuppens, N. Cuppens-Boulahia, J. G. Alfaro, L. Toutain and Y. Elrakaiby, "Semantic Context Aware Security Policy Deployment," *Proceedings of the 4th International Symposium on Information, Computer, and Communications Security (ASIACCS'09)*, Sydney, 10-12 March 2009, pp. 251-261.

[10] D. Xu and K. E. Nygard, "Threat-Driven Modeling and Verification of Secure Software Using Aspect-Oriented Petri Nets," *IEEE Transactions on Software Engineering*, Vol. 32, No. 4, 2006, pp. 265-278.

[11] "A Complete Guide to the Common Vulnerability Scoring System Version 2.0.," 2011. http://www.first.org/cvss/cvss-guide.html.

[12] "CMLA Service Provider Agreement," 2011. http://www.cm-la.com/documents/CMLA%20Service%20Provider%20Agreement%20V1.42%2020110712%20final.pdf.

[13] PostgreSQL, 2011. http://www.postgresql.org/

[14] V. E. Sower, R. Quarles and E. Broussard, "Cost of Quality Usage and Its Relationship to Quality System Maturity," *International Journal of Quality & Reliability Management*, Vol. 24, No. 2, 2007, pp. 121-140.

[15] M. Lazzaroni, "A Tool for Quality Controls in Industrial Process," *IEEE Instrumentation and Measurement Technology Conference*, Suntec City, 3-6 March 2009.

[16] H. De Koning and J. De Mast, "ASQ: The CTQ Flowdown as a Conceptual Model of Project Objectives," *Quality Management Journal*, Vol. 14, No. 2, 2007, pp. 19-28.

[17] L. Grunske, R. Colvin and K. Winter, "Probabilistic Model-Checking Support for FMEA," *4th International Conference on the Quantitative Evaluation of Systems (QEST 2007)*, Edinburgh, 16-19 September 2007, pp. 119-128.

[18] National Vulnerability Database (NVD), 2011. http://nvd.nist.gov/home.cfm

[19] H. P. Barringer, "Process Reliability and Six Sigma," *National Manufacturing Week Conference*, Chicago, 13-16 March 2000.

[20] C. Hsieh, B. Lin and B. Manduca, "Information Technology and Six Sigma Implementation," *Journal of Computer Information Systems*, Vol. 47, No. 4, 2007, pp. 1-10.

[21] A. Takanen, J. DeMott and C. Miller, "Fuzzing for Software Security Testing and Quality Assurance," 1st Edition, Artech House, London, 2008.

[22] "The ANOVA Procedure, SAS/STAT(R) 9.2 User's Guide," 2nd Edition, 2011. http://support.sas.com/documentation/cdl/en/statuganova/61771/PDF/default/statuganova.pdf

[23] M. Tanco, E. Viles, L. Ilzarbe and M. Álvarez, "Manu-
facturing Industries Need Design of Experiments (DoE),"
*Proceedings of the World Congress on Engineering*
(*WCE* 2007), London, Vol. 2, 2-4 July 2007.

[24] D. M. Ferrin, M. J. Miller and D. Muthler, "Six Sigma
and Simulation, So What's the Correlation," *Proceedings*

*of the* 2002 *Winter Simulation Conference*, 8-11 December 2002, pp. 1439-1443.

[25] M. J. McDonald, "Quality Prediction and Mistake Proofing," *Technical Report*, Sandia National Laboratories,
Washington, DC, 1998.

# 13

# Identifier Migration for Identity Continuance in Single Sign-On

**Yoshio Kakizaki, Kazunari Maeda, Keiichi Iwamura**
Tokyo University of Science, Tokyo, Japan

## ABSTRACT

Single sign-on (SSO) is an identity management technique that provides the ability to use multiple Web services with one set of credentials. However, when the authentication server is down or unavailable, users cannot access these Web services, regardless of whether they are operating normally. Therefore, it is important to enable continuous use alongside SSO. In this paper, we present an identity continuance method for SSO. First, we explain four such continuance methods and identify their limitations and problems. Second, we propose a new solution based on an identifier migration approach that meets the requirement for identity continuance. Finally, we discuss these methods from the viewpoint of continuity, security, efficiency, and feasibility.

Keywords: Identity Management; Single Sign-On; Identifier Migration; Identity Continuance

## 1. Introduction

User authentication is typically required when using personalized online services. We often need to memorize a username (identifier) and password (secret) pair for each service. From a security viewpoint, the use of the same identifier and/or password for multiple service providers is undesirable; however, it is difficult to remember many separate identifier and password pairs. This results in lower usability, with users opting not to register for online services.

Single sign-on (SSO) is an identity management technology that provides multiple applications and supports multiple service providers through a single user authentication. In other words, users enjoy "one-stop authentication" because further authentication is not required. More specifically, with SSO, the user is authenticated only once by the authentication server. The user presents authentication results to other service providers and receives their services. Therefore, the number of username and password pairs that the user must memorize decreases compared to separate authentication for each service provider; as a result, usability dramatically improves.

However, the authentication may be unsuccessful on occasions when the server is unavailable for some reason (e.g., outage, hardware/software failure); in this case, the user cannot receive any of the multiple services provided by the SSO environment. This holds true even when service providers are operating normally. Therefore, a reliable method for receiving continuous service is needed, even when the authentication server is temporarily unavailable.

The key requirements for enabling users to continue using services when the authentication server stops responding are as follows:

1) Continuity: this ensures that users are able to keep using services after the problem occurs.

2) Security: this ensures that a malicious attacker cannot masquerade as a user.

3) Efficiency: this ensures that the user does not experience a slowdown or other such problems during the outage or lack of authentication server availability.

In this paper, we describe four conventional methods for achieving identity continuance in SSO—the Redundant SSO Auth Server method, Alias SSOID method, Multiple SSOID method, and Different SSO combination method. We identify the limitations and problems encountered by these conventional methods, and propose a new solution based on the identifier migration approach. Our method meets the requirement for identity continuance. To evaluate each method, we apply the three requirements introduced above; furthermore, we discuss the range of influence and feasibility of each method.

The remainder of this paper is organized as follows: Section 2 describes the concept of SSO, and Section 3 gives a detailed definition of some useful terms in the SSO model, as well as defining the problem we attempt to solve in this paper. Section 4 presents four conventional solution methods and a discussion of their limitations, and we describe our identity continuance method in Section 5. Section 6 summarizes our evaluation and discusses the relative merits and limitations of each system, and Section 7 presents our conclusions and ideas for future work.

## 2. Identity Management and Single Sign-On

Identity management concerns the management of individual identities, their privileges, attributes, and permissions, with the aim of improving security and usability [1,2]. We can divide identity management technologies into three models [3]: isolated, centralized, and federated. Under isolated identity management, each service provider manages the user independently and for a long time. Centralized identity management is implemented in a client-server model, separating the functions of service provider and identity provider. Federated identity management has gained in popularity in recent years [4]; for example, OpenID [5,6], Liberty/ID-WSF [7], Shibboleth [8], and InfoCard/Cardspace all use this method [9,10]. Identity management technology supports the following [3]: 1) End-user requirements; 2) Network operator requirements; 3) Service provider requirements; 4) Administrative requirements; and 5) Legal requirements.

SSO is achieved with centralized and federated identity management. Under SSO, the user does not need to login repeatedly to use multiple services if they have been authenticated once.

SSO techniques can be categorized as agent types or reverse-proxy types [11]. **Figure 1** shows the composition of the agent approach to SSO. An agent, which is part of the service provider, communicates with both the user and the authentication server to exchange authentication results, thus achieving SSO. **Figure 2** shows the composition of the reverse-proxy approach to SSO. The proxy server exists between the user and the service provider. When the user logs in to the proxy server, the service provider receives authentication from the proxy ser-

ver instead of the user.

OpenID [5,6] is a de facto standard user-centric authentication that uses URIs (Uniform Resource Identifiers) and XRIs (eXtensible Resource Identifiers) to authenticate users. OpenID is expressed by a three-party model consisting of an OP (OpenID Provider), RP (Relying Party), and UA (User Agent).

An authenticator requires credentials, such as an identifier (username) and password pair, in order to authenticate a user. It is often assumed that, for their own convenience, users set the same identifier and password pair for different authenticators. In such cases, a malicious authenticator can masquerade as an authenticatee using the credentials it has received. Under OpenID, the RPs do not have credentials: only the OP does. Therefore, an RP requests user authentication from an OP and receives the authentication result from the OP; in other words, the RP cannot authenticate a user itself. In OpenID authenticcation, only one identifier and password pair are required to achieve SSO for multiple RPs.

## 3. Terms and Problem Statement

In this paper, we adopt and transform the agent type SSO approach illustrated in **Figure 1**. In this section, we introduce relevant terms, present a model for SSO, and summarize the problem we are addressing.

### 3.1. Terms

**SSO Auth Server**: An SSO Auth Server is an entity that authenticates users within the SSO environment. First, the SSO Auth Server issues an SSOID to a user. Next, the server attempts to authenticate a user who presents an unauthenticated SSOID as well as authentication credentials. If successful, an authenticated SSOID is issued to the user.

**SSO Client**: An SSO Client is an entity that provides services to a user within the SSO environment. The SSO Client requests user authentication from an SSO Auth Server, because the SSO Client cannot verify the credentials of a user who claims an unauthenticated SSOID. The SSO Client verifies an authenticated SSOID using the authentication result from the SSO Auth Server and, if successful, provides services to the user. The SSO Client binds an authenticated SSOID to a LocalID to manage the user and their information.

**User**: A user is an entity who receives service from an SSO Client within the SSO environment. A user must be authenticated by an SSO Auth Server in order to receive services from an SSO Client. Moreover, a user can receive services from different SSO Clients once they have been authenticated by the SSO Auth Server.

**SSOID**: An SSOID is an identifier that is uniquely assigned to each user within the SSO environment. The

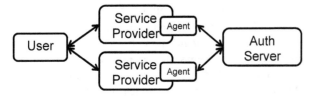

**Figure 1. An agent type SSO technique.**

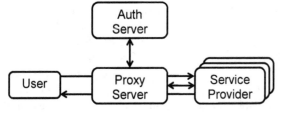

**Figure 2. A reverse-proxy type SSO technique.**

SSO Auth Server and SSO Client identify the user by their SSOID. Each SSOID is a unique and permanent identifier of an individual user. As noted above, we use "unauthenticated SSOID" to indicate the SSOID of a user who has not been authenticated by the SSO Auth Server and "authenticated SSOID" when a user's SSOID has been successfully authenticated by the SSO Auth Server.

**LocalID**: A LocalID is an identifier used by each SSO Client to manage a user. Each SSO Client binds an authenticated SSOID to a LocalID; therefore, the LocalID is only effective in that SSO Client (*i.e.*, it is unique to each SSO Client).

## 3.2. Abstraction of Single Sign-On

**Figure 3** shows the general model of SSO. In this model, a user obtains services from an SSO Client using an SSOID, which is issued by the SSO Auth Server. There are two fundamental procedures for obtaining services from an SSO Client:

**Procedure A**: the user presents an unauthenticated SSOID to the SSO client;

**Procedure B**: the user presents an authenticated SSOID to the SSO client.

In Procedure A, the SSO Client redirects the user to the SSO Auth Server, which authenticates the user with credentials corresponding to the unauthenticated SSOID. If successful, the authenticated SSOID is returned to the user, allowing the user to receive the desired services from the SSO Client by presenting this authenticated SSOID. Procedure B is identical to the latter portion of Procedure A once the user has acquired the authenticated SSOID. In either case, the user can receive services from multiple SSO Clients without further authentication once an authenticated SSOID has been issued by the SSO Auth Server.

The SSO Client manages each user by binding the authenticated SSOID to a LocalID, which is only valid for that particular SSO Client. In **Figure 3**, as an example, SSOID1 and SSOID2 are bound to LIDAA and LIDBB, respectively. Hence the SSO Client maintains that SSOID1 and SSOID2 correspond to different users.

## 3.3. Problem Statement

Continuing the example above, a user who is issued SSOID1 from SSO Auth Server A receives services from multiple SSO Clients, who each map SSOID1 to a unique LocalID. If we assume that SSO Auth Server A is unavailable for some reason, then users cannot receive service from SSO Clients via SSOID1, because they cannot be authenticated.

Users can receive services by obtaining SSOID2 from, say, SSO Auth Server B; however, each SSO Client views SSOID1 and SSOID2 as belonging to different users, because they are bound to different LocalIDs. Therefore, a user cannot access any information and/or history related to SSOID1 from the SSO Clients.

The key problem we aim to address is how to continuously use the information and history that a user has stored in the past. **Figure 4** shows an overview of the problem.

This problem occurs because the SSO Client, which does not have the credentials of its users, cannot authenticate users. Thus, the SSO Client behaves as if there are different users with different SSOIDs, even if it is the same entity. In this case, one solution is to authenticate a User using a LocalID in each SSO Client. However, the User must give their credentials to each SSO Client, which does not align with the SSO function, so we do not assume this solution.

In conclusion, SSOID continuance is crucial in order to solve this problem and provide users with a less interrupted service.

## 4. Identity Continuance in Single Sign-On

In this section, we describe four conventional methods for solving the problem of SSOID continuance described above.

### 4.1. Redundant SSO Auth Server Method

The Redundant SSO Auth Server method involves multiplexing authentication across multiple servers. Server functions can be used continuously as long as at least one server is running in this redundant configuration. **Figure 5** shows a model of the Redundant SSO Auth Server method. In the figure, SSO Auth Server A consists of a two-server redundant configuration, which is transparent to the user. In this case, SSO Auth Server A can be used

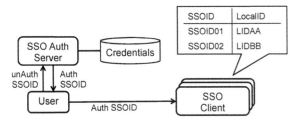

**Figure 3. General model of single sign-on.**

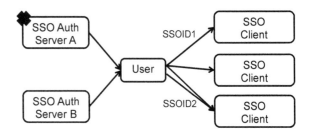

**Figure 4. Overview of problem.**

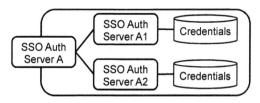

**Figure 5. Redundant SSO Auth Server.**

continuously as long as one of SSO Auth Server A1 or SSO Auth Server A2 is operational.

To implement the Redundant SSO Auth Server method, the type of redundancy required (either in the same domain or between different domains) must be considered. It is easier to compose a redundant configuration in the same domain; however, functions cannot be continuously used when a problem occurs in a higher-layer network, even if each server is operating normally. Unfortunately, it is more difficult to implement redundancy across different domains, and there is the operational problem of sharing or duplicating user credentials on the different domains.

### 4.2. Alias SSOID Method

The Alias SSOID method uses a different (or "alias") SSOID as a pseudonym for the SSOID described above.

**Figure 6** illustrates the relationship between an alias SSOID and its "canonical" SSOID. In the figure, SSOID0A is an alias SSOID that binds to the canonical SSOID01. SSOID0A is presented to an SSO Client, and the SSO Auth Server that issued SSOID01 authenticates the user. When SSOID01 cannot be used, the user can present SSOID0A to the SSO Client, even though SSOID0A binds to another canonical SSOID.

### 4.3. Multiple SSOID Method

The Multiple SSOID method binds SSOIDs to LocalIDs. Services can be accessed continuously by submitting other SSOIDs when one particular SSOID cannot be used due to an outage. **Figure 7** illustrates the multiple SSOID method. An SSO Client specifies a user by assigning a LocalID, which binds to the user's SSOID. In the figure, SSOID01 and SSOID11, which are issued from different SSO Auth Servers, both bind to LocalID LIDAA. Therefore, the SSO Client can treat different SSOIDs as the same user. Moreover, this does not require any changes in the SSO Auth Server; it is possible to use any SSOID, issued by any SSO Auth Server.

Users should perform a similar procedure with all SSO Clients. In **Figure 7**, a user with SSOID01 uses SSO Clients 1 and 2. SSOID11 was not added to SSO Client 2, although the user added SSOID11 to SSO Client 1. Therefore, another LocalID, such as LIDEE, is assigned when the user accesses SSO Client 2 with SSOID11, and

SSO Client 2 identifies the user as LIDEE. Thus, this method impairs the convenience of SSO.

### 4.4. Different SSO Combination Method

The Different SSO combination method binds multiple SSO methods to LocalIDs, and is an expansion of the Multiple SSOID method. In this method, users can login via any SSO method that binds to a LocalID.

Protocol translation is another approach. For example, Project Concordia aimed to permit interconnection by translating Security Assertion Markup Language (SAML) and OpenID protocols. In this approach, interconnection can be achieved between an OpenID server and an SAML client, or between an SAML server and an OpenID client. However, as the translation server becomes a single point of weakness, this does not solve the issue of SSO.

## 5. SSOID Migration Method

We propose the SSOID Migration method to allow an SSOID to be migrated or transferred to another SSOID Auth Server by a pre-arranged mutual agreement between SSO Auth Servers. **Figure 8** illustrates the SSOID Migration method. In the figure, SSO Auth Server A is the migration source; SSO Auth Server B is the migration destination.

Our method uses the Multiple SSO Auth Server and Redundant SSO Auth Server methods. In the Redundant SSO Auth Server method, it is necessary to transfer user credentials, which is problematic. Our method binds both SSOID1 and SSOID2, which are issued by SSO Auth

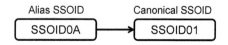

**Figure 6. Alias SSOID.**

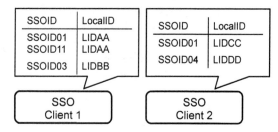

**Figure 7. Multiple SSOID.**

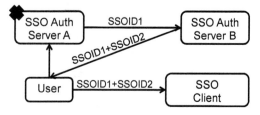

**Figure 8. SSOID migration.**

Server A and SSO Auth Server B, respectively.

## 5.1. Migration Phase

We consider the case of binding SSOID1 to SSOID2. SSO Auth Server B, being a different entity than SSO Auth Server A, cannot authenticate a user who presents SSOID1.

At first, the user logs in to SSO Auth Server B. Next, the user logs in to and accesses SSO Auth Server A from SSO Auth Server B as a SSO Client, and prepares to migrate. SSO Auth Server A binds SSOID1, which is issued by itself, to SSOID2, issued by SSO Auth Server B. The additional information transmitted during this binding process includes:

* information showing that both SSOID1 and SSOID2 are bound;
* information showing that SSO Auth Server A permits this binding in agreement with the user;
* information showing that the additional data has not been modified.

SSO Auth Server A redirects the user to SSO Auth Server B with SSOID2 and SSOID1, as well as the additional information specified above. Finally, SSO Auth Server B binds SSOID1 and SSOID2, and stores SSOID1 and the additional information. The migration phase is now complete.

## 5.2. Continuance Phase

When SSO Auth Server A is unavailable, the user logs in to SSO Auth Server B. SSO Auth Server B redirects the user to SSO Clients with SSOID2, the migrated SSOID1, and the additional information. The SSO Client verifies the additional information and confirms that SSOID1 and SSOID2 are bound. As a result, the SSO Client can assign the same LocalID to both SSOID1 and SSOID2. Henceforth, the user can access services continuously in the SSO Client via SSOID2.

## 5.3. Summary

Our method uses multiple SSO Auth Servers, and requires users to follow a predetermined procedure for identity continuance. Our method makes it possible to transfer an SSOID to other SSO Auth Servers alongside additional information, which is used to identify the owner of SSOID1 and SSOID2 to SSO Clients. Therefore, our method of SSOID migration can achieve the requirements of SSO in any circumstances.

However, our method does have some shortcomings. SSO Clients cannot verify whether the binding is still valid, even if both SSOID1 and SSOID2 are confirmed as bound by the additional information. To solve this, we can include a validity period as part of the additional

information, although we cannot check the revocation time, meaning that additional information is still alive at the end of the validity period.

A second issue concerns the frequency with which the additional information is updated. The user should lie between SSO Auth Servers A and B during the update, because the exchange of additional information requires the user's agreement. As a solution, we propose to use an authorization protocol, such as OAuth [12].

# 6. Evaluation and Discussion

In this section, we consider the requirements described in Section 1. Furthermore, we discuss the range of influence and feasibility of each of the methods described in Sections 4 and 5. **Table 1** provides a summarized comparison of each method.

## 6.1. Requirement 1: Continuity

In the Redundant SSO Auth Server method, a user can continuously access a service by changing (transparently) from SSO Auth Server A1 to SSO Auth Server A2, and in the Alias SSOID method, users can continuously access a service by changing their canonical SSOID.

In the Multiple SSOID method, a user is authenticated by the LocalID belonging to each SSO Client, rather than the SSOID. Thus, a user can access a service if each SSO Client is operational, even when the SSO Auth Server has stopped; however, SSO cannot be used because the user is authenticated and now identified using a LocalID.

In the Different SSO combination method, a user can continuously access a service using other SSO methods.

In the SSOID Migration method, it is possible to continuously access a service if the SSO Client accepts and verifies the additional information described previously. Otherwise, the SSO Client cannot verify the relationship between SSOID1 and SSOID2, and the user cannot continuously access the given service.

## 6.2. Requirement 2: Security

The Redundant SSO Auth Server method faces a security problem when additional information is transmitted between servers. It is necessary to transmit additional information securely, especially if redundancy is achieved across different domains. Moreover, authentication results

**Table 1. Comparison of identity continuance methods.**

| Methods | Req. 1 | Req. 2 | Req. 3 | Range | Feasibility |
|---|---|---|---|---|---|
| Redundant | good | | good | all | easy to adopt |
| Alias | good | | | all | [6] |
| Multiple | | good | | edrestrict | [13] |
| Combination | | good | | restricted | [14,15] |
| Ours | good | good | good | all | [16] |

may not be reliable when the authentication policy at the destination server is different from that of the source server.

The Alias SSOID method is only secure if a user is revocable. Otherwise, it is possible to masquerade as another user, because the canonical SSOID is easily revocable.

In the Multiple SSOID method, the influence of masquerading as another user is confined to individual SSO Clients. Thus, this method is secure because of its reliance on individual authentication for each SSOID.

In the Different SSO combination method, the overall security level is defined by the lowest of the multiple SSO methods that can be accepted to login. Therefore, security problems will occur when vulnerable SSO methods are accepted, even if other SSO methods have a high level of security.

The SSOID Migration method uses additional information describing the relationship between SSOID1 and SSOID2. If this additional information is modified, a malicious attacker can masquerade as a user; however, the additional information includes modification detection codes. Moreover, this method is secure because of its reliance on individual authentication for each SSOID. Therefore, if a malicious attacker attempted to use SSOID2 fraudulently, the attempt would fail.

## 6.3. Requirement 3: Efficiency

In the Redundant SSO Auth Server method, it is necessary to select the SSO Auth Server to authenticate SSOIDs. This process is performed on the SSO Auth Server side; users and SSO Clients do not require any changes.

In the Alias SSOID method, the user prepares and binds the alias SSOID to a canonical SSOID. Hence, it is necessary for the entity to resolve the alias SSOID. Furthermore, the user must bind alias SSOIDs to other canonical SSOIDs when the canonical SSOID changes.

In the Multiple SSOID and Different SSO combination methods, the SSO Client binds multiple SSOIDs to a LocalID; therefore, no changes are required in the SSO Auth Servers. Users must perform a similar procedure for all SSO Clients; thus, the user procedure is more complex.

In the proposed SSOID Migration method, SSO Clients and users do not require any changes. The SSO Auth Server must manage the bound SSOIDs and the corresponding additional information, presenting such information on demand; however, the SSOID Migration method is more usable than the Multiple SSOID method, because many SSO Clients exist.

## 6.4. Range of Influence and Effect

In this section, we discuss the range of influence by applying identity continuance solutions, and this evaluation

indicates user experience.

Using the Redundant SSO Auth Server method, the Alias SSOID method, or the SSOID Migration method ensures that the effect reaches all SSO Clients. In the Redundant and Alias methods, the influence extends to all SSO Clients after acquiring an authenticated SSOID. In the SSOID Migration method, the influence does not extend from the SSO Client, which is presented with additional information and an authenticated SSOID.

Conversely, the influence and effect of the Multiple SSOID method and the Different SSO combination method only reaches SSO Clients handled by the user. Of course, influence and effect are not exerted on other SSO Clients at all. Hence, the influence and effect of the Multiple SSOID method has a restricted range, whereas the other methods have a wide range.

## 6.5. Feasibility

In this section, we discuss the feasibility of each of the four methods, as well as the problems that may occur in their operation. Moreover, we refer to examples of actual use.

The Redundant SSO Auth Server method is easy to adopt. However, it is necessary to select an SSO Auth Server that authenticates any unauthenticated SSOIDs, as described in Section 6.3. Thus, a higher-layer entity (e.g., SSO Auth Server A in **Figure 5**) is needed to implement this method.

An example implementation of the Alias SSOID method is the HTML-based Discovery method of OpenID 2.0 [6]. This method discovers the claimed identifier by showing the OP endpoint URL as a LINK element within the HEAD of an HTML document. HTML-based Discovery is a working example of the Alias SSOID method, if we assume the URL of the HTML document to be an alias and the OP endpoint URL to be canonical.

Similarly, SourceForge [13] is an actual example of the Multiple SSOID method in OpenID. SourceForge supports login with any OpenID that has been registered beforehand.

ATND [14] is a concrete example of the Different SSO combination method. ATND can bind two SSO authentication methods, Twitter OAuth authentication and OpenID authentication. As a result, users can access services from either SSO authentication with one account. Another example is that of Stack Overflow [15], which supports Facebook OAuth authentication and OpenID authentication.

Reference [16] provides an example of the SSOID Migration method in OpenID. This method helps users who utilize other SSO Auth Servers. It is thought that SSO Auth Servers are passive with respect to cooperation in the identity continuance of others, because it is beneficial for them to issue a lot of identifiers. Hence, an SSO Auth Server will see a chance to acquire new users when another server is unavailable. For this reason, it is difficult to achieve a system that incorporates our proposed method, even though it is suitable from a user aspect.

## 7. Conclusions

In this paper, we presented four methods for SSO continuance in the event that the authentication server was not available. We then proposed an identity continuance method based on an identifier migration approach. For each method, we discussed the continuity, security, efficiency, range of influence, and feasibility. Our proposed method has advantages over the four conventional methods from the viewpoint of identity continuance requirements. However, our method also has some shortcomings. To address these issues, we propose the use of an authorization protocol, such as OAuth, for achieving updates without user agreements.

In future work, we will study cloud identity management. This will increase in importance with the popularization of cloud technologies, and the SSO concept will spread widely. We expect to develop a trouble-resistant, non-stop SSO system.

## REFERENCES

[1]    A. Josang and S. Pope, "User Centric Identity Management," *Proceedings of AusCERT Asia Pacific Information Technology Security Conference: R&D Stream*, Gold Coast, 22-26 May 2005, pp. 77-89.

[2]    J. Goode, "The Importance of Identity Security," *Computer Fraud & Security*, Vol. 2012, No. 1, 2012, pp. 5-7.

[3]    Y. Cao and L. Yang, "A Survey of Identity Management Technology," 2010 *IEEE International Conference on Information Theory and Information Security*, Beijing, 17-19 December 2010, pp. 287-293.

[4]    D. Smith, "The Challenge of Federated Identity Management," *Network Security*, Vol. 2008, No. 4, 2008, pp. 7-9.

[5]    D. Recordon and D. Reed, "OpenID 2.0: A Platform for User-Centric Identity Management," *Proceedings of the 2nd ACM Workshop on Digital Identity Management* (*DIM'*06), Alexandria, 30 October-3 November 2006, pp. 11-16.

[6]    "OpenID Authentication 2.0," 2007. http://openid.net/specs/openid-authentication-2_0.html

[7]    "Liberty Alliance Project." http://www.projectliberty.org/

[8]    "Shibboleth." http://shibboleth.internet2.edu/

[9]    T. Miyata, Y. Koga, P. Madsen, S. Adachi, Y. Tsuchiya, Y. Sakamoto and K. Takahashi, "A Survey on Identity Management Protocols and Standards," *IEICE Transactions on Information and Systems*, Vol. E89-D, No. 1, 2006, pp. 112-123.

[10]   T. El Maliki and J.-M. Seigneur, "A Survey of User-Centric Identity Management Technologies," *International Conference on Emerging Security Information, Systems, and Technologies*, Valencia, 14-20 October 2007, pp. 12-17.

[11]   D. Nobayashi, Y. Nakamura, T. Ikenaga and Y. Hori, "Development of Single Sign-On System with Hardware Token and Key Management Server," *IEICE Transactions on Information and Systems*, Vol. E92-D, No. 5, 2009, pp. 826-835.

[12]   E. Hammer-Lahav, "The OAuth 1.0 Protocol," *RFC*5849, 2010.

[13]   "SourceForge." http://sourceforge.net/

[14]   "ATND." http://atnd.org/

[15]   "Stack Overflow." http://stackoverflow.com/

[16]   K. Maeda, Y. Kakizaki and K. Iwamura, "Identifier Migration in OpenID," *Proceedings of the Fifth International Conference on Innovative Mobile and Internet Services in Ubiquitous Computing* (*IMIS*-2011), Seoul, 30 June-2 July 2011, pp. 612-617.

[17]   Y. Kakizaki, K. Maeda and K. Iwamura, "Identity Continuance in Single Sign-On with Authentication Server Failure," *Proceedings of the 5th International Conference on Innovative Mobile and Internet Services in Ubiquitous Computing* (*IMIS*-2011), Seoul, 30 June-2 July 2011, pp. 597-602.

# 14

# MAMNID: A Load Balance Network Diagnosis Model Based on Mobile Agents

**Thomas Djotio Ndié[1], Claude Tangha[2], Guy Bertrand Fopak[1]**
[1]Lirima/Masecness, University of Yaounde 1, Yaounde, Cameroon
[2]Lirima/Aloco, University of Yaounde 1, Yaounde, Cameroon

## ABSTRACT

In this paper, we propose MAMNID, a mobile agent-based model for networks incidents diagnosis. It is a load-balance and resistance to attack model, based on mobile agents to mitigate the weaknesses of centralized systems like that proposed by Mohamed Eid which consists in gathering data to diagnose from their collecting point and sending them back to the main station for analysis. The attack of the main station stops the system and the increase of the amount of information can equally be at the origin of bottlenecks or DDoS in the network. Our model is composed of $m$ diagnostiquors, $n$ sniffers and a multi-agent system (MAS) of diagnosis management of which the manager is elected in a cluster. It has enabled us not only to reduce the response time and the global system load by $1/m$, but also make the system more tolerant to attacks targeting the diagnosis system.

**Keywords:** Diagnosis; Incident; Intrusion; MAMNID; MAS

## 1. Introduction

The popularization of new strategies of systems attacks mobilizes more researchers for the development of adequate defense strategies. That is how we assist today to an explosion of incident diagnosis methods in computer systems generally group into two main classes [1,2]: the behavioral-based approach and the scenario-based approach. Among these methods, others are based on mobile agents. The first is based on the research of known intrusion signature in audit data trail. The second hypotheses that normal activity of the system can be modeled after its observation during a sufficient period of time or according to the instructions of the adopted security policy, and that computer attacks generate abnormal activities that are different from known normal activities. These methods give satisfaction but the increasingly high volume of information, as well as unceasingly crescent network bandwidth puts in badly these last which cannot any more give efficient result at relatively reasonable time. These reports resulted in thinking that a good organization of data to be diagnosed could reduce this time.

Mohamad Eid proposed a mobile agents-based distributed diagnosis model [3]. It consists in deploying the diagnosis system in a central point of the network. This model integrates a manager agent whose role is to create mobiles agents which are going to collect data at the local level (a network node where a sniffer captures network traffic) and send them to a central point for diagnosis purpose. By analyzing this model, we wonder about the availability and response time of the central diagnosis system. Indeed, if the central system is attacked, the whole system disappears. Moreover, the increase of the number of sniffers considerably augments the load of the system and therefore its response time. That can lead to two problems: the scalability and the denial of service (DoS). Considering the importance of diagnosis system in the information availability, integrity and confidentiality, we are interested in the implementation of a network size and bandwidth independent, highly available and fast diagnosis system. Our aim in this paper is to present a load-balance diagnosis model based on mobile agents which consists of several diagnostiquors and a balance manager elected in a cluster.

The rest of the paper is structured in 4 sections. In Section 2 we make a brief overview of related agent-based works in incident/intrusion diagnosis systems. Section 3 is dedicated to the presentation of our load-balance diagnostic model based on mobile agents. The analysis of our model is presented in Section 4 by focusing on its advantages compared to the one proposed by Mohamad Eid in [3]. Before concluding, we proposed in Section 5 a prototype built using Snort open source IDS and JADE (Java Agent Development Framework), to show the operational of our model.

## 2. Related Works in Network Diagnosis

The term diagnosis can be defined as a process of data-gathering in order to build, rebuild, discover, prove or understand a fact or information. In the network area, this term is strongly associated to detection and prevention terms. We will particularly focus on the detection aspect and especially we will address the diagnosis in intrusion detection system (IDS). Several diagnosis methods are integrated in IDSs. We start this section by firstly presenting a brief review on diagnosis methods. We will then state a point on network intrusions diagnosis in distributed systems. We will finally present diagnosis techniques based on multi-agent systems (MAS) and distributed systems.

### 2.1. Intrusion Diagnosis Methods

There are two main approaches of intrusions diagnosis: scenario-based and behavioral-based [1,2,4]. The first is focused on the search for already-known intrusion signature in audit data. A scenario indicates detailed description of actions and elementary steps constituting an intrusion. A signature indicates all concrete traces left by the attack during its execution. The main drawback of this diagnosis approach is its inability to detect new intrusions. To challenge this drawback, the behavioral approach proposes an alternative based on the modeling of the normal activity and any deviation will be interpreted during the diagnosis process like a possible intrusion. This approach hypotheses that the normal activity of a system can be modeled after its observation during a sufficient period of time or following instructions of the adopted security policy.

Finally, the diagnosis principle is based either on the research of anomalies and/or abnormal activities in comparison with known models of activities, or on the research of signatures of known intrusions. Another idea consists in making a coupling of both methods to have a hybrid method which benefits from advantages of both approaches. Besides, the introduction of agents in diagnosis systems can make us profit from their properties. We briefly introduce agent concepts in the following paragraph.

### 2.2. MAS, Distributed Systems and Diagnosis of Network Intrusions

#### 2.2.1. Agents and Multi-Agents Systems (MAS)
The MAS concept proposes an answer framework to applications and objects distribution in order to satisfy users while it guarantees more autonomy and initiative in different software modules. There is no consensus yet, as for the definition of the word "agent"; nevertheless, we retain here that it is an autonomous, real or abstract entity, that is able to act on itself and on its environment which, in a multi-agents universe, can communicate with other agents, and behavior of which is the consequence of its observations, knowledge and its interactions with other agents [5]. An agent is characterized by its goals and means of reaching them, it is rational, cooperative and adaptive. A mobile agent is an agent which can move through a heterogeneous network under its own control [6]. A MAS is a set of agents interacting according to cooperation, competition and/or coexistence modes. It is generally characterized by the total absence of system control, of data decentralization, asynchronous calculation and possession by each agent of a local knowledge of the environment with limited capacity of problem solving [7-9].

#### 2.2.2. Distributed Systems and Peer-to-Peer Systems
A distributed information system is a collection of autonomous stations or calculators interconnected by means of communication network. Each host executes components, for example sequences of calculations, resulting from the splitting of a global calculation project. It uses a middleware which deals with activating components and coordinating their activities so that a user perceives the system like a single integrated system [10]. The consequence to distribute tasks on network computers increases the available resources. Thus, incidents diagnosis system must necessary be distributed to efficiently and pertinently succeed in diagnosing the great amount of network information and to resist faults. This motivated us to propose a distributed architecture-oriented model.

The characteristics of distributed systems are the following: transparency, interoperability management, scalability, faults, heterogeneity and security management. The Amdhal and Gustafson law is a function which determines the gain in terms of speed which will bring the parallelization of a calculation or more generally of an activity according to the number of nodes used or involved. In the expression of acceleration hereafter, $f$ represents the fraction in percentage of the task which must be sequentially executed. The smaller is this fraction, the more the addition of a node will increase the execution speed. This law is written as follows [11].

$$\text{Acceleration } (N) = \text{time with 1 processor/time with } N$$
$$\text{processors} = N/\left(1+\left(N-1\right)*f\right)$$

Unfortunately, the increase of the speed is not linear. At the level of a critical point, the addition of a node will instead marginally increase the execution speed. After the critical point, it is not beneficial to add nodes. We thus see all the importance of the distributivity of a network diagnosis system. Moreover, for the high availability of the system, we found it better to make groups of equivalent nodes: peer-to-peer (P2P). A P2P network is a network composed of group of entities in which each can play indifferently the role of client and/or of server. P2P networks are a type of distributed systems, and one distinguishes pure P2P networks, hybrid P2P networks and those based on structured virtual networks [3].

The P2P helps in file-sharing, using various algorithmic techniques for file access (the first problem is to find the file), and equally applying on the same file techniques of equal share (to ensure the files persistence in time and a fast and reliable download). However, the P2P is not only for file-sharing, it also has many other applications. To quote only some of them: 1) The sharing of computing power and memory capacity; 2) Instant messaging and IP telephony software; 3) Mailing lists with persistent research mechanisms. In this paper, we use the P2P in our load-balance diagnosis principle among IDS instances to increase fault-tolerance. In the next subsection, we will explore aspects which twin distributed systems, MAS in networks incidents diagnosis.

## 2.3. Agent-Based IDS and Agent-Based Distributed IDS: Our Positioning

Historically, the network intrusions diagnosis dated from 1980 and developed with intrusions detection model presented by Denning [12]. Until there, diagnosis systems are centralized. One station installed at a strategic point of the network reads and analyzes systems logs, what gives the possibility to an attacker to destabilize the station and to reach the network with complete freedom. It is to correct this defect that was born distributed systems of diagnosis. In the majority of these systems, agents and especially mobile agents play a central role [3]. For this reason, we have Karima Boudaoud works on the design of MAS-based IDS for fast and effective intrusions diagnosis [13]. The principle in her work is based on a coordinating agent that interacts with the administrator who specifies attacks schemas to be detected and distributes them to deployed agents that are intended to supervise each network area (set of equipments). Each local agent analyzes the traffic and filters attacks according to these schemas and informs the coordinator.

Jean-Marc Percher and Bernard Jouga in [14] proposed a security architecture for ad hoc networks. In this architecture, each node (computer, PDA...) is equipped with a local IDS (which detects by analysis of MIB information) and autonomous mobile agents are implemented, if necessary, to collect information (by SNMP agents) stored on other nodes, proposes an architecture for the diagnosis of distributed intrusions based on MAS. This system consists in collecting data coming from each host to diagnose, this last being in fact a combination of a host-based IDS (HIDS) and a network-based IDS (NIDS).

The problems raised by this architecture can be: network extensibility, performance, security and the administration interface. Moreover, the possibility of automatically adding and withdrawing agents in the system gives a new form of attack which can consist in automatically injecting a hacker agent in the system. Fopak in [4] presents a completely distributed system where the collected data are locally diagnosed without referring to a central management system. Mohammad Eid [3] proposes a distributed diagnosis system based on agents mobile. Its system, intended to detect internal as well as external attacks, is based on the following principle: distant sniffers are controlled via a mobile agent created and controlled by a central station responsible at the same time to diagnose the data gathered by mobile agents and coming from distributed probes. Its prototyping consists in deploying Snort on the central machine to diagnose data from distributed probes and gathered by the mobile agents.

We presented in this section some concepts relating to the construction of our model. Distributed systems are going to enable us to distribute IDS instances and components of our system in the network. Agents constitute the base of our system. P2P systems will be used to ensure the evolution of managers in a cluster in order to guarantee the system availability. After a rapid panorama of agents-based IDS, we saw that the concern of diagnosing all data in the network in spite of their response time led to agents-based distributed models. Mohammad Eid [3] thus proposed a system coordinated by a central agent with the responsibility of diagnosing network data gathered by distributed probes and transported towards this central agent by mobile agents. This system solves the problem of full network data diagnosis while revealing certain concerns namely: 1) The availability. Indeed, if the central agent breaks down, the entire supervised sub network becomes again vulnerable; 2) The whole network data overloads the IDS and increases its response time. In the optics of staging these problems, we propose a mobile agents-based model which consists in deploying several diagnostiquors (in relation to network size), several probes and at any moment, an elected manager undertakes the diagnosis load balance between different available diagnostiquors. The following section presents this model in detail.

## 3. MAMNID: Mobile Agent Based Model for Network Incident Diagnosis

Here we present our load balance network diagnosis model based on mobile agents which overcomes overload and response time problems that currently face diagnosis systems in a distributed context. Our distributed mobile agents-based diagnosis model is consisted of diagnosis units (IDS), of data-gathering units (sniffers) and a MAS for data transfer towards diagnostiquors (sensors).

## 3.1. Model Elements

### 3.1.1. Diagnosis Unit (DU)
In our model, a diagnosis unit diagnoses the flow of data in the network. This diagnosis consists in data analysis coming from sniffers to look for attacks signatures. In case of detection, all diagnostiquors log intrusions traces in the same database in order to facilitate the administration task. Let us mention that the system can have several diagnostiquors according to the network size and bandwidth, and of a desired response time. The DU will be for us an instance of IDS.

### 3.1.2. Data-Gathering Unit (DGU)
A data-gathering unit (DGU) is mainly made up of a sniffer whose role is to collect the traffic at its installed point to send it to the diagnosis manager (an agent) which cares of redirecting the data gathered towards the most available diagnostiquor that we will thereafter qualify. This action is ensured by a mobile agent. As for DUs, the system can have several sniffers according to the network size.

### 3.1.3. A Multiagent System for Data Transfer (MAS-DT)
A MAS is consisted of a the MAS platform and agents in the following manner:
- Each participating station to the system hosts an agent platform. They are machines equipped with sniffers, diagnostiquors and machines hosting manager agents;
- Each machine hosting a sniffer has a sniffer agent to create a mobile agent for each data unit;
- The traffic manager has of a redirection agent of a mobile agent and an election agent of the manager. Let us recall that for needs for the manager security, a set of eligible agents for this role (manager) existing in a cluster;
- Each machine equipped with a DU has a diagnostiquor agent which gets, kills the mobile agent, and transfers received data to the UD in this case Snort IDS.

## 3.2. Genaral Architecture of the Model

This diagram (**Figure 1**) shows how the information circulating in the network is collected and introduced into the model thanks to the sniffer (a) and how results are logged if positive match (e). The diagram equally shows how the sniffer send data to be analyzed to load balance SMA (b) and how the SMA passes data to IDS (c). The MAS is mainly made up of four agents (sniffer agent, manager agent, diagnostiquor agent and mobile agent) that are going to be described more in detail in the fol-

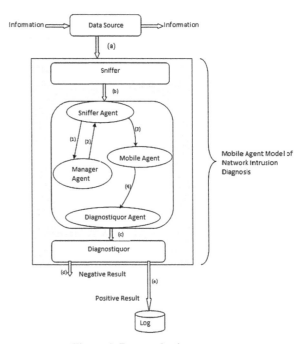

**Figure 1. Data gathering process.**

lowing sections.

### 3.2.1. Description Model Agents
Here we describe agents of our MAS.
- Sniffer agent: this agent is in charge of requesting the load-balancer agent to get parameters of the most available diagnostiquor agent. It has a queue of data units to diagnose. After the reception of parameters of the most available diagnostiquor agent, it creates a mobile agent to convey the data unit. Characteristics of the sniffer agent are the following: its state (parameter for requesting the load-balancer (IP, DNS…), a queue of data units.); its behavior (to transform the data flow sent by the sniffer into data units, to receive parameters of load-balancer agent, to request load-balancer agent for parameters of the diagnostiquor agent, to create mobile agents, to launch the mobile agent);
- Note: here we define the data unit as a complete information bloc for a diagnostiquor (an instance of IDS);
- Mobile agent: this agent's role is to transport a data unit to the most available diagnostiquor. It has the data unit ontology in its state and in its behavior; it has the possibility of initiating communication with the diagnostiquor agent to transfer to him the data unit it carries;
- Load-balancer agent: this agent is in charge of diagnosis load balancing. Its characteristics include 1) Its state constituted of its parameters (IP, DNS…), active load balancer parameters (IP…), and balance management queue. It is a queue (of size of diagnos-

tiquors) in which each node contains the number of data units transferred to the diagnostiquor, connection parameters to the diagnostiquor and an indicator bit that indicates if the diagnostiquor is functional or not. It is set to 0 when one sends a data unit to the diagnostiquor and it will later come to set it to 1 when it finished processing the data unit; 2) Its behavior is consisted of the following methods: answering the sniffer request and updating the queue (++number of data unit to transfer), taking part in the load-balancer election, receiving indications about diagnostiquors activities, broadcasting its parameters to sniffers.

- Diagnostiquor agent: its role is to transfer the data unit it receives to an IDS. Its state is consisted of its operation indicator which is a bit it sends to the load-balancer agent 1) and a queue of data units. Its behavior comprises in: transforming a data unit into flow to send to IDS, receiving data unit, sending its activity indicator and to kill mobile agents.

The diagram (**Figure 2**) below shows how: a) a diagnostiquor is managed at one moment by one and only one manager agent whereas a manager can manage several diagnostiquors; b) A sniffer can create several mobile agents and at each creation, an instance of its DU is made; c) An diagnostiquor receives several mobile agents whereas a mobile agent is intended for one and only one diagnostiquor.

Note: here, the diagnostiquor represents the diagnosis unit (Snort in our case) whereas the diagnostiquor agent is in charge of gathering information to diagnose from the system for diagnosis unit. Also, the sniffer (Wireshark for example) captures network information to be diagnosed and send it to the sniffer agent for the diagnosis system (MAS for diagnosis management).

### 3.2.2. Operation of the Model
Here we present the functioning of MAMNID. We will particularly focus on its components and interaction diagram. These components are the following:
- Sniffer: software able to collect or capture network data. In our model, the sniffer agent takes data gathered from this latter and splits them into data unit.

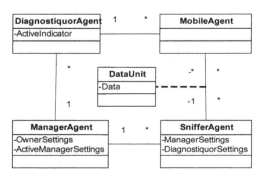

**Figure 2. The MAS AUML diagram.**

- MAS platform: software environment in which an agent can be created and evolve. We will thus use a platform to deploy our different agents.
- Agent: in our model, an agent represents a software entity that will be developed. Each agent will later contributes to the implementation of the diagnosis load balance in our model.
- Database: will help to store attacks traces.

The interaction schema (**Figure 3**) shows how different system components interact together in the model. For the implementation of MAMNID, a participating machine in the model must have as mentioned above following elements: sniffer and MAS platform for agents' evolution for a host which only collects data. On the host able of diagnostic load-balancing, one can have in addition a manager agent (or load-balancer agent) whose role will be described further in the operation section. A host able of data diagnosing will have an IDS.

From the interaction diagram, from bottom upwards, we have a double-direction link (p) which represents exchanges between a station of data collection and the active load-balance station, with aim of having parameters of the most-available diagnostiquor. Links (d) represent information transfers between the data collection host and the host of the most-available diagnostiquor. Links (e) represent exchanges of activity indication between the diagnosis manager and diagnostiquors. Links (l) represent log of attacks in databases in case of detection. The link (a) symbolizes the result analysis. A host may not have a manager; but if it has some, this last can be active or not. In the whole system, only one manager must be active at a time. In addition, a manager or diagnostiquor host may not have a sniffer.

### 3.3. Algorithms Description

We argue in this paragraph how agents of MAMNID operate to balance loads and to ensure the network data diagnosis.

### 3.3.1. Starting of the Manager: The Clustering
In MAMNID, the manager agent has the role of redirecting traffic coming from a sniffer towards the most-available diagnostiquor which we will thereafter qualify. As several hosts can play the manager role, we present here the election principle of the active manager: 1) At the starting of a platform equipped with a manager (agent), this last broadcasts a message to all other managers. If it receives no feedback, it therefore becomes the active manager and it broadcasts its parameters (IP address, domain name...) to all other platforms; 2) If there is one active manager, each manager draws a random latency random $(1,X)$ to the end of which it remakes a broadcasting to test the presence of an active manager. If

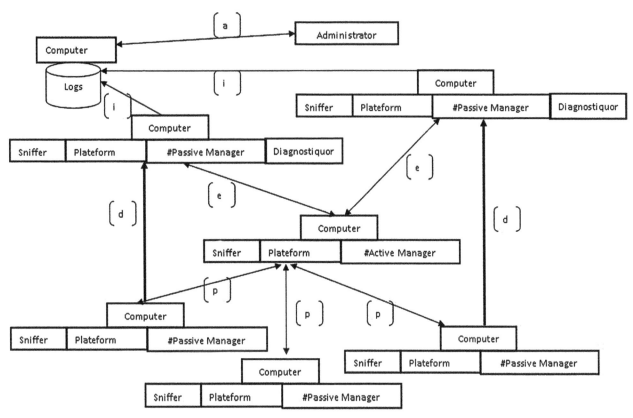

**Figure 3. Interaction diagram of MAMNID.**

once more it receives no answers, it becomes active manager and broadcasts its parameters to all platforms. Let us note here that $X$ is the maximum latency. We signal that these two points constitute the principle of manager election; 3) The manager knowing the parameters of all diagnostiquors redirects in a cyclic way towards the latter, mobile agents carrying data to be analyzed. It results from this that the most-available diagnostiquor is that of the next index in the cycle modulo number of diagnostiquors.

The algorithm of redirection (daemon) is the following: let $m$ be the number of diagnostiquors, we have parameters of these diagnostiquors in a list of $m$ elements.

    While True
      For integer $i$ from 1 to $m$ do
        Receive the request of obtaining parameters of the most available diagnostiquor from a sniffer,
        Send parameters of the diagnostiquor of node $i$ of the list of diagnostiquors,
      EndFor
    EndWhile.

### 3.3.2. Sniffer Agent and Mobile Agent

At the starting of the sniffer agent, it requests the manager for its parameters. For each $\Delta d$ data unit sniffed, each sniffer agent creates a mobile agent which will transport this data unit towards the most-available diagnostiquor

(that of which parameters were received from the manager). During the transport of the information from one host towards the diagnostiquor station, if the mobile agent does not find the diagnostiquor station, it gets back to its origin with the data unit.

### 3.3.3. Diagnostiquor Agent and Diagnosis

At the start-up, each diagnostiquor agent broadcasts its parameters to managers until it receives an acknowledgement. At the reception of a mobile agent, the diagnostiquor agent extracts mobile agent's data, sniffer's parameters and kills the mobile agent. Data are then deposited in the traditional diagnostiquor (IDS) queue; in our case, the Snort queue.

### 3.3.4. Diagnosis Sequence Diagram

To summarize, we show with the following sequence diagram (**Figure 4**), how a data unit $k$ is diagnosed by the diagnostiquor $i\% m$ ($i$ modulo $m$) where $m$ is the number of diagnostiquors, and $i$ the sequential variable of the diagnostiquor's selection.

In this section we presented our mobile agent-based model for networks incidents diagnosis (MAMNID). This model is in the continuation of the one of Mohammad and corrects the overload and the diagnosis delay in this last. In the following section, we will illustrate MAMNID advantages compared to the Mohammad model.

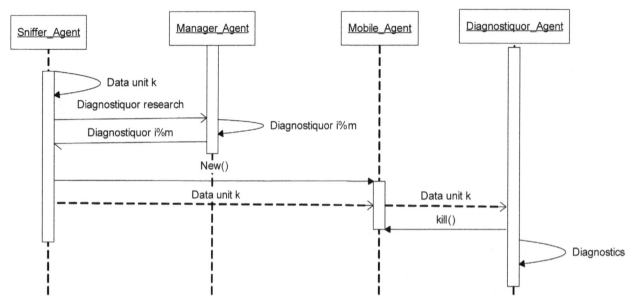

Figure 4. Diagnosis sequence diagram.

## 4. Analysis of MAMNID

It is question in this section of showing the relevance of MAMNID compared to an existing model. Here, we took as reference model, the one of Mohammad Eid. Let us recall that he presents a centric mobile agent model in which mobile agents are created and controlled by a central station at the same time in charge of diagnosing data gathered from remote sniffers and distributed probes. Its prototyping consisted in deploying Snort on the central machine to diagnose data from the distributed probes. For this comparison, we will make a diagnosis time-saver, overload and availability analysis. We will also present the limits of our model.

### 4.1. Diagnostic Time-Saver Analysis

Here we make an analysis in time of our model. If we suppose that the processing time of a data unit in the Mohammad Eid model is $t$, we will have for $t$ probes a processing time of O $(tn)$. In our case we will have for $n$ probes and $m$ diagnostiquors, a processing time of O $(tn/m)$. Thus a time-saver out of O $(tn [1 - 1/m])$. So far, we will equally note that, more $m$ will tend towards $n$, more we will gain in processing time. It also appears that if $n = m$ one obtains an almost constant processing time. Moreover, if we are in a network with high bandwidth, volumes of data to be diagnosed become important. In this case, if we are in a small network with high bandwidth with 1 probe and $m$ diagnostiquors, we obtain a response time of about O $(t/m)$. Let us mention that in this case, each machine plays the role of a diagnostiquor.

We make a theoretical presentation of these time-savers in the summary **Table 1** in which one has on the first line, the number of data units to be diagnosed and on the first column, the number of diagnostiquors in the system. By hypothesizing that a data unit is diagnosed in a unit of time, each box represents the time necessary to diagnose the corresponding number of data units on the first line with the corresponding number of diagnostiquors of the system on the first column.

**Figure 5** graphically highlights the time-saver on the basis of theoretical data contained in **Table 1**. We represent there time variations according to the number of data unit projected on 1, 2, 4, 8, 16 diagnostiquors of our model. Each curve of the graph corresponds to a line of the table.

### 4.2. Overload Analysis

Let us see now what our model brings for the reduction of an IDS load. Indeed, if for 1 diagnostiquor, the workload at one moment $t$ is $k$ data units, we will have a reduction at $k/m$ with $m$ diagnostiquors. This means a reduction of $k (1 - 1/m)$. Once more, we notice that more $m$ tends towards $n$ more this reduction is important. Here are **Tables 2** and **3** of theoretical reduction in the IDS load. In these tables, we suppose that we have $k$ data units at each time unit.

**Table 2** represents the case where $m < k$; *i.e.* the case where the number of diagnostiquor is inferior to the number of data unit at a time unit. **Table 3** presents the case where $m \geq k$.

As consequence, according to obtained results; the number of diagnostiquors must be lower or equal to the round part from the division of network bandwidth by the size of a data unit: $m \leq [D/T]$ where D = network bandwidth of and T = size of a data unit. **Figure 6** represents a pace of load reduction compared to the number of

**Table 1. Reduction of the diagnosis time with the number of diagnostiquors.**

| Data units | | 1 | 2 | 3 | 4 | 5 | | | | n − 1 | N |
|---|---|---|---|---|---|---|---|---|---|---|---|
| | 1 | 1 | 2 | 3 | 4 | 5 | . | . | . | n − 1 | N |
| | 2 | 1/2 | 1 | 3/2 | 2 | 5/2 | | | | (n − 1)/2 | n/2 |
| | 3 | 1/3 | 2/3 | 1 | 2/3 | 5/3 | | | | (n − 1)/3 | n/3 |
| Number of diagnostiquors | . | | | | | | | . | | | |
| | . | | | | | | | . | | | |
| | . | | | | | | . | | | | |
| | m − 1 | 1/(m − 1) | 2/(m − 1) | 3/(m − 1) | 4/(m − 1) | 5/(m − 1) | | | | (n − 1)/(m − 1) | n/(m − 1) |
| | m | 1/m | 2/m | 3/m | 4/m | 5/m | | | | (n − 1)/m | n/m |

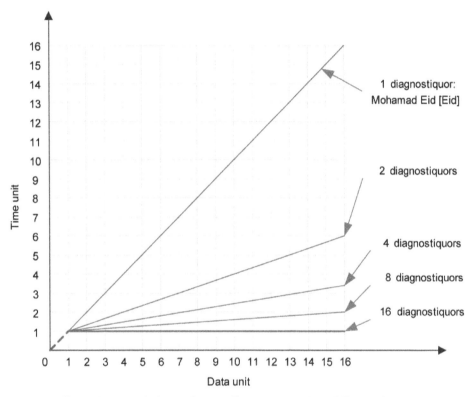

**Figure 5. Time of diagnostic according to the number of diagnostiquors.**

**Table 2. Diminution of the diagnostic load: case where $m < k$.**

| Number of diagnostiquors | 1 | 2 | 3 | 4 | 5 | | $m − 1$ | $m$ |
|---|---|---|---|---|---|---|---|---|
| Diagnosis theorical load | $k$ | $k/2$ | $k/3$ | $k/4$ | $k/5$ | $\cdots$ | $k/m − 1$ | $k/m$ |

**Table 3. Reduction of the diagnosis load: case where $m \geq k$.**

| Number of diagnostiquors | 1 | 2 | | $k − 1$ | $k$ | $k + 1$ | | $m − 1$ | $m$ |
|---|---|---|---|---|---|---|---|---|---|
| Diagnosis theorical load | $k$ | $k/2$ | $\cdots$ | $k/(k − 1)$ | 1 | 1 | $\cdots$ | 1 | 1 |

diagnostiquors at a fixed time T for a load $k = 16$ data units.

Noting the amount of data received by each instance of Snort server (diagnostiquors), we see that this charge decreases that it adds instances of Snort. So, the schema in **Figure 6** represents this decrease when adding the number of snort server instances. Note to fully understand that the dependent ordinate is assessed in the unit of data (more small indivisible, complete and indivisible that can be analyzed). You can see for example that if in one snort instance 16 data unit are analyzed, it will only concern 8 for two diagnostiquors.

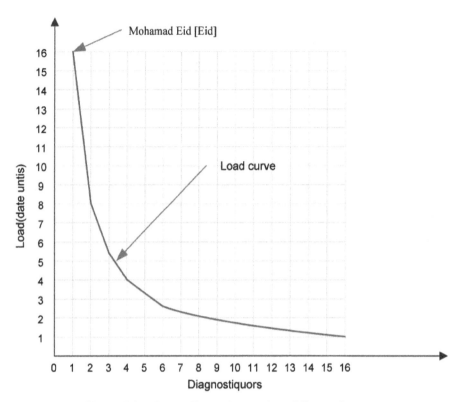

**Figure 6. Load according to the number of diagnostiquors.**

## 4.3. Availability

We can affirm that MAMNID is more available compared with the model proposed by Mohammad. Indeed, contrary to his approach which has one diagnostiquor on a host which is at the same time responsible for the creation and management of mobile agents, we have a system of agents manager which evolve in a cluster and a completly decentralized creation of mobile agents. In fact, it is each data collecting point which creates its mobile agent. It is therefore important to highlight that event in the case of a manager loss; the system remains available because another will be directly elected.

We presented in this section advantages of our model. However, we can note some doubts for borderline cases. Indeed when the number of diagnostiquors is equal to the number of probes, one can note a waste of time of information transfer in the network whereas a host-based diagnostiquor would do the work. Moreover as it is probable that several data units resulting from one source are analyzed by different diagnostiquors, distributed attacks on several data units could escape our system.

## 5. Implementation of MAMNID [6]

We present in this section an implementation of MAN-NID based on Snort IDS and agents from JADE platform. Snort is signatures-based IDS. It has several components that work together for attacks detection. Among these

components, principal ones are the following: packet decoder; preprocessors; detection engine; logging and alerting system, output modules.

## 5.1. Realization of Snort Decoupling Preprocessor

The Snort IDS offers various functions that help to implement a preprocessor. Mainly these functions are: SetUp and Init. To these functions one can add functions which allow to manipulate packets and to possibly carry out preliminary operations to analysis.

### 5.1.1. The SetUp Function

This function is called at a preprocessor's initialization. It helps to record the preprocessor's identifier, because in Snort, any preprocessor has a single identifier which will be setup in the configuration file snort.conf. The following code is an illustration of the SetUp function of our preprocessor: we will call it linkjade. The SetUp function of the file spp_java_agen.c is the following:

```
#include "spp_template.h"
void Setuplink_jade()
{
    RegisterPreprocessor("link_jade", link_JadeInit);
    DebugMessage (DEBUG_PLUGIN," Preprocessor: Template is setup...\n");
}
```

The first line of the program allows including the header file which contains declarations specific to each preprocessor and will be used by Snort as shown in the following example:

```
#ifndef __SPP_LINKJADE_H__
#define __SPP_LINKJADE_H__
void Setuplink_jade ();
#endif  /* __SPP_LINKJADE_H__ */
```

### 5.1.2. The Init Function
It is in this function that one has the possibility of making reference to other functions for data or network packets processing. It is thus thanks to this function that functions specific to a processor will be added to the list of Snort preprocessors.

### 5.1.3. Snort Part Which Feeds the MAS (Snort Client)

Here is C language code of our preprocessor, which will allow sending Snort packets (here playing the snifer role) towards the MAS. This code is shown below:

```
connect(sock, (SOCKADDR *)&sin, sizeof(sin));
  convert 123 to string [buf]
  itoa(num, buf, 50);
 printf("valeur                                  :
%d",(packet->orig_tcp_header)->checksum);
  send(sock, buf, sizeof(), 0);
  send(sock,"Sending of TCP header \r\n",14,0);
  sendValue = htonl(*(packet->pkt_data));
  send(sock, (char const*)&sendValue, sizeof
sendValue, 0);
  send(sock, "\r\n", 2, 0);
 recv(sock, buffer, sizeof(buffer), 0);
 closesocket(sock);
 WSACleanup();
```

### 5.1.4. Snort Part Which Takes MAS Packets for Analysis (Snort Server)
Here is C language code of our preprocessor at the diagnostiquor side, which will allow receiving packets sent by a MAS analyzer. It must then be present on all hosts which will have to receive certain number of packets coming from the MAS.

```
  if ((sock = socket(AF_INET, SOCK_STREAM,
0)) == -1) {
        perror("Socket");
        exit(1);
    }
        if                              (set-
sockopt(sock,SOL_SOCKET,SO_REUSEADDR,&tru
e,sizeof(int)) == -1) {
        perror("Setsockopt");
```

```
    exit(1);
    }
    server_addr.sin_family = AF_INET;
    server_addr.sin_port = htons(5000);
    server_addr.sin_addr.s_addr         =
INADDR_ANY;
    bzero(&(server_addr.sin_zero),8);
    if (bind(sock, (struct sockaddr
*)&server_addr, sizeof(struct sockaddr))
                == -1) {
        perror("Unable to bind");
        exit(1);
    }

    if (listen(sock, 5) == -1) {
        perror("Listen");
        exit(1);
    }
    printf("\nTCPServer Waiting for client on
port 5000");
    fflush(stdout);
    while(1)
    {
        sin_size = sizeof(struct sockaddr_in);
        connected = accept(sock, (struct
sockaddr *)&client_addr,&sin_size);
        printf("\n I got a connection from
(%s ,%d)",inet_ntoa(client_addr.sin_addr),ntohs(client
_addr.sin_port));
        bytes_recieved             =
recv(connected,recv_data,1024,0);
        recv_data[bytes_recieved] = '\0';
        if (strcmp(recv_data , "q") == 0 ||
strcmp(recv_data , "Q") == 0)
        {
            close(connected);
            break;
        }
        else
        printf("\n RECIEVED DATA = %s
\n" , recv_data);
        fflush(stdout);
        break;
    }
    close(sock);
```

## 5.2. Realization of the MAS

The MAS of our application includes three resident agents (the Sniffer agent, the Manager agent, and the Analyzor agent) and a mobile agent.

### 5.2.1. The Sniffer Agent
This agent directly communicates with JADE platform,

for which it has a socket for listening Snort client in charge of sending packets. The implementation of this package is done using SnifferAgent, SnifferBehaviour and SnifferFrame UML classes as shown in the diagram (**Figure 7**):

As we can note on the diagram (**Figure 7**), the Sniffer agent has a cyclic behavior; thus the agent execution does not end. At the reception of an address sent by the manager agent, it creates a mobile agent which will be given the responsibility to transport the packet towards an analyzer.

### 5.2.2. The Manager Agent
The Manager agent (**Figure 8**) is in charge of indicating to the agent towards which network host it must send the packet so that it is analyzed. For that, at the reception of the packet, it sends a message to the Manager agent which in its turn will answer.

### 5.2.3. The Analyzor Agent
It is the Analyzor agent which is going to undertake the packet analysis and to redirect it towards a host in waiting of the packet. For that it has a client which is going to be connected to the Snort server in waiting of a packet. The following AUML diagram (**Figure 9**) is obtained:

### 5.3. Compilation and Launching of MAMNID

MAMNID is implemented in NETBEANS 6.7 IDE, while the snort source code is modified with the Microsoft Visual C++ 6 IDE.

### 5.3.1. Snort Configuration
We start by installing Snort and Winpcap for Windows (**Figure 10**). After the modification (addition of our pre-processor) and compilation of the Snort sources, we obtain a set of DLL generated in the Snort's folder lib\ snort_dynamicpreprocessor. We copy and paste our pre-processor's DLL in the Snort's DLLs folder. In the Snort configuration file, in the "configure dynamic loaded library" section; we indicate the path of the DLL there containing our preprocessor of connection to the MAS. Finally, Snort is launched.

### 5.3.2. MAS Launching and Visualization
While launching our MAS, we start MAMNID. We can indeed see the supervision interfaces: **Figure 11** for managing the supervisor and **Figure 12** for snifer agent. The supervision of Analyser agent is similar.

### 5.3.3. Results Analysis
The principle is the following. On the client machine we install the Snort client with winPcap to read and sniff the network. We also install jade and the client part of our MAS. On the server machine, are installed: Snort server, JADE and the server part of our MAS. At the start of the 4 modules (snort client and server, MAS client and server), each instance will operate on the port 1099 as long as it runs. Thus, WinPcap from the client machine that is strongly coupled to Snort client will capture traffic and file on port 1099. The MAS_Client will read this port to put the paquet in the MAS. The latter will do the work of redirection to find the most available MAS_Server.

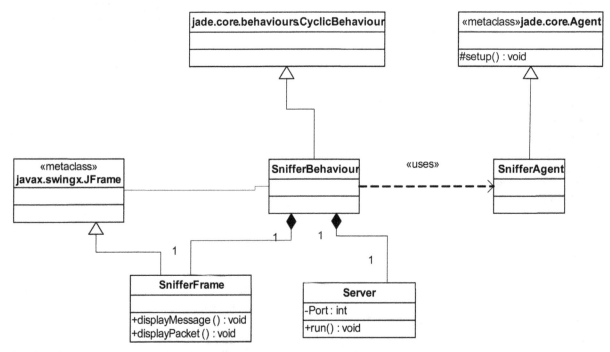

**Figure 7. Diagram of Sniffer agent.**

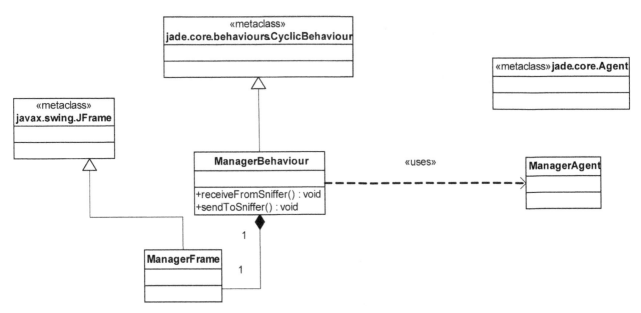

**Figure 8. Diagram of Manager agent.**

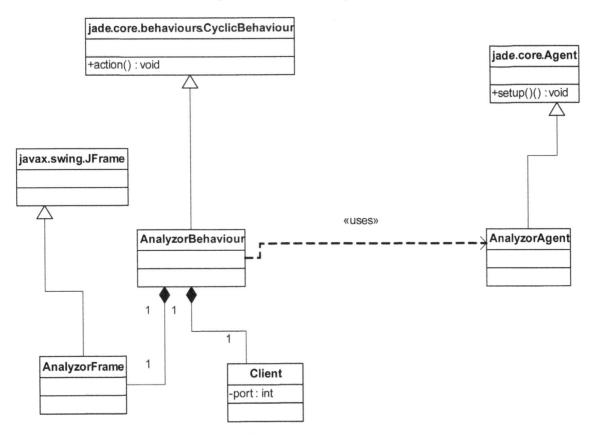

**Figure 9. Diagram of the Analyzor agent.**

The latter will therefore retrieve packet and position it on port 1099 of the machine. The Snort server listening on this port retrieves it to analyze. Note that the part value is customizable; its default value is 5000.

After start of snort (**Figure 10**), one stops on screens that inform us about the status of snort client and server and indicate on which port they are listening (**Figures 11** and **12**). The representation of the MAS sequences in JADE (**Figure 13**) translates the background communication activity that takes place between the client and the server. It is noted that the final server behavior will depend on its configuration file *i.e.*, log data for detection

Figure 10. Starting of Snort.

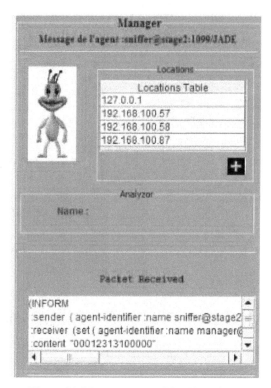

Figure 11. Manager supervision' interface.

Figure 12. Snifer agent supervision interface.

in a file or in a database.

## 6. Conclusions and Perspectives

The aim of our paper was to propose a mobile agent model for network intrusions diagnosis (MAMNID). After a literature review, we saw that the concern of diagnosing all the data of the network in spite of the response time of IDS led to the distributed models. Mohammad Eid proposed a system coordinated by a central agent which undertakes the responsibility of diagnosing network data gathered by distributed probes and relayed to this last by mobile agents. The limits of this system led us to propose a more profitable model in terms of response time, load and availability of the diagnostiquor. Proofs of time-savings, better availability and better overload manage-

ment were illustrated compared to the Mohamed's model considered in our context as reference model.

As future works, we have the resolution of data transfer problem of information if the case where the number of diagnostiquors is equal to the number of probes by the

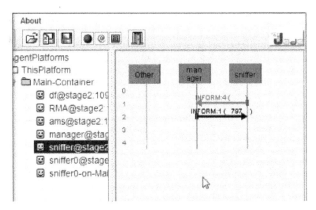

**Figure 13. MAS sequences in JADE.**

addition of another behavior to the manager and sniffer which would enable them to stop any transfer as soon as the number of diagnostiquors is equal to the number of probes.

# REFERENCES

[1] W. Lee and S. Stolfo, "A Framework for Constructing Features and Models for Intrusion Detection Systems," *ACM Transactions on Information and Systems Security*, Vol. 3, No. 4, 2000, pp. 227-261.

[2] K. Tabia, "Graphical Models and Behavioral Approaches for Intrusions' Detection," Ph.D. Thesis, University of Artois, Arras, 2008.

[3] M. Eid, "A New Mobile Agent-Based Intrusion Detection System Using Distributed Sensors," American University of Beirut, Department of Electrical and Computer Engineering, Washington DC, 2004.

[4] G. B. Fopak, "MAMDIR: A Mobile Agent Model of Network Incidents Diagnosis," Master 2 of Research Thesis, National Advanced of Engineering, Unviersity of Yaoundé 1, Yaounde, 2011.

[5] J. Ferber, "Multi-Agent Systems. An Introduction to Distributed Artificial Intelligence," Addison Wesley, Boston, 1999.

[6] M. Tchikou, "A Multiagents Design Environment for the Piloting of Production Systems," Master's Thesis, University of Pau and Pays de l'Adour, France, 2004.

[7] G. Picard, "Development Methodology of Adaptative Multi-Agents Systems and Design of Software with Emerging Functionalities," Ph.D. Thesis, University Paul Sabatier of Toulouse III., France, 2004.

[8] J. B. Voron, "Automatic and et Particularized Construction of Intrusion Detection Systems for Parallel Systems Based on Petri Networks," Ph.D. Thesis, University Pierre et Marie Curie, France, 2009.

[9] S. F. Wu, *et al.*, "JiNao: Design and Implementation of a Scalable Intrusion Detection System for the OSPF Routing Protocol," *IEEE Workshop on Information Assurance and Security*, West Point, June 2001, pp. 91-99.

[10] W. Emmerich, "Engineering Distributed Objets," John Wiley & Sons Ltd., Chichester, 2000.

[11] J. P. Sansonnet, "Parallel Architectures Online Course," 2011. www.limsi.fr/~/enseignementtutoriels/archi/archi.html

[12] D. E. Denning, "An Intrusion-Detection Model," *IEEE Transactions on Software Engineering*, Vol. SE-13, No. 2, 1987, pp. 222-232.

[13] K. Boudaoud, "Networks Security Management: A New Approach by Multi-Agents System," University of de Geniva, Geniva, 2001.

[14] Percher, *et al.*, "Intrusions Detection in Ad Hoc Network," West Higher Ectronic School (ESEO), France, 2004.

# iPhone Security Analysis

**Vaibhav Ranchhoddas Pandya, Mark Stamp**
*Department of Computer Science, San Jose State University, San Jose, USA*

## Abstract

The release of Apple's iPhone was one of the most intensively publicized product releases in the history of mobile devices. While the iPhone wowed users with its exciting design and features, it also angered many for not allowing installation of third party applications and for working exclusively with AT & T wireless services (in the US). Besides the US, iPhone was only sold only in a few other selected countries. Software attacks were developed to overcome both limitations. The development of those attacks and further evaluation revealed several vulnerabilities in iPhone security. In this paper, we examine some of the attacks developed for the iPhone as a way of investigating the iPhone's security structure. We also analyze the security holes that have been discovered and make suggestions for improving iPhone security.

**Keywords:** iPhone, Wireless, Mobile, Smartphone, Jailbreaking, Reverse Engineering

## 1. Introduction

The release of Apple's iPhone on June 29, 2007 was one of the most heavily publicized events in the history of mobile electronics devices. Thousands of people lined up outside Apple stores prior to its release. Approximately three and half million iPhones were sold within the first six months of its release in the U.S. alone [1]. By any measure, the iPhone has been a commercial success—in spite of being a first-timer in the smart phone industry, Apple immediately outpaced traditional cell phone giants like Nokia, Motorola, and LG. The iPhone is an all-in-one package including a cell phone, a digital music and video player, a camera, a digital photo, music, and video library, and more [2]. It has helpful widgets for maps, weather, in addition to email and other Internet capabilities [2].

### 1.1. Features

The iPhone confirms that Apple understands consumers' desires, not only in terms of functionality, but also in terms of appearance and style. While other smart phone companies have offered products that include features offered by the iPhone, none have approached the iPhone in terms of popularity and sales. Phone features include a soft keypad with the ability to easily merge calls and visually obtain voicemail information. Apple took advantage of iPod's popularity by including complete iPod

functionality in the iPhone. A full-functional web browser with zoom in/out functionality made internet surfing experience on a mobile phone better than ever. The Multi-Touch touch screen display allows for gliding and scrolling besides zooming. The accelerometer detects the orientation of the phone. These features put iPhone above and beyond other smartphones such as Blackberry and Motorola Q.

### 1.2. Hardware

The iPhone uses the ARM 1176JZF-S processor, which offers good power management for superior battery life and powerful processing for 3D graphics. Further details regarding this processor are available on the ARM product website [3]. **Figure 1** shows how different functions within the iPhone interface with one another [4]. **Figure 2** shows an image of the board inside an iPhone.

## 2. Motivation

iPhones are supposed to only be used with AT & T wireless service (in the US). AT & T agreed to give a portion of its revenue to Apple per each new contract it signed with iPhone users. This agreement spawned outrage among users of other GSM-based wireless services such as T-Mobile since they could not offer services to iPhone customers. Many people viewed this as an "unfair" move by the two companies. People felt that they should be

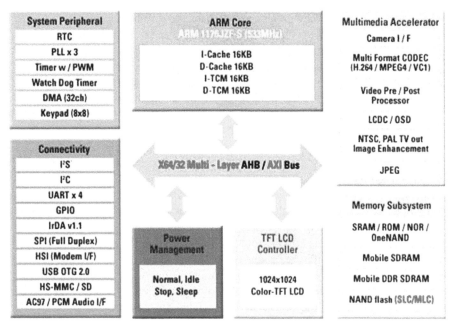

Figure 1. iPhone architecture from a high level [4].

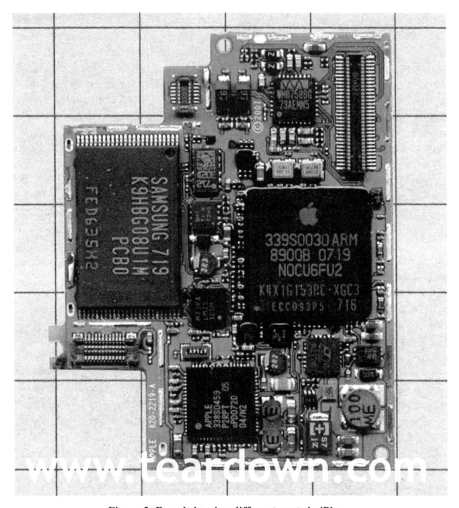

Figure 2. Board showing different parts in iPhone.

able to choose whatever wireless service they prefer and should not be forced to use a particular one.

There was another reason that some iPhone users became irritated. Apple designed iPhone as a closed system that does not allow installation of third-party applications. Users can only access a very small subset of the file system, a "sandbox" where they can add and remove music and other files via iTunes. Users who wanted to install third-party applications such as widgets and games were unable to do so.

These two limitations placed on iPhone users prompted a series of hack and attack efforts by iPhone enthuseasts and hackers. "Jailbreak" is an iPhone hack that permits the addition of third-party applications or gadgets on the iPhone by permitting read/write access to the root file system. Without "jailbreaking" an iPhone, a customer is limited to the factory-installed tools included with it. "Unlock" is an attack on iPhone that allows it to be used with any wireless service offering the GSM standard, not just AT & T. Without "unlocking" an iPhone, one can only use AT&T's wireless services. Perhaps surprisingly, jailbreaking is the more important of the two because it is the first step to unlocking. We look at a jailbreak attack in detail and also discuss different unlocking solutions.

Due to the commercial success of the iPhone, it makes a good candidate for security analysis. Having close to a million iPhones jailbroken and unlocked within first six months of its release, iPhone security obviously has had significant financial implications. In addition, with more millions of users worldwide, any security holes in iPhone can jeopardize the privacy of millions of people. We believe that these issues make the security analysis of iPhone a worthwhile and important topic.

## 3. Jailbreaking

The process of gaining root access to the iPhone so that third party tools can be installed is called Jailbreaking [5]. Without gaining read-write access to the root system, one cannot install third party applications. Note that this limitation prevents users from doing what they want to do with their iPhones—products that they own. This is somewhat analogous to buying a computer and not being allowed to install new programs on it. There are several websites (see, for example, [6]) that provide interesting gadgets and games for iPhone. Some of the most popular games are iSolitaire, iZoo, Tetris, iPhysics, and NOIZ2SA. Beyond providing access to such applications, jailbreaking is essential for another reason: it is the first step in unlocking.

Without jailbreaking, one cannot install the necessary application to use a wireless service other than AT & T.

Close to a million new iPhones were not activated with AT & T in the first six months after its release [1]. Without jailbreaking, these iPhone owners would not be able to use the phone part of the iPhone unless they signed a contract with AT & T after switching from their existing GSM wireless service provider. Even for AT & T customers, jailbreaking is still necessary to enable the addition of third party applications to the iPhone.

### 3.1. Looking for Ideas

Immediately after its release, iPhone enthusiasts and hackers all around the world were looking for a way to gain root access. A feasible solution has to be reasonably easy to use and should not take several hours to complete. Hackers investigated various techniques for meeting these requirements. They evaluated existing hacks for other phones and devices and searched for similar vulnerabilities in the iPhone [7,8].

A previous hacker success was using buffer overflow techniques on the Sony PSP. By exploiting vulnerability in the Tag Image File Format (TIFF) library, libtiff, used for viewing TIFFs, hackers were able to hack PSP to run homebrew games, which was otherwise prohibited [9].

Hackers inspected Apple's MobileSafari web browser to see if it could be targeted for the same vulnerability. It turned out that for firmware version 1.1.1 of the iPhone, MobileSafari uses a vulnerable version of libtiff [10,11]. The exploitable vulnerability in libtiff is documented as entry CVE-2006-3459 in Commom Vulnerabilities and Exposures, a database tracking information security vulnerabilities and exposures [10]. This vulnerability is also documented and tracked in the U.S. National Vulnerability Database [12]. A malicious TIFF file can be created to include the desired rogue code. When attempting to view the malicious tiff file in a vulnerable version of MobileSafari, the vulnerabilities in libtiff are exploited to create a stack buffer overflow, and the malicious code is injected and executed.

### 3.2. Stack Buffer Overflow and Return-To-Libc Attacks

The attack we review, which exploits the libtiff vulnerability, uses a stack buffer overflow to inject code and the "return-to-libc" technique to execute it. To illustrate how a stack buffer overflow can be created and how a return-to-libc attack works, we first consider a generic example.

Consider the piece of code below [13]:
```
void func (char *passedStr) {
        char localStr[4]; // Note that only 4 bytes allocated
```

```
        strcpy(localStr, passedStr); // length of pass-
edStr is not checked
    }
    int main (int argc, char **argv) {
        func(argv[1]);
    }
```

Suppose that we have a program is called myprog. Now, let us look at a simplified representation of the stack when myprog is executed with "hi" as the input parameter—see **Table 1** below.

Now, consider the stack when myprog is executed with the string "goodsecurity."

As it is clear from the tables above(**Table 1, 2**), our program is only capable of handling a string with three characters plus NULL. When a string of more than three characters is passed, the extra characters cause stack buffer overflow and overwrite other sections of the stack [14]. Of course, the function func() should have performed a string length check on passedStr to ensure that it has three characters or fewer before the NULL. Any piece of code that makes a mistake similar to this is potentially vulnerable to a stack buffer overflow [14,15].

Instead of entering "good security," a carefully crafted string could be used. In the example above, suppose we replace "good security" with, say, "good secu\x12\x34\x56\x78." In little-endian, the last 4 bytes are 0x78563412, which might be the address of a function, say, system(). Then when the stack unwinds, instead of execution returning to the calling function, the pre-existing function indicated by the overwrite bytes will be executed—in this case, system(). Moreover, the stack could be overwritten so that desired parameter values are passed to a pre-existing function [16]. Such an attack is generally known as the return-to-libc attack. By discovering the address of such a desirable function, an attacker can potentially exploit a buffer overflow to execute the function and thereby achieve the desired behavior. Furthermore,

**Table 1. Simplified stack representation with proper input.**

| |
|---|
| Parent function's stack |
| Return address (4 bytes) |
| char* passedStr |
| hi\0   (4 bytes allocated for localStr. so String up to 3 characters is a good input) |

**Table 2. Simplified stack representation with corrupting input.**

| |
|---|
| Parent function's stack |
| "rity" (return address overwritten) |
| "secu" (char* passedStr overwritten) |
| "good"   (expected 3 characters + \0, got 12) |

by passing a carefully crafted malicious input that exploits a stack overflow, an attacker can even inject malicious code that results in a chain of calls to such pre-existing functions.

### 3.3. Libtiff Vulnerability

A vulnerability similar to that in the example above is found in libtiff version 3.8.1 and earlier—an area of memory is accessed without performing an out-of-bounds check. The vulnerability is in function TIFFFetchShortPair in the tif_dirread.c file [10]. That function fetches a pair of bytes or shorts, as the name implies. It should throw an error if the request is to fetch more than two bytes or shorts. Instead, it fetches any arbitrary number of bytes requested. This vulnerability was fixed in libtiff version 3.8.2. The source code for both versions of libtiff can be downloaded from the Maptools.org website [17]. Below we give excerpts of this function as it appears in libtiff versions 3.8.1 and 3.8.2. First, we look at the snippet from version 3.8.1:

```
static int
TIFFFetchShortPair(TIFF* tif, TIFFDirEntry* dir)
{
        switch (dir->tdir_type) {
            case TIFF_BYTE:
            case TIFF_SBYTE:
                {
                uint8 v[4];
                return TIFFFetchByteArray(tif, dir,
v)
                        &&           TIFFSetField(tif,
dir->tdir_tag, v[0], v[1]);
                }
            case TIFF_SHORT:
            case TIFF_SSHORT:
                {
                uint16 v[2];
                return TIFFFetchShortArray(tif, dir,
v)
                        &&           TIFFSetField(tif,
dir->tdir_tag, v[0], v[1]);
                }
            default:
                return 0;
        }
}
```

Now, let us look at the snippet from version 3.8.2, which has the fix for the vulnerability. The fix is obvious from the developer's comments.

```
static int
TIFFFetchShortPair(TIFF* tif, TIFFDirEntry* dir)
{
```

```
/*
 * Prevent overflowing the v stack arrays be-
low by performing a sanity
 * check on tdir_count, this should never be
greater than two.
 */
if (dir->tdir_count > 2) {
    TIFFWarningExt(tif->tif_clientdata,
tif->tif_name,
    "unexpected count for field \"%s\", %lu,
expected 2; ignored",
    _TIFFFieldWithTag(tif,
dir->tdir_tag)->field_name,
        dir->tdir_count);
    return 0;
}

switch (dir->tdir_type) {
    case TIFF_BYTE:
    case TIFF_SBYTE:
        {
        uint8 v[4];
        return TIFFFetchByteArray(tif, dir,
v)
            && TIFFSetField(tif,
dir->tdir_tag, v[0], v[1]);
        }
    case TIFF_SHORT:
    case TIFF_SSHORT:
        {
        uint16 v[2];
        return TIFFFetchShortArray(tif, dir,
v)
            && TIFFSetField(tif,
```
```
dir->tdir_tag, v[0], v[1]);
        }
    default:
        return 0;
    }
}
```

To take advantage of the vulnerability in the TIFF library, a malicious TIFF file must be constructed. To accomplish that requires a reasonable working knowledge of the TIFF file format. There are two important objectives to keep in mind while constructing a malicious TIFF file: causing buffer overflow and injecting code. The iPhone is constructed around an ARM processor, thus some knowledge of it is required for successful code injection. Next, we discuss the TIFF format and give a brief overview of the ARM processor.

### 3.4. TIFF

The TIFF standard is owned and maintained by Adobe. It is tag-based format used primarily for scanned images [18]. A TIFF file has a header section and descriptive sections at the top of the file with offsets pointing to the actual pixel image data [19]. This means that a poorly constructed file may have tags pointing to incorrect offsets or offsets beyond the end of the file. Such aberrations can be used to exploit a buffer overflow in poorly written programs that read and manipulate tiff images [19]. Some examples of tags include image height, image width, planar configuration, and dot range. Different tags give necessary information about the image including color, compression, dimensions, and location of data. Below is an example of a tiff file ("value" column) with corresponding descriptions [18].

| Offset (hex) | Description | Value (numeric values are expressed in hexadecimal notation) |
|---|---|---|
| *Header:* | | |
| 0000 | Byte Order | 4D4D |
| 0002 | 42 | 002A |
| 0004 | 1st IFD offset | 00000014 |
| *IFD:* | | |
| 0014 | Number of Directory Entries | 000C |
| 0016 | NewSubfileType | 00FE 0004 00000001 00000000 |
| 0022 | ImageWidth | 0100 0004 00000001 000007D0 |
| 002E | ImageLength | 0101 0004 00000001 00000BB8 |
| 003A | Compression | 0103 0003 00000001 8005 0000 |
| 0046 | PhotometricInterpretation | 0106 0003 00000001 0001 0000 |
| 0052 | StripOffsets | 0111 0004 000000BC 000000B6 |
| 005E | RowsPerStrip | 0116 0004 00000001 00000010 |
| 006A | StripByteCounts | 0117 0003 000000BC 000003A6 |
| 0076 | XResolution | 011A 0005 00000001 00000696 |
| 0082 | YResolution | 011B 0005 00000001 0000069E |
| 008E | Software | 0131 0002 0000000E 000006A6 |

| 009A | DateTime | 0132 0002 00000014 000006B6 |
| 00A6 | Next IFD offset | 00000000 |

***Values longer than 4 bytes:***

| 00B6 | StripOffsets | Offset0, Offset1, ... Offset187 |
| 03A6 | StripByteCounts | Count0, Count1, ... Count187 |
| 0696 | XResolution | 0000012C 00000001 |
| 069E | YResolution | 0000012C 00000001 |
| 06A6 | Software | "PageMaker 4.0" |
| 06B6 | DateTime | "1988:02:18 13:59:59" |

***Image Data:***

| 00000700 | Compressed data for strip 10 |
| xxxxxxxx | Compressed data for strip 179 |
| xxxxxxxx | Compressed data for strip 53 |
| xxxxxxxx | Compressed data for strip 160 ... |

The first two bytes in an Image File Directory (IFD) represent the number of directory entries (14 in the example above). The IFD then consists of a sequence of tags, 12 bytes each, where the first two bytes identify the field, and the next two identify the field type: short int, long int, byte, or ASCII. The next four bytes specify the number of values, and the final four specify the value itself or an offset to the value [18]. Since TIFF files are not intended to be human-readable, their contents are best viewed in a hex editor.

### 3.5. Arm Processor

Since the ARM1176JZF-S processor is used in the iPhone, some working knowledge regarding its architecture and instruction set is required for this study. ARM is a RISC-based processor. **Figure 3** gives a high-level diagram of ARM1176JZF-S.

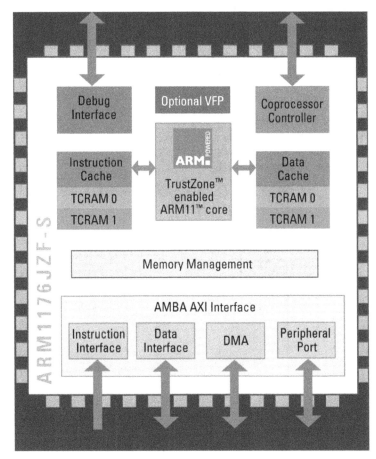

**Figure 3. ARM 1176JFZ-S processor [3].**

The ARM processor can be configured in either little- or big-endian modes to access its data [20]. The iPhone runs the ARM processor in little-endian mode. For example, if a value in a register is 0x12345678, in little-endian mode it appears in memory "byte-reversed", that is, as 0x78 0x56 0x34 0x12. This is illustrated in the **Figures 4** and **5** below.

The ARM processor can be configured in either little- or big-endian modes to access its data [20]. The iPhone runs the ARM processor in little-endian mode. For example, if a value in a register is 0x12345678, in little-endian mode it appears in memory "byte-reversed", that is, as 0x78 0x56 0x34 0x12. This is illustrated in the **Figures 4** and **5** below.

### 3.6. Dre And Niacin'S Tiff Exploit Jailbreak

We now have accumulated the background required to understand and reverse-engineer the libtiff exploit for jailbreaking developed by two teenagers known as Dre and Niacin. The source code for the attack is available on Dre and Niacin's website [23]. However, little explanation is provided, so we found it necessary to reverse engineer various aspects of the attack.

First, we verify and demonstrate the overflow problem. Though the exploit was created for the iPhone, we demonstrate the overflow on a Windows PC in cygwin to mimic a Unix-like environment. First the exploit source code was downloaded and compiled. Then, a malicious TIFF badDotRange.tiff was created.

An interesting outcome occurred when we attempted to create the code badDotRange.tiff. The file creation was blocked by Norton AntiVirus software running on the machine, and it claimed the file was "Bloodhound. Exploit.166" [24]. Further information on the vulnerability shows Norton characterizing badDotRange. tiff as a Trojan and a Virus, as shown in **Figure 6** [24].

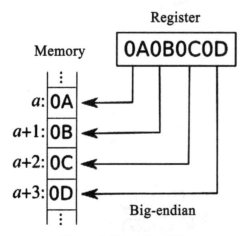

**Figure 4. Big-endian [22].**

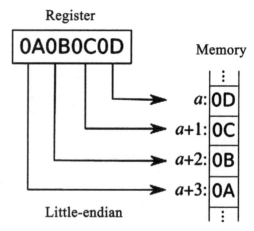

**Figure 5. Little-endian [22].**

Once the work area was put in the list of directories to be excluded by Norton AntiVirus, badDotRange.tiff was created; a hex editor view of the file is available in [25].

Next, we demonstrate the malicious TIFF file causing a buffer overflow in libtiff. We also show a well formed TIFF file being handled properly by libtiff. A program was written to simulate the stack buffer overflow. Below is a snippet from driver.cpp file.

```
int main() {
    cout << "Start!" << endl;
    TIFF*  tif  =  TIFFOpen("c:/thesis/tiffExp/t1.tiff", "r");
    if (tif) {
        cout << "Opened file successfully" << endl;
    } else {
        cout    << "FAILED to open tiff file" << endl;
    }
    TIFFClose(tif);
    cout << "End!" << endl;
    return 0;
}
```

Next, badDotRange.tiff is copied to t1.tiff and driver.cpp is compiled, linked with libtiff.a, and run, which results in a segmentation fault, as shown below.

```
$cp badDotRange.tiff t1.tiff
$g++ -I /usr/local/include –g driver.cpp –c
$g++ driver.o –L. –ltiff –o driver.exe
$./driver.exe
Start!
Segmentation fault <core dumped>
```

The program execution sequence is the following: TiffOpen() calls TIFFReadDirectory(), which upon encountering the DotRange tag calls TIFFFetchShortPair () as can be seen from the following snippet from tif_dir-read.c.

```
case TIFFTAG_DOTRANGE:
    (void) TIFFFetchShortPair(tif, dp);
```

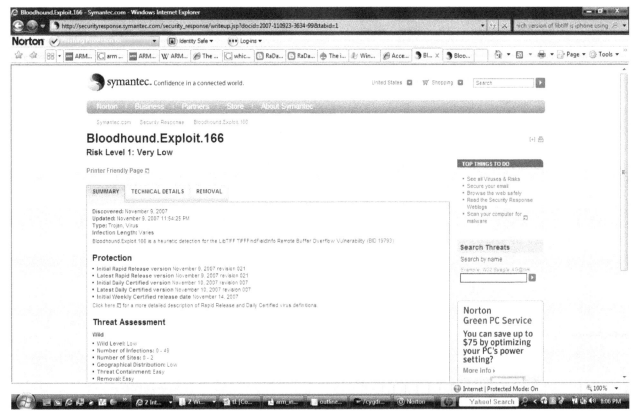

**Figure 6. Bloodhound.Exploit.166 trojan [24].**

break;
case TIFFTAG_REFERENCEBLACKWHITE: ...

As seen earlier, that function allocates memory for two shorts, but instead receives the request to fetch 255 of them. Below is the corresponding line in the source code of the attack.

0x50,0x01,0x03,0x00,0xff,0x00,0x00,0x00,0x84,0x00,0x00,0x00,

Since we are assuming little-endian representation, the first two bytes become 0x0150, which represents the DotRange tag. The next two bytes give us the value 0x0003, which means the data type is SHORT. The next four bytes give us the number of different values for this tag, which is 0x000000ff or 255 in decimal. Finally, the final four bytes give us 0x00000084, which is the offset to the actual values for the tag [18].

By looking at the TIFF specification [18] and also looking at the code for the version of libtiff with sanity check [17], we see that the number of parameters expected by DotRange is two. As seen in the stack buffer overflow example, attempting to fetch 255 shorts causes a stack buffer overflow. In our example, the program overwrites the return value in the stack, changing it to some area in memory that is not accessible, resulting in a segmentation fault. Below, the line in badDotRange.tiff corresponding to the DotRange tag is shown, as it appears in Hex Editor. The twelve bytes corresponding to the DotRange tag appear from 0x74 to 0x7f.

0000070: 0100 0000 5001 0300 ff00 0000 8400 0000
    ....P...........

Thus far, we have solved half of the problem of creating an attack by gaining control of the stack. Before we move on to injecting particular code and executing it, we first confirmed that a well-formed TIFF file is not recognized as a virus by Norton AntiVirus and does not cause a crash when opened with our program.

We now consider the code that provides root access to the iPhone and observe how it is executed. As mentioned earlier, this exploit uses the return-to-libc technique to execute a sequence of pre-existing functions. These pre-existing functions come from the dynamically loaded libSystem. dylib, which can be disassembled and searched for blocks of code that perform desired tasks [26]. The iPhone only allows access to a small section of the file system to add and remove music and other files. This "sandbox" area is the directory /var/root/Media. The algorithm used in the exploit renames /var/root/Media to /var/root/OldMedia. It then creates a symbolic link with /var/root/Media pointing to root, "/" and next it remounts root with the "MNT_UPDATE" flag to make it writable

[23]. The malicious tiff file is crafted skillfully to set up the stack to call the necessary functions from libSystem.dylib. Each of those functions must be studied carefully to discover how many values it reads from the stack and in what registers. The stack pointer must be set appropriately, and the link registers must be set properly for the next function call. With this method the exploit uses pre-existing functions to make the iPhone root writable—in other words, it "jailbreaks" the iPhone.

### 3.7. Summary of Jailbreaking

Let's recap the tools needed and the process taken for jailbreaking method used above. Vulnerability in tiff library was targeted to create a stack buffer overflow and inject desired code. Then return-to-libc technique was used to execute desired code to make the root directory of iPhone writeable – i.e. to jailbreak it. During the process knowledge of TIFF was necessary in order to construct a vulnerable TIFF file. Also, knowledge of ARM processor architecture and it's deficiencies were required to ensure the attack works consistently on any given iPhone. Furthermore, knowledge of ARM instructions was required to construct the code for the attack. In summary, a great deal of research and learning was required in order to pick up the necessary tools to successfully create the Jailbreak attack.

### 4. Unlocking

The iPhone is considered unlocked when it is able to use a cellular service other than that of AT & T. There are several free and paid software unlocking solutions available on the Internet including AnySIM, TurboSIM, and SimFree. Among these solutions, AnySIM seems to be quite popular, likely because it is free. It is developed by a group of people who call themselves the iPhone dev team.

AnySim works by patching the firmware on the baseband [27]. We can predict that somewhere in the baseband firmware, there is code that checks whether the SIM card being used is AT & T's. If the check passes, the baseband allows the phone part of the iPhone to work normally; conversely, if the check fails, the phone function does not work. AnySim performs a patch to the firmware so that it skips the above check and jumps to the section of code that executes when the check passes [27]. This procedure unlocks the iPhone because a SIM card from any GSM wireless carrier can then be used to make phone calls. If the baseband firmware is upgraded or downgraded, the iPhone gets "un-unlocked", as the patch that skips the check will almost certainly no longer be part of the code.

SimFree, also known as iPhone SimFree or IPSF, is unlocking software that currently sells for approximately $60, and at one point cost $99 [28]. Since it is a paid product, details about how it works are not revealed. It claims not to rely on firmware patching, so a phone unlocked with SimFree should remain unlocked even when a baseband upgrade is performed [27].

TurboSim is another paid solution for unlocking. It tricks the iPhone SIM card checking function into thinking it is an AT & T SIM card by providing an International Mobile Subscriber ID (IMSI) and an Integrated Circuit Card ID (ICC-ID)—also known as SIM Serial Number (SSN). For TurboSim to work, it must be programmed with a valid AT & T SIM, which it copies for later use [29].

Following table summarizes the above mentioned unlocking methods.

| Unlocking Method | Technique used |
| --- | --- |
| AnySim | Patch the baseband to skip AT & T SIM card check. |
| SimFree | Proprietary software application that patches the iPhone firmware |
| TurboSim | Tricks iPhone into thinking that it's SIM card is an AT & T SIM card |

### 5. Jailbreaking and Unlocking Newer Versions of Iphone

As mentioned earlier, for the purposes of this project, iPhone firmware version 1.1.1 and baseband bootloader version 3.9 are assumed. As of 2008, Apple had released versions 1.1.2, 1.1.3, and 1.1.4 of the firmware. Also, the baseband bootloader version is 4.6 in some of the phones. Can these phones be jailbroken and unlocked?

We use a simple approach: on newer versions of the iPhone, we downgrade the firmware to version 1.1.1 and the bootloader to version 3.9. Then we use the known attacks to jailbreak and unlock the iPhone. Several hacker websites, including iphone.unlock.no, offer instructions on how to downgrade the firmware and bootloader, and they also have different firmware files available for download [27].

Unlocking is not possible if the iPhone has version 4.6 or higher of bootloader because that version requires a secpack—a special password—to modify the baseband [30] and unlocking cannot be achieved without modifying the baseband. Since version 3.9 of the bootloader does not require any passwords, the baseband can be modified, and unlocking can be achieved. For that reason a "bootloader downgrader" tool *gbootloader* was developed by George Hotz and made available to iPhone users [31]. The tool downgrades the bootloader from version

4.6 to version 3.9 so that a patch to the baseband can be made and the iPhone can be unlocked.

Several other small utilities have been developed in addition to the ones mentioned here, which allows users to sort out different versions of firmware, baseband, and bootloader and make appropriate choices. Tools have been developed to upgrade the firmware on jailbroken phones to pick up some of the latest features developed by Apple for the iPhone.

## 6. Other Malicious Attacks

Attacks that we have examined so far do not carry the intention to be malicious, though the libtiff attack certainly could be malicious, depending on the type of code injected. For jailbreaking, the code injected was non-malicious—both behavior and intention-wise. However, using the libtiff vulnerability, malicious code could certainly be injected for a malicious attack. Now, let us examine a couple of malicious attacks created by a group of researchers at Independent Security Evaluators by exploiting other vulnerabilities; those attacks give us further insight into iPhone security. Details of the attacks discussed below are not revealed; the goal of the researchers was to make Apple aware of some of the issues and not to let the hackers find out the details of the vulnerabilities and the attacks. The attacks expose well-known security weaknesses in the OS X operating system used in the iPhone, including lack of address randomization and an executable heap [32].

The first attack consists of an exploit written to attack Safari on the iPhone. When a malicious HTML document was visited using MobileSafari, the iPhone was forced to make a connection to an outbound compromised server controlled by the attackers. The attackers were then secretly and automatically able to obtain personal data including contacts, call history, text message, and voice mail from the attacked iPhone. Attackers concluded that further personal information including passwords and emails could have been obtained had they chosen to do so [32]. What makes this attack even more dangerous is the ease with which it can be carried out. A link to a compromised website could be sent via email, and the iPhone owner could be lured into visiting it. That is all it would take to capture all of the personal data of the iPhone owner.

A second exploit was written to perform physical actions on the phone such as making a system sound and vibrating [32]. This exploit was run on the iPhone when another malicious HTML was viewed using Safari browser. To make matters worse, certain API functions discovered during this exploit could have allowed it to send text messages, dial phone numbers, or even record audio and transmit it over the network [32]. This vulnerability is particularly dangerous since the phone bill or text message bill could be increased by the attacker, which could cost the iPhone's owner a significant sum. The attacker could also send maliciously provocative messages to the owner's contacts, which could result in personal or professional relationship problems.

These malicious exploits are, collectively, comparable to having one's iPhone stolen. If attacks like these become widespread, there is a potential that customers would reconsider buying the iPhone.

While details of the attacks above were not disclosed, let us look at the high level approach used in the above MobileSafari attacks. This information could certainly be used as a guideline for the attacks above, provided one is able to write appropriate payloads. The iPhone uses Webkit, an open source web browser engine used by Mobile Safari [33], which in turn uses the Perl Compatible Regular Expression Library (PCRE). One of the first versions of iPhone used a version of PCRE that was more than a year old. Several versions of PCRE had been released with several bug fixes since the version used by iPhone. One of the bug fixes found in the change log of a newer version 6.7 [34] follows.

*A valid (though odd) pattern that looked like a POSIX character class but used an invalid character after [ (for example [[,abc,]]) caused pcre_compile() to give the error "Failed: internal error: code overflow" or in some cases to crash with a glibc free() error. This could even happen if the pattern terminated after [[ but there just happened to be a sequence of letters, a binary zero, and a closing ] in the memory that followed.*

Now, one can review the bug fix and immediately get ideas for possible attacks on the iPhone. Attackers used the above vulnerability and constructed a regular expression in an HTML file that attacked the vulnerability when the file was viewed in Safari. The HTML document used was constructed as below [35]:

```
<SCRIPT LANGUAGE="JavaScript"><!--
var re = new RegExp("[[**]][[**]][[**]][[**]][[**]][[**]][[**]][[**]]
[[**]][[**]][[**]][[**]][[**]][[**]][[**]][[**]][[**]][[**]][[**]]
[[**]][[**]][[**]][[**]][[**]][[**]][[**]][[**]][[**]][[**]][[**]]
[[**]][[**]][[**]][[**]][[**]][[**]][[**]][[**]][[**]][[**]][[**]]
[[**]][[**]][[**]][[**]][[**]][[**]][[**]][[**]][[**]][[**]][[**]]
```

```
[[**]][[**]][[**]][[**]][[**]][[**]][[**]][[**]][[**]][[**]][[**]][[**]]
[[**]][[**]]ABCDEFGHIJKLMNOPQRSTUVWXYZAB-
CDEFG[\x01\x02\x03\x04\x05\x06\x07\x09\x0b\x0e\x0f\x11\x12\x13\x14\x15\x17\x19\x1b\x1c\x1d\x1f\x20\x21\x22
\x23\x25\x26\x27\x29\x2a\x2b\x2c\x2d\x2f\x30\x32\x33\x35\x37\x39\x3a\x3b
\x3c\x3e\x3f]XYZABCDEFGHIJKLMNOPQR");
</script>
```

To develop the exploit, attackers resorted to a technique called "fuzzing" [35], which involves passing different inputs that cause a given program to crash and then analyzing the crash to gain insight about the program. From the crash reports, they were able to get useful information such as the stack pointer and values in different registers. They then employed a technique to overwrite the return address on the stack to point to the heap area where shell code was injected [35]. The shell code then executed and did the job of stealing private information. The code consisted of typical socket connect, open, read, and write functions. The researchers have revealed some of the functions they used to perform physical actions on the phone including making a system sound, dialing phone calls, and sending SMS text messages. Those functions include AudioServicesPlaySystemSound from the Audio Toolbox library and CTCallDial, CTSMSMessageCreate, and CTSMSMessageSend from the Core Telephony library [35]. The purpose of each function is clear from its name.

To summarize, vulnerabilities in PCRE were targeted by creating a malicious HTML file to create a buffer overflow, which facilitated injection and execution of malicious code.

## 7. Security Analysis

Having briefly examined several vulnerabilities in the iPhone and attacks that exploit those vulnerabilities, we now analyze the iPhone security structure from a high level. What was the approach Apple took while designing the security architecture for the iPhone? Were there flaws in this philosophy? What high-level approaches can be used to exploit the security flaws? What are some of the ways that Apple can either fix some of the vulnerabilities or at least make it difficult for an attacker to exploit them? Let us try to answer some of these questions.

It is clear that iPhone is a vulnerable device with several security holes. The iPhone security philosophy itself has a signifcant flaw. Apple's approach to making the iPhone a secure device was to reduce "the attack surface of device" or "the device's exposure to vulnerabilities" [32]. To achieve this, Apple allowed write access only to a sandbox area in the file system and disallowed installation of third-party applications. Several features of Safari were removed in Mobile Safari, including the ability to use plug-ins like Flash and the ability to download certain file types. Mobile Safari was restricted to only execute Javascript code, and only do so in the sandbox area. In short, Apple's approach was to make a controlled, essentially closed-box device. Apple's security approach might be summed up by the following analogy: rather than teaching a child how to swim to prevent him from drowning, he is simply not allowed to jump in a lake.

While the security philosophy is debatable, the architecture has significant holes. Since Apple banked on preventing the iPhone from being compromised in the first place, it put very little effort into protecting different parts of the device individually. This conclusion is supported by the fact that all significant processes run as a super user or with administrative privileges—a major mistake from a security perspective. A result of this configuration is that an attacker is likely able to control the entire iPhone if he is able to exploit any vulnerability in any of its applications [32]. For example if Mobile Mail were compromised by an attack, the attacker could also gain access to contacts and pictures. In simple terms, the iPhone's security architecture looks like a home owner putting all effort for securing his or her home into buying a strong lock to stop an intruder from getting in. No effort is made to, say, secure individual room, to put valuables in a safe-deposit box, to use a home security system, etc. While it may be difficult to enter the house, if a thief can do so, he can easily steal all its contents.

A security hole is also created by the fact that the iPhone uses several applications including MobileSafari and MobileMail that are based on open source projects. While the use of open source is itself likely a good idea, using (and sharing) of open source projects with old and outdated versions of those projects is clearly a problem. Earlier we looked at examples of an old version of libtiff library facilitating the jailbreak attack, and an old version of the PCRE library allows another malicious attack. By using outdated versions of open source projects, Apple made it relatively easy for hackers to develop ideas and approaches for attacks attacks.

Apple also failed to make the exploitation of vulnerabilities challenging for hackers. By not utilizing common techniques such as Address Space Layout Randomization (ASLR) or non-executable heap in the version of OS X used for iPhone, Apple has not posed any particular difficulties for hackers in the development and distribution of buffer overflow exploits [32].

The table below summarizes the attacks discussed in this paper.

| Attack | Vulnerability targeted | Tools used | Effects |
|---|---|---|---|
| Jailbreaking | Vulnerable libtiff | TIFF, buffer overflow, return-to-libc, ARM architecture and instructions | Get root access |
| Unlocking | Jailbroken phones allow for installation of unauthorized applications | Installation of unauthorized application | Being able to use the iPhone with non-AT&T wireless services |
| Mobile safari (malicious) | Vulnerable PCRE | Malicious HTML, fuzzing, buffer overflow | Stolen personal data and other malicious effects |

Apple did employ some good practices and has shown more effort recently in making the iPhone more secure. That has not stopped the hackers, however, as they have found solutions to the obstacles presented by Apple. For example, the stack is non-executable in the iPhone, so an attacker cannot simply add payload to the stack via a buffer overflow and execute it. However, a non-executable stack does not protect against the return-to-libc attack, which was employed in the jailbreaking attack, as we observed earlier. New versions of firmware have been released with certain vulnerabilities fixed to prevent jailbreaking. Unfortunately, these have been somewhat countered by the ability to downgrade the firmware. Apple also attempted to prevent unlocking by using a new version of the bootloader. That attempt failed because hackers found a way to downgrade the bootloader as well.

After evaluating Apple's security for the iPhone, one can safely conclude that overall the company failed to make the iPhone as secure as it could possibly have been. Looking at the security approach and the decisions the company made, it is no surprise that the initial iPhones were considered a fairly vulnerable device.

## 8. Analysis of Sample Decisions by Apple

Now that we have had a chance to analyze the iPhone's security structure, we can ask several questions regarding different choices Apple has made. Why are they using versions of open-source based packages that are about a year out of date? Why did they choose to have almost all important processes run as super user? Why did they not use ASLR? Why did they use a vulnerable version of the tiff library? This final question is particularly important because even after three new versions of firmware and a new version of the bootloader, Apple was still paying for this mistake.

It seems implausible that Apple had no knowledge of the vulnerability in libtiff that causes buffer overflow, since this vulnerability is well known in the hacking community and other mobile devices including Sony's PSP had been hacked using it. We can only speculate as

to why Apple used the vulnerable version of libtiff. Perhaps there was an existing version of Safari with the vulnerable version of libtiff ready to be used with iPhone. One can certainly see that there is some cost involved in using a new version of libtiff in Safari, which would have to be thoroughly tested prior to being deployed in a new version for iPhone. Perhaps Apple found that there were other known vulnerabilities in the version used anyway. Perhaps Apple performed a cost analysis of losses suffered by delaying the new version of firmware versus losses due to the number of people who would hack the iPhone to jailbreak it and eventually unlock it and use a wireless service other than that of AT & T. Such a decision would express disregard for consumer security, since the same vulnerability could be also used to perform truly malicious acts.

From a short-term perspective, it is hard to argue with the success of the iPhone. However, from the consumer confidence or reputation perspective, the situation is not so clear. Apple is generally regarded as a company that delivers secure and robust products. They may have lost some of that sheen with the iPhone.

## 9. Suggestions to Improve Security Structure

We have pinpointed several flaws in the initial iPhone security structure. A large security hole would have been filled if most of the processes were not run with administrative privileges, or as the super user. This would generally make it more difficult for an attacker to gain full control of an iPhone.

While using open-source based applications is a good idea, Apple needs to be more cognizant about using versions that do not have serious known bugs. Apple should also use a technique such as ASLR for heap and stack address randomization to make it more difficult for hackers to develop stable attacks and distribute them [32]. Moreover, it could develop a mechanism that prohibits both writing to and executing an area of the heap. Some attacks copy the exploit payload into the heap area that is both writeable and executable, and they execute it there. If an area in heap was not both writeable and executable, such attacks would be thwarted. Also, if ASLR were employed, even if an attacker could successfully write an attack that relies on an address in the stack or heap, distribution of the attack would be difficult, as the target address is unreliable due to randomization.

## 10. Conclusions

In this paper, we considered the iPhone security structure and its vulnerabilities. The Jailbreaking attack analyzed here relied on a known vulnerability in the TIFF library. The analysis of the attack required some knowledge of the ARM architecture and the TIFF file format. We showed that using a vulnerable version of the TIFF library proved costly for Apple, in the sense that updates could not easily prevent "rollback" attacks. Interestingly, hackers found ways to jailbreak later iPhone without even losing the new features introduced in newer versions. Perhaps predictably, the attacks on the iPhone and the countermeasures by Apple quickly devolved into a cat and mouse game.

The security problems discussed here have resulted in financial losses for both Apple and AT&T and, arguably, a reputation loss for Apple. For each iPhone that was unlocked to access an alternate wireless carrier, AT & T stood to lose about $1500 in revenue for the two-year contract period. As we noted earlier, the number of unlocked iPhones was estimated at nearly a million in just its first six months [1]. Apple too missed out on some gains, as it receives a certain amount from AT & T for each iPhone activated with AT&T. The security vulnerabilities of the iPhone have also affected Apple's reputation as a company, as it had been generally believed to deliver relatively secure products. While Apple's exclusive deal with AT & T and its decision to use a closed system undoubtedly increased the motivation to attack the iPhone.

We have also explained that malicious attacks can be created for the iPhone. However, the significant attacks have not been malicious, but were instead focused on enabling people more freedom to do what they want with their telephone product.

We conclude that Apple's initial effort in making the iPhone a secure device was somewhat disappointing. While Apple worked to improve iPhone security, the initial release unnecessarily gave hackers the upper hand, which, to some extent, has continued to this day.

## 10. References

[1]  C. Maxcer, "Apple Minus AT&T Equals Lots of iPhones Somewhere Else," Mac News World. http://www.mac-newsworld.com/story/61389.html?welcome=1209968031

[2]  iPhone, Apple–iPhone. http://www.apple.com/iphone/

[3]  ARM, ARM1176 Processor. http://www.arm.com/products/CPUs/ARM1176.html

[4]  A. L. Shimpi, "Apple's iPhone Dissected: We did it, so you don't have to," Anandtech, 29 June 2007. http://www.anandtech.com/mac/showdoc.aspx?i=3026&p=3

[5]  In brief, Network Security, Vol. 2009, No. 7, July 2009, pp. 3.

[6]  Best iPhone Apps. http://www.Installerapps.com

[7]  K Dunham, "Mobile Malware Attacks and Defense," Elsevier 2009, pp. 197-265.

[8]  B. Haines, "Seven Deadliest Wireless Technologies Attacks," Syngress, 2010.

[9]  Max Console. http://www.maxconsole.net/?mode=news&newsid=9516

[10]  Common Vulnerabilities and Exposures, 2006. http://cve.mitre.org/cgi-bin/cvename.cgi?name=CVE-2006-3459

[11]  TIFF Library and Utilities, 15 January 2008. http://www.libtiff.org/

[12]  National Vulnerability Database, 2006. http://nvd.nist.gov/nvd.cfm?cvename=CVE-2006-3459

[13]  "Stack buffer overflow," Wikipedia. http://en.wikipedia.org/wiki/Stack_buffer_overflow

[14]  M. Stamp, "Information Security: Principles and Practice," Wiley 2005.

[15]  C. Cowan, et al., "StackGuard: Automatic Adaptive Detection and Prevention of Buffer-Overflow Attacks," Proceedings of the 7th USENIX Security Symposium, San Antonio, Texas, January 26-29, 1998.

[16]  "Return-to-libc," Wikipedia. http://en.wikipedia.org/wiki/Return-to-libc

[17]  Maptools, 15 January 2008. http://dl.maptools.org/dl/libtiff/

[18]  Adobe Developers Association, TIFF Revision 6.0 Final, 3 June 1992. http://partners.adobe.com/public/developer/en/tiff/TIFF6.pdf

[19]  "Tagged Image File Format," Wikipedia. http://en.wikipedia.org/wiki/TIFF

[20]  Simple Machines, The ARM instruction set. http://www.simplemachines.it/doc/arm_inst.pdf

[21]  "1176JZF-S Technical Reference Manual Revision r0p7," ARM. http://infocenter.arm.com/help/topic/com.arm.doc.ddi0301g/DDI0301G_arm1176jzfs_r0p7_trm.pdf

[22]  "Little-endian," Wikipedia. http://en.wikipedia.org/wiki/Little_endian

[23]  Toc2rta, TIFF exploit. http://www.toc2rta.com/files/itiff_exploit.cpp

[24]  "Bloodhound.Exploit.166 Technical Details," Symantec, 9 November 2007.

[25]  V. Pandya., IPhone security analysis, Masters Thesis, Department of Computer Science, San Jose State University, 2008. http://www.cs.sjsu.edu/faculty/stamp/students/pandya_vaibhav.pdf

[26] Metasploit. http://www.metasploit.com

[27] iPhone UnlockUSA.com. http://iphone.unlock.no

[28] iPhone Sim Free. http://www.iphonesimfree.com

[29] Hackintosh, Turbosim Technical Background. http://hackint0sh.org/forum/showthread.php?t=18048

[30] Hackintosh, iPhone. http://www.hackint0sh.org

[31] G. Hotz, "On the iPhone," 15 February 2008. http://iphonejtag.blogspot.com/

[32] C. Miller, J. Honoroff and J. Mason, "Security Evaluation of Apple's iPhone," Independent Security Evaluators, 19 July 2007. http://securityevaluators.com/files/papers/exploitingiphone.pdf

[33] The Webkit Open Source Project. http://webkit.org/

[34] Perl Compatible Regular Expressions, Change log. http://www.pcre.org/changelog.txt

[35] C. Miller, "Hacking Leopard: Tools and Techniques for Attacking the Newest Mac OS X," Black Hat Media Archives, 2 August 2007. https://www.blackhat.com/presentations/bh-usa-07/Miller/Presentation/bh-usa-07-miller.pdf

# 16

# Design and Implementation of Multilevel Access Control in Synchronized Audio to Audio Steganography Using Symmetric Polynomial Scheme

**Jeddy Nafeesa Begum[1], Krishnan Kumar[1], Vembu Sumathy[2]**
[1]*Department of Computer Science and Engineering, Government College of Engineering, Bargur, India*
[2]*Department of Electronics and Communications Engineering, Government College of Technology, Coimbatore, India*

## Abstract

Steganography techniques are used in Multimedia data transfer to prevent adversaries from eaves dropping. Synchronized audio to audio steganography deals with recording the secret audio, hiding it in another audio file and subsequently sending to multiple receivers. This paper proposes a Multilevel Access control in Synchronized audio steganography, so that Audio files which are meant for the users of low level class can be listened by higher level users, whereas the vice-versa is not allowed. To provide multilevel access control, symmetric polynomial based scheme is used. The steganography scheme makes it possible to hide the audio in different bit locations of host media without inviting suspicion. The Secret file is embedded in a cover media with a key. At the receiving end the key can be derived by all the classes which are higher in the hierarchy using symmetric polynomial and the audio file is played. The system is implemented and found to be secure, fast and scalable. Simulation results show that the system is dynamic in nature and allows any type of hierarchy. The proposed approach is better even during frequent member joins and leaves. The computation cost is reduced as the same algorithm is used for key computation and descendant key derivation. Steganography technique used in this paper does not use the conventional LSB's and uses two bit positions and the hidden data occurs only from a frame which is dictated by the key that is used. Hence the quality of stego data is improved.

**Keywords:** Steganography, Multilevel Access Control, Synchronized Audio, Symmetric Polynomial, Dynamic, Scalable

## 1. Introduction

Transmission of audio files is very important for many applications and it is found that this transmission takes place through an insecure medium. For a live session where on the go audio transmission takes place, efficient techniques should be used. One way of preventing the dissemination of secret audio is through digital audio stenography. This protects valuable information from unauthorized persons. For real time audio transmissions the secret data is recorded and send subsequently to the receivers. For hiding the message there is a need for a secret key that is available with all receivers. This key has to be changed to preserve forward and backward secrecy. There is an additional very important requirement called the multilevel access control. There are many scenarios in which situation arises, that only some users should be able to hear the data or all higher level users should also be able to hear the message that are relayed to the descendant users. To implement such a multilevel access control in steganography symmetric polynomial approach is used. In most existing schemes, key derivation is different from key computation. Key derivation needs iterative computation of keys for nodes along the path from a node to its descendant, which is inefficient if the path is long. In this scheme, both operations are same by substituting (different) parameters in the same polynomial function assigned to node *v*. Thus, the key derivation efficiency can be improved. Our scheme also supports full dynamics at both node and user levels and permits any random access hierarchies. More importantly, removing nodes and/or users is an operation

Design and Implementation of Multilevel Access Control in Synchronized Audio to Audio Steganography Using Symmetric Polynomial Scheme

147

as simple as adding nodes and/or users in the hierarchy. A trusted Central Authority (CA) can assign secrets (*i.e.*, polynomials) to corresponding nodes so that nodes can compute their keys. Also, nodes can derive their descendants' keys without involvement of the CA once polynomial functions were distributed to them. In addition, the storage requirement and computation complexity at the CA are almost same as that at individual nodes, thus, the CA would not be a performance bottleneck and can deal with dynamic operations efficiently.

The rest of the paper is as follows, Section 2 deals with related work Section 3 gives an insight into multilevel access control problem. Section 4 gives the system Overview, Section 5 describes the audio steganography method Section 6 deals about the symmetric polynomial approach Section 7 shows the simulation results and Section 8 gives the performance analysis and Section 8 concludes the paper.

## 2. Related Work

### 2.1. Related Work in Steganography

Information hiding using steganography [1] relates to protection of text, image, audio and digital content on a cover medium [2-5]. The cover media in many cases has been an image [1]. Aoki presented a method in which information that is useful for widening the base band is hidden into the speech data [6]. Sub band Phase shifting was also proposed for acoustic data hiding [3]. All these schemes focus on data that is stored in a hard disk or any other hardware whereas there are many applications like military warfare where the audio data is to be given in real time as in live broadcast system. Techniques for hiding the audio in real time came into existence [7] and systems for synchronized audio steganography has been developed and evaluated [8]. In our scheme secret speech data is recorded and at the same time it is sent to the receiver and a trusted receiver extracts the speech from the stego data using the key which is shared between the server and the receiver.

### 2.2. Related Work in Multilevel Access Control

The first multi level access solution was proposed by Akl *et al.* [9,10] in 1983 and followed by many others [11-21]. These schemes basically rely on a one-way function so that a node *v* can easily compute *v*'s descendants' keys whereas *v*'s key is computationally difficult to compute by *v*'s descendant nodes. In this paper, we propose a new scheme based on symmetric polynomials for synchronized audio data. Unlike many existing schemes based on one-way functions, our scheme is based on a secret sharing method which makes the scheme unconditionally secure [21,22]. Also, this multilevel access con-

trol requires two types of key operations: (1) key computation. A node *v* computes its own key and (2) key derivation. A node *v* computes its descendants' keys.

## 3. Multi Level Access Control Problem

In practice, many group applications contain multiple related data streams and have the members with various access privileges. These applications prevail in various scenarios.

1) Multimedia applications distributing data in multi-layer coding format. For example, in a video broadcast, users with a normal TV receiver can receive the normal format, while others with HDTV receivers can receive both the normal format and the extra information needed to achieve HDTV resolution.

2) Communications in hierarchically managed organizations, such as military group communications where participants have different access authorizations.

3) Multilevel access control can be effectively used in Audio library and patient monitoring system.

4) E-newspaper subscription service may have multiple data streams. The service provider classifies the users into membership groups and provides data streams according to the subscription.

5) Video multicasting service in which users can subscribe to services with different video quality.
Defense messaging systems where the server sends messages and one or more can see the message according to the access rights.

In these applications, group members subscribe to different data streams, or possibly multiple of them. Thus, it is necessary to develop group access control mechanism that supports the multi-level access privilege, which is referred to as the Multilevel Access Control.

## 4. System Overview

Multilevel Access Control applied to real time audio to audio steganography is useful for organizations which have a hierarchical structure. e.g., in the Indian Military system the following hierarchy exists in "**Figure 1**".

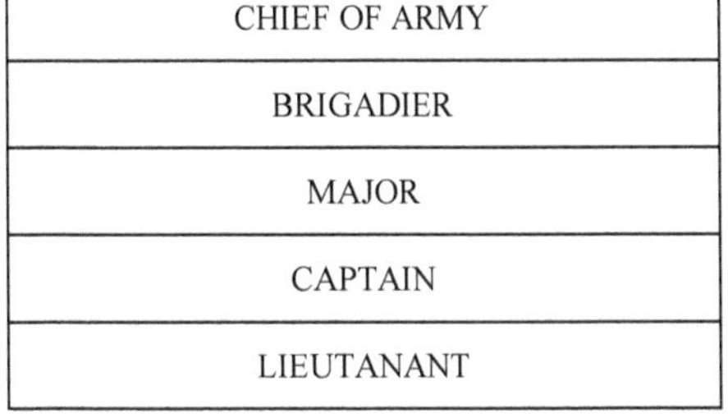

| CHIEF OF ARMY |
| BRIGADIER |
| MAJOR |
| CAPTAIN |
| LIEUTANANT |

**Figure 1. Military hierarchy.**

In such a type of system, audio messages sent to a lower class should be heard by the active members of lower class and also by all active members of the higher class. It is not only essential to maintain the access control but the data should be hidden as well. The sequence of events is as follows.

*At the server*:

1) Generate a general polynomial.

2) Give a symmetric polynomial to each of the classes.

3) Record the real time audio on a microphone.

4) Use Steganography technique to hide the audio into another audio.

5) A text can also be hidden in an audio file.

6) The file is encrypted by the class key for whom the Message is to be relayed.

7) The symmetric polynomial generates a key in this case. The server takes care to include class dynamics so the hierarchy can be changed at any time.

8) Users can join or leave a class at all instances. Keys are recalculated so that Forward and Backward secrecy is maintained.

9) If the users within the group need to transfer message among themselves. The private key of the users is used.

The above steps are given pictorially in "**Figure 2**".

*At the receiver*:

1) All the active receivers will receive the audio file.

2) If the recipient belongs to the actual intended class he can use the polynomial to get the hidden audio file instantaneously.

3) If the recipient belongs to a class lower than the Actual intended class in the hierarchy, he will not be able to derive the key .The polynomial derivation method will give a null value.

4) If the recipient belongs to a higher class he can derive the key and hear to the audio file and in case a text message was sent it can be seen.

5) The users at the same class can transfer messages among them.

6) When a user leaves or joins. The new polynomials are given by the server and the private keys also get updated according to the new polynomial. Other classes are not affected by this.

7) Service messages can be sent from higher class users to lower class users.

The above steps are explained pictorially in "**Figure 3**".

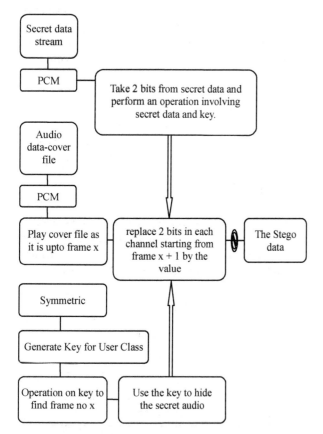

**Figure 2. At the server.**

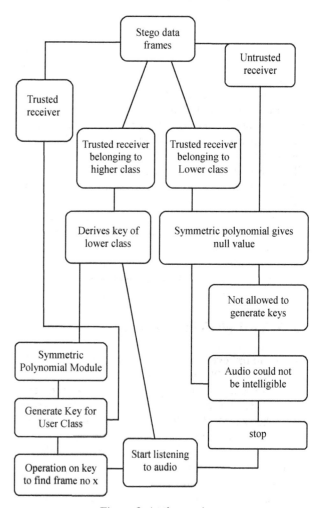

**Figure 3. At the receiver.**

Design and Implementation of Multilevel Access Control in Synchronized Audio to Audio Steganography Using
Symmetric Polynomial Scheme

149

## 4.1. Features of our Model

Solutions of a synchronized steganography have been given in past [8]. In this once the stego data reaches the destination the audio can be listened by the trusted receiver. Our contributions are

1) The key is used during the embedding process also.

2) The key is not a simple key it identifies a class of users.

3) If the key used belongs to a low level group in the hierarchy, the higher level class of user can derive the key using the symmetric polynomial approach and listen to it.

4) There can be normal message transfer among the Group elements and also service messages from higher classes.

5) Forward and backward secrecy is maintained.

6) It is a dynamic one where new hierarchies can be introduced, User level and class level dynamics are taken care.

## 5. Synchronized Audio to Audio Steganography

The data to be sent is not available. It is recorded in real time before starting the steganography scheme. When the covering media is being played at the same time the audio file is recorded and put into the cover file. The stego bit stream is then transmitted to the receivers. Multilevel Access control using symmetric polynomial is used at this stage to generate the key to make secure transmission of the audio file. According to the hierarchy the trusted users are able to retrieve the hidden audio file.In this system, both of cover data and secret data are divided into fix-sized frames according to pulse code modulation setting. To cover low size and high phonetic quality the sampling rate of the hidden audio is set to 8 kHz. Three main processes are involved in the synchronized audio to audio steganography.

1) Using data sampling, acoustic signals are embedded into another audio.

2) Bit Embedding: The key used helps in hiding the audio file in bit positions and once the bit positions are found data is hidden after performing an operation on secret data and the key.

3) Synchronized Process: Malicious and intentional attacks can be avoided as the secret data is real time.

### 5.1. Algorithm

Step 1: Record the Secret Speech Data: The audio files are divided into fix-sized frames and set to be specific PCM format. PCM quantification is decided by sampling rate, sampling size, and sampling channel. The PCM property of cover audio wav is set to be 32kHz-16bit-2ch, while the secret wav data is 16kHz-8bit-1ch.

Formula used for steganography:

Steganography process:

cover_medium + hidden_data + stego_key
= stego_medium

Part of The Wave File Format opened using Notepad:
52 49 46 46 24 40 01 00 57 41 56 45 66 6D 74 RIFF $ @.
Wave Fmt10 00 00 00 01 00 02 00 11 2B 00 00 44 AC 00 00 ....... + ...D...04 00 10 00 64 61 74 61 00 40 01 00 00 00 00 00 .... data. @..........
Wave_Format_PCM: 01 11 channel count: 02 00
Samples: 11 2B 00 00 bytes: 44 AC 00 00
Block align: 04 00 bits per sample: 10 00
Step 2: Use Symmetric Polynomial to calculate key of the class
Step 3: Perform calculation and decide the frame from which the data is to be embedded.
Step 4: Decide two bit locations in each frame and clear the bit in the locations.

$$cmask1 = (2^{loc1}-1) \text{ xor (keybit)}$$

$$cmask2 = (2^{loc2}-1) \text{ xor (Keybit)}$$

$$cmask = cmask1 \wedge cmask2$$

hide the secret data bits into these bit locations by again performing an operation on the secret data along with the key. The cover media has two channels so data is written on both the channels. Other bits are not changed.
Step 5: The next set of data will go to the next frame.
Step 6: Do the repetitive process till the recoding is over.
Step 8: Transmit using sockets.
Step 9: At the receiving end, use the key and play the audio.
Step 10: If the receiving user belongs to higher class, he can derive the key and listen to the audio.

## 6. Symmetric Polynomial Approach

### 6.1. Symmetric Polynomial

A CA selects a large positive integer $P$ as the system modulus, $p$ need not be a prime and a threshold number $t$ so that less than $t + 1$ users cannot collaborate together to disclose their ancestors' keys. Then, the CA can randomly generate a symmetric polynomial in $m$ variables with co-efficient from $Z_p$ in which the degree of any variables is at most $t$ as:

$$P(x_1, x_2, \ldots, x_m) = \sum_{i_1=0}^{t} \sum_{i_2=0}^{t} \cdots \sum_{i_m=0}^{t} a_{i_1,i_2,\ldots,i_m} x_1^{i_1} x_2^{i_2} \cdots x_m^{i_m} \pmod{P}$$

where $a_{i_1,i_2,\ldots,i_m}$ are randomly generated coefficients by the CA. The polynomial function $P(x_1, x_2, \ldots, x_m)$ is kept as a secret to the CA. Every class in the hierarchy has a polynomial function which is derived from $P(x_1, x_2, ..., x_m)$ and the polynomial function is transmitted to each class securely by the CA.

*Example for Symmetric Polynomial*
The following polynomial function is a suitable example for symmetric polynomials.

$$f(x_1, ..., x_n) = \sum_{i_1=0}^{w} \cdots \sum_{i_n=0}^{w} a_{i_1, i_2, ..., i_n} x_1^{i_1} ... x_n^{i_n}$$

where $a_{i_1, i_2, ..., i_n} = a_{\pi(i_1, i_2, ..., i_n)}$

For all permutations $\pi$ of $\{1, ... n\}$
For example,
suppose $n = 3$ and $w = 2$,
Let $i_1, i_2, i_3$ be as follows

$a_{0,0,0} = 13$

$a_{0,0,1} = a_{0,1,0} = a_{1,0,0} = 3$

$a_{0,0,2} = a_{0,2,0} = a_{2,0,0} = 7$

$a_{0,1,1} = a_{1,0,1} = a_{1,1,0} = 4$

$a_{0,1,2} = a_{0,2,1} = a_{1,0,2} = a_{2,0,1} = a_{2,1,0} = 8$

$a_{0,2,2} = a_{2,0,2} = a_{2,2,0} = 9$

$a_{1,2,2} = a_{2,1,2} = a_{2,2,1} = 11$

$a_{2,2,2} = 5$

## 6.2. Polynomial Function

To derive proper keys in the hierarchy, the CA generates some publicly known numbers
1) $n$ random numbers $s_i$ associated with $C_i$ for $i = 1, 2, ... n$ and 2) and $(m - 1)$ additional random numbers $r_j$ for $j = 1, 2, ..., m - 1$
(Note: $s_i$ and $r_j$ belong to $Z_p$).

For each class $C_i$ with an ancestor set $S_i = \{C_{i_1}, C_{i_1}, ..., C_{i_n}\}$ where $i_j$ is an ordinal number such that $1 \le i_j \ne i \le n$, class $C_i$ is given a polynomial function, $g_i$ derived by the CA as,

$$g_i(x_{m_i+2}, x_{m_i+3}, ..., x_m) = P(s_i, s_{i_1}, s_{i_2}, ..., s_{i_m},$$
$$x_{m_i+2}, x_{m_i+3}, ..., x_m)$$

A symmetric polynomial based scheme:

$A$ is an set of n classes – $\{C_1, C_2, C_3, ..., C_n\}$

$B$ is a set of ancestral classes of set $A$.

$$B = \{S_1, S_2, S_3, ..., S_n\}$$

*mi* is calculated as the number of the ancestral classes $m_i = |S_i|$. We choose m such that $m \ge \max\{m_1, m_2, ..., m_n\} + 1$. Here $m$ is the number of parameter in the polynomial function $P$, where $P$ is to construct our multi level access control scheme.

We illustrate with a sample hierarchy "**Figure 4**"
Here we have nine classes

$\{C_1, C_2, C_3, C_4, C_5, C_6, C_7, C_8, C_9\}$
Ancestral classes' sets are

$S_1 = \{\varphi\}, S_2 = \{\varphi\}, S_3 = \{C_1, C_2\}, S_4 = \{C_2\}$

$S_5 = \{C_2\}, S_6 = \{C_1, C_2, C_3\},$

$S_7 = \{C_1, C_2, C_3, C_4\}$

$S_8 = \{C_2, C_3, C_5\}, S_9 = \{C_2, C_5\}$

From the previous step, we need to choose m such that $m \ge \max\{m_1, m_2, m_3, ..., m_9\}$. Let us choose $m = 7$, it will allow to expand the hierarchy without changing the value of $m$.

Symmetric polynomial, we are using here is as follows

$$P(x_1, x_2, ... x_m) = \sum_{i_1=0}^{t} \sum_{i_2=0}^{t} \cdots \sum_{i_m=0}^{t} a_{i_1, i_2, ... i_m},$$
$$x_1^{i_1}, x_2^{i_2}, ... x_m^{i_m} \bmod P$$

Here $t$ is threshold number. We can classify our work into two Key Calculation and Key Derivation.
Key Calculation:
We can calculate key $K_i$ of class $C_i$ as follows

$$K_i = P\left(s_i, s_{i_1}, s_{i_2}, ..., s_{i_m}, s_1', s_2', ..., s_{m-m_i-1}'\right) \quad (1)$$

Key Derivation:
In key derivation, we are using a term $Sj/I$ which is

$$S_{j/I} = S_j / (S_i U \{C_i\}) = \{C_{(j/i)1}, C_{(j/i)2}, ..., C_{(j/i)rj}\}$$

Consider a class $C_i$ which is ancestor to class $C_j$ and key $K_j$ can be calculated by $C_i$ as,

$$K_j = g_i\left(s_j, s_{(j/i)1}, s_{(j/i)2}, ..., s_{(j/i)r_j}, s_1', s_2', ..., s_{m-m_i-2-r_j}'\right)$$
$$= P\left(s_i, s_j, s_i, s_{i_1}, s_{i_2}, ..., s_{i_{m_i}}, s_{(j/i)1}, s_{(j/i)2}, ..., s_{(j/i)r_j},\right.$$
$$\left. s_1', s_2', ..., s_{m-m_i-2-r_j}'\right)$$

$$(2)$$

*Example Key Derivation*
Consider that $C_3$ is an ancestor class to class $C_7$.

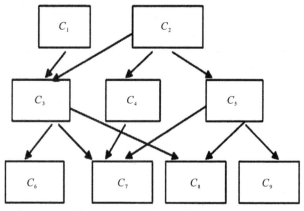

**Figure 4. A typical hierarchy.**

Design and Implementation of Multilevel Access Control in Synchronized Audio to Audio Steganography Using Symmetric Polynomial Scheme

151

Then $K_7$ can be derived by $C_3$ in the following steps.

$$S_{7/3} = \{C_4\}$$
$$K_7 = P\left(s_3, s_7, s_1, s_2, s_4, s_1{}', s_2{}'\right)$$

Key Calculation for the Classes using Equation (1)

$$K_1 = P\left(s_1, r_1, r_2, r_3, r_4, r_5, r_6\right)$$
$$K_2 = P\left(s_2, r_1, r_2, r_3, r_4, r_5, r_6\right)$$
$$K_3 = P\left(s_1, s_2, s_3, r_1, r_2, r_3, r_4\right)$$
$$K_4 = P\left(s_4, s_1, s_2, r_1, r_2, r_3, r_4\right)$$
$$K_5 = P\left(s_5, s_1, s_2, r_1, r_2, r_3, r_4\right)$$
$$K_6 = P\left(s_6, s_1, s_2, s_3, r_1, r_2, r_3\right)$$
$$K_7 = P\left(s_7, s_1, s_2, s_3, s_4, r_1, r_2\right)$$
$$K_8 = P\left(s_8, s_1, s_2, s_3, s_4, s_5, r_1\right)$$
$$K_9 = P\left(s_9, s_1, s_2, s_3, s_4, s_5, r_1\right)$$

Key Derivation of class 7 by class 3 using Equation (2)

$$S_3 = \{C_1, C_2\}$$
$$S_7 = \{C_1, C_2, C_3, C_4\}$$
$$S_3 U \{C_3\} = \{C_1, C_2, C_3\}$$
$$S_{3/7} = \{C_4\}$$
$$K_7 = P\left(s_3, s_7, s_1, s_2, s_4, r_1, r_2\right)$$

Which is equal to the key calculated by class7 itself.

Key Derivation of class 3 by class 7 using Equation (2)

$$S_3 = \{C_1, C_2\}$$
$$S_7 = \{C_1, C_2, C_3, C_4\}$$
$$S_7 U = \{C_7\} = \{C_1, C_2, C_3, C_4, C_7\} \qquad (3)$$
$$S_{7/3} = \{\varphi\}$$
$$K_7 = P\left(s_7, s_3, s_1, s_2, s_3, s_4, s_1{}'\right)$$

It can be seen that when the class derives its own key and when a ancestor of this class derives the key same parameters are passed in the polynomial but the combination differs when a wrong ancestor derives the key, the parameters are not the same.

The default values, we have taken are $m = 7$, $P = 2147483646$, $s_1 = 5$, $s_2 = 10$, $s_3 = 13$, $s_4 = 9$, $s_5 = 6$, $s_6 = 22$, $s_7 = 18$, $s_8 = 30$, $s_9 = 39$, $r_1 = 11$, $r_2 = 12$, $r_3 = 13$, $r_4 = 14$, $r_5 = 15$, $r_6 = 16$, $r_7 = 17$, $r_8 = 18$, $r_9 = 19$ (instead of $s'$ we have used $r$)

For a small Hierarchy "**Figure 5**", with more than two classes, we can easily illustrate our key calculations, where each class consists of several users.

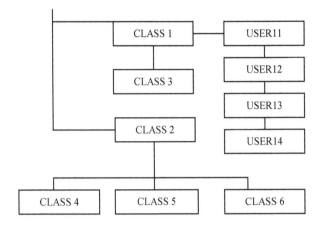

Figure 5. Sample hierarchy to illustrate calculations.

Key Calculations:
The parameters to be passed for calculating group key class 2 are $P(S_2, r_1, r_2, r_3, r_4, r_5, r_6)$
Group key class $C_2 = 699615258$
1) Private key for user 21 = 699615258 + (699615258/21) = 732930270
2) Private key for user 22 = 699615258 + (699615258/22) = 731415951
3) Private key for user 23 = 699615258 + (699615258/23) = 730033312
4) Private key for user 24 = 699615258 + (699615258/24) = 728765893
Key Derivation:
Deriving the group key of class $C_4$ using its ancestral class $C_2$

$$S_2 = \{\ \} \quad S_4 = \{s_2\}$$

Sj|i can be calculated as
$$S_{4|2} = \{s_4\} \big| \left(S_2 U \{C_2\}\right) \text{ Set Difference } S_{4|2} = \{\Phi\}$$

The parameters to be passed for deriving the key of class $C_4$ using $C_2$

$$\text{Key} = p\left(s_2, s_4, r_1, r_2, r_3, r_4, r_5\right) = p\left(10, 9, 11, 12, 13, 14, 15\right)$$
$$= 1947982264$$

Private Keys are used for local communication.

## 6.3. Class Level Dynamics

### 6.3.1. Adding a Class
When a new class $C_r$ is added, we need to verify whether m value satisfies the new node constraints
1) If $m < \max\{m_1, m_2, ..., m_n, m_r\} + 1$, a new m value will be generated so that $m \geq \max\{m_1, m_2, ..., m_n, m_r\} + 1$. Also, the CA will regenerate a new polynomial functions $P(x_1, x_2, ..., x_m)$ accordingly. In addition, all polynomial functions of classes are recomputed and retransmitted securely.

2) If $m \geq \max\{m_1, m_2, ..., m_n, m_r\} + 1$, the CA selects a random number $s_r$ for the new class $C_r$ so that a new polynomial function $g_r$ can be computed and transmitted to class $C_r$ securely. However, if class $C_r$ is added as a parent class of any existing classes, we need to modify keys of $C_r$'s descendant classes to prevent class $C_r$ from obtaining old keys of its descendant.

## 6.3.2. Deleting a Class

When a class $C_r$ is removed from the hierarchy, we need to determine whether the class $C_r$ is a leaf node or a parent node. Here, a leaf node is defined as a node without any descendant:

1) class $C_r$ is a leaf node: The CA can simply discard the public parameter $s_r$ without changing any other keys.

2) class $C_r$ is a parent node: Once class $C_r$ is deleted from the hierarchy, we cannot allow it to compute keys of $C_r$'s descendant classes using polynomial function $g_r$. We need to prevent class $C_r$ from accessing its descendants' resources.

## 6.3.3. Moving a Class

A class $C_r$ can be moved from one node to another node in the hierarchy. There are four cases:

1) leaf node to another leaf node: the CA simply recomputes new polynomial function $g_r$ according the new hierarchy and securely transmits $g_r$ to $C_r$.

2) leaf node to parent node: the CA recomputes polynomial functions of class $C_r$ and $C_r$'s new descendant classes according to the new hierarchy. The CA securely transmits polynomial functions to the affected classes;

3) parent node to leaf node: the CA recomputes polynomial functions of previous descendant classes of $C_r$ and class $C_r$ according to the new hierarchy and then, securely transmits these polynomial functions to the affected classes

4) parent node to parent node: the CA recomputes polynomial functions of previous and present descendant classes of $C_r$ and class $C_r$ according to the new hierarchy and then, securely transmits these polynomial functions to the affected classes.

## 6.3.4. Merging a Class

Two or more classes can merge together and become one class $C_r$. Similarly, the CA needs to find previous and present descendant classes of the merging classes. The CA randomly chooses a new number sr and then, generates polynomial functions for all corresponding classes.

## 6.3.5. Splitting a Class

A class $C_r$ splits into two classes $C_{r1}$ and $C_{r2}$. Depending on whether $C_r$ is a parent node or leaf node, the CA has to determine what previous and present descendant cla-

sses are associated with these classes ($C_r$, $C_{r1}$ and $C_{r2}$). The CA then selects two new numbers $s_{j1}$ and $s_{j2}$ and generates polynomial functions for these affected classes.

## 6.3.6. Adding a Link

If two classes $C_r$ and $C_k$ are linked together, we establish a new direct parent-child relationship between two classes, say class $C_r$ is the parent of class $C_k$. There are two different cases: 1) class $C_r$ was an ancestor of class $C_k$ through other classes. The CA does not need to perform anything; and 2) class $C_r$ is the only parent for class $C_k$ in the new hierarchy. The CA selects a new number $S_k$, and generates new polynomial functions for class $C_k$ and its descendants classes. The CA securely transmits new polynomial functions to these affected classes.

## 6.3.7. Deleting a Link

If two linked classes $C_r$ and $C_k$ are disconnected, we destroy a direct parent-child relationship between two classes, say class $C_r$ will not be the parent of class $C_k$ in the new hierarchy. Again, there are two different cases: 1) class $C_r$ is still an ancestor of class $C_k$ through other classes in the new hierarchy. The CA does not need to perform anything; and 2) class $C_r$ is not an ancestor for class $C_k$ in the new hierarchy. The CA selects a new number $S_k$, and generates new polynomial functions for class $C_k$ and its descendants classes. The CA securely transmits new polynomial functions to these affected classes.

## 6.4. User Level Dynamics

In this scheme, every class represents certain access privileges. Also, a group of users in a class can share a key if they belong to the same class. For example, all users in class $C_j$ can compute the keys of class $C_j$ and its descendant classes. Dynamic user operations deal with how a user can join in a class or leave from a class, and possible displacement from one class to a different class. They all require the class key to be changed after any user operation is completed so that the issue of backward secrecy and forward secrecy can be addressed. Specifically, our scheme can revoke a user from a class $C_j$. It is as quick and efficient as to join a user in the class $C_j$. Both operations require that the CA randomly select a new public parameter $s_j$ for $C_j$ and recompute a new polynomial function $g_j$ by using the new $s_j$. Since the polynomial function $g_j$ is newly produced, other polynomial functions and keys are also recomputed for the descendant classes of $C_j$. This will guarantee both backward secrecy and forward secrecy. The efficiency can be improved if backward secrecy or forward secrecy is not required. Another common user operation is to allow a

Design and Implementation of Multilevel Access Control in Synchronized Audio to Audio Steganography Using Symmetric Polynomial Scheme

153

user to move from one class $C_j$ to another class $C_k$. Here, the CA will randomly choose two new public parameters $s_j$ and sk for $C_j$ and $C_k$ so that new polynomial functions and keys are recomputed and transmitted to $C_j$, $C_k$ and their descendants respectively. Thus, both backward secrecy and forward secrecy are guaranteed.

### 6.4.1. User Join
Every time if a single user wants to join a group the CA just allows the user to be added to the hierarchy and generates a private for that user by providing the corresponding group key. When a new user joins the hierarchy, it should be provided with a group key and there are no changes to be made on the user's key.

### 6.4.2. User Leave
When a user wants to leave from the hierarchy the CA change the group key by making changes on anyone of the following changing the polynomial or changing the value factor $P$.

## 7. Simulation Results

The system is developed using .NET and found to be secure and fast. The system takes care of USER level and class level dynamics. The large number of numbers prevents a possible guessing. e.g., for a eight parameter polynomial, 16! (*i.e.*, 10922789888000) combinations possible. Bursty leave and join operations also are possible and the system can be used for any hierarchy. The outputs are shown in **Figures 6-10**.

## 8. Performance Analysis

Performance and security: Each user $u_i$ will receive

$$g_i = f\left(s_i, x_2, \ldots x_n\right) = g\left(x_2, \ldots x_n\right)$$
$$= \sum_{i_2=0}^{i_2=w} \cdots \sum_{i_n=0}^{i_n=w} a_{i_2, \ldots i_n}, x_2^{i_2}, \ldots x_n^{i_n}$$

The time complexity for computing the group key is $O$ $(w^{2n})$. An important measure for a secure group communication scheme is the number of rekeying messages. Suppose that t users will be joining the group. The TA will send $k$ and $g_i$ to each of them respectively ($2t$ messages) and broadcast one message to tell which users are joining. The total number of rekeying messages is $O$ ($2t$). Suppose that $t$ users are leaving the group. The TA only broadcasts one message to tell which users are leaving, thus the number of rekeying messages is $O$ (1). Suppose that t users are joining and another $v$ users are leaving the group, the total number of rekeying messages is still $O$ ($2t$).

As for the security of the scheme, if $w + 1$ class collude, then they can Figure out the function f entirely. Therefore, the scheme is $w$-resilient. Moreover, if less than $w + 1$ classes collude, they cannot get any information about the key, *i.e.*, any value in the key space looks like a valid and equiprobable key to these colluding users. It follows that the scheme is unconditionally secure.

### 8.1. Memory

Each user will be able to calculate the key based on the

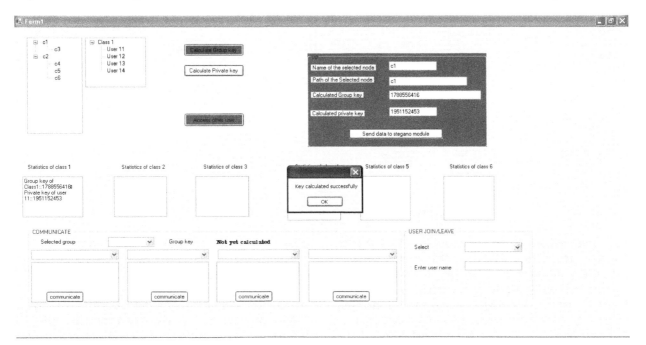

**Figure 6. Users and classes.**

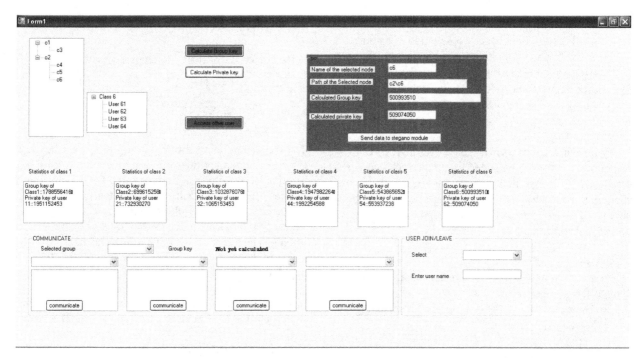

**Figure 7. Key calculation for all classes.**

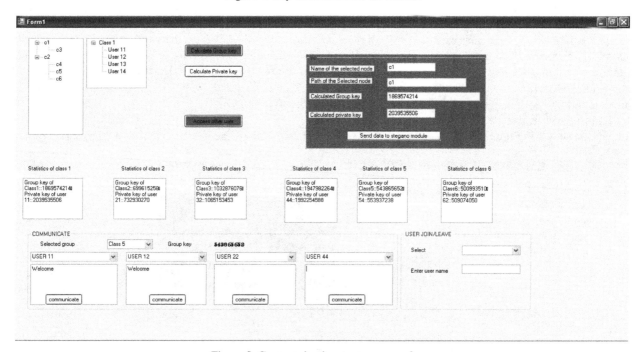

**Figure 8. Communication among same class.**

polynomial and hence very less memory is used. All parameters are publicly available and using the same method keys of lower hierarchy can be derived by substituting the corresponding parameters as given by the derivation module. The steganography module does not involve any storage for storing the already recorded data as always data is recorded and subsequently sent to the receivers. The size of the cover medium does not in-

crease because only two bits are used in each channel.

## 8.2. Computation Cost

When the user joins there is no need for recalculation because the recorded message has already been played. When a user leaves a group key is recalculated and given to the class. Private keys are generated from this. The

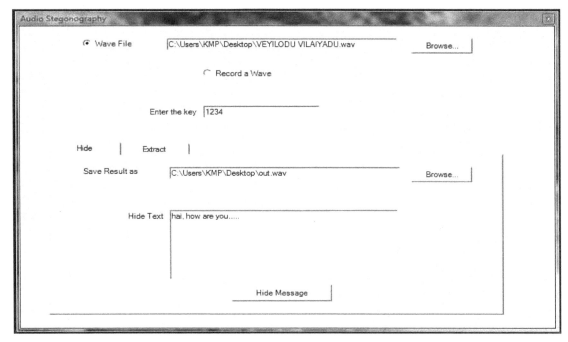

**Figure 9. Hiding the message.**

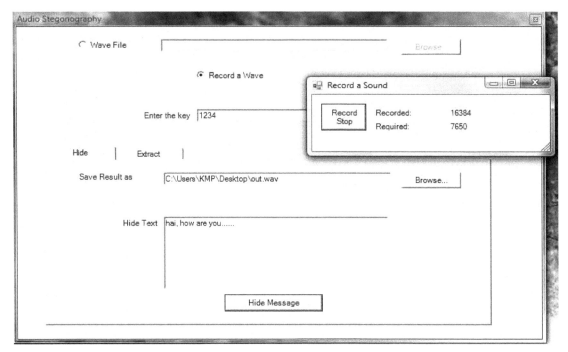

**Figure 10. Recording the message.**

value of the new key involves not a change of parameters but a change of mod $P$ value. Hence each class will be able to get a new polynomial value by passing the same parameters. Any left user will not be able to get the key. Only one key is used during creation of stego data. The higher class users need not remember the keys of all their descendant classes but rather using a simple scheme derive the exact parameters to generate the key. Hence the

computation cost is reduced.

## 8.3. Communication Cost

The P value is changed by the Trusted Authority and when the users try to calculate the key the new key will be generated. The computation cost is reduced because, the class users are not bothered about the key transmission. Once the polynomial is given the users can calculate their own key.

## 8.4. Dynamics

Class joining, Class leaving, Dynamic Hierarchy and New user joining a class are all done by the trusted authority in a phased manner thereby allowing the scheme to scale to greater hierarchy. Additionally local messaging and service messages are taken care in this system.

## 8.5. No of Rekeys

To calculate the no of changes might be made on the user's key based on user join/leave. Key must be changed when a new user is being joined/left from the hierarchy In the Hierarchy "**Figure 11**" for analyzing the no. of rekeys there are 50 classes and Let every classes consists of four users each, then we can calculate an unique key for every class based on this group key, we can generate a private key for every single user.

Classes:
Totally fifty classes of eight levels

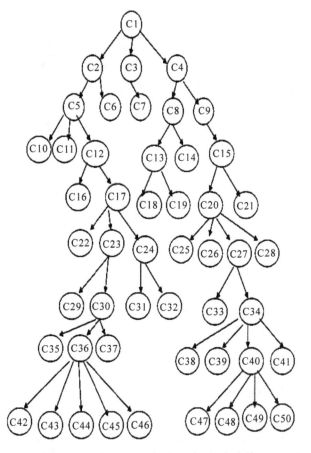

**Figure 11. Hierarchy analyzed for calculating the no. of rekeys.**

Users:
Every class is consists of 4 users
User joins:
Every time if a single user wants to join a group the CA just allows the user to be added to the hierarchy and generates a private for that user by providing the corresponding group key. The secrecy is maintained as the audio is real time.
User leave:
When a user wants to leave from the hierarchy the CA change the group key by making changes on anyone of the following Changing the polynomial, or by Changing the value factor P. The total no of key changes to be made = No. of Ancestor classes + 1 as shown in **Table 1**.

## 9. Conclusions and Future Work

### 9.1. Conclusions

Thus in this Paper, Design And Implementation Of Multilevel Access Control In Synchronized Audio To Audio Steganography Using Symmetric Polynomial Scheme is implemented successfully .The implementation results show that any type of hierarchy can be introduced and all dynamics can be done. For a 8 parameter polynomial that can have use 8 among the 16 values there are 16! combinations. Also, nodes can derive their descendants' keys without involvement of the CA once polynomial functions were distributed to them. In addition, the storage requirement and computation complexity at the CA are almost same as that at individual nodes, thus, the CA would not be a performance bottleneck and can deal with dynamic operations efficiently.

**Table 1. No of rekeys for user leaving from a corresponding class.**

| | | | | |
|---|---|---|---|---|
| Class 1: 1 | Class 11:4 | Class 21:5 | Class 31:7 | Class 41:8 |
| Class 2:2 | Class 12:4 | Class 22:6 | Class 32:7 | Class 42:9 |
| Class 3:2 | Class 13:4 | Class 23:6 | Class 33:7 | Class 43:9 |
| Class 4:2 | Class 14:4 | Class 24:6 | Class 34:7 | Class 44:9 |
| Class 5:3 | Class 15:4 | Class 25:6 | Class 35:8 | Class 45:9 |
| Class 6:3 | Class 16:5 | Class 26:6 | Class 36:8 | Class 46:9 |
| Class 7:3 | Class 17:5 | Class 27:6 | Class 37:8 | Class 47:9 |
| Class 8:3 | Class 18:5 | Class 28:6 | Class 38:8 | Class 48:9 |
| Class 9:3 | Class 19:5 | Class 29:7 | Class 39:8 | Class 49:9 |
| Class 10:4 | Class 20:5 | Class 30:7 | Class 40:8 | Class 50:9 |

Design and Implementation of Multilevel Access Control in Synchronized Audio to Audio Steganography Using Symmetric Polynomial Scheme

157

## 9.2. Future Work

1) The Trusted authority can still made secure by changing the value of the parameters.

2) A symmetric polynomial can be changed by the trusted authority.

3) Bit selection for steganography can be made by using some pseudo random generator.

# 10. References

[1]  W. Stallings, Ed., "Network and Internetworking Security," Pearson Education Asia, Singapore, 2001.

[2]  N. F. Johnson, Z. Duric and S. Jajodia, "Information Hiding Steganography and Watermarking-Attacks and Countermeasures," Kluwer Academic Publishers, Boston, 2001.

[3]  F. A. P. Petitcolas, R. J. Anderson and M. G. Kuhn, "Information Hiding - A Survey," *Proceedings of IEEE*, Vol. 87, No. 7, 1999, pp. 1062-1078.

[4]  M. Hosei, "Acoustic Data Hiding Method Using Sub-Band Phase Shifting," *Technical Report of IEICE, EA*, Vol. 106, No. 205, 2006, pp. 7-11.

[5]  M. Wu and B. D. Liu, "Multimedia Data Hiding," Springer-Verlag, New York, 2003.

[6]  T. Aoki and N. Homma, "A Band Widening Technique for VoIP Speech Using Steganography Technology," *Report of IEICE, SP*, Vol. 106, No. 333, 2006, pp. 31-36.

[7]  X. P. Huang, R. Kawashima, N. Segawa and Y. Abe, "The Real-Time Steganography Based on Audio-to-Audio Data Bit Stream," *Technical Report of IEICE, ISEC*, Vol. 106, No. 235, September 2006, pp. 15-22.

[8]  X. P. Huang, R. Kawashima, N. Segawa and Y. Abe, "Design and Implementation of Synchronized Audio-to-Audio Steganography Scheme," *IEEE Explore*, 2008, pp. 331-334.

[9]  S. G. Akl and P. D. Taylor, "Cryptographic Solution to a Problem of Access Control in a Hierarchy," *ACM Transactions on Computer Systems*, Vol. 1, No. 3, March 1983, pp. 239-247.

[10] S. J. MacKinnon, P. D. Taylor, H. Meijer and S. G. Akl, "An Optimal Algorithm for Assigning Cryptographic Keys to Control Access in a Hierarchy," *IEEE Transactions on Computers*, Vol. 34, No. 9, September 1985, pp. 797-802.

[11] S. Chen, Y.-F. Chung and C.-S. Tian, "A Novel Key Management Scheme for Dynamic Access Control in a User Hierarchy," *COMPSAC*, September 2004, pp. 396-397.

[12] I. Ray, I. Ray and N. Narasimhamurthi, "A Cryptographic Solution to Implement Access Control in a Hierarchy and More," *SACMAT'02: Proceedings of the 7th ACM Symposium on Access Control Models and Technologies*, ACM Press, New York, 2002, pp. 65-73.

[13] R. S. Sandhu, "Cryptographic Implementation of a Tree Hierarchy for Access Control," *Information Processing Letter*, Vol. 27, Vol. 2, February 1988, pp. 95-98.

[14] G. C. Chick and S. E. Tavares, "Flexible Access Control with Master Keys," *Proceedings on Advances in Cryptology: CRYPTO'89, LNCS*, Vol. 435, 1989, pp. 316-322.

[15] M. L. Das, A. Saxena, V. P. Gulati and D. B. Phatak, "Hierarchical Key Management Scheme Using Polynomial Interpolation," *SIGOPS Operating Systems Review*, Vol. 39, No. 1, January 2005, pp. 40-47.

[16] L. Harn and H. Y. Lin, "A Cryptographic Key Generation Scheme for Multilevel Data Security," *Computers and Security*, Vol. 9, No. 6, October 1990, pp. 539-546.

[17] V. R. L. Shen and T.-S. Chen, "A Novel Key Management Scheme Based on Discrete Logarithms and Polynomial Interpolations," *Computers and Security*, Vol. 21, No. 2, March 2002, pp. 164-171.

[18] M.-S. Hwang, C.-H. Liu and J.-W. Lo, "An Efficient Key Assignment for Access Control in Large Partially Ordered Hierarchy," *Journal of Systems and Software*, February 2004.

[19] C. H. Lin, "Dynamic Key Management Scheme for Access Control in a Hierarchy," *Computer Communications*, Vol. 20, No. 15, December 1997, pp. 1381-1385.

[20] S. Zhong, "A Practical Key Management Scheme for Access Control in a User Hierarchy," *Computers and Security*, Vol. 21, No. 8, November 2002, pp. 750-759.

[21] X. Zou, B. Ramamurthy and S. Magliveras, "Chinese Remainder Theorem Based Hierarchical Access Control for Secure Group Communications," *Lecture Notes in Computer Science (LNCS)*, Vol. 2229, November 2001, pp. 381-385.

[22] X. Zou, B. Ramamurthy and S. S. Magliveras, Eds., "Secure Group Communications over Data Networks," Springer, New York, October 2004.

# 17

# Eliminating Forgers Based on Intra Trial Variability in Online Signature Verification Using Handglove and Photometric Signals

**Andrews Samraj[1], Shohel Sayeed[1], Loo Chu Kiong[1], Nikos E. Mastorokis[2]**
[1]*Faculty of Information Science and Technology, Multimedia University, Malacca, Malaysia*
[2]*Faculty of Engineering, Industrial Engineering Department, Technical University of Sofia, Sofia, Bulgaria*

## Abstract

The novel reinforcement to the data glove based dynamic signature verification system, using the Photometric measurement values collected simultaneously from photo plethysmography (PPG) during the signing process is the emerging technology. Skilled forgers try to attempt the genuine signatures in many numbers of trials. The wide gap in the Euclidian distances between forgers and the genuine template features prohibits them from successful forging. This has been proved by our repeated experiments on various subjects using the above combinational features. In addition the intra trial features captured during the forge attempts also differs widely in the case of forgers and are not consistent that of a genuine signature. This is caused by the pulse characteristics and degree of bilateral hand dimensional similarity, and the degrees of pulse delay. Since this economical and simple optical-based technology is offering an improved biometric security, it is essential to look for other reinforcements such the variability factor considerations which we proved of worth considering.

**Keywords:** Photo Plethysmography, Data Glove, Signature Verification, Multimodal Biometrics

## 1. Introduction

Enhancements to the signature verification systems has been suggested by many researchers [1-3] and bio signal based security features are also considered as a unique alternatives for applications that require some document evidence like signing cheques and security documents. The signal based biometrics in the only applicable means for people with physical disability [4].

Making use of multimodal biometric technology which provides unique and robust identification features for every individual is in great demand in security environments that require high quality authentication methods. Using PPG wave forms to distinguish individuals using their biometric component was suggested by researchers in 2007 [5] and is employed in protected applications like e-transactions and access control mechanisms.

As a fortification to the current signal based dynamic signature verification system, we have used a new method by using the combination of the plethysmographic component along with the data glove signals to make the authentication process more robust and distinctive.

The possibility of skilled forging is reduced by the PPG feature that brings in the hand and heart dimensions of an individual into the signature feature vector. In order to further reinforce the effectiveness of the system here in this research work we have considered the intra trial variation approach to further validate the signature process. This method assures the elimination of skilled forging by a multi level authentication.

## 2. The Equipment

The plethysmographic system, a simple equipment that functions on the intensity of light reflected from the skin's surface. The red cells count below the skin is considered to determine the volume of blood in the particular area. The recorded signal posses the measurement of changes in venous blood volume and the arterial blood pulsation in the arterioles, hence representing the heart rate. There are two values supplied by the system and are the measurements of transmission and reflectance. A sam-

Eliminating Forgers Based on Intra Trial Variability in Online Signature Verification Using Handglove and
Photometric Signals

159

ple signal produced by the PPG is shown in **Figure 1**.

Similarly, the data glove is used for dynamic signature verification and that is easy to use, free from image and material of signature medium as well as no scanning processes is required. It involves only a direct acquisition of signals from the subjects while they write down their signatures, preprocess it, extract the feature, match it to classify and decision making. The data glove offers the users comfort, ease of application, and it comes with a small form factor with multiple application drivers, high data quality, low cross-correlation and high frequency data lodging. It measures finger flexure (2 sensors per finger) as well as the abduction between fingers. The system interfaces with the computer via a cable to the USB port (Platform Independent). It features an auto calibration function, 8-bit flexure and abduction resolution, extreme comfort, low drift and an open architecture. It can also be operated wirelessly to interface with the computer via Bluetooth technology up to 20 m distance.

Similarly, the data glove is used for dynamic signature verification and that is easy to use, free from image and material of signature medium as well as no scanning processes is required. It involves only a direct acquisition of signals from the subjects while they write down their signatures, preprocess it, extract the feature, match it to classify and decision making. The data glove offers the users comfort, ease of application, and it comes with a small form factor with multiple application drivers, high data quality, low cross-correlation and high frequency data lodging. It measures finger flexure (2 sensors per finger) as well as the abduction between fingers. The system interfaces with the computer via a cable to the USB port (Platform Independent). It features an auto calibration function, 8-bit flexure and abduction resolution, extreme comfort, low drift and an open architecture. It can also be operated wirelessly to interface with the computer via Bluetooth technology up to 20 m distance.

One glove fits many hands since it is made-up of stretchable material "A".

The data Glove and the signature verification process using the glove is shown in **Figure 2**. The output of the probe is fed into the serial port of a pulse oximetry module (from Dolphin Medical, Inc.) Measurements were taken for 50 signatures from 14 sensors of the data glove, and four led's of plethysmogram fixed on the subject as seen in **Figure 3**.

## 3. The Fusion of Photo Plethysmography System with Data Glove Signals

### 3.1. Subjects and Signal Acquisition Methods

In this study, the data glove signals and photo plethysmographic signals were recorded from 6 volunteered

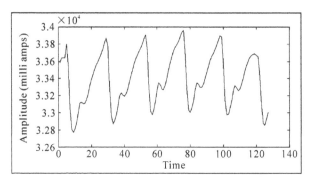

**Figure 1. The PPG signal pattern during one signature.**

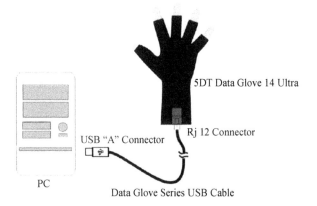

**Figure 2. The data glove.**

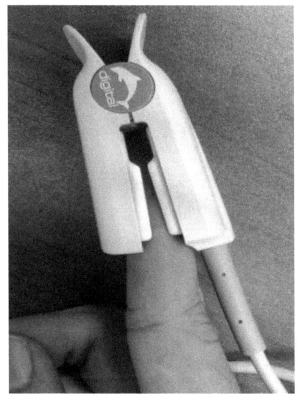

**Figure 3. The plethysmogram.**

subjects. Two subjects were considered as original signers and other four were the skilled forgers. The data glove signals and the peripheral volume pulses (PPG) were sampled at 61 Hz. Both the signals were recorded from the subjects simultaneously while they were signing.

The subjects were selected among our co-researchers and the average age of the subjects is 34.

The dynamic features of the data glove signal comprises of

1) Distinctive patterns to an individual's signature,
2) The hand dimensions,
3) Time taken to complete a signature process,
4) Hand trajectory dependent rolling.

These factors contributes to the feature of the signal captured from the data glove and make it more suitable to trust for use in signature verification since it provides data on the dynamics of pen movement and the individual's hand dimensions. Along with these four components that represent a person's identity, the heart rate reflected by the plethysmographic signals is also measured as the fifth component to reinforce the system's distinctiveness. The photometric signal consists on the volume of blood that flows through the blood vessels per pulse during every beat of the heart.

## 3.2. Experimental Setup

The recordings of signals are arranged in such a way that one of the subject writing original signatures was allowed to sign 50 original (own) signatures and the subjects who are assigned to forge are allowed to observe it to do the skilled forgery [6].

The forgers are given generous exercise to forge against the two genuine signatures by giving special sessions to practice the original signatures. The subjects are seated in a comfortable chair located in a sound protected room. The data glove was fixed on their right hand and the photoelectric probe was fixed to the index finger of their left hand.

All the subjects appointed for forging were allowed to sign 50 forge signatures one by one each with the help of a tracing paper placed on the original signatures after successful training. The subjects were asked to write the signatures, in two sessions, with an interval of 24 hours. Fifty signatures were collected per subject in one session. The skilled forging of the original signatures from forging subjects were also collected in the same intervals. Forging with 50 signatures per original subject takes a total of 100 signatures per session for two original signatures.

The PPG signal during the signing in process was also recorded for every subject from all the 14 electrodes embedded in the data glove.

Hence there were 200 original signatures and 800 forgings were recorded and considered for analysis. Similarly 1000 simultaneous PPG recordings were also included in the analysis.

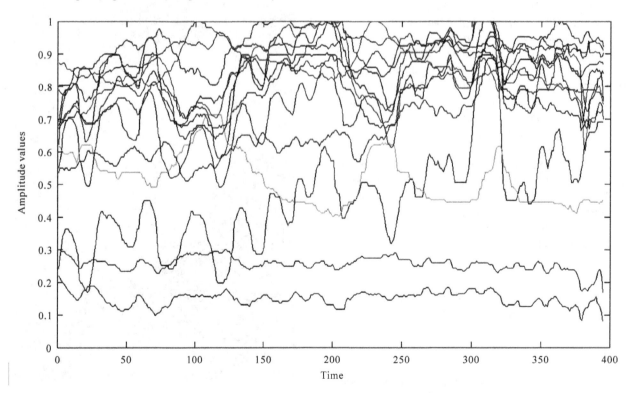

**Figure 4. The data glove signal pattern during one signature.**

Eliminating Forgers Based on Intra Trial Variability in Online Signature Verification Using Handglove and Photometric Signals

161

## 3.3. Preprocessing and Feature Vector Construction

The dimension of each recordings of hand glove signal, $A$ is of order $n$ by $m$, where $n$ is the number of electrodes and $m$ is the number of sequential samples per second. $n$ was fixed as 14 throughout the experiment, and $m$ differs in milliseconds as the intra and inter subject vary in signature timings. A sample of the plotted handglove signals are shown in **Figure 4**.

The dimension of every PPG, matrix $B$ is $j$ by $k$, where $j$ is the number of LEDs and $k$ is the number of sequential samples in one second. Throughout the experiment, $j$ was fixed as 4 and $k$ was taken up to the exact time length of $m$.

To condense the dimension and to reduce the effects of overlapping spectral information between noise and signature features, singular value decomposition (SVD) approach was applied to both matrix $A$ and $B$.

Since there is a real factorization for any real $nX$ $m$ matrices, The SVD of matrix $A$ & $B$ are is given by

$$A = U.S.V^T \qquad (1)$$

$$B = R.F.Q^T \qquad (2)$$

where $U$ (m by m), $R$ ($j$ by $j$) $Q$ ($k$ by $k$) and $V$ ($n$ by $n$) are orthogonal matrices and $S$ ($m \times n$) and $F$ ($j \times k$) are the diagonal matrices. The columns, $u_i$ and $v_i$ of $U$ and $V$ are the left and right singular vectors respectively, and the diagonal elements of $\sigma_i$ of $S$ are called the singular values. The columns, $r_i$ and $q_i$ of $R$ and $Q$ are the left and right singular vectors respectively, and the diagonal elements of $\sigma_i$ of $S$ are called the singular values.

Next, the singular values for each signal are arranged on the main diagonal in such an order:

$$\sigma_1 \geq \sigma_2 \geq \sigma_3 \cdots \geq \sigma_{r+1} = \cdots = \sigma_p = 0 \qquad (3)$$

The singular values calculated from the Matrix A are considered as the total Energy of matrix $A$. [7], and are measured in the direction of ith left singular vector of the matrix $A$.

$$E[A] = \|A\|_F^2 = \sum_{i=1}^{n} \sum_{j=1}^{m} a_{ij}^2 \qquad (4)$$

Similarly through SVD, the diagonal entries $\sigma_i$ are the singular values of any matrix $A$, $A$ can be written as the sum of rank one matrices as $r = \text{rank}(A)$.

$$A = \sum_{i=1}^{r} ui.\sigma i.v_i^T \qquad (5)$$

where $(u_i, \sigma_i, v_i)$ is the ith singular triplet of matrix $A$. The oriented energy of matrix $A$, $E_q$ is measured in direction $q$ is delineated as

$$E_q[A] = \sum_{K=1}^{n} \left(q^T.a_k\right)^2 \qquad (6)$$

In general the energy $E_Q$ measured in subspace $Q \in R^m$ is given as

$$E_Q[A] = \sum_{K=1}^{n} \left\|P_Q\left(a_k\right)\right\|^2 \qquad (7)$$

The SVD can be related to the minima or maxima of the oriented energy distribution as follows.

$$max_{q \in UB} E_q[A] = E_{u1}[A] = \sigma_1^2 \qquad (8)$$

$$min_{q \in UB} E_q[A] = E_{un}[A] = \sigma_n^2 \qquad (9)$$

From this it is proved that the oriented energy measured in the direction of the ith left singular vector of the matrix $A$ is equal to the square of ith singular value. Hence it is determined that the singular value decomposition protects the characteristics of the source signal matrix given by the $m$ signal samplings from $n$ electrodes.

Matrix $B$, used to incorporate PPG representation was also subjected to exactly similar SVD process to estimate the singular values for use in feature vector.

The average size of the glove signature matrix is (14,234) as well as the average size of the PPG signal matrix is (4,234). After the application of SVD the features are reduced to (14,1) and (4,1) respectively.

We were used the $l$-largest singular values of $A$ as well as $q$-largest singular values of $B$ as feature contents representing every single data glove signal and PPG respectively. Therefore, the entire signal $A$ is now represented by a highly discriminate feature vector of length $A$ ($l$) and the entire PPG is represented by $B$ ($q$). These $l$ and $q$ largest singular value features of $A$ and $B$ contain the feature component of the subjects' unique signature ID that discriminates the original from forge signatures. To minimize computational complexity, we set the $l$ value to be five and $q$ to 2 throughout these experiments, subsequent to its superior performance during our preliminary simulations.

$$Fs = \left[A_i, \ldots A_j\right] \qquad (10)$$

$$Fp = \left[B_i, \ldots B_q\right] \qquad (11)$$

where $i = 1$, $J = 5$ and $q = 2$;

The fused feature

$$F = \left[F_s, F_p\right] \qquad (12)$$

reflects the pattern of integrated signature components with the heart rate variability for further matching and classification.

## 3.4. Matching and Classification

The reference signature along with the reference PPG $F_G$ (Genuine Factor) was computed from a set of reference enrollment samples. The pair having minimal overall angle to the rest of signature, PPG pairs was selected as the reference signature to which all the comparisons where carried out. The genuineness of any factor pair $F_i$

is decided by the similarity factor (SF) to both the components of $F_G$ & $F_i$ are calculated as the angle between their principle subspaces.

## 4. Results and Discussions

**Figure 5** gives Euclidean distance between the genuine reference signature PPG fusion factors with other genuine signature and forge signatures with the corresponding PPG of the subjects. The Euclidian distance is calculated using

$$d = \sqrt{\sum_{j=1}^{L}\left(x_j - t_j\right)^2} \qquad (13)$$

Ten random sample distances across the two sessions were shown taken for considerations and other signatures were also giving similar results. These results were reported in our previous works [4].

The Equal Error Rate (EER) can be calculated if and only if a set of False Acceptance rate (FAR) and False Rejection Rate (FRR) are available. In this experiment, both are found to be zero and hence could not able to draw a curve of FAR and FRR to find the intersection point which is EER.

As an enhancement to this system we intended to find the consistency of the signatures written by the forgers with that of the consistency of the genuine signatories. This is to identify the best forger and later this factor may be used to enhance the authenticity of the entire system using the distinct quality of inter trial coherence.

**Table 1** shows the results in terms of Euclidian distance between the signatures cum PPG fusion template to every subject's with their own signature cum PPG features found in different trials. We found that the consistency of the genuine signatory is consistence and all the other four skilled forgers were not able to retain their consistency across the trails. This can be seen from the zigzag lines from **Figure 6**.

The performance of the data glove declines with the reduction of sensors. The performance degradation with the reduction of electrode channels from the hand glove were reported in our previous works [8] to minimize the

hardware and volume overheads in data processing. But the proposed technique of this paper helps to eliminate the said problem by providing strong reinforcements provided in two levels. The first one being the PPG factors and the second one is the intra trial variability. Table 1 shows the values of intra trial variability with the corresponding reference temples of every subject.

In all the ten trials the Euclidean distance is calculated against the templates of the individual subjects' training to write the same signature. The proposed signature and PPG combination is not altered through out the experiment.

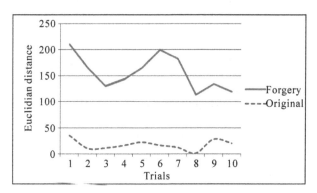

**Figure 5. Euclidian distance between genuine signature + ppg factors and forgery.**

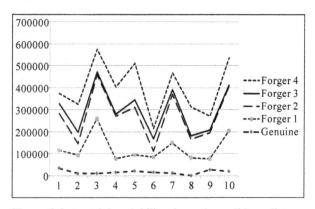

**Figure 6. Intra trial variability shown in euclidean distance across ten trials among individual forgers compared with the intra trial variability of genuine features.**

**Table 1. Intra trial variations in euclidian distance between individual templates to corresponding individual signatures.**

|         | Trial1 | Trial2 | Trial3 | Trial4 | Trial5 | Trial6 | Trial7 | Trial8 | Trial9 | Trial10 | Average Rnd |
|---------|--------|--------|--------|--------|--------|--------|--------|--------|--------|---------|-------------|
| Genuine | 34370  | 9934   | 10759  | 15392  | 21582  | 15866  | 11819  | 875.38 | 27423  | 19917   | 16793       |
| Forger1 | 165410 | 53161  | 198290 | 191950 | 215300 | 28236  | 218790 | 83738  | 118500 | 201180  | 147455      |
| Forger2 | 44223  | 51702  | 12488  | 8906.1 | 33876  | 54862  | 21046  | 15533  | 12128  | 6096.4  | 26086       |
| Forger3 | 46886  | 127180 | 103760 | 123760 | 165250 | 46779  | 75789  | 129740 | 62206  | 124990  | 100634      |
| Forger4 | 82633  | 82805  | 249120 | 62179  | 73780  | 68638  | 138800 | 81469  | 49637  | 184130  | 107319      |

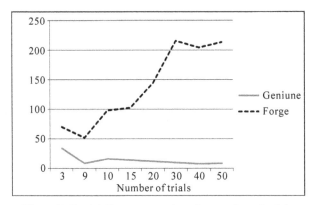

**Figure 7. Variability rates against the number of trials.**

This wide gap between the intra trial variability shown in **Figure 7** reveals that this factor can be considered as an improvement factor in reinforcing the robustness of data glove + PPG based signature verification system.

## 5. Conclusions

The proposed intra trial variability measurement of multi-modal signature + PPG based signature verification system, is found to be reliable in strengthening the identification of genuine subjects of Data glove based signature verification system. The novelty lies in two levels of using PPG factors and its augment to the robustness of the data glove features as well as the counting of Intra trial variability factors against the reference signatures. In feature the data glove may be fabricated as additionally accommodating the PPG sensor to make it easy for everyone. This technique is verified with the present easy modeling of data glove signals using SVD. Two sets of singular vectors produced by SVD are fused as the feature, where the primary set is from data glove with the maximum energy of the signature during the process of signature writing, and the secondary set is derived from the photometric signals extracted by PPG simultaneously during the process has been presented. These selected set of vectors are known as the principle subspace of data glove output matrix $A$ and PPG output matrix $B$ respectively. These principle subspace set are used to model a reinforced signature feature robust against any forge attack.

This research work is a venture to demonstrate the intra trial variability factor enhances the signature verification system that uses the PPG as its combination. This novel system is much potential to offer a sensitive high level security for applications like banking, electronic commerce and legal proceedings, than the existing similar systems. On the other hand this founding strongly supports the reduction in hardware by manufacture data glove integrated with PPG with minimum sensors so that the size of the equipment can be made simple and efficient for handling by a single hand. Since the possibility of reducing the feature size by means of reducing sensor in the data glove as well as reducing timing in the PPG, we can achieve a low cost signature verification system suitable to a common user in common place.

## 6. References

[1]   R. Plamondon and S. N. Srihari, "On-Line and Off-Line Handwriting Recognition: A Comprehensive Survey," *IEEE Transactions on Pattern Analysis and Machine Intelligence*, Vol. 22, No. 1, 2000, pp. 63-84.

[2]   S. Rhee, B.-H. Yang and H. H. Asada, "Modelling of Finger Photoplethysmography for Wearable Sensors," *Proceedings of 21st Annual International Conference of the IEEE Engineering in Medicine and Biology Society*, Atlanta, 1999.

[3]   Y. Y. Gu, Y. Zhang and Y. T. Zhang, "A Novel Biometric Approach in Human Verification by Photophlytesmograpic Signals," *Proceedings of the 4th IEEE conference on Information Technology Applications in Biomedicine*, Birmingham, 2003, pp. 13-14.

[4]   A. Samraj, N. G. Noma and S. Sayed, "Quantification of Emotional Features on Phtoplethysomogrpic Wave Forms Using Box Counting Method of Fractal Dimention," *Proceedings of the 8th WSEAS International Conference on Circuits, Systems, Electronics, Control & Signal, Processing (CSECS'09)*, Puerto De La Cruz, 2009, pp. 24-29.

[5]   J. C. Yao, X. D. Sun and Y. B. wan, "A Pilot Study on Using Derivatives of Photop Phlythesomogrpic Signals as Biometric Identifier," *Proceedings of 24th Annual International Conference of the IEEE EMBS*, 2007, pp. 4576-4579.

[6]   B. Majhi, Y. Santhosh Reddy and D. Prassanna Babu, "Novel Features for off-Line Signature Verification," *International Journal of Computers Communication & Control*, Vol. 1, No. 1, 2006, pp. 17-24.

[7]   "SVD and Signal Processing: Algorithms, Applications and Architectures," F. Deprettere, Ed., North Holland Publishing Co., Amsterdam, 1989.

[8]   N. S. Kamel, S. sayeed and G. A. Ellis, "Glove Based Approach to Online Signature Verification," *IEEE Transactions on Pattern Analysis and Machine Intelligence*, Vol. 30, No. 5, 2008, pp. 1-5.

# 18

# Fast Forgery Detection with the Intrinsic Resampling Properties

Cheng-Chang Lien, Cheng-Lun Shih, Chih-Hsun Chou

*Department of Computer Science and Information Engineering,*
*Chung Hua University, Hsinchu, Taiwan, China*

## Abstract

With the rapid progress of the image processing software, the image forgery can leave no visual clues on the tampered regions and make us unable to authenticate the image. In general, the image forgery technologies often utilizes the scaling, rotation or skewing operations to tamper some regions in the image, in which the resampling and interpolation processes are often demanded. By observing the detectable periodic distribution properties generated from the resampling and interpolation processes, we propose a novel method based on the intrinsic properties of resampling scheme to detect the tampered regions. The proposed method applies the pre-calculated resampling weighting table to detect the periodic properties of prediction error distribution. The experimental results show that the proposed method outperforms the conventional methods in terms of efficiency and accuracy.

**Keywords:** Image Forgery, Resampling, Forgery Detection, Intrinsic Properties of Resampling

## 1. Introduction

In recent years, with the rapid progress of image processing software, it becomes a great challenge to verify whether the digital image is tampered or not because the image processing software can create a sophisticated digital forgery and leave no visual clues on the tampered regions. For example, the *Liberty Times* newspaper in January 2008 (newspaper in Taiwan) published a photograph shown in **Figure 1(b)** in which the picture "Miss Wang" had been removed intentionally.

In general, the digital forgery detection methods can be roughly categorized into the active [1-4] and passive methods [5-16]. In the active methods [1-4], the digital watermarking or signatures are hid in the image for the purpose of authentication [1-4]. In addition, the embedded watermarks need to be robust enough to resist the various kinds of image attacks. On the contrary, the passive approaches [5-17] do not need any prior information for the forgery detection and can be further categorized into the methods of detecting copy-pasted regions, defocus blur edges, resampling, sensor noise pattern, different lighting conditions and block artifact inconsistency.

In [5], the author provided a method to identify the digital forgery regions that are copied and pasted from the same image by applying the method of block matching. However, the matching process can fail if the tampered region is cropped from different images. Zhou *et al.* [6] proposed a method to identify the digital forgeries by using the edge preserving smoothing filter in which the manual blur edge is discriminated from the defocus blur edge and the erosion operation is applied for detecting the manual blur edge. Another typical method developed by Popescu [7] detected the digital forgeries by tracing the characteristic of the resampled signals. The major concept of this method is to apply the EM (expectation/ maximization) algorithm to acquire the resampling coefficients and then calculate the resampling probability map. Based on the spectral analysis of the probability map, the magnitude peak can be used to identify the forgery patterns. Moreover, Popescu [8] utilized the specific interpolation coefficients of color filter array for each brand of digital camera to identify the digital forgery. Kirchner [9] proposed a more efficient method by directly applying the converged resampling coefficients to detect the tempered regions. As same as tracing the periodic characteristic of the resampled signals, Prasad [10] and Mahdian [11,12] proposed their method to extract the periodical property of the resampled signals based on analyzing the periodic characteristic of the covariance of the second order derivatives. In [13,14], Lukáš *et al.*

(a)

(b)

**Figure 1. (a) The original image; (b) The tampered image.**

proposed a method that utilize the imaging sensor noise as a unique stochastic characteristic to detect the forgeries. Johnson *et al.* [15] discovered that the light condition of the tampered area will be inconsistent to the original image. For the compressed image, Ye *et al.* [16] proposed a method based on the different block artifacts caused by different quantization tables.

Generally, each kind of digital forgery detection method can solve only one kind of forgery pattern. In this study, we only address on the detection of resampling forgery. Two related researches addressed on the detection of resampling forgery are the methods proposed by Popescu [7] and Mahdian [11]. However, there exist two major drawbacks in the above-mentioned algorithms. For the Popescu's method [7], high computation cost in the iterative computing procedure is required. It takes almost 5 minutes to generate the probability map for the image with resolution 512 × 512 pixels. For the method proposed by Mahdian [11], we found that the derivative kernel used in [11] will destroy the periodicity of the correlation function at the high texture regions. Hence, in

this study, we try to investigate and analyze the intrinsic properties of resampling scheme and develop a new more efficient algorithm based on the intrinsic properties of resampling.

Based on the periodical property that the original values can be selected from the resampling process, some of the reconstructed values would exactly overlap the original values in resampled signal and then the error between the predicted value and the resampled value would be very small. By analyzing the prediction error distribution generated by the weighting tables from different resampling rates, we can detect the digital forgeries. To enhance the periodical property, the projection operation is used for creating one-dimensional prominent periodical patterns. In addition, both of the vertical and horizontal predicting error variations are considered simultaneously.

The rest of this paper is organized as follows. In Section 2, two typical forgery detection methods are described. In Section 3, a new forgery detection method based on the intrinsic properties of resampling is proposed, which can detect the tampered regions more efficiently. In Section 4, we present the efficiency and accuracy analyses among the proposed method and other approaches. Finally, we summarize the contributions and future works in Section 5.

## 2. Related Works

In this section, two typical forgery detection methods for the resampling forgery techniques are introduced. These methods detect the forgery by tracing the interpolation clues of resampled signal

### 2.1. The Popescu's Method

A well known forgery detection method proposed by Popescu [7] assume that the interpolated samples are the linear combination of their neighboring pixels and try to train a set of resampling coefficients to estimate the probability map. In this method, a digital sample can be categorized into two models: $M_1$ and $M_2$. $M_1$ denotes the model that the sample is correlated to their neighbors; while $M_2$ denotes that the sample isn't correlated to its neighbors. The resampling coefficients can be acquired by the EM algorithm. In the E-step, the probability for $M_1$ model for every sample is calculated. In the M-step, the specific correlation coefficients are estimated and updated continuously. The detailed description of the forgery detection algorithm is described in the sequel.

#### 2.1.1. E-Step
The conditional probability for sample $y[i]$ belonging to $M_1$ model is calculated by the following formula.

$$\Pr\left\{y[i]\big|y[i]\in M_1\right\}$$

$$=\frac{1}{\sigma\sqrt{2\pi}}\exp\left[\frac{-\left(y[i]-\sum_{k=-N}^{N}\alpha_k y[i+k]\right)^2}{2\sigma^2}\right] \quad (1)$$

### 2.1.2. M-Step

Minimize the quadratic error function defined in Equation (2) by updating the correlation coefficients $\alpha$ iteratively.

$$E(\vec{\alpha})=\sum_i \omega(i)\left(y[i]-\sum_{k=-N}^{N}\alpha_k y[i+k]\right)^2 \quad (2)$$

where $\omega(i)\equiv\Pr\left\{y[i]\in M_1\big|y[i]\right\}$.

After applying the Popescu's method to the image, we can obtain a probability map. The peak ratio of frequency response of the probability map can be used to identify the digital forgery. **Figure 2** illustrates that the peaks of frequency response exist in the tampered image. On the contrary, no peaks exist in the original image shown in **Figure 2(a)**.

## 2.2. The Mahdian's Method

Another method proposed by Mahdian and Saic [11] demonstrates that the interpolation operation can exhibit periodicity in their derivative distributions. To emphasize the periodical property, they employ the radon transformation to project the derivatives along a certain orientation. The radon transformation is defined as:

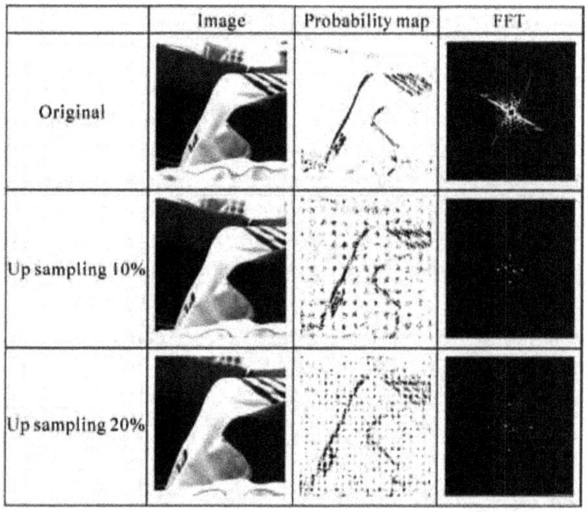

**Figure 2. The frequency response of the probability maps generated from Popescu's method for the original image, resampled images with up-sampling rate 10% and 20% respectively.**

$$\rho D^2\{b\}(x,y)=\int_L \left|D^2\{b(x,y)\}\right|dl \quad (3)$$

where, $b(x,y)$ denotes the pixel in the block with size of $R\times R$ and $D^2\{*\}$ denotes the derivative kernel of order 2. The radon transform along angle $\theta$ ($0\sim 179°$) is defined in Equation (4).

$$\rho_\theta(x')=\int_{-\infty}^{\infty}\left|D^2\{b(x,y)\}\right|\cdot(x'\cos\theta$$
$$-y'\sin\theta, x'\sin\theta+y'\cos\theta)\,dy' \quad (4)$$

After projecting all the derivatives to one direction and forming 1-$D$ projection vectors, the autocovariance function can be used to emphasize the periodicity and defined as:

$$R_{\rho_\theta}(k)=\sum_i\left(\rho_\theta(i+k)-\overline{\rho_\theta}\right)\left(\rho_\theta(i)-\overline{\rho_\theta}\right) \quad (5)$$

Then, the Fourier transformation of $R_{\rho_\theta}$ are also computed to identify the periodic peaks which can indicate the existing of digital forgery. The simulation results are shown in **Figure 3**. It shows that the resampled image can have strong peaks in the frequency response of the derivative covariance.

## 3. Forgery Detection Using the Resampling Intrinsic Properties

There exist two major drawbacks in the above-mentioned algorithms. For the Popescu's method [7], high computation cost in the iterative computing procedure is required. It takes almost 5 minutes to generate the probability map for an image with resolution $512\times 512$ pixels. For the method proposed by Mahdian [11], we found that the derivative kernel used in [11] can reduce the periodicity of the correlation function at the high texture region. Hence, in this study we try to investigate and analyze the intrinsic properties of resampling process and develop a new more efficient algorithm. The system flowchart is shown in **Figure 4** and the detailed function for each block will be described in the following subsections.

### 3.1. Intrinsic Properties of Resampled Signal

In this section, we firstly introduce the procedures of general resampling process. The up-sampling process is illustrated in **Figure 5(a)** and the original values are denoted as red bars. **Figure 5(b)** shows that interpolation operation fills the empty points with the linear combination of the adjacent signals' values which are denoted as yellow bars. Finally, the samples selected for decimation process which are denoted as blue bars are shown in **Figure 5(c)**. Through the observation of the resampling process, it gives us an important clue to design a new

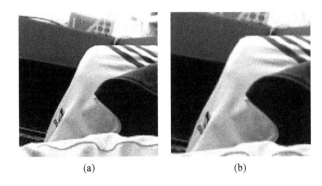

(a)                                    (b)

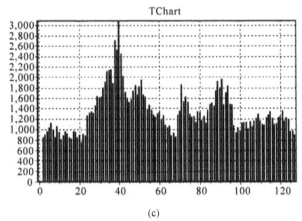

(c)

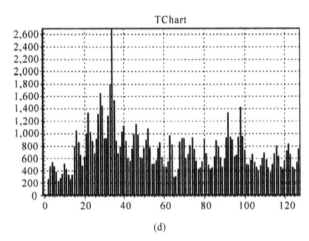

(d)

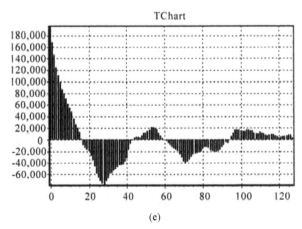

(e)

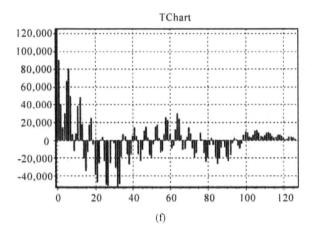

(f)

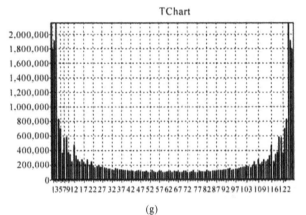

(g)

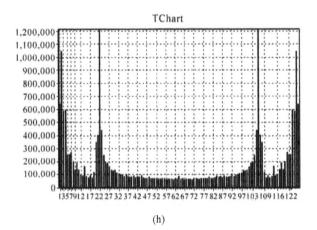

(h)

Figure 3. (a) The original image; (b) Resampled image with up-sample rate 20%; (c) The magnitudes of row-based derivative projection for $\theta = 90^\circ$ of (a); (d) The magnitudes of row-based derivative projection for $\theta = 90^\circ$ of (b); (e) The auto-covariance of (c); (f) The auto-covariance of (d); (g) The frequency response of (e); (h) The frequency response of (f).

forgery detection algorithm, *i.e.*, the original value will appear periodically in the resampling process. According to this property, the new detection scheme can be developed that will be illustrated in the Subsection 3.2.

## 3.2. Periodicity of the Prediction Error

Every resampled value denoted as blue bar in **Figure 5** can be approximated by the linear combinations of the adjacent original values denoted as red bar with different weights according to their positions, *i.e.*, the weighting in the linear interpolation algorithm is propositional to the distance to their neighbors. Here, we pre-calculate the weighing table (shown in **Table 1**) for each resampling rates. If the resampling rate is known, then the original values can be approximated by the linear combination of the interpolated values. Based on the periodical property of the original values selected from resampling, some of the approximated values would exactly overlap the original values in resampled signal (see the green bar in **Figure 6**). Ideally, the error between the predicted value and the resampled value would be very small at the position where the original value is resampled (the green bar in **Figure 6**). Moreover, the variation of the prediction error will distribute periodically. The weighting table $WT$ $[i]$, $i$ = 1, 2,..., $N$, should be calculated in advance for

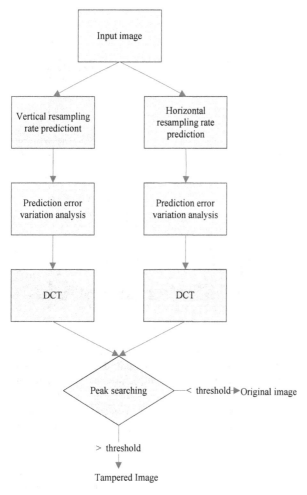

**Figure 4. Flowchart of the proposed forgery detection system.**

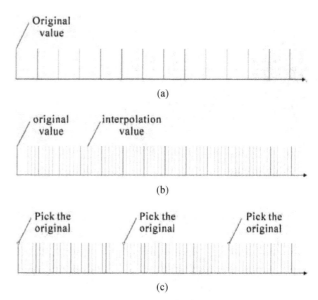

**Figure 5. An example for illustrating the intrinsic property of resampled signal. The scaling factor used here is 6/5. (a) The up-sampling for the original values (red bars); (b) Linear interpolation denoted as yellow bars; (c) Down sampling of signal in (b). The resampled signal is denoted as blue bars. The blue bars labeled the white node denote that the original values are chosen.**

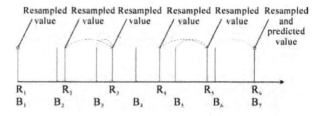

**Figure 6. The values (red bar) could be predicted by the resampled values (blue bar). After a certain periodical time interval, the predicted value will overlap the original value denoted as green bar.**

**Table 1. Weighting table for resampling rate 6/5.**

|   | $WT_L[i]$ | $WT_R[i]$ |
|---|---|---|
| 1 | 1/6 | 5/6 |
| 2 | 2/6 | 4/6 |
| 3 | 3/6 | 3/6 |
| 4 | 4/6 | 2/6 |
| 5 | 5/6 | 1/6 |

each resampling rate. The prediction process is described in **Figure 6**.

In **Figure 6**, the interpolated values can be computed as:

$$B_i = R_{i-1} \times WT_L[i-1] + R_i \times WT_R[i-1] \qquad (6)$$

Then, the predicted resampling values can be computed as:

$$pre_1 = R_2 = \frac{B_2 - R_1^* WT_L[i]}{WT_R[i]}$$

$$pre_2 = R_3 = \frac{B_3 - pre_1^* WT_L[i]}{WT_R[i]}$$

. (7)

.

$$pre_m = R_N = \frac{B_N - pre_{m-1}^* WT_L[i]}{WT_R[i]} = B_{N+1}$$

Finally, the prediction error within the certain sliding window can be computed as:

$$\text{Prediction error} = |B_{N+1} - pre_m| \qquad (8)$$

For the case of resampling rate 120%, the difference between $pre_5$ and $B_7$ will be very small. When the sliding window for calculating the sample prediction is moving (shown in **Figure 7**), the prediction error will increase and then decrease to the minimum value until the sliding window moves to the next periodical position ($B_{14}$, $B_{21}$…). Such a periodical property makes the sequence of prediction error distribute periodically shown in **Figure 8**. In order to enhance this property, the projection operation is also performed for every row and column (two directions are considered separately) before we utilize the frequency analysis to detect the forgery patterns (peaks in frequency response). If the test samples are not resampled or the wrong weighting table is selected, the distribution of prediction error would be irregular.

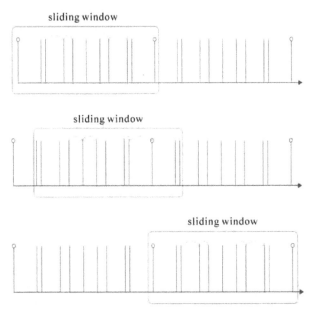

Figure 7. **The sliding window for calculating the sample prediction using the pre-calculated weighting table.**

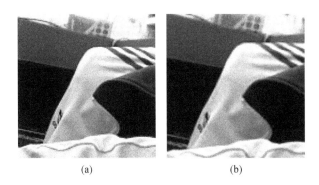

(a)                    (b)

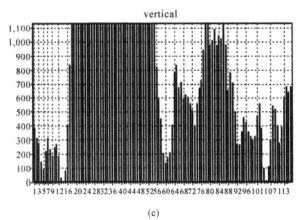

(c)

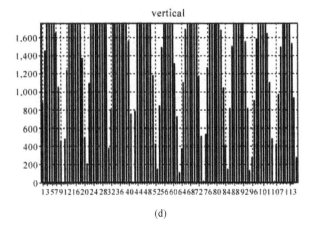

(d)

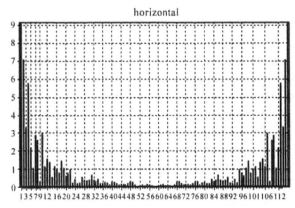

(e)

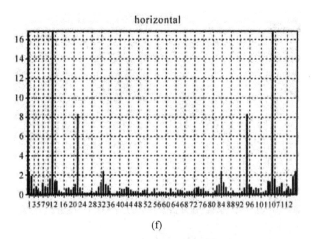

(f)

**Figure 8. (a) The original image; (b) Resampled image with up-sampled rate 10%; (c) The magnitudes of row-based prediction error variation projection of (a); (d) The magnitudes of row-based prediction error variation projection of (b); (e) The frequency response of (c); (f) The frequency response (d).**

To develop an automatic forgery detection method, there are two main criteria should be considered. The first one is the position where the peak occurs and the second one is the peak ratio. According to the different weighting tables (different resampling rate) for the forgery detection and the specific periodical property for each resampling rate, the expected position where the peak occurs could be forecasted. Then, we can match the peak position to the forecasted position where the specific resampling rate generates for identifying the existence of digital forgery. If the ratio is larger than a specified threshold, we can identify that existence of digital forgery. Finally, the flowchart of the proposed system is shown in **Figure 9**. To detect the tampered region, the image is scanned from left-top to right-bottom with different block sizes. In each block, the proposed method is applied to detect the tampered regions.

## 4. Experimental Results

In this section, the efficiency and accuracy for Popescu'd method [7], Mahdian's method [11], and the proposed method are analyzed. The experimental database is constructed with 160 gray level images with resolution 512 × 512 and each image is partial tampered in BMP format. The image tampering is based on the resampling process with the different bi-linear sampling rates: 105%, 110%, 120% and 125%. The forgery detections are performed by scanning the image with the block size of 128 × 128 pixels.

Before analyzing the accuracy of forgery detection, we firstly describe the detection rules for the Popescu's [7], Mahdian's [11], and our methods. Here, the forgery detection of Popescu's and Mahdian's methods is deter-

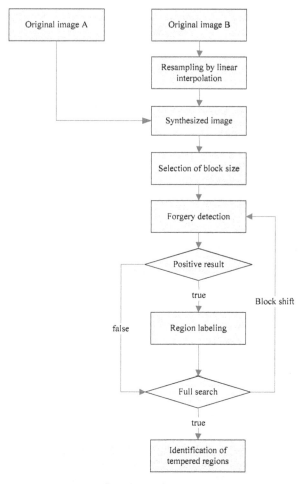

**Figure 9. The flowchart of the proposed method.**

mined by evaluating whether the ratio of peak-to-average frequency response is larger than a predefined threshold value or not. The ratio of peak-to-average frequency response is defined as:

$$R_{Pop\,sec\,u} = R_{Mahdian} = \frac{magnitude_{maximum}}{magnitude_{average}}$$

For our method, the forgery detection is determined by evaluating whether the ratio of forecasted peak-to-average frequency response is larger than a predefined threshold value or not. The ratio of forecasted peak-to-average frequency response is defined as:

$$R_{our} = \frac{magnitude_{forecasted\,position}}{magnitude_{average}}$$

The resampled image with rate 120% shown in **Figure 10(a)** is used as the tampered image for analyzing the detection accuracy for the three methods. **Figure 10(b)** shows the probability map produced by the Popescu's method and **Figure 10(c)** shows the frequency response of the probability map. **Figure 11(a)** shows the radon transformation of the derivative along horizontal direction generated by Mahdian's method and **Figure 11(b)** shows its auto-covariance. **Figure 11(c)** shows the frequency response of the auto-covariance values. Based on the proposed method, the prediction error generated by the novel algorithm is shown in **Figure 12(a)**. **Figure 12(b)** presents the frequency response of the prediction error. An obvious drawback of the Mahdian's method is that the weak periodical patterns occur at the high texture regions shown in **Figure 11(c)**. The accuracy analyses of forgery detections for different resampling rates are analyzed in **Table 2**.

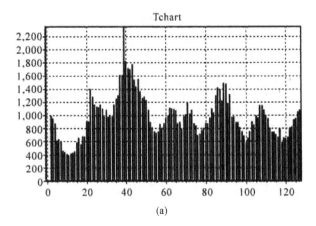

(a)

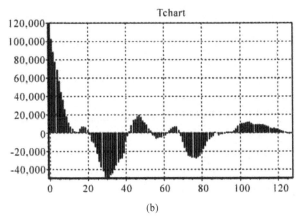

(b)

(a)

(b)

(c)

Figure 10. (a) The tampered image; (b) The probability map generated by the Popescu's method; (c) The frequency response of (b).

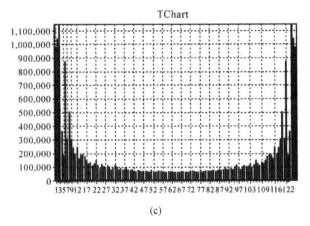

(c)

**Figure 11. (a) The radon transformation output of Figure 13 by the Mahdian's method; (b) The autocovariance of (a); (c) The frequency response of (b).**

The ROC curves with different up-sampling rates for Popescu's, Mahdian's and our methods are shown in **Figure 13**. In this Figure, the detection accuracy of Popescu's method is the highest one and the detection accuracy of our method is close to the Popescu's curve. However, our method is the fastest one that will be mentioned later. The detection accuracy of Mahdian's method is the lowest because the detection accuracy is affected by the high texture regions.

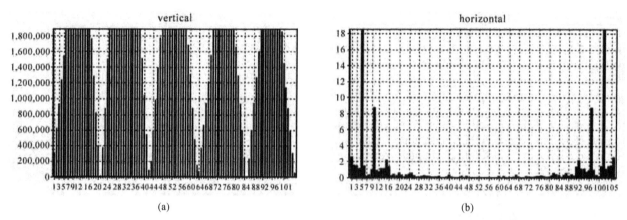

**Figure 12. (a) The prediction error of the tampered image shown in Figure 10, which is generated by the proposed method; (b) The frequency response of (a).**

**Table 2. The accuracy analysis for the methods of our, Popescu's and Mahdian's with 40 resampled images for different rates.**

|  | Popescu's method | | | | Our method | | | | Mahdian's method | | | |
|---|---|---|---|---|---|---|---|---|---|---|---|---|
| Up-sampling | 5% | 10% | 20% | 25% | 5% | 10% | 20% | 25% | 5% | 10% | 20% | 25% |
| Positive | 40 | 40 | 40 | 40 | 40 | 40 | 40 | 40 | 40 | 40 | 40 | 40 |
| Negative | 40 | 40 | 40 | 40 | 40 | 40 | 40 | 40 | 40 | 40 | 40 | 40 |
| True positive | 40 | 39 | 40 | 40 | 38 | 39 | 40 | 40 | 21 | 22 | 37 | 37 |
| True negative | 40 | 40 | 40 | 40 | 35 | 37 | 38 | 38 | 25 | 33 | 28 | 30 |
| Accuracy | 100% | 98.7% | 100% | 100% | 91.2% | 95% | 97.5% | 97.5% | 57.5% | 68.7% | 81.2% | 83.7% |

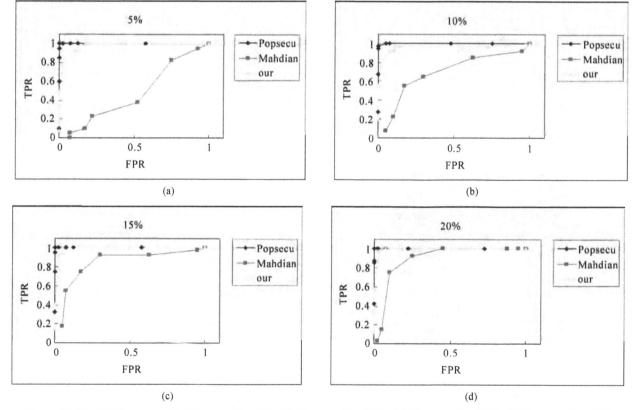

**Figure 13. The ROC curves of (a) Up-sampling 5%; (b) Up-sampling 10%; (c) Up-sampling 20%; (d) Up-sampling 25%.**

In addition, we compare the efficiency among Popescu's [7], Mahdian's [11] and our methods with the PC of 1.8 GHz. The efficiency analysis is shown in **Figure 14**. Here, we perform the efficiency analysis from block size 64 × 64 to 512 × 512 and assume there are 21 weighting tables for 21 resampling rates used in [7]. Because the iterative EM algorithm is very time-consuming, the efficiency of Popescu's method is the lowest. On the contrary, the highest efficiency is presented in Mahdian's method because the operations in his method are very simple. It's worthy to conclude that detection accuracy and efficiency of our method can approach both of the benefits of Popescu's and Mahdian's methods.

**Figures 15-16** show the detection results of the pro-

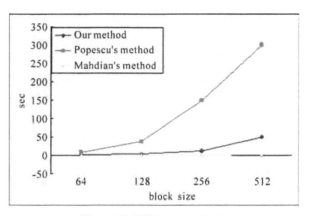

**Figure 14. Efficiency analysis.**

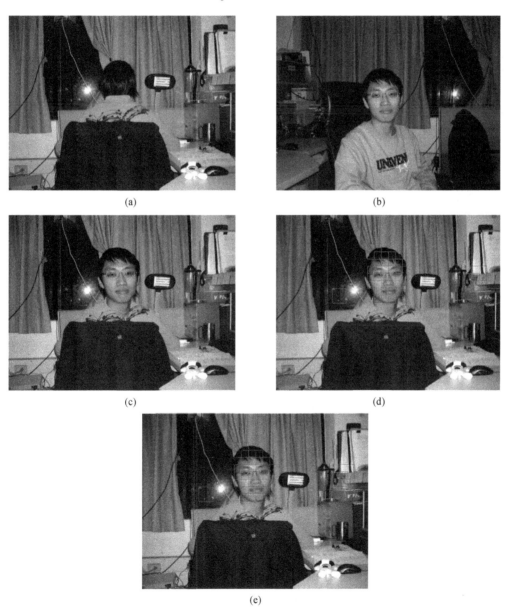

(a)

(b)

(c)

(d)

(e)

**Figure 15. (a) Original image; (b) Image with up-sample rate 5%; (c) Forgery image composed from (a), (b); (d) Detection result with 64 × 64 block size; (e) Detection result with 128 × 128 block size.**

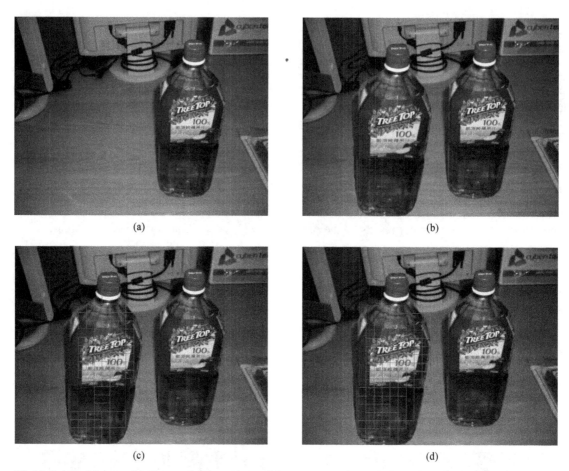

(a)     (b)

(c)     (d)

**Figure 16. (a) Original image; (b) Forgery image composed from up-sample (a) 10% and put the bottle near beside; (c) Detection result with 64 × 64 block size; (d) Detection result with 128 × 128 block size.**

-posed method for different resampling rates with two block sizes. In **Figure 15**, the man's head in **Figure 15(b)** is cropped and replaced the head region in **Figure 15(a)** to synthesize the forgery image shown in **Figure 15(c)**. **Figure 15(d)** and **Figure 15(e)** show the detection result with 64 × 64 and 128 × 128 block sizes. **Figure 16(a)** shows an original bottle image and **Figure 16(b)** shows that a resized bottle is put on the left side of the tampered image. **Figures 16(c)** and **16(d)** show the detection results with different block sizes. Here, we observe that the detection accuracy for the smaller block size is lower than the accuracy with larger block size because more periodical patterns can be collected in larger blocks.

## 5. Conclusions

In this paper, we propose a novel method based on the intrinsic properties of resampling scheme to detect the forgery regions with the pre-calculated resampling weighting tables and the detecting of periodic patterns for the vertical and horizontal prediction error. In Popescu's method, high accuracy can be obtained with high computation cost. On the contrary, in Mahdian's method, the

detecting accuracy can be affected on the high texture regions. The detection accuracy and efficiency of our method can approach both of the benefits of Popescu's and Mahdian's methods. The detection accuracy of our method is about 95% and the time for detecting a 512 × 512 image needs only 50 seconds.

## 6. References

[1]  R. B. Wolfgang and E. J. Delp, "A Watermark for Digital Image," *Proceedings of the International Conference on Image Processing*, Vol. 3, 1996, pp. 219-222.

[2]  R. B. Wolfgang, C. I. Podilchuk and E. J. Delp, "Perceptual Watermarks for Digital Images and Video," *Proceedings of the IEEE, Special Issue on Identification and Protection of Multimedia Information*, Vol. 87, No. 7, 1999, pp. 1108-1126.

[3]  M. Wu and B. Liu, "Watermarking for Image Authentication," *IEEE International Conference on Image Processing*, Vol. 2, 1998, pp. 437-441.

[4]  M. Yeung and F. Mintzer, "An Invisible Watermarking Technique for Image Verification," *Proceedings of the International Conference on Image Processing*, Vol. 1,

1997, pp. 680-683.

[5]  J. Fridrich, D. Soukal and J. Lukáš, "Detection of Copy-Move Forgery in Digital Images," *Proceedings of the Digital Forensic Research Workshop*, Cleveland, 2003.

[6]  L. Zhou, D. Wang, Y. Guo and J. Zhang, "Blue Detection of Digital Forgery Using Mathematical Morphology," *Technical Report, KES AMSTA*, Springer-Verlag, Berlin, Heidelberg, 2007, pp. 990-998.

[7]  A. C. Popescu and H. Farid, "Exposing Digital Forgeries by Detecting Traces of Resampling," *IEEE Transactions on Signal Processing*, Vol. 53, No. 2, 2005, pp. 758-767.

[8]  A. C. Popescu and H. Farid, "Exposing Digital Forgeries in Color Filter Array Interpolated Images," *IEEE Transactions on Signal Processing*, Vol. 53, No. 10, 2005, pp. 3948-3959.

[9]  M. Kirchner, "Fast and Reliable Resampling Detection by Spectral Analysis of Fixed Linear Predictor Residue," *MM & Sec'08, Proceedings of the Multimedia and Security Workshop*, 2008, pp. 11-20.

[10] S. Prasad and K. Ramakrishnan, "On Resampling Detection and its Application to Detect Image Tampering," *Proceedings of the 2006 IEEE International Conference on Multimedia and EXPO*, 2006, pp. 1325-1328.

[11] B. Mahdian and S. Saic, "Blind Authentication Using Periodic Properties of Interpolation," *IEEE Transactions on Information Forensics and Security*, Vol. 3, No. 3,

2008, pp. 529-538.

[12] B. Mahdian and S. Saic, "Detection of Resampling Supplemented with Noise Inconsistencies Analysis for Image Forensics," *International Conference on Computational Sciences and its Applications*, Vol. 81, No. 4, 2008, pp. 546-556.

[13] J. Lukáš, J. Fridrich and M. Goljan, "Detecting Digital Image Forgeries Using Sensor Pattern Noise," *Proceedings of the SPIE Conference on Security, Steganography and Watermarking of Multimedia Contents*, Vol. 6072, 2006, pp. 362-372.

[14] J. Lukáš, J. Fridrich and M. Goljan, "Digital Camera Identification from Sensor Pattern Noise," *IEEE Transactions on Information Security and Forensics*, Vol. 1, No. 2, 2006, pp. 205-214.

[15] M. K. Johnson and H. Farid, "Exposing Digital Forgeries in Complex Lighting Environments," *IEEE Transactions on Information Forensics and Security*, Vol. 2, No. 4, 2007, pp. 450-461.

[16] S. Ye, Q. Sun and E. Chang, "Detecting Digital Image Forgeries by Measuring Inconsistencies of Blocking Artifact," *IEEE International Conference on Multimedia and EXPO*, 2007, pp. 12-15.

[17] M. C. Stamm and K. J. R. Liu, "Forensic Detection of Image Tampering Using Intrinsic Statistical Fingerprints in Histograms," *Proceedings of the APSIPA Annual Summit and Conference*, Sapporo, 2009.

# 19

# Micro-Architecture Support for Integrity Measurement on Dynamic Instruction Trace

**Hui Lin[1], Gyungho Lee[2]**
[1]*ECE Department, University of Illinois at Chicago, Chicago, USA*
[2]*College of Information and Communications, Korea University, Seoul, Korea*

## Abstract

Trusted computing allows attesting remote system's trustworthiness based on the software stack whose integrity has been measured. However, attacker can corrupt system as well as measurement operation. As a result, nearly all integrity measurement mechanism suffers from the fact that what is measured may not be same as what is executed. To solve this problem, a novel integrity measurement called dynamic instruction trace measurement (DiT) is proposed. For DiT, processor's instruction cache is modified to stores back instructions to memory. Consequently, it is designed as a assistance to existing integrity measurement by including dynamic instructions trace. We have simulated DiT in a full-fledged system emulator with level-1 cache modified. It can successfully update records at the moment the attestation is required. Overhead in terms of circuit area, power consumption, and access time, is less than 3% for most criterions. And system only introduces less than 2% performance overhead in average.

**Keywords:** Integrity Measurement, Remote Attestation, Software Vulnerability, Trusted Computing

## 1. Introduction

Nowadays, computer under different platforms interacts with each other through internet environment. Although this provides convenience and increased functionality, it is necessary to securely indentify software stack running in remote systems. Effective remote attestation mechanism has drawn lots of research interests. Trusted Computing Group (TCG) first standardized the procedure to launch a remote attestation [1]. As defined, the protocol consists of three stages: integrity measurement, integrity logging, and integrity reporting [2]. The function of integrity measurement is to derive a proper measure that is an effective representation of a given platform status. In order to narrow down the range of such measures, Trusted Computer Base (TCB) is defined as hardware components and/or software modules whose integrity decides the status of a whole platform. Consequently, integrity measurement can simply based on measures from the TCB, which reduce performance overhead in measurement and attestation. Integrity logging is the process of storing aforementioned integrity measure in protected storing space. This process is not mandatory, but highly recommended to reduce the overhead due to

repeated calculation for integrity measurement. The last step, which is called integrity reporting, is to attest system based on the stored or calculated integrity measures.

Computer systems emphasize different security goals per contexts. While system integrity is more important in one situation, the other may concern more about data privacy. Integrity measurement is strongly related to security policy applied to specific computer system and consequently results in different attestation mechanism. TCG's specification describes an integrity measurement during system's booting process. This mechanism is called "trusted boot". At the very beginning, a hardware signature, which is stored in some security-related hardware components, is used as the root of the trust. Current hardware vendors design Trusted Platform Module (TPM) to provide such functionality. As each entity is loaded into memory, the integrity measures on the binaries are calculated one by one and form a trust chain at last. Unlike secure booting, system takes measurements and leaves them to the remote party to determine system's trustworthiness. TCG's attestation based on such a trusted booting is also called binary attestation [2].

Other integrity measurements still follow TCG's "measure-before-load" principle. Property attestation and semantic attestation both try to extract the high level property or semantic information from binary measurement. So it will be more efficient and effective to validate whether a security policy is hold or violated on such a measured property a priori. IBM's Integrity Measurement Architecture (IMA) based on the TCG's trusted booting extends the approach into application software stack. IMA is now a security module provided by Linux kernel since version 2.30 [3].

A good integrity measurement should be able to derive a reliable measure that represents the status of computer system. From the resulting measure, a challenger (the remote entity which is interested in attesting the system) should be able to tell the system's updated security-related capability such as whether the memory has been ever corrupted by attacker, or whether programs can be properly executed in isolation, or whether cryptography keys are securely stored, and so on. On the other hand, measurement procedure should be transparent to the local user and introduces little performance overhead.

Current integrity measurements face problems of gathering sufficient history information on what has been done to the computing device. When each entity is loaded into memory, measurement of its binary codes is recorded. However, there will be a "measurement gap" at the moment when measurement results are requested. System status may be different from the recording in measure. Furthermore, measurements are made directly on program's executable code residing in main memory. There exists another "behavior gap" between instructions executed in the processor and executable codes in the memory. The integrity measure of executable code in the memory can be a good measure to represent the system state. However, as different attacks occur from internet, this is becoming less sufficient for a remote challenger. For those programs running for a long time, such as server programs, a static measurement prior to execution may have little relation to the system status at the current moment. As a result, more accurate measurement, which can include program behavior, needed to tell challenger all history of bad behavior. This results in a better decision on trustworthiness of the system.

However, with more information included, overhead to measure programs' state increases. As a result, some measurements are targeted to specific data, such as processor control data, function pointer in memory, network traffic, intrusion detection, and so on. Measurement is often restricted in order to utilize only limited amount of information. Consequently validation of system against a certain security policy introduces little performance overhead. This policy-driven attestation or validation schemes are largely based on limited information specific per intended attack scenarios. The problem is that although it is efficient in their proposed situation, portability of such measurement is very low. In different situation, attestation may require a big modification which also exerts a large performance penalty.

In order to provide updated integrity measurement as system evolves, we propose an original dynamic instruction trace measurement (DiT) to include in the metric dynamic instructions-level behaviour in the processor with the help of simple micro-architecture modification. However, instruction-level trace can vary from time to time, with some part of the program being executed more frequent than the other. Directly recording the processor behavior causes lots of performance overhead and without increasing any accuracy. In stead of applying measurement in processor, we still perform the operations on the memory. As a result, most function interfaces provided before, such as the ones proposed in TCG or IBM's IMA, can be maintained.

Cache is an evolutionary design building a bridge between the memory and processor to reduce access delay. However, in this paper, we modify the structure of the instruction cache to the one similar to the data cache. The consequence is that instructions can also be written back to the memory. As program continues its execution, code region in its address space no longer stores codes loaded before execution but records instructions which are executed. We improve the integrity measurement for trusted computing in the following aspects:

1) Extending the measurement scope. When the security-sensitive program is loaded and starts execution, DiT writes back instructions into memory. Consequently, binary code located in its address space records instructions which are actually executed.

2) Facilitating attestation for different security policy. DiT only replaces static measurement with dynamic one. As a result, it changes little on the high level interface and provides a better general solution to diverse scenarios.

3) Writing back instructions does not require the involvement of operating system. Thus, DiT builds a connection between what has seen inside processor and what resides in memory. This procedure does not require trusting operating system, which in some cases can be corrupted by attackers.

The paper is structured as follows. Section 2 presents the background on trusted computing and integrity measurement. In Section 3, we present DiT's design in details. To avoid potential hazards from attacks, we propose several hardware-wise recommendations in Section 4. The experimental results and analysis are given in Section 5. Finally, the related work and conclusion are made in Section 6 and Section 7.

## 2. Background

### 2.1. Trusted Computing

Trusted computing deals with computer system in a hazard environment. Though there is lack of ubiquitous definition of trust, this paper refers the one from Trusted Computing Group (TCG) specification. Trust is mentioned as the expectation that a device will behave in a particular manner for a specific purpose [2].

Trusted Computing Base (TCB) is specified as any hardware and/or software components within the interested platform, whose safety can affect the status of the whole system. The assumption is made that if TCB is safe, system can be trusted. However, TCB's components vary from systems. In some situations, it may work with integrity validation mechanism; as a result, run-time critical data values are included in TCB. However, on other situations, execution of security-sensitive programs, such as encryption/decryption operation, is important to system's proper function; some architecture components, which guarantee privacy of such application program, are chosen in TCB. TCG has summarized diverse application scenarios and concludes that it should include the following two characteristics:

1) Isolated Execution, or protected execution. The computing platform should be able to equip security-related application program with an isolated environment. As a result, no other legacy programs can access or corrupt information it relies on. To achieve this property, many researchers adopt the virtualization approach or hardware extension to legacy computer architecture [4].

2) Remote Attestation. Each computing platform should be able to provide mechanisms to: (1) securely measure TCB's safety state; (2) protect measure log stored locally; (3) transmit measure to remote challenger.

## 2.2. TCG's Binary Attestation

TCG defines a binary attestation to provide a trusted booting. Whenever an entity is loaded into memory from the moment machine is physically turned on, TPM applies cryptographic hash function, say *Hash*, on its executable code to make a measurement result, say *M*. The binary measurement for each entity is logged separately. Additionally, each measurement is also stored in one of Platform Configuration Registers (PCRs) in TPM by making the cryptographically *extend* operations with PCR's current value, PCR$_t$, *i.e.*, new PCR values PCR$_{t+1}$ = $Hash$(PCR$_t$|$M$), where|denotes concatenation. When verifier requires attestation, TPM sends measurement logs (in local hard disk) and the corresponding PCR value to the verifier. He will recalculate hash result based on measurement logs. The comparison between newly-computed hash result and PCR value can tell whether untrusted behaviour within the environment has ever modified PCR value, measurement log, or executable code itself.

Using binary attestation facilitate verification in mainly two aspects. 1) measurement with such format hides

many different high-level implementations and reduces the complexity to calculate measure log and PCR value; 2) It successfully separates measuring and verification. Attestation does not try to prevent a system from illegal behaviour that might compromise system. It only records the history of loaded code, securely sends them to the verifier and leaves the verifier to make trustworthiness decision.

## 2.3. Integrity Measurement on the Application Program

Starting from the root of trust provided by TCG, Integrity measurement architecture (IMA) from IBM takes the first step to extend measurements from booting process to application level programs. IMA is provided as a software module to Linux kernel from the version 2.30. It provides measurements regarding to current system's software stack. The whole project provides integrity measurement but does not propose any detailed attestation mechanism. Measurements provide evidences showing whether system is corrupted by certain rootkit attacks or not.

IMA measures each individual component before it is loaded. With the help of *extend* operation, trusted booting forced execution to follow only one legal order. However, in application level, programs can execute different threads in parallel; program order does not related to trusted condition any more. So IMA groups measure together instead of applying extend operation one by one.

But IMA's is following TCG's "measure before loading" principle, therefore it inevitable maintains shortcomings of the binary attestation, such as its ineffectiveness to reveal hardware attacks or the software attacks after the program is loaded and executing.

## 3. Architecture Extension to Measure Instruction Level Behaviour

### 3.1. Design of Integrity Measurement in Application Level

DiT is based on IBM's IMA which provides comprehensive measurement over software stack. In IMA, all executable codes and chosen structured data are included in the measurement log. Any data which are loaded by operating system, dynamic loaders, or applications with identifiable integrity semantics are hashed. Measurement can be made automatically at the moment when codes or data are loaded into main memory. As programs continue their execution, kernel is able to measure its own changes. Similarly, every user level process can measure its own security sensitive inputs, such as its configuration files or scripts. The consequent 160 bit value from hash calculation becomes an unambiguous identity for such software module. Challenger can distinguish different file types, versions, and extensions by this unique fingerprint.

As system evolves, IMA collects hash results into a measurement list which is stored locally. The integrity of this list is of a great importance. Therefore, IMA uses TPM to prevent any modifications made on measurement list. Platform Configuration Register whose value can only be changed by physically system rebooting or TPM extend operation provides protected storage. Extend operation is applied on each value stored in the measurement list. Since it is impossible to restrict application-level softwares into a small number of orders, order of each value in the list is not used to validate the trustworthiness of the system.

## 3.2. Writing Back the Instructions

Although IMA provides measurement of all loaded software, it still follows TCG's "measure-before-loading" mechanism. As a result, "metric gap" and "behaviour gap" can largely degrade efficacy of measure log.

The "metric gap" occurs when measurement does not represent the updated state of the system. Application program can run for a long time, such as server program. So it may be a long period since the measurement is made. During this time interval, memory is possible to be corrupted. Attacks, who can take root privilege, can modify loaded executable codes. However, it is possible to detect such modification when the codes are being executed again. This is the basic assumption made in former tamper resistance design [5]. As executable code is hashed again, resulting measure will be different. However, attestation is made asynchronously to system's operation. It is possible that attestation is made before executable codes are hashed again. As a result, measurements may give challenger a misinformation about what is running at the moment.

**Figure 1** makes a comparison between three measurement mechanisms: DiT proposed in this paper, IMA and Aegis which is a typical secure processor design to achieve tamper evidence and resistance environment [5]. When IMA measures executable code, it makes comparison to values which are calculated before. In Aegis, if software's execution relies on a program, the measurement of this program is calculated again and comparison is made to former calculated value. In these two situations, the challenger may still get measurements from which the system can regarded as trusted but actually the memory is already corrupted.

"Metric gap" can be resolved by applying a measure to executable code at the moment of attestation is made

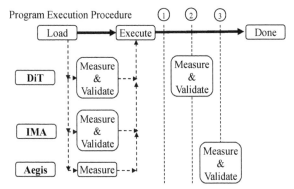

① Represent the event of possible attacks which corrupt memory
② Represent the event that remote attestation is required
③ Represent the event the program is used by other application

**Figure 1. "Metric Gap" occurs in the design of IMA and Aegis.**

(which is also reflected in **Figure 1**). However, "behaviour gap" can further introduce more severe problem. This describes the fact that static codes in memory are different from instructions executed in processor. But it is instructions executed in processor finally corrupt the system. On the other words, executing instructions are truly represent the trustworthiness of the system. What makes things worse is that many attacks do not rely on the modification on program's executable code to launch malicious behaviour any longer. For example, buffer overflow attack has diverse implementations. One of them is to insert codes directly in stacks which make detection only possible for a very short period of time. Challenger should also be able to know such deleterious execution since this system is vulnerable to attacks in the future.

No matter how attacks exploit software vulnerability, it finally needs to execute its code in the processor. As a result, researchers also propose to records behaviour in the processor. To reduce performance overhead, they only analyse behaviour of critical instructions, such as indirect branch or critical data. Measuring those data may work for certain security policy but lacks of portability and extendibility to future unknown attacks.

Measuring all instructions is a challenge. Instructions are fetched from memory, but dynamic execution flow varies from situation to situation. It is impossible to provide limited number of unique state to represent safety of such execution. On the other hand, collecting all possible states are computationally impossible to make.

DiT does not directly measure all executed instruction in processor. It maintains large part of original measurement interfaces which measure codes in memory. What DiT successfully makes is to extend architecture's pipeline to build connection between processor and memory (**Figure 2**). It proposes to store back instructions into its original locations after they are fetched into pipeline. The

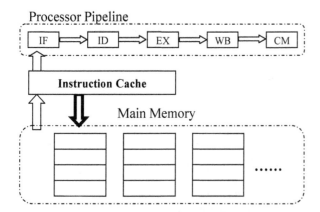

Figure 2. Strcture to measure dynamic instruction trace.

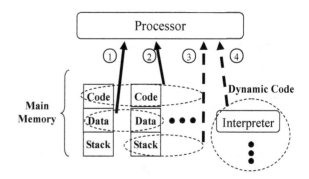

①: Data with integrity semantic is loaded by operating
②: Executable codes are fetched from memory
③: Malicious codes are fetched in statck or other illegal location
④: Codes are executed dynamically

Figure 3. Behavior gap occurs due to attacks or dynamic generated code.

purpose is to resolve "behaviour gap" between processor and memory. This is not an intention to record all possible run-time execution paths but to store instructions which are truly executed into measure log.

With such modification, what to measure and when to measure have to be carefully designed. Program's address space consists of data region, code region, and stack to record program execution context. In IMA, all executable code and part of related data, which are dynamically loaded by operating system, are measured (**Figure 3**). DiT will cover all code regions, data regions and stack as long as there are some instructions being written back to them.

Due to attacks, instructions can come from other locations rather the code region. This not only makes DiT to expand measurement range to include memory region such as stack, but also require it to add several temporal points to make such measurement. We can still use the aforementioned buffer overflow as the example. Stack contents vary as program enters into different contexts. Malicious code hidden there may soon be overlapped by unrelated information, such as parameter passed by following function call. As a result, malicious code should be measured on time before it is eliminated by legal ones.

To insert proper temporal points is a trade-off between detection ability and performance overhead. The performance overhead in original integrity measurement mechanisms is amortized, which is due to the fact that hash calculation is made at the frequency of program loading. From many former anomaly-detection approaches, successful corruption usually results in some changes in instructions level behaviour, such as cache miss, prediction miss and so on [6]. Furthermore, hash operation, which calculates memory code, is easily performed in parallel with program's normal operation. In the current work, one inevitable measurement is added. DiT launches the measurement at the moment of attestation requirement is made, which at least resolve the metric gap between measure and system state.

## 3.3. Introduce Randomization through the Use of Cache

Most personal computers usually have two level caches. Instruction and data are divided in the level-1 cache while level-2 cache is usually a unified cache which stores them together. DiT includes cache into the procedure of writing back instructions to the memory which "reverse" the procedure when instructions are fetching from it. In order to make write back work, instruction cache should be appended with few state bit just as data cache does.

By replacing structure of individual cache to the one of data cache, processor actually does not need to have the actual action of "writing back". It only needs to set a corresponding status bit and leave the work to cache and memory management unit. Whenever cache miss occurs, instruction cache first stores values in cache entry back to the memory and then read other instructions instead of overwriting it directly.

Usually, it is hard to predict cache miss. This randomizes the time to write back instructions. As a result, another level of protection which prevents attacks from learning this measurement and hide its malicious codes can be made. Besides, this operation does not need the involvement of operating system. Even when OS is not trusted, such as the kernel is corrupted, writing back operation can always be executed properly.

Current micro-architecture design can further help our design to write back instructions. Since level-2 cache is unified, only level-1 instruction cache requires modification. And the modification is restricted to small number of status bits added to each cache entry. As a result, overhead on chip area, power consumption and access time to cache entry (which is also called cache hit latency) is reasonable. Furthermore, instructions usually holds much better locality references than data cache which results in much less cache miss. Consequently, performance effect from writing back instructions is also possible to be restricted to a small amount.

# 4. Further Micro-Architecture Recommendations

With the proposed design, DiT is able to measure large amount of program's execution. However, it may still miss some situation due to current operating system design as well as diverse attacking mechanism. In this section, we propose several extra hardware recommendations to further resolve those issues.

## 4.1. Adding Measurement Point

With the aid of DiT, measurement will be recalculated with program's execution. There is still a possible hazard that attacker replaces correct codes to the malicious ones (that he injects before) in memory to avoid proper measuring (similar to the way he/she can insert malicious code) after malicious codes are stored back. As a result, adding more measurement points is necessary to provide another protection level on DiT itself.

The cache miss or branch prediction miss indicate a behaviour change in instruction level, which can be used as a point to recalculate measurement. To further reduce performance, we propose to make the measurement at the moment when the potential attacks are going to happen. However, from current study in software vulnerability, to detect the proper attacking potential is proved to be another difficult issue. As program is running, its address space records its execution state through the use of stack and/or heap and so on. However, its code space remains stable. Operating system design provides a good protection when it launches different code space to execute, such as the design of context switch. However, attackers successfully inject or exploit new or existing code space to avoid reliable operation provided from operating system.

As a result, we can make measurement when instructions are written back to the memory location which is outside of the code region (not address space) for the current running programs. As each program is loading its code, we can records its physical address in memory into a table and store it in a memory management unit. A comparison between written back instruction and each physical address of a code region can indicate which program this instruction is belong to. If it does not belong to any legal program, we can raise an exception. On seeing this exception, measurement is not also necessary since action of avoiding measurement is made.

By such architecture recommendation, DiT can achieve the validation such that every instruction executed in processor should be from executable code space which is properly loaded into memory before. Consequently, DiT can prevent injected code attacks while making measurement.

## 4.2. Measuring the Run-Time Generated Code

Different from compiler which generates executable codes, interpreter executes machine instructions on the fly. In our proposed design, integrity measurement is only capable of measuring binary codes of interpreter itself, dynamic codes generate by interpreter to processor are not recorded (**Figure 3**). On the other hand, more popular attacks begin to adopt this mechanism. Such attacks, including sql injection, cross script attacks, dominate current web applications. This presents a big challenge to provide accurate measurements to remote challenge, as malicious behaviours are extracted from user input and getting execution one instruction by another. Measuring executable codes from memory becomes impossible.

When instructions are generated from interpreter, DiT finds that there is no source memory location to which such dynamic instructions can transmit. Our proposed method is to "deceive" the interpreter that the dynamic executed codes is actually dynamic loaded. As a result, it can follow the predefined procedure to make such measurement.

This is achieved by creating a new memory region which can be linked to the memory space of interpreter's process. Current operating system, such as Linux kernel, provides safe interface to dynamically add or remove memory region from process' address space. It will be easy to include such secondary code region to interpreter's address space.

This is equivalent to adding a container to store dynamically executed code; however, the measurement will not be possible at the "load" time, since the container is empty at this moment. Only at the end of execution when all executed codes are written back, proper measure is going to be made on the full container.

# 5. Experiment and Result Analysis

In order to analyse applicability of DiT, two sets of experiments are conducted respectively. The first one simulated measurement mechanism, especially the situation to hash program's code upon asynchronous attestation. Then another set of experiments are made to detect hardware and performance overhead caused by modification on level-1 instruction cache.

## 5.1. Implementing Measurement

Different from IBM's IMA which implements all integrity measurements within Linux kernel, we implement it in the hardware level. DiT is integrated into Bochs which is a full-fledged open source × 86 PC emulator. It is used to emulate entire system from × 86 architecture to virtually instrumented monitor.

Through our experiment, we find that write back instructions to memory causes some instability for emulated system. As a result, DiT focuses on certain target program and only stores its on-fly instructions into memory. As mentioned before, TCB provides an isolation execution environment for the security-related programs. By implementing writing back instructions for only interested program, we believe that DiT can more practically simulate TCB's execution model.

We install Gentoo Linux with the kernel of version 2.6.29 in the emulation. To track process information, kernel is modified so that hardware emulator becomes aware of software context switch. Since version 2.6.x, kernel introduces the late binding for the context switch, so both *exec* () and *sched* () functions are modified. Consequently, process identity, such as Process ID and Process name is updated into a global variable as soon as process is created and loaded into memory.

Besides the operating system modification, we also implement several virtual debugging monitor. One of the most critical interfaces which DiT inserts is the one that halts the execution of current program in emulated operating system and hashes the code region in the address space of current active process. This efficiently emulates the situation that measurement is made upon the attestation request is sent from remote challenger.

## 5.2. Performance Overhead

In order to make instructions cache to write back, several extra status bits are required to each cache entry which is similar to the structure in data cache. Since in most micro-architecture design, level-2 cache is designed as a unified cache, only level-1 instructions cache needs modifications. To make a comprehensive analysis of such change, area, power consumption and access time is emulated under CACTI 5.0 [7]. The parameter of unmodified cache is the same as the one used in **Table 1**, which is also used in SimpleScalar for performance experiment. Five extra bits are added to each entry of the instruction cache to implement the write back mechanism. With the simulation results given from **Table 2**, largest power overhead is less than 10%. Overhead of other criterion is actually ignorable. Especially, modification has little effect on access time of level-1 cache.

**Table 1. Architecture parameters.**

| Parameter | Value |
| --- | --- |
| Fetch/dispatch/issue width | 4 |
| Instruction window | 128 entries |
| register update unit size | 128 entries |
| Load/Store Queue | 64 entries |
| I-cache | 128K 1 way set-asso., 1-cycle hit time |
| D-cache | 128K 1 way set-asso., 1-cycle hit time |
| L2 cache | Unified, 1M, 4 way set-asso, 6 –cycle hit time |
| Memory | 100 cycles access time, 2 memory ports |
| Function unit | 4 Int ALUs, 1 Int MUL/DIV, 4 FP Adder, 1 FP MUL/DIV |

**Table 2. Area, power and access time overhead for modified L1 cache.**

| Technology node | Overhead criterion | Normal L1 Cache | Modified L1 Cache | Overhead |
| --- | --- | --- | --- | --- |
| 90 nm | Area (mm^2) | 2.59811765 | 2.66909173 | 2.73% |
| | Power (W) | 5.23044172 | 5.23787143 | 0.142% |
| | Access time (ns) | 1.40756434 | 1.40756434 | 0.00% |
| 32 nm | Area (mm^2) | 0.36714162 | 0.36929974 | 0.588% |
| | Power (W) | 3.54005779 | 3.87976541 | 9.59% |
| | Access time (ns) | 0.43442463 | 0.43875809 | 0.998% |

We tested SPEC2000 benchmarks running in Simplescalar which models an out-of-order superscalar processor [8]. Reference inputs are adopted and we skip instructions of the number which is specified by SimPoint [9].

Writing back instructions are not supported in Simplescalar, as a result, we modify source codes of sim-outorder (the out of order simulators) such that right after each time a read access is performed to the level-1 cache, a write access to the same entry in the cache is launched. The parameter to run Simplescalar is given in **Table 1**.

We collect all number of level 2 cache access and cache misses for each program in SPEC 2000. The number of level-2 cache access varies to different programs. In *eon*, *perlbmk* and *vortex*, the modified level-1 cache increases more than 50% of level 2 cache accesses. But for other benchmarks, the change is not that obvious. We only select the increase of level-2 cache access with more than 0.01% among all 26 programs (**Figure 4**).

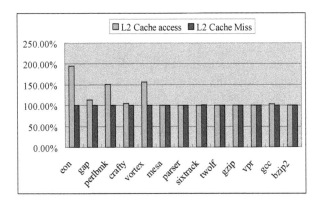

**Figure 4. Normalized Level-2 cache access and cache misss.**

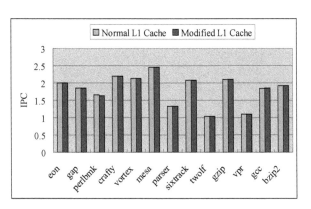

**Figure 5. Comparison of IPC number with normal Level-1 cache and modified L1 cache in processor.**

Although there are big increases in level-2 caches access, this does not simply increase the corresponding cache miss. All cache miss due to the modification of level-1 cache is increased with less than 1%. This is probably due to the fact that level-2 cache holds a good locality references for instructions. As a result, performance overhead for all benchmark programs is ignorable as shown in **Figure 5**. The largest performance overhead measured in IPC is less than 5%.

# 6. Related Work

## 6.1. Tamper Resistance Design

Execute Only Memory (XOM) has included whole memory space in the trusted computing base as most adversaries launch the attacks to corrupt memory [10]. In order to guarantee both integrity and privacy of the data in memory, encryption components are included in the legacy architecture design. Data transmitted from processor to memory is encrypted and reversely, they are decrypted for execution in processor

Aegis [5] follows the same assumption that memory can not be trusted. It hashes executable code when a program is loaded into the memory for execution. At this moment, any other code and data that the program relies on is checked to guarantee that the program is started in a trusted environment. In the situation that operating system can not be trusted, Aegis introduce security related module and hardware component into the legacy processor. Tamper resistance design does not make assumption on how memory is corrupted thus it is able to detect simple hardware attacks.

Tamper resistance design is similar to our approach in the way of measuring untrusted code. However, they are holding the assumption that detection of static code can be found on moment the software is used again. As mentioned before, attestation can be made before next-use of

software modules, so directly adopting tamper resistance approach introduces "metric gap". On the other hand, they are unable to measure program's runtime behaviour as well.

## 6.2. Integrity Measurement

TCG first standardize the procedure to make a remote attestation, besides, it also recommends an integrity measurement methods which is efficient during system booting. This binary attestation can only record what the programs are running on the platform and use the identity and the loading order of programs to system state after booting.

IBM's IMA, Integrity Measurement Architecture, inserts measurement interface into Linux kernel. As each program is loaded into memory, its executable code is hashed. When a program is further loading other codes or security-critical data structure, measurement is made as program transfer its control flow. However, software vulnerability which is exploited by attackers during each individual program's execution can also spoil measurement.

Based on the observation that modifications made in kernel space is usually permanent, Loscocco *et al.* propose to measure dynamic data structure which is critical to kernel control flow [11]. Such dynamic data structure is called contextual information, which is used to represent the state of the whole computing system. But this method is not efficient to be used in the user space operations.

## 6.3. Property Driven Remote Attestation

Binary measurement has the advantage of easy calculation and application-independence. Since hash calculation is irreversible, directly exploiting such metrics provides a big challenge and performance overhead. As a result, different attestation, which adopts different metrics, is proposed.

With specific security policy being set for the attesting system, property attestation and semantic attestation [12-14] propose to derive system high level information instead of the pure software stack. The extracted metrics can be directly used against security policy. Measurement methods may be implemented differently, but measurement is decided by security policy. As security policy changes, it is less flexible to change measurement implementation accordingly. As they indirectly include validation part into attesting platform, attesting platform's performance overhead is increased and validation procedure is also put under the hazardous environment. We propose DiT which designs an application-independent measurement which separates validation and measurement just as binary attestation does.

Some other researches also consider that program's run-time behaviour as a validation metrics, however, with many limitations. Alam *et al.* propose a behaviour attestation method [15]. However, the behaviour is defined as the quality of service the system can provide, connection latency, and so on. Consequently, this attestation implementation designed for web services only which lack the portability to be applied to other applications programs.

## 7. Conclusions

Ever since TCG standardized the procedure to launch a remote attestation, how to exchange the trust measure efficiently between computer systems under diverse platoforms has been a popular open research issue. Locally, attesting mechanism derives integrity measure based on software stacks on which trust decision is made. TCG introduces a binary attestation during system booting and many integrity measurement implementations are proposed following the "measure-before-loading" principle. Those measurements do not take into the account the actions after each program begins its execution. As a result software vulnerability which can corrupt both system status as well as measurement operation can introduce the "behavior gap" and the "metric gap" between program runtime behavior and consequent measurement. DiT, the dynamic instruction trace integrity measurement, is proposed as assistance to the current integrity measurement methods. By changing the structure of instruction cache, instructions are stored back into memory when cache miss occurs. As a result, code region in programs address space actually contains dynamic instructions trace executed in processor. By applying integrity

measurement based on this change, DiT successfully include most updated system state to the moment when attestation is required.

We have experimented this attestation mechanism in *bochs*, a full-fledged emulator, with a current updated version of Linux kernel installed. We have successfully simulated the procedure of measuring program's code (or trace) at the time when attestation is made. To further analyze the change made in level-1 instruction cache, Cacti is exploited to check area, power consumption and access time overhead. SPEC2000 benchmarks are run on the modified Simplescalar to analyze the performance overhead. As we only limit our small modification in level 1 instruction cache, the overhead in terms of circuit area, power consumption, and access time are all reasonable, and also the performance overhead is marginal.

## 8. Acknowledgement

This work was supported by the IT R&D Program of MKE/KEIT (2010-KI002090, Development of Technology Base for Trustworthy Computing).

## 9. References

[1] "Trusted Computing Group." http://www.trustedcomputinggroup.org

[2] TCG Specification Architecture Overview Specification Revision 1.4, Trusted Computing Group (TCG), 2007.

[3] IBM Integrity Measurement Architecture (IMA). http://domino.research.ibm.com/comm/research_people.nsf/pages/sailer.ima.html

[4] J. M. McCune, B. Parno, A. Perrig, M. K. Reiter and A. Seshadri, "How Low can you Go Recommendations for Hardware-Supported Minimal TCB Code Execution," *Proceedings of ASPLOS'08*, Seattle, Vol. 43, No. 3, 2008, pp. 14-25.

[5] G. Edward Suh, D. Clarke, B. Gassend, M. Dijk and S. Devadas, "AEGIS: Architecture for Tamper-Evident and Tamper-Resistant Processing," *Proceedings of ICS'03*, San Francisco, 2003, pp. 160-171.

[6] Y. X. Shi and G. H. Lee, "Augmenting Branch Predictor to Secure Program Execution," *Proceedings of DSN* 07.

[7] http://www.hpl.hp.com/research/cacti/

[8] T. Austin and D. Burger, "The SimpleScalar Tool Set," University of Wisconsin CS Department, Technical Report No. 1342, June 1997.

[9] T. Sherwood, E. Perelman, G. Hamerly and B. Calder, "Automatically Characterizing Large Scale Program Behavior," *Proceedings of the* 10*th ASPLOS*, California, Vol. 37, No. 10, 2002, pp. 45-57.

[10] D. Lie, C. Thekkath, M. Mitchell, P. Lincoln, *et al.*, "Archi-

tectural Support for Copy and Tamper Resistant Software," SIGPLAN Notice, Vol. 35, No. 11, 2000, pp. 178-179.

[11]  P. Loscocco, P. Wilson, A. Pendergrass and C. McDonell, "Linux Kernel Integrity Measurement Using Contextual Inspection," *STC'07: Proceedings of the 2007 ACM Workshop on Scalable Trusted Computing,* Virginia, 2007.

[12]  L. Chen, R. Landfermann, H. Lohr and C. Stuble, "A Protocol for Property-Based Attestation," *Proceedings of STC'06,* the ACM Press, Virginia, 2006, pp. 7-16.

[13]  A. Sadeghi and C. Stuble, "Property-Based Attestation for Computing Platforms: Caring about Properties, not Mechanisms," *Proceedings of NSPW'04,* New York, 2004, pp. 67-77.

[14]  V. Haldar, D. Chandra and M. Franz, "Semantic Remote Attestation: A Virtual Machine Directed Approach to Trusted Computing," *Proceedings of VM'04,* San Jose, 2004, p. 3.

[15]  M. Alam, X. W. Zhang, M. Nauman and T. Ali, "Behavioral Attestation for Web Services (BA4WS)," *Proceedings of the 2008 ACM Workshop on Secure Web Services,* 2008.

# 20

# Game Theory Based Network Security

**Yi Luo[1], Ferenc Szidarovszky[1], Youssif Al-Nashif[2], Salim Hariri[2]**
[1]*Department of Systems and Industrial Engineering, University of Arizona, Tucson, USA*
[2]*Department of Electrical and Computer Engineering, University of Arizona, Tucson, USA*

## Abstract

The interactions between attackers and network administrator are modeled as a non-cooperative non-zero-sum dynamic game with incomplete information, which considers the uncertainty and the special properties of multi-stage attacks. The model is a *Fictitious Play* approach along a special game tree when the attacker is the leader and the administrator is the follower. Multi-objective optimization methodology is used to predict the attacker's best actions at each decision node. The administrator also keeps tracking the attacker's actions and updates his knowledge on the attacker's behavior and objectives after each detected attack, and uses it to update the prediction of the attacker's future actions. Instead of searching the entire game tree, appropriate time horizons are dynamically determined to reduce the size of the game tree, leading to a new, fast, adaptive learning algorithm. Numerical experiments show that our algorithm has a significant reduction in the damage of the network and it is also more efficient than other existing algorithms.

**Keywords:** Multi-Stage Attack, Dynamic Game, Multi-Objective Optimization, Adaptive Learning

## 1. Introduction

The increased dependence on networked applications and services makes network security an important research problem. Detection of intrusions and the protection of the networks against attacks is the central issue. Game theory is an appropriate methodology to model the interactions between attackers and network administrator and to determine the best countermeasure strategy against attacks. There are however some difficulties in directly applying classical game theory, since the attackers' strategies are uncertain, their steps are not instantaneous, the rules of the games might change in time, and so on. Therefore any game theory based methodology has to take these difficulties into account.

There are many types of intrusions. Multi-stage attacks are the most destructive and most difficult kinds for any defense system. They use intelligence to strategically compromise the targets in a planned sequence of actions, so the usual methodology designed to protect against single-stage attacks cannot be used.

Network intrusion response mechanisms have been

intensively developed and studied in recent years. Several authors used Markov Games (MG) as a model and methodology. Lye and Wing [1] viewed the interactions between the attacker and the administrator as a two-player Markov game and modeled it by an intrusion graph. The recovery effort was considered as the cost of the response. The payoff for the attacker was defined by the amount of effort the administrator needed to spend in order to bring the network back to normal state. The equilibrium was obtained by using nonlinear programming and dynamic programming for infinite and finite horizon games, respectively. The main disadvantage of this approach is the huge size of the state space which makes extremely difficult to compute the equilibria. Shen *et al.* [2] used a piecewise linearized Markov game model with estimated beliefs of the possible cyber attack patterns obtained by data fusion and adaptive control. They also recognized that larger time-step horizons result in increased computation complexity. Another approach is based on Partially Observable Markov Decision Processes (POMDP) which results in more complex computation problems. Carin *et al.* [3] introduced the protection map and used reverse-engineering methodology to build an attack graph. Zhang and Ho [4] presented a model to characterize multi-stage collusive attacks in terms of key spatio-temporal properties. The attacker's behavior was modeled as a reward-directed partially observable Markov

The research presented in this paper is supported in part by National Science Foundation via grants numbers CNS-0615323 and IIP-0758579, and by Electronic Warfare Associates, Inc. via the grant number ewagsi-07-LS-0002, and it is conducted as part of the NSF Center for Autonomic Computing at University of Arizona.

decision process and the administrator was assisted by identifying the potential causal relationships between the different system vulnerabilities. This approach also suffered from serious computation difficulties because of the very large state space. Liu *et al.* [5] introduced a dynamic game approach based on modeling the Attacker Intent, Objectives and Strategies (AIOS) which resulted in a much smaller state space, so this approach is more efficient than the application of Markovian games. A similar concept was applied in Siever *et al.* [6] for the security of electric power transmission grids, when the goals of the attacker were used in formulating the attacker's game, which optimizes the difference of its reward and the amount of power delivered. The objective function of the defender is the sum of the amount of delivered power and a special reward function. The approach introduced by Luo *et al.* [7] was based on POMDP, however a reduced special game tree structure was used and a new stochastic multi-stage defense algorithm was developed.

All models and algorithms are based on assessing all damages and costs of the cyber attacks. The uncertainty in the knowledge of the network, its vulnerabilities, possible actions and counteractions, damages and costs, etc. make the mathematical modeling more complicated. In the economic literature this issue has been known and treated by the deterministic equivalent, which is a linear combination of the expected value ($\mu$) and variance ($\sigma^2$) of a random outcome: $\mu - \alpha\sigma^2$, where $\alpha$ shows the level of willingness of the decision maker to take risk.

Almost all models of multi-stage attacks are based on special game trees. It is well-known from the game theory literature (see for example, Forgo *et al.*, [8]) that such games with full information always have at least one Nash equilibrium, which can be computed by using backward induction. This general result however cannot be used in computer network security, since the game tree and the possible strategies of the players are not completely known by all participants. The administrator and the attacker might believe in different game trees with different possible actions.

## 2. Consequence Modeling

We have adopted the approach given in Richardson and Chavez [9]. The consequence of any attack and any action during a multi-stage attack is based on the following six steps:

1) Define the categories of impact;
2) State the importance of each category relative to the others;
3) Define the measures of impact for each category;
4) Define the relationships between physical effects and impact measures;
5) Define the system and its users;
6) Define the events in terms of scales and network system impact.

Impact categories include and not restricted to economic, image, safety, security, intelligence, and privacy concerns. Their relative importance factors can be assessed by any one of the well known procedures from multi-criteria decision making (see for example, Szidarovszky *et al.*, [10]). A common approach of obtaining the weights is based on pair-wise comparisons, when all participants in the decision making process are asked to give relative importance factors for all pairs of categories. Then the results are summarized into a final set of importance weights either by averaging them or by using the Analytic Hierarchy Process (AHP). The measures of the impact in different categories are usually given in different units, and they can be combined by using multi-attribute utility theory or weighting method with normalized evaluations. Performance measures can be defined for the impact categories, and each performance measure can be divided into a set of constructed scales representing the amount of impact the physical consequences have on the network and its users including lost revenue, repair and/or replacement cost, damage by lost or stolen information, etc. Any actual attack has impacts on different categories with different levels. Using the consequence modeling tool, the overall consequence of the different types and scales of events on the system and its users can be assessed into one combined value. This value has to be computed at all states of the multistage attack and will be used in the game tree analysis.

## 3. Game Tree and Decision Nodes

Multi-stage attacks are represented by special game trees. **Figure 1** shows the first two interactions on a game tree. The attacker is the leader, the administrator is the follower. The root of the tree is the initial decision node of the attacker, and the possible initial moves of the attacker are represented by the arcs originating at the root. These actions might include attacking the server with different intensity levels, sending a virus to a group of customers, etc. At the end point of each arc the administrator has to

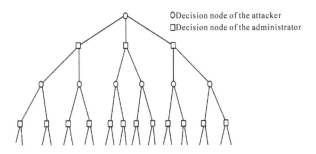

**Figure 1. Special game tree.**

respond, so they are its decision nodes. After the administrator's response the attacker makes the next move, and so on. This tree continuous until the intruder gives up the attack or reaches its goals. This tree can become very large and the payoff values at the decision nodes are uncertain, therefore the classic method, known as backward induction, cannot be used in this case.

## 4. Determining Optimal Responses

The algorithm to be described in this section is an on-line procedure, it provides the best response of the administrator at each of its decision nodes, when a multi-stage attack reaches that particular node of the game tree. So during an attack the algorithm can be used at each stage to find the best next move of the administrator starting just after the first action of the attacker and continuing until the end of the game.

Consider now a particular decision node of the administrator and the sub-game tree having this node as its root. The time horizon for this sub-game tree is obtained as follows. We have to check all end points of this sub-game tree where the attacker reaches its goals during smallest number of steps, so we select the shortest path with smallest number of arcs from the root to such end points. The length of the shortest path is the time horizon, and then all paths starting at the root will be considered only until this time horizon. The utility function of the attacker is then assessed at all endpoints of this truncated sub-game tree. The utility function is the linear combination of the expected payoff of the attacker and its variance as it was explained earlier. The risk taking coefficient of the attacker can be updated after each attack, since the administrator has estimates of the expectations and the variances of its utility values for all possible moves and also observes the actual move. The administrator then has to assess the probability distributions of the attacker's actions at all of its decision nodes. The probability values are computed based on the assessed utility values of the intruder as well as previous interactions with the attacker. First the probability values are computed proportionally to the utility values at the endpoints of the different arcs representing the next moves of the attacker, and if previous interactions provide relative frequencies, they are averaged with the computed probabilities. Using these probability distributions the expectation and the variance of the cumulative impact up to the time horizon for the administrator can be computed for each of its possible responses, and the corresponding utility values are obtained by combining expectations and variances with the risk acceptance coefficient of the administrator. The best response of the administrator is the arc which has its highest utility value.

The attacker makes the first move. At the end point of the corresponding arc the administrator has to respond.

Using the above procedure the administrator finds its response. Then the attacker makes the next step, and the best next response of the administrator is obtained again by using the same algorithm with updated data based on the information obtained from the previous actions of the attacker. Then the attacker has the next move, the administrator responds by using the same algorithm, and so on until the game ends, which occurs when the attacker stops attacking by reaching its goals or giving up.

## 5. Numerical Example

**Figure 2** shows a network structure. It is assumed that the HTTP server, Database 2, the FTP1 server and the information in the CEO are the vulnerable components in the network system, and access to the information in the CEO is the attacker's objective. It is also assumed that the CEO needs services provided by the HTTP server, Database 2 and the FTP1 server to do its jobs. The attacker can launch multi-stage attacks to obtain the information from the CEO in many different ways. Then the administrator can respond to it by selecting from a set of options, and so on, which leads to the game tree.

Next we assume that in addition to the sensitive data in the CEO the data in the Accounting is another vulnerability of the system. The attacker has now two objectives: the information in CEO and the data in Accounting. The Accounting also needs services provided by Database 2 and the HTTP server, etc. Our computer study assumed that the attacker always selects the action leading to maximal impact, and the administrator always selects its best action at its decision nodes by using one of the three tested algorithms.

We applied three methods to find the best responses of the administrator: One is a greedy algorithm (GA) in which the administrator completely blocks the traffic of

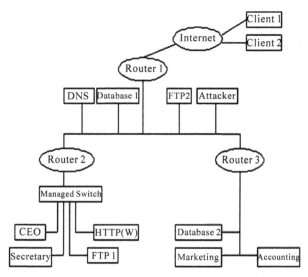

**Figure 2. Network structure.**

**Table 1. The performances of the three algorithms.**

| The total losses of the system occurred during the life-cycle of the multi-stage attacks | | Administrator | | |
|---|---|---|---|---|
| | | GA Algorithm | SO Algorithm | Our Algorithm |
| Attacker | Risk Seeking — Single Objective | 4,694 | 3,608 | 2,781 |
| | Risk Seeking — Two Objective | 9,597 | 6,741 | 4,689 |
| | Risk Neutral — Single Objective | 4,694 | 3,176 | 2,252 |
| | Risk Neutral — Two Objective | 9,597 | 6,325 | 4,021 |

corresponding services on routers, firewall, or disconnect the machines using managed switches, etc. regardless of what kind of attack occurs or what is the intensity levels of the attack. Another algorithm is also myopic, single-interaction optimization algorithm (SO) in which the administrator tries to minimize the loss from the most current attack at each interaction without considering future interactions with the attacker. The third algorithm is the one we developed. The results are shown **Table 1**. Two types of attacks were assumed. The risk seeking attacker worried about only the expectation of the impact ($\alpha = 0$), while the risk neutral intruder selected a relatively high risk taking coefficient ($\alpha = 1$). The two scenarios refer to the cases of one or two objectives of the attacker. The last three columns indicate the three methods which were used for comparison. The numbers in the last three columns of the table show the total losses of the system with using different methods. Clearly our method resulted in the smallest overall losses in all cases, where the loss reduction was 41%, 51%, 52% and 58% in comparison to the Greedy Algorithm, and 23%, 30%, 29% and 36% in comparison to single-interaction optimization. In assessing the numerical values of the impacts in the consequence analysis, we used only economic impact. A more complex consequence analysis would not alter the main steps of the algorithms.

# 6. Conclusions

This paper introduced a multi-stage intrusion defense system, where the interactions between the attacker and the administrator are modeled as a two-player non-cooperative non-zero-sum dynamic game with incomplete information. The two players conduct *Fictitious Play* along the game tree, which can help the administrator to find quickly the best strategies to defend against attacks launched by different types of attackers. Our algorithm is

an online procedure, which gives the most appropriate response of the administrator at any stage of the game. So it has to be repeated at all actual decision nodes of the administrator. Our algorithm is different than the usual methods based on decision trees, since at each step only a finite horizon is considered, instead of expected outcomes certain equivalents are used and the probabilities of the different arcs are continuously updated based on new information. In our numerical example our approach was compared to two other algorithms and the total network losses were compared. The loss reduction by using our approach varied between 23% and 58%. The performance of our algorithm is much better than that of other algorithms based on the results of our numerical experiments.

# 7. References

[1]  K. Lye and J. Wing, "Game Strategies in Network Security," *International Journal of Information Security*, Vol. 4, No. 1-2, 2005, pp. 71-86.

[2]  D. Shen, G. Chen, E. Blasch and G. Tadda, "Adaptive Markov Game Theoretic Data Fusion Approach for Cyber Network Defense," *IEEE Military Communications Conference* (*MILCOM* 2007), Orlando, 2007.

[3]  L. Carin, G. Cybenko and J. Hughes, "Cybersecurity Strategies: The QuERIES Methoddology," *Computer*, Vol. 41, No. 8, 2008, pp. 20-26.

[4]  Z. Zhang and P. Ho, "Janus: A Dual-Purpose Analytical Model for Understanding, Characterizing and Countermining Multi-Stage Collusive Attacks in Enterprise Networks," *Journal of Network and Computer Applications*, Vol. 32, No. 3, 2009, pp. 710-720.

[5]  P. Liu and W. Zang, "Incentive-Based Modeling and Inference of Attack Intent, Objectives, and Strategies," *CCS'03*, Washington, DC., 2003.

[6]  W. M. Siever, A. Miller and D. R. Tauritz, "Blueprint for Iteratively Hardening Power Grids Employing Unified Power Flow Controllers," *SoSE'07, IEEE International Conference on System of Systems Engineering*, Tampa, 2007.

[7]  Y. Luo, F. Szidarovszky, Y. Al-Nashif and S. Hariri, "Game Tree Based Partially Observable Stochastic Game Model for Intrusion Defense Systems (IDS)," *IIE Annual Conference and EXPO* (*IERC* 2009), Miami, 2009.

[8]  F. Forgo, J. Szep and F. Szidarovszky, "Introduction to the Theory of Games," Kluwer Academic Publishers, Dordrecht, 1999.

[9]  B. T. Richardson and L. Chavez, "National SCADA Test Bed Consequence Modeling Tool," *Sandia National Laboratory Report, SAND*2008-6098, Albuquerque, 2008.

[10] F. Szidarovszky, M. Gershon and L. Duckstein, "Techniques for Multiobjective Decision Making in Systems Management," Elsevier, Amsterdam, 1986.

# 21

# Sustainable Tourism Using Security Cameras with Privacy Protecting Ability

**Vacharee Prashyanusorn[1], Yusaku Fuji[2], Somkuan Kaviya[1], Somsak Mitatha[3], Preecha Yupapin[3]**
[1]*Innovative Communication Program, Krirk University, Bangkok, Thailand*
[2]*Gunma University, Kiryu, Japan*
[3]*King Mongkut's Institute of Technology Ladkrabang, Bangkok, Thailand*

## Abstract

For sustainable tourism, a novel method of security camera operation is proposed. In the method, security cameras, which encrypt the taken images and store them into the memory card inside, are used. Only when crimes occur, the memory cards are taken out from the cameras and the images are decrypted with the key and viewed by the city government and/or the police. When no crimes occur, images are overwritten by the new ones after a week automatically without being viewed by anyone. By using the stand-alone cameras without wiring to the control center, the installation cost and the operation cost are much lower than CCTV cameras. By using image encryption, the privacy of the tourists is protected. Using this system, high density installation of the security cameras with very low cost can be realized in encryption with image encryption privacy protection function.

**Keywords:** Innovative Communication, Security Camera, Privacy, Safety, Sustainable Tourism, Crime Prevention

## 1. Introduction

In the sightseeing places, security camera systems, such as Closed-circuit Television (CCTV) system, are now widely used and can be found in ordinary shops and citizens' houses. These systems sometimes play an important role in reducing crime and identifying suspects. However, many problems seem to arise with regard to such security camera systems because of the fact that they are introduced only for the benefit of the owners. One problem is that an expensive high-end security camera system is required for maintaining complete surveillance of an owner's property. The second problem is that a typical system usually keeps watch only inside the owner's property; therefore, it cannot be used for the overall safety of the community. The third problem is that if the system keeps a watch outside the owner's property, it could amount to invasion of the privacy of neighbour. We argue that these problems can be solved if the camera systems are introduced within an altruistic, community-minded framework.

Recently, many security camera systems have been in-

stalled in some countries such as the United Kingdom and the United States of America, by the national and the local governments. Although, it is difficult to evaluate the effectiveness of the security camera system in preenting crime [1,2], which are obvious that they can capture images of any person or car passing within their range. If a considerable number of security cameras are installed without any dead angles on every road, then every criminal who uses the roads can be captured and traced.

However, a center-controlled real-time monitoring system such as the typical systems costs a considerable amount of money and cannot be introduced everywhere without any dead angles. Therefore, we propose a new concept according to which a community can effectively prevent crime if some residents keep watch on what happens around their houses with the aid of their own home computers, cheap commercially available cameras, and free software. **Figure 1** shows the concept of the e-JIKEI Network.

Many types of software applications for capturing video images are available; however, we could not find a

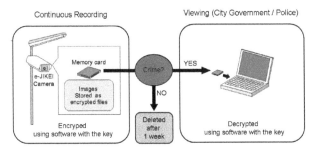

**Figure 1. Concept of "e-JIKEI with privacy protection".**

 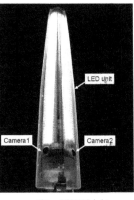

(a) e-JIKEI Camera                    (b) e-JIKEI Light

**Figure 2. Prototype of the e-JIKEI camera and e-JIKEI Light.**

free one that could be used to implement our concept. Therefore, we have developed asoftware with the minimum necessary functions and distributed it free of charge through our website [3]. The software supports both English and Japanese languages. The software simply selects relevant pictures and saves them to the hard disk [4]. This concept has been discussed from the viewpoints of social science [5], homeland security [6] and e-Government [7].

## 2. Personal Computer (PC)-Based System Using Free Software

We have provided the first version of the free software "Dairy EYE standard." Its functions are very limited but essential. The major features of the software are as follows:

• High stability: It can be run continuously for more than 300 days.

• High operation of file storage: The file name and its path express time and location information.

• Minimum necessary storage: Simple picture selection software has been adapted. The software saves a picture only when the difference between two consecutive pictures exceeds the threshold.

• Automatic delete: Folders that are older than the save period set by the owner are automatically deleted.

• Compatibility with many types of cameras: The software can operate in the VFW mode (PC cameras and USB video adapters) and the FTP mode (network cameras).

• Simultaneous operation: The software can operate several cameras connected to a PC.

• No Internet connection: Because of concerns related to privacy, the function of connection to the Internet was disabled in the distributed version of the software. Even in this case, the e-JIKEI Network can be formed, where the word "Network" refers not to the Internet but to the personal network of the residents.

We think that the e-JIKEI Network system should be easily installed in a D.I.Y. (Do It Yourself) manner at a low cost. **Figure 2** shows the examples of camera set-

tings. In one case, an inexpensive network camera is installed outside a house. In the other case, an inexpensive USB PC camera is installed inside a house by using adhesive tape.

## 3. E-JIKEI with Privacy Protection

We propose a new concept regarding the management of security cameras, e-JIKEI with Privacy Protection, in which those who own and manage images (owners) and those who have the right to view these images (viewers) are separated by means of the encryption of the images [8]. On the basis of this concept, encrypted images are transferred from an owner to a viewer only when both the owner and the viewer consider it necessary, such as in the case of crimes; then, the encrypted images are restored for viewing by the viewer. By this method, the images can be viewed only when absolutely necessary. This concept has been proposed to prevent the risk of privacy violation, as well as to reduce the unnecessary psychological burden that third parties may be subjected to, with the aim of promoting the placement of security cameras throughout local communities.

By managing the security camera system using our concept, it is possible to markedly reduce the negative effects associated with the introduction of security cameras, such as concerns over the violation of privacy, without reducing the positive effects, such as crime prevention at places other than those requiring high-level security and constantly manned surveillance, i.e., most communities, while providing recorded images to investigating authorities in the case of crime.

In a practical example carried out in Kiryu City, Gunma Prefecture, a PC-based security camera system is owned and managed by the owners of retail stores affiliated with the merchant association "Suehirocho Shotengai Shinkokyokai," and images are encrypted and stored in the system. To view the stored images, special software installed in the PCs at the Police Department of Kiryu City must be used. Only when the owners of the retail stores and the police determine that it is necessary to view these images, are the stored images transferred from the owners of the retail stores to the police. Then, the stored images are viewed by the police and used as information for investigations. The encrypted images that are stored at retail stores are automatically deleted after 30 days if no incidents or accidents have occurred.

To prove that the software installed in the PC definitely encrypts the images with the cipher-key owned by only the police, a paper on which the owner states the purpose of the camera system and allows the investigations by the merchant association at any time is posted near the cameras. Because the owners of retail stores purely wish to safeguard their shopping street and the customers, and do not intend to violate the privacy of their customers, the installed system is ideal for them.

## 4. All-in-One System "E-JIKEI Camera"

In the experiments of the PC-based system, we have realized that the PC-based system is not very user-friendly since it is difficult for ordinary residents to maintain and operate PCs. In the near future, when home automation is widespread, this problem of PC operation will be solved. However, at this time, it is a serious obstacle for the widespread nationwide use of the e-JIKEI Network. Therefore, we decided to develop an all-in-one system without the use of a PC.

We have developed a prototype of security camera systems "e-JIKEI Camera," which can realize the concept of "e-JIKEI with Privacy Protection." **Figure 3** shows the prototype of the e-JIKEI Camera. It only requires an AC power supply and can be attached outdoors just like a streetlamp. If it is mass produced, the cost per camera will be less than 200 USD. The features of the developed camera are as follows:

1) It can realize the concept of "e-JIKEI with Privacy Protection."

2) All images are encrypted and stored in the memory.

3) To decrypt and view the image, both the special software and the secret key are required.

4) It has a card-type memory of 16 GB, in which the images for the last 1 week are recorded.

5) It can be placed outside.

6) It requires an AC power supply of only 100-240 ACV.

7) The price of the prototype, the first 1000 pieces, is 500 USD/piece.

There are many types of security camera systems available; however, a system with the above features does not exist, except for the newly developed e-JIKEI Camera.

The e-JIKEI Camera is used for realizing our concept of a security camera system in which those who own images (owners) and those who have the right to view the images (viewers) are separated by means of image encryption. This concept was suggested with the aim of preventing the risk of privacy violation, reducing the unnecessary psychological burden that third parties may experience, and promoting the placement of security cameras in local communities.

In Kiryu city, Japan, a social experiment has been conducted since 30 May 2009, in which eleven cameras are installed on the poles of the street lamps in a residential area, as illustrated in **Figure 3(b)**. **Figure 4** shows the location of the 11 e-JIKEI Cameras and the 411 street lamps in the area, where 2218 homes are located. In the experiment, the owner of the images is the PTA (Parent-Teacher Association) of the Higashi Elementary School, and the viewer is the Kiryu Police Station.

(a) Setting of e-JIKEI Camera　　　(b) Setting of e-JIKEI Light

**Figure 3. Examples of camera installation in walking street in Pattaya City.**

**Figure 4. Locations of e-JIKEI cameras and street lamps.**

**Figure 5** shows the procedure for using the e-JIKEI camera in the experiment. Before the experiment, we explained the concept of e-JIKEI with Privacy Protection to the residents of all the 2218 homes by circulating a notice for the same and in an explanation meeting held at the community hall. Our proposal for this experiment was granted by the residents without any negative opinions. During the first six months of the experiment, three crimes were committed. In each case, the police asked the PTA to provide the images, and the PTA decided to grant the police request. During the experiment, many residents expressed their opinion that the e-JIKEI Cameras were very effective in improving the safety of the community but the number of cameras was still very small compared to the number of street lamps.

Recently, we held a discussion with the residents, PTA, and police. The residents and the PTA provided the following opinions about the installed system:

1) It seems very effective in improving the safety of the community.

2) Number of cameras is very small.

3) Privacy violation seems to be perfectly prevented.

4) The cost is comparable to that of the usual street lamps and therefore affordable.

(a) Picture taken by e-JIKEI Camera-1

(b) Picture taken by e-JIKEI Camera-5

**Figure 5. Pictures taken by the cameras.**

The police had the following opinions:

1) The reliability of the system is very high. (There has been no trouble for more than six months now.)

2) The quality of the images is acceptable but can be improved.

3) We hope this camera system spreads all over the city.

If our concept on the security camera system with privacy protection is accepted by society, then a considerable number of cameras, which is comparable to the number of streetlamps, will be introduced in communities throughout the country and the world. Then, every street will be watched by numerous cameras, and photographs of suspects can be provided to the police once a crime occurs in a community.

In the current all-in-one security camera in the e-JIKEI Network, the camera has to be opened to remove the memory card. However, this inconvenience is preferred from the viewpoint of privacy protection, especially in the initial stage of the society's gradual acceptance of our concept. However, in the near future, the cameras will be connected to the Internet after the information security system between the owners and the viewers is established. Thereafter, online operations of solving crime, such as the rescue of kidnapped child CCTV camera system [11,12] is suitable for the real time monitoring of the very important points. However, the cost of installation/maintenance/operation is high, Then the number of the cameras are strictly limited due to such costs.ren, can be implemented.

## 5. Discussions

Comparing to the existing the CCTV camera system in Pattaya City, the e-JIKEI Camera has the following features,

1) Low installation cost: The wiring to the control room and control room itself are not necessary. Only AC power supply is required.

2) Low maintenance/operation cost: The memory cards of the cameras are only taken, when the city government thinks that necessary.

3) Privacy Protection: Only crime occurs, only the certain officers of the city government can view the images.

In the case of the Pattaya City, we propose that the combination the existing CCTV system and the e-JIKEI Cameras. 300 pieces CCTV system watches for only the very busy points, and the huge number of the e-JIKEI Cameras watch the dead-angle of the CCTV in the busy area. In addition, if a huge number of the e-JIKEI Cameras are installed to the quiet residential area, the safety of the whole city will be increased significantly.

If the memory capacity is sufficiently large, the selection of images, in which only the images that are sufficiently different from the previous ones are saved, is not necessary. If the memory capacity is small and memory needs to be conserved, then the selection of images is useful. However, in general, there is no selection algorithm that has a zero failure rate with respect to the selection of necessary images. If all the images are saved without image selection, then the failure of saving a necessary image is prevented. In addition, without this selection, the CPU power can be saved.

At this moment, only the software and programmable stand-alone camera devices, which do not connect to the Internet, have been developed. If the system of security cameras connected to computers and to the Internet spreads nationwide, a very powerful and flexible social structure can be formed. In addition, the software installed in each system can be easily upgraded. This means that this social structure can lead to very interesting research subjects and applications for software research, such as research involving image processing, security systems, and artificial intelligence.

If the security cameras are to be connected to the Internet, the protection of the privacy of the ordinary citizen has to be considered very seriously. A different social structure, including increased social awareness and a revised legal system, will be required for the society; in this structure, every outdoor location will be monitored by security cameras, but the privacy of ordinary citizens will be highly protected, being understood and accepted.

If the appropriate legal, social, and administrative systems are established, most residents will allow appropriate third parties, such as the police department and the city hall, to access their PCs and the saved information through the Internet in the case of a community emergency. In such a case, it will be necessary to ensure that the access rights to the images saved on the PCs can be separately, strictly, and flexibly defined and given to the appropriate third parties by the owner of each system.

If the security cameras are connected to the Internet and can be accessed by the police in the case of serious crimes, the real-time chasing of criminals and rescue of kidnapped children will be possible. A single control station manned by the police, where many operators can access images from cameras spread throughout the nation, is required to realize such a social system.

## 6. Conclusions

We are asking citizens to compare the responsibility of watching what happens around their houses with the risk of violation of their privacy. In the meanwhile, we are trying to increase the advantages of the security camera such as crime prevention and identification of suspects and to reduce its disadvantages such as violation of privacy. We are now commencing tests to assess the true contribution of our concept toward the realization of a safer and more comfortable community.

## 7. Acknowledgements

The Japanese team was supported by the research aid fund of the Research Foundation for Safe Society and the Grant-in-Aid for Scientific Research (B) 21300268 (KAKENHI 21300268).

The authors would also like to give their acknowledgement to Pattaya City Council, Chonburi, Thailand for the research facility under the tourism with safety and privacy project.

## 8. References

[1]   C. Welsh and D. Farrington, "Crime Prevention Effects of Closed Circuit Television: A Systematic Review," Home Office Research Study, 252, 2002.

[2]   M. Gill and A. Spriggs, "Assessing the Impact of CCTV," Home Office Research Study, 292, 2005.

[3]   NPO, The e-JIKEI Network Promotion Institute. http://www.e-jikei.org/index_e.htm/.

[4]   Y. Fujii, N. Yoshiura and N. Ohta, "Community Security by Widely Available Information Technology," JoCI 2005, 2. http://ci-journal.net/index.php/ciej/article/view/285/.

[5]   Y. Fujii, N. Yoshiura and N. Ohta, "Creating a Worldwide Community Security Structure Using Individually Maintained Home Computers: The e-JIKEI Network Project," Soc. Sci. Comput. Rev., Vol. 23, 2005, pp. 250-258.

[6]   N. Yoshiura, Y. Fujii and N. Ohta, "Using the Security Camera System Based On Individually Maintained Computers For Homeland Security: The e-JIKEI Network Project," Proc. IEEE IMTC, Ottawa, Canada, 2005, pp. 101-105.

[7]   H. Ueda, Y. Fujii, S. Kumakura, N. Yoshiura and N. Ohta, "e-JIKEI Network Project/Japan: Enhancing Community Security," eGov., Vol. 11, 2009, pp. 9-11.

[8]   Y. Fujii, K. Maru, N. Yoshiura, N. Ohta, H. Ueda and Y. Sugita, "New Concept Regarding Management of Security Cameras," JoCI 2008, 4. http://www.ci-journal.net/index.php/ciej/article/view/442/427/

[9]   Y. Fujii, K. Maru, K. Kobayashi, N. Yoshiura, N. Ohta, H. Ueda and P. P. Yupapin, "e-JIKEI Network Using e-JIKEI Cameras: Community Security Using Considerable Number of Cheap Stand-Alone Cameras," Safety Science, Vol. 48, No. 7, 2010, pp. 921-925.

[10]  V. Prashyanusorn, S. Kaviya and P. P. Yupapin, "Surveillance System for Sustainable Tourism with Safety and Privacy Protection," Procedia—Social and Behavioral Sciences, Vol. 2, 2020, pp. 74-78.

[11]  M. Zhang, B. Yang, S. Zhu and W. Zhang, "Ordered

semiring-Based Trust Establish Model with Risk Evaluating," *International Journal of Network Security*, Vol. 8, No. 2, 2009, pp. 101-106.

[12] S. H. Chiu, C. P. Lu and C. Y. Wen, "A Motion Detection-Based Framework for Improving Image Quality of CCTV Security Systems," *Journal of Forensic Sciences*, Vol. 51, No. 5, 2006, pp. 1115-1119.

# 22

# Denial of Service Due to Direct and Indirect ARP Storm Attacks in LAN Environment*

**Sanjeev Kumar, Orifiel Gomez**

*Department of Electrical/Computer Engineering, University of Texas—PanAm, Edinburg, USA*

## Abstract

ARP-based Distributed Denial of Service (DDoS) attacks due to ARP-storms can happen in local area networks where many computer systems are infected by worms such as Code Red or by DDoS agents. In ARP attack, the DDoS agents constantly send a barrage of ARP requests to the gateway, or to a victim computer within the same sub-network, and tie up the resource of attacked gateway or host. In this paper, we set to measure the impact of ARP-attack on resource exhaustion of computers in a local area network. Based on attack experiments, we measure the exhaustion of processing and memory resources of a victim computer and also other computers, which are located on the same network as the victim computer. Interestingly enough, it is observed that an ARP-attack not only exhausts resource of the victim computer but also significantly exhausts processing resource of other non-victim computers, which happen to be located on the same local area network as the victim computer.

**Keywords:** ARP Attack, Computer Network Security, Computer Systems, Direct Attack, Distributed Denial of Service Attacks (DDoS), Indirect Attack, Local Area Networks

## 1. Introduction

A Distributed Denial of Service (DDoS) attack [1,2] involves multiple DoS agents configured to send attack traffic to a single victim computer. DDoS is a deliberate act that significantly degrades the quality and/or availability of services offered by a computer system by consuming its bandwidth and/or processing time. As a result, legitimate users are unable to have full quality access to a web service or services. A Denial of Service attack consumes a victim's system resource such as network bandwidth, CPU time and memory. This may also include data structures such as open file handles, Transmission Control Blocks (TCBs), process slots etc. Because of packet flooding in a DDoS attack that typically strives to deplete available bandwidth and/or processing resources, the degree of resource depletion depends on the traffic type, volume of the attack traffic, and the processing power of the victim computer.

According to Computer Emergency Response Team Coordination Center (CERT/CC) [3], there has been an

increase in use of Multiple Windows-based DDoS agents. There has been a significant shift from Unix to Windows as an actively used host platform for DDoS agents. Furthermore, there has been an increased targeting of Windows end-users and servers. To raise awareness of such vulnerabilities, the CERT/CC published a tech tip entitled "Home Network Security" in July of 2001 [4]. According to the CERT/CC [3], there is a perception that Windows end-users are generally less security conscious, and less likely to be protected against or prepared to respond to attacks compared to professional industrial systems and network administrators. Furthermore, large populations of Windows end-users of an Internet Service Provider are relatively easy to identify and hence the attackers or intruders are leveraging easily identifiable network blocks to selectively target and exploit Windows end -user servers and computer systems.

In this paper, we consider a Distributed Denial of Service (DDoS) attack that can be caused by a barrage of ARP-requests sent to a victim computer. In order to understand the intensity of the attack, we conduct experiments in a controlled lab environment to measure the

---
*Work of Dr. Kumar is supported in part by funding from CITeC, FRC, FDC, OBRR/NIH, digital-X Inc, and US National Science Foundation.

availability of the processing power and memory resources of the victim computer during an ARP-attack. Since, windows based servers are very commonly deployed, we consider a Window-XP server with a 3.06 GHz Pentium-IV processor and 512 Mbytes of RAM to be used as the victim computer in the ARP-attack experiments. Section II presents a background on ARP and how it is used to exploit vulnerability of a computer system; Section III presents detail on use of ARP requests, ARP format, types of ARP-request traffic, and the processing that needs to be done for ARP-request messages; Section IV presents the experimental-setup, systems configuration for DDoS attacks in the controlled lab environment, and attack measurement results under direct ARP attack traffic and Indirect ARP attack traffic; and Section V provides discussion on detection and prevention schemes for ARP storm attacks, Section VI concludes the paper.

## 2. Arp-As an Attack Bullet

The Address Resolution Protocol (ARP) requests are legitimate and essential for the operation of the network. However, ARP can be used in more than one way to exploit the vulnerability of a computer system or a network. Some of the security attacks involving ARP can cause Denial of Service (DoS) attack by sending a massive amount of ARP requests to a victim computer and tying up its resource [5]. ARP can also be used to create Denial of Service attack by sending a victim computer's outgoing data to a sink by the technique of ARP cache poisoning. Other ARP based attacks can result in unauthorized sniffing of packets, or hijacking of secured Internet sessions. The Denial of Service attacks due to ARP storms can also be caused by worms such as code red due to their rapid scanning activity [6,7]. The worm initiated ARP storms have been commonly found in networks with high numbers of infected and active computers and servers. In ARP storm, an attacked victim (the gateway or a server) may receive a constant barrage of ARP requests from attacking computers in the same sub-network, and this ties up not only the network bandwidth but also the processing resource of the victim computer.

The worm Code-Red's rapid scanning activity can result in a denial-of-service attack against a Windows NT 4.0 IIS 4.0 server with URL redirection enabled [6]. The worm Code-Red can easily spread to new vulnerable systems, and there is a patch available for this vulnerability. Applying the patch can keep a server from being infected by the worm Code-Red. Nevertheless, it is still possible for the worm in other infected computers on the network to attack the same chain of IP addresses over

and over again. This can generate a high-traffic overload due to massive amount of ARP requests generated in the network, which in turn can still affect the server's performance (despite the patch).

In this paper, we investigate the brute force of ARP attack where a constant barrage of ARP requests is directed to a victim computer. In this experiment, we set out to measure how bad the effect of the ARP attack was on the victim computer. Furthermore, we also measure the extent of resource exhaustion due to the ARP attack traffic on other computers located on the same LAN segment as the victim computer. To understand the degree of resource exhaustion, we measure performance in terms of processor exhaustion, occupancy of systems' memory and the page-file size. Since Microsoft Windows-XP based computers and servers with high performance Pentium-IV processors are becoming quite affordable and popular with small businesses, we use a Windows-XP based computer as a victim computer to be stress-tested for the extent of resource exhaustion under the ARP attack.

## 3. Processing an Arp-Request Message

### 3.1. Use of ARP-Request Message

A gateway or a host on a local area network uses ARP request broadcast messages [8] for IP and hardware address bindings. The ARP message contains the IP address of the host for which a hardware address needs to be resolved (**Figure 2**). All computers on a network receive ARP message and only the matching computer responds by sending a reply that contains the needed hardware address.

### 3.2. ARP Message Format

ARP is used for a variety of network technologies. The ARP packet format varies depending on the type of network being used. The ARP packet format used in Ethernet is shown in **Figure 1**. While resolving IP protocol address, the Ethernet hardware uses 28-octet ARP message format [8]. The ARP message format contains fields to hold sender's hardware address and IP address, shown as SENDER-HA and SENDER-IP fields in **Figure 1**. It also has fields for the target computer's hardware and IP address, which is shown as TARGET-HA and TARGET-IP fields in **Figure 1**. When making an ARP request, the sender supplies the target IP address, and leaves the field for the target hardware address empty (which is to be filled by the target computer).

In the broadcasted ARP request message, the sender also supplies its own hardware and IP addresses for the target computer to update its ARP cache table for future correspondence with the sender. Other fields in the ARP packet format in **Figure 2** are HARDWARE TYPE of 2 Bytes (shown as 2B in **Figure 1**), which specifies the type of network being used such as Ethernet in this case. The PROTOCOL TYPE field of 2 Bytes specifies the high-level protocols address used such as the IP addresses. The fields HLEN and PLEN of one Byte each specify the length of hardware address and high-protocol address, in the case of ARP protocol use in the arbitrary networks. The OPERATION field of 2 Bytes specifies if the message is one of the four possible types *i.e.* 1 for ARP-request, 2 for ARP-reply, 3 for RARP-request and 4 for RARP-reply.

## 4. Types of ARP-Request Traffic on a LAN

A computer on the LAN will receive two different types of ARP-request packets from the network. The first type of ARP request packets can be named as the *direct ARP request traffic* where the IP address in the ARP request packet matches the local IP address of the computer *Pi*. The second type of ARP request traffic that is received by the computer on a LAN can be named as *indirect ARP request traffic* where the IP address in the ARP request packets doesn't match the local IP address of the computer $P_i$.

In other words, a computer *i* on a LAN with IP address

| Harware Type (2b) | | Protocol Type (2b) |
|---|---|---|
| Hlen (1b) | Plen (1b) | Operation (2b) |
| Sender Ha (Octets 0-3) | | |
| Sender Ha (Octets 4-5) | | Sender Ip (Octets 0-1) |
| Sender Ip (Octets 2-3) | | Target Ha (Octets 0-1) |
| Target Ha (Octets 2-5) | | |
| Target Ip (Octets 0-3) | | |

**Figure 1. ARP mssage frmat**

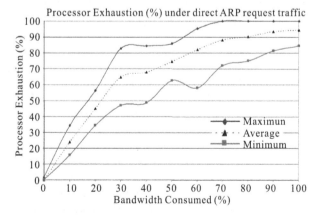

**Figure 2. Processor exhaustion under direct ARP- attack traffic with IP address = {χ | χ = *P*ᵢ}.**

of $P_i$ may receive one of the two possible types of ARP request traffic during an ARP-attack –

a) *Direct ARP traffic* – it is a traffic comprising of ARP request messages with IP address = {χ | χ = $P_i$}

b) *Indirect ARP traffic* – it is a traffic comprising of ARP request messages with IP address = {χ | χ ≠ $P_i$}

The target or victim computer will primarily be inundated with the direct-ARP attack traffic, whereas the other computers (non-victim computers) located on the same LAN segment will be inundated with the indirect ARP-attack traffic.

The main task of the processor in the target computer after receiving the ARP request message is to make sure the ARP request message is for it. In the case of direct ARP frames, the processor proceeds to fill in the missing hardware-address in the ARP request format-header, swaps the target and sender hardware & IP address pair, and changes the ARP-request operation to an ARP-reply. Thus the ARP reply carries the IP and hardware addresses of both, the sender and the target computers. Unlike the ARP request message, the ARP replies are directed to just the sender computer and it is not broadcasted. In the case of indirect ARP frames received, the computer still does some processing to determine if the ARP request message is for the local computer. In this case, once it is determined that the frame is not for the local computer, the indirect ARP message is simply dropped.

The processing needed for an ARP-request message is fairly simple, however there is more processing involved when direct ARP request frames are received by a victim computer, compared to that of the indirect ARP-request frames received by non-victim computers present on the same LAN. Even though, there is comparatively less processing involved when an indirect ARP request message is received, a barrage of such requests can still exhaust the processing power of a non-victim computer just because it happens to be sitting on the same LAN segment as the victim computer or server. The degree of processor exhaustion for a given computer will of course depend on the processor speed and the bandwidth consumed by ARP-request messages. In the following sections, we discuss our experiment to measure the extent of resource exhaustion of two different types of computers on a LAN under an ARP attack – the first type of computer, being the victim computer, which is inundated with direct ARP-request frames. We also measure the computing resource exhaustion of the second type of computers (the non-victim computers, which happen to be on the same LAN as the victim computer or server), when inundated with indirect ARP-request frames.

# 5. Performance Evaluation

## 5.1. Experimental Setup

In this experiment, an ARP-storm was generated in a controlled environment of the network security research lab at the UTPA by having different computers send a barrage of ARP-request messages to a victim computer on the same local area network. A Windows-XP based computer was used as the attack target of the ARP-storm. The computer under attack deployed a Pentium IV processor with a speed of 3.06 GHz with 533 MHz Bus, 512 kb Cache, a physical memory of 512 Mbytes (RAM), and a NIC card from 3 Com. Furthermore, other computers (that received indirect ARP request traffic) on the LAN deployed exactly the same resources as the victim computer on the LAN. Computers under attack on the LAN deployed Windows-XP Service-Pack 2 (SPK 2). We also used the network observer software to collect traffic detail and the applied load on the LAN.

This experimental setup and results obtained in this paper are much more detailed compared to the one presented in [9] where a different system was used for the victim computer, which deployed a Pentium-4 processor with a speed of 2.66 GHz. Furthermore, the NIC card used in [9] were the Intel's NIC card, which could not support full speed of 100 Mbps of network traffic. Whereas, in this experiment, the 3 Com's NIC card was used that supported full speed of 100 Mbps. Furthermore, in [9] only the effect of direct ARP traffic was measured and no indirect ARP traffic was considered.

## 5.2. Attack Measurements

Parameters of performance evaluation considered for this attack experiment were the applied load of the ARP-attack traffic, processor exhaustion during the attack and memory occupied while processing the attack traffic by the target computer. The DDoS attack was simulated as ARP packets coming from multiple different attacking-computers at a maximum aggregate speed of 100 Mbps towards the target server. The attack traffic (while simulating ARP storm) load was started with 0 Mbps (the background condition) and was increased by 10 Mbps *i.e.* from 0% load to 100% load (= 100 Mbps). In the ARP-storm experiment, the attacked target computer continued to receive a barrage of ARP-requests for a period of 60 minutes for a given load, and was obligated to process them by creating an ARP-reply. In this experiment, a total of 10 different loads were generated, *i.e.* 10% - 100%. A total of 10 hours of ARP attack traffic were experienced at the victim computer and another non-victim computer on the local network. The CPU

time is termed as processor exhaustion in these measurements, which gives an indication of the rate of processor exhaustion for a given bandwidth consumed by the attack-traffic during the ARP storm. It is observed that as the network bandwidth is increasingly consumed by the ARP-attack traffic, the processor is exhausted at a much faster rate, and hence this type of attack can be classified under computing-resource starvation attack.

## 5.3. Resource Exhaustion of the Victim Computer Due to Direct-ARP Request Traffic

Direct ARP request traffic comprises of ARP-request frames that have

$$\text{IP address} = \{\chi \mid \chi = P_i\}$$

In this experiment, we measure, processor exhaustion, memory used and the page file size under direct-ARP request traffic. Page file size gives indication of virtual memory activity, if any, during the attack.

**Figure 2** shows minimum and maximum CPU time observed (called processor exhaustion in the attack experiments) for a given load of the direct ARP-attack traffic. Average CPU time is also shown in the graph so that we can get an idea if the majority of observations are closer to the maximum CPU time or closer to the minimum CPU time. It can be seen that a bandwidth consumption of 40% by direct ARP-attack traffic in a fast Ethernet environment exhausts a Pentium-IV processor to up to 85% of its 3.06 GHz processing capacity. Due to the processing of a barrage of ARP-requests the CPU resource is easily consumed and this in turn can degrade the quality and availability of associated web services.

Furthermore, it is obvious that if such servers are operated in a Gigabit network deploying higher interfaces such as 1 Gbps then it will be easier for such CPU of 3.06 GHz to be completely consumed by the Gigabit-flood of ARP-attack traffic, and attacks in such Gigabit environment can completely stall the system. Complete stalling of system means that one cannot even move the cursor on the attacked computer, let alone running the security diagnostics. It is also obvious from this experiment that a lower capacity (< 3.06 GHz) processor can easily be frozen (consumed 100%) by this type of ARP-storm in commonly available fast Ethernet environment of local area networks.

**Figure 3** shows the memory-usage of the victim computer under direct ARP-attack traffic, as the network bandwidth is increasingly consumed by the ARP-storm. The memory consumed due to direct ARP attack traffic is observed to be within a range of 6 Mbytes, which seems to be not much of an issue for a 3.06 GHz processor with 512 Mbytes of RAM. However, for a slower

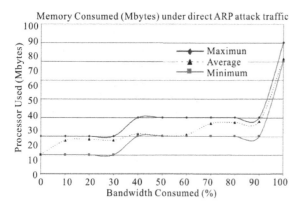

**Figure 3. Memory usage under the direct ARP-attack traffic with IP address = {χ | χ = $P_i$}.**

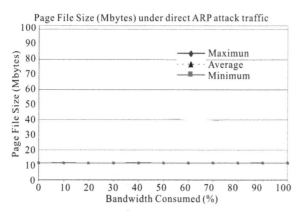

**Figure 4. Page-file size is visibly unaffected under direct-ARP-attack traffic with IP address = {χ | χ = $P_i$}.**

processor with processing power less than 3.06 GHz, a greater amount of computer's memory resource can be wasted. Slower processing power in the fast Ethernet environment can cause the queue of ARP packets to build up waiting for address resolution and computer's response. Hence a slower processor will exhaust a relatively greater amount of memory resource of the victim computer under ARP storm. In any case, the memory usage is so insignificant that it is not really a problem in these ARP attacks.

Another parameter of interest is the Page file size. Page File size is the current number of bytes that the active processes have used in the paging file(s). We measure the page file size during the attack to observe for activities in the virtual memory.

**Figure 4** shows that there is no change in the page-file size before and during the direct ARP attack. Page-file size measurement at 0% load mainly provides the size due to the background processes running in the computer in the absence of any ARP request traffic. Furthermore, as the load of incoming direct ARP traffic is increased, there is really no impact on the virtual memory of the computer.

## 5.4. Resource Exhaustion of a (Non-Victim) Computer Receiving Indirect Frames

If $i^{th}$ computer in the broadcast domain has an IP address of $P_i$ then the indirect ARP-request frames arriving to the computer can be described as the frames with

$$\text{IP addresses} = \{\chi \mid \chi \neq P_i\}$$

**Figure 5** shows minimum, maximum and average value for the processor exhaustion for a given load of the indirect ARP-attack traffic. It can be seen that a bandwidth consumption of 40% by indirect ARP-attack traffic in a fast Ethernet environment exhausts a Pentium-IV based non-victim computer to up to 55% of its 3.06 GHz processing capacity. Indirect ARP requests are still being processed by the computers on the network even though they are not directed towards them. Due to the processing of a barrage of indirect ARP-request messages, the CPU resource is still getting significantly consumed, however the processor exhaustion rate is relatively less intense compared to the one under direct ARP attack traffic. This is understandable as there is relatively more processing involved in direct ARP attack traffic compared to that of indirect ARP attack traffic.

**Figure 6** shows the memory-usage of a non-victim computer, which is located on the same LAN segment as that of the victim computer, as the network bandwidth is increasingly consumed by the indirect ARP attack traffic. The memory consumed due to such indirect-ARP attack traffic is observed to be within 3 Mbytes, which is comparatively less than that consumed by the direct ARP attack traffic in **Figure 3**. Consumption of physical memory in the range of 3 Mbytes is not much of an issue for a 3.06 Hz computer with 512 Mbytes of RAM.

In this experiment, we also measure the page-file size before the onset of indirect ARP attack, and during the indirect ARP attack (**Figure 7**). The page-file size at 0% ARP traffic indicates the page-file size before the onset

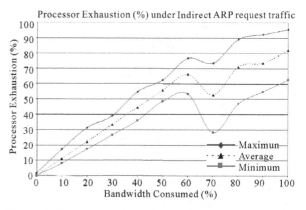

**Figure 5. Processor exhaustion under the indirect ARP-attack traffic with IP address = {χ | χ ≠ $P_i$}.**

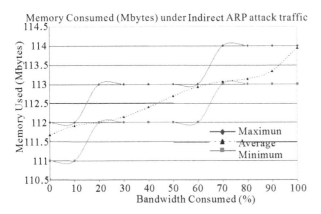

**Figure 6. Occupancy of the computer's memory under indirect ARP-attack traffic with IP address = $\{\chi \mid \chi \neq P_i\}$.**

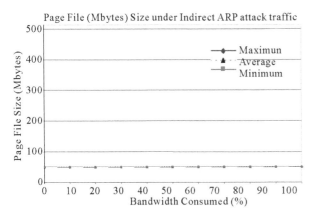

**Figure 7. Page-file size is visibly unaffected under the indirect ARP-attack traffic with IP address = $\{\chi \mid \chi \neq P_i\}$.**

of the ARP-attack, which is mainly due to the processes running in the background. The page-file size of the victim computer is measured as the network bandwidth is increasingly consumed by the indirect ARP-attack traffic. **Figure 7** shows that the page-file size is not affected by the indirect ARP attack traffic, as it stays the same before and after the onset of the indirect ARP attack. This is obviously due to the fact that the memory-consumed by the indirect ARP traffic (**Figure 6**) is quite minimal, and stays within the range of 3 Mbytes (out of a total 512 Mbytes) of RAM space, and hence no incoming ARP messages spill to the page-file.

## 6. Detection and Prevention

It can be seen from the prior experiments that the ARP storms can consume the computing resources rapidly for all the computers on the affected LAN segment. Hence it is important to detect the ARP storms immediately and raise alarm for its possible prevention before the entire LAN segment is brought down by such ARP storms. In

order to detect these types of ARP attacks, it is important to monitor the ARP traffic on each LAN segments. Programs such as ARPwatch [10] can be used to monitor ARP traffic on each LAN segments and raise alarm when ARP storms or ARP poisoning tools are detected. One can also use SNMP to monitor changes in ARP table in routers and switches to raise alarm for onset of such ARP attacks.

One way to prevent ARP storm is to involve layer-2 switches in controlling the ARP broadcast floods at the source where the storm starts building up. This can be achieved by allowing for threshold limits for broadcast/multicast traffic on a per-port basis. Furthermore, these thresholds per-port basis should be set up by limiting the bandwidth consumed by ARP broadcasts on a switch port.

In order to support multiple layers of prevention, the routers can also be used in controlling ARP storm from spreading to others LAN segments. A network manager can configure the router (using its control policy) to impose a limit on the rate of ARP requests that can be allowed for the associated LAN segments. When the imposed threshold for the ARP requests is exceeded then the ARP request packets are dropped by the router. The router hardware should be fast enough to examine and drop the ARP request packets that exceed the imposed threshold, otherwise it is possible for the router to crash or experience slowdown of its operation and itself become a bottleneck resulting in eventual denial of service (DoS).

## 7. Conclusions

According to Computer Emergency Response Team (CERT/CC), there has been an increased targeting of Windows end-users' computer systems and servers for security attacks. Distributed Denial of Service (DDoS) attacks due to ARP-storms can be found in local area networks where many computer systems are infected by worms such as Code Red or by DDoS agents. In this paper, we present results of our experiments to measure the impact of ARP-storms on systems resource exhaustion of a Window-XP based computer system deploying a high performance Pentium-IV processor. It is observed that ARP-storms not only waste the communication bandwidth but also exhaust a processor's resource of a victim computer even more rapidly by forcing it to reply to a barrage of ARP-request messages. It is also observed that when the network bandwidth is consumed 40% by the ARP-attack traffic in a fast Ethernet environment, a computer system with a high-performance Pentium-IV processor of 3.06 GHz speed wastes up to 85% of its (victim computer) raw CPU-time in processing direct

ARP attack traffic and 55% of its (non-victim computers) raw CPU-time in processing indirect ARP attack traffic. This attack is found to be more processor intensive which means that it exhausts processor resource more rapidly than other computing resources such as memory. The memory exhaustion is found to be not significant when compared with the corresponding processor exhaustion. Memory usage is observed to be quite insignificant compared to the memory resource deployed in the system. The virtual memory or the page file of the victim computer is observed to be completely unaffected. Based on these experimental results, the ARP-attack can be categorized as the attack that causes computing resource starvation more rapidly than the bandwidth starvation, especially that of the processor of the victim and non-victim computer systems on the affected network. It is interesting to notice the collateral damage done by this attack on a given LAN, according to which it not only exhausts the resource of the victim computer but also exhausts computing resource of other non-victim computers present on a given LAN where the victim computer resides. The rate of resource exhaustion in this type of experiment can help network security engineers design efficient flow-control and threshold based attack prevention schemes at the switches and routers used in the LAN.

## 8. Acknowledgements

The authors would like to thank Uriel Ramirez and Sumanth Avirneni for equipment support, data collection and verification efforts in the Network Security Research Lab (NSRL) at UTPA. The work in this paper is supported in part by funding from US National Science Foundation under grant # 0521585.

## 9. References

[1] L. Gerber, "Denial of Service Attacks Rip the Internet," *IEEE Computer*, April 2000.

[2] P. G. Neumann, "Denial-of-Service Attacks," *ACM Communications*, Vol. 43. No. 4, April 2000, p. 136.

[3] K. J. Houle and G. M. Weaver, "Trends in Denial of Service Attack Technology," Computer Emergency Response Team (CERT)® Coordination Center, V1.0, October 2001.

[4] Computer Emergency Response Team (CERT)® Advisory, "Home Network Security," CA-2001-20. http://www.cert.org/tech_tips/home_networks.html

[5] A. Householder, A. Manion, L. Pesante and G. M. Weaver, "Managing the Threat of Denial-of-Service Attacks," CERT Coordination Center, October 2001.

[6] CERT® Incident Note IN-2001-10, "Code-Red Worm Crashes IIS 4.0 Servers with URL Redirection Enabled," CERT Coordination Center, August 2001. http://www.cert.org/incident_notes/IN-2001-10.html

[7] Cisco Security Advisory, "Code-Red Worm—Customer Impact," Cisco Networks, July 2001. http://www.cisco.com/warp/public/707/cisco-code-red-worm-pub.shtml

[8] D. C. Plummer, "Ethernet Address Resolution Protocol," IETF Network Working Group, RFC-826, November 1982.

[9] S. Kumar, "Impact of a Distributed Denial of Service (DDoS) Attack Due to ARP Storm," *International Conference on Networking*, to be published in *Lecture Notes in Computer Science (LNCS)*, April 2005.

[10] ARPwatch. http://en.wikipedia.org/wiki/Arpwatch

# Permissions

The contributors of this book come from diverse backgrounds, making this book a truly international effort. This book will bring forth new frontiers with its revolutionizing research information and detailed analysis of the nascent developments around the world.

We would like to thank all the contributing authors for lending their expertise to make the book truly unique. They have played a crucial role in the development of this book. Without their invaluable contributions this book wouldn't have been possible. They have made vital efforts to compile up to date information on the varied aspects of this subject to make this book a valuable addition to the collection of many professionals and students.

This book was conceptualized with the vision of imparting up-to-date information and advanced data in this field. To ensure the same, a matchless editorial board was set up. Every individual on the board went through rigorous rounds of assessment to prove their worth. After which they invested a large part of their time researching and compiling the most relevant data for our readers. Conferences and sessions were held from time to time between the editorial board and the contributing authors to present the data in the most comprehensible form. The editorial team has worked tirelessly to provide valuable and valid information to help people across the globe.

Every chapter published in this book has been scrutinized by our experts. Their significance has been extensively debated. The topics covered herein carry significant findings which will fuel the growth of the discipline. They may even be implemented as practical applications or may be referred to as a beginning point for another development. Chapters in this book were first published by Scientific Research Publishing Inc.; hereby published with permission under the Creative Commons Attribution License or equivalent.

The editorial board has been involved in producing this book since its inception. They have spent rigorous hours researching and exploring the diverse topics which have resulted in the successful publishing of this book. They have passed on their knowledge of decades through this book. To expedite this challenging task, the publisher supported the team at every step. A small team of assistant editors was also appointed to further simplify the editing procedure and attain best results for the readers.

Our editorial team has been hand-picked from every corner of the world. Their multi-ethnicity adds dynamic inputs to the discussions which result in innovative outcomes. These outcomes are then further discussed with the researchers and contributors who give their valuable feedback and opinion regarding the same. The feedback is then collaborated with the researches and they are edited in a comprehensive manner to aid the understanding of the subject.

Apart from the editorial board, the designing team has also invested a significant amount of their time in understanding the subject and creating the most relevant covers. They scrutinized every image to scout for the most suitable representation of the subject and create an appropriate cover for the book.

The publishing team has been involved in this book since its early stages. They were actively engaged in every process, be it collecting the data, connecting with the contributors or procuring relevant information. The team has been an ardent support to the editorial, designing and production team. Their endless efforts to recruit the best for this project, has resulted in the accomplishment of this book. They are a veteran in the field of academics and their pool of knowledge is as vast as their experience in printing. Their expertise and guidance has proved useful at every step. Their uncompromising quality standards have made this book an exceptional effort. Their encouragement from time to time has been an inspiration for everyone.

The publisher and the editorial board hope that this book will prove to be a valuable piece of knowledge for researchers, students, practitioners and scholars across the globe.

# List of Contributors

**Yogendra Narain Singh**
Department of Computer Science & Engineering, Institute of Engineering & Technology, Gautam Buddh Technical University, Lucknow, India

**S. K. Singh**
Department of Computer Engineering, Institute of Technology, Banaras Hindu University, Varanasi, India

**Sandeep K. Sood**
Department of Computer Science & Engineering, Regional Campus Gurdaspur, Gurdaspur, India

**Maurizio Talamo**
Department of Engineering, University of Rome Tor Vergata, Rome, Italy
Nestor Laboratory, University of Rome Tor Vergata, Rome, Italy

**Christian H. Schunck and Franco Arcieri**
Nestor Laboratory, University of Rome Tor Vergata, Rome, Italy

**Maulahikmah Galinium**
Department of Information Science, University of Rome Tor Vergata, Rome, Italy

**Yuji Waizumi, Hiroshi Tsunoda, Masashi Tsuji and Yoshiaki Nemoto**
Graduate School of Information Sciences (GSIS), Tohoku University, Miyagi, Japan

**Youssef Gahi and Zouhair Guennoun**
Laboratoire d Electronique et de Communications − LEC, Ecole Mohammadia d Ingénieurs − EMI, Université Mohammed V-Agdal − UM5A. BP, Rabat, Morocco

**Khalil El-Khatib and Mouhcine Guennoun**
University of Ontario Institute of Technology, Oshawa, Canada

**Shay Gueron**
Department of Mathematics, University of Haifa, Haifa, Israel
Intel Corporation, Israel Development Center, Haifa, Israel

**Vlad Krasnov**
Intel Corporation, Israel Development Center, Haifa, Israel

**Fabio Garzia**
Department of Information, Electronics and Telecommunications Engineering, University of Rome, Rome, Italy
Wessex Institute of Technology, Southampton, UK

**Alfredo Maesa, Michele Scarpiniti and Roberto Cusani**
Department of Information, Electronics and Telecommunications Engineering, University of Rome, Rome, Italy

**Tahir Amin and Dimitrios Hatzinakos**
Department of Electrical and Computer Engineering, University of Toronto, Toronto, Canada

**Ilung Pranata, Geoff Skinner and Rukshan Athauda**
Faculty of Science and IT, University of Newcastle, Callaghan, Australia

**Peter Schartner**
System Security Group, Klagenfurt University, Klagenfurt, Austria

**Amir Mohamed Talib, Rodziah Atan, Rusli Abdullah and Masrah Azrifah Azmi Murad**
Faculty of Computer Science & IT, University Putra Malaysia UPM, Serdang, Malaysia

**Vijay Anand, Jafar Saniie and Erdal Oruklu**
Department of Electrical and Computer Engineering, Illinois Institute of Technology, Chicago, USA

**Yoshio Kakizaki, Kazunari Maeda and Keiichi Iwamura**
Tokyo University of Science, Tokyo, Japan

**Thomas Djotio Ndié and Guy Bertrand Fopak**
Lirima/Masecness, University of Yaounde 1, Yaounde, Cameroon

**Claude Tangha**
Lirima/Aloco, University of Yaounde 1, Yaounde, Cameroon

**Vaibhav Ranchhoddas Pandya and Mark Stamp**
Department of Computer Science, San Jose State University, San Jose, USA

**Jeddy Nafeesa Begum and Krishnan Kumar**
Department of Computer Science and Engineering, Government College of Engineering, Bargur, India

**Vembu Sumathy**
Department of Electronics and Communications Engineering, Government College of Technology, Coimbatore, India

**Andrews Samraj, Shohel Sayeed and Loo Chu Kiong**
Faculty of Information Science and Technology, Multimedia University, Malacca, Malaysia

**Nikos E. Mastorokis**
Faculty of Engineering, Industrial Engineering Department, Technical University of Sofia, Sofia, Bulgaria

**Cheng-Chang Lien, Cheng-Lun Shih and Chih-Hsun Chou**
Department of Computer Science and Information Engineering, Chung Hua University, Hsinchu, Taiwan, China

**Hui Lin**
ECE Department, University of Illinois at Chicago, Chicago, USA

**Gyungho Lee**
College of Information and Communications, Korea University, Seoul, Korea

**Yi Luo and Ferenc Szidarovszky**
Department of Systems and Industrial Engineering, University of Arizona, Tucson, USA

**Youssif Al-Nashif and Salim Hariri**
Department of Electrical and Computer Engineering, University of Arizona, Tucson, USA

**Vacharee Prashyanusorn and Somkuan Kaviya**
Innovative Communication Program, Krirk University, Bangkok, Thailand

**Yusaku Fuji**
Gunma University, Kiryu, Japan

**Somsak Mitatha and Preecha Yupapin**
King Mongkut's Institute of Technology Ladkrabang, Bangkok, Thailand

**Sanjeev Kumar and Orifiel Gomez**
Department of Electrical/Computer Engineering, University of Texas–PanAm, Edinburg, USA

Printed in the USA
CPSIA information can be obtained
at www.ICGtesting.com
JSHW052020301024
72690JS00004B/121